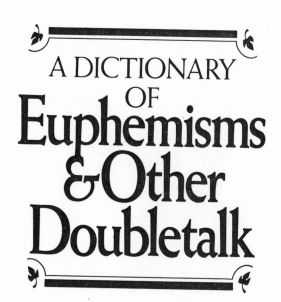

A DICTIONARY
OF
Euphemisms & Other Doubletalk

A DICTIONARY
OF
Euphemisms
&Other
Doubletalk

Being a Compilation of Linguistic
Fig Leaves and Verbal Flourishes for
Artful Users of the English Language

HUGH RAWSON

Crown Publishers, Inc.
New York

Published by Crown Publishers, Inc.,
One Park Avenue, New York, New York 10016
and simultaneously in Canada by General Publishing Company Limited

Manufactured in the United States of America
CROWN is a trademark of Crown Publishers, Inc.

Library of Congress Cataloging in Publication Data

Rawson, Hugh
A dictionary of euphemisms & other double talk
    Includes bibliographical references.
    1. English language—Euphemisms.   I. Title.
II. Title: Fig leaves and flourishes.
PE1449.R34 1981   428.1   81-4748
ISBN: 0-517-55710-X (pbk.)   AACR2

Designed by Fran Gazze Nimeck

10 9 8 7 6 5 4 3 2 1

First Paperback Edition, 1985

For Margaret, finally

The tongue of man is a twisty thing,
there are plenty of words there
of every kind, the range of words is wide,
and their variance.

The Iliad of Homer, ca. 750 B.C.
Richmond Lattimore, trans., 1951

There is nothing unclean of itself:
but to him that esteemth any thing
to be unclean, to him it is unclean.

Romans, XIV, 14, ca. A.D. 56
King James Version, 1611

Acknowledgments & a Request

Most sources are given in the text, but the influence of a few is so pervasive as to require special acknowledgment. First is the *Oxford English Dictionary*, edited by Sir James Murray, which I have used in the compact edition, published by Oxford University Press in 1971. The *OED* is a monument to the English language and it is hard to imagine any other dictionary—or compilation of euphemisms—being made without continually consulting it, as well as its recent supplements, edited by R. W. Burchfield (the first two volumes, issued in 1972 and 1976, go through the letter "N"). Nearly as well-thumbed were *A Dictionary of American English on Historical Principles* (Sir William A. Cragie and James R. Hurlburt, eds., University of Chicago Press, 1938–44, four volumes) and *A Dictionary of Americanisms* (Mitford M. Mathews, University of Chicago Press, 1951, two volumes). Also of great use were various works on slang: for British usage, *A Dictionary of Slang and Unconventional English* (Eric Partridge, Macmillan, 1970) and *A Classical Dictionary of the Vulgar Tongue* (Capt. Francis Grose, ed. and annotated by Partridge, Barnes & Noble, 1963); for American usage, the *Dictionary of American Slang* (Harold Wentworth and Stuart Berg Flexner, Thomas Y. Crowell, 1975), *The Underground Dictionary* (Eugene E. Landy, Simon & Schuster, paperback, 1971), *The American Thesaurus of Slang* (Lester V. Berrey and Melvin Van den Bark, Thomas Y. Crowell, 1953), and *Playboy's Book of Forbidden Words*, (Robert A. Wilson, ed., Playboy Press, 1972).

Other particularly helpful books included *A Dictionary of Contemporary American Usage* (Bergen Evans and Cornelia Evans, Random House, 1957), *I Hear America Talking* (Stuart Berg Flexner, Van Nostrand Reinhold, 1976), *Word Origins and Their Romantic Stories* (Wilfrid Funk, Funk & Wagnalls, paperback, 1968), *Personalities of Language* (Gary Jennings, Thomas Y. Crowell, 1965), *You English Words* (John Moore, J. B. Lippincott, 1962), *Safire's Political Dictionary* (William Safire, Random House, 1978), and *In Praise of English* (Joseph T. Shipley, Times Books, 1977). One of the principal points of departure for the present work, as well as a valuable reference thereafter, was H. L. Mencken's *The American Language* (Alfred A. Knopf, 1936, and its supplements, 1945 and 1948). Back issues of the quarterly *American Speech*, published since 1925, also provided joy, inspiration, and information.

The *New York Times* comes the closest to being the newspaper of record in the United States and, as such, preserves on its pages most of the best euphemisms of our time. It has been used accordingly. Another work that has been extremely valuable, not only for the intrinsic interest of the subject matter but as an unusual record of the way people actually talk in private, is *The White House Transcripts* (Richard M. Nixon, et al., introduction by R. W. Apple, Jr., Bantam Books, 1974).

The manuscript benefitted from the readings of Patrick Barrett and Margaret Miner, most of whose criticisms were accepted gracefully as well as gratefully. The first draft was typed single-space on small slips of paper, which were easy for me to keep in alphabetical order but not so easy for typists to handle, and I wish to thank Gladys Garrastegui, Irene Goodman, Cynthia Kirk, and Karen Tracht-

Acknowledgments

man for so carefully, and cheerfully, converting the slips into usable copy. I also am indebted to Brandt Aymar and Rosemary Baer for shepherding the manuscript through to publication.

Individuals who supplied euphemisms are too numerous to name: A few are mentioned in the citations for particular entries; many other people made suggestions that led to entries that are now tied to written sources. All contributors are greatly, and equally, thanked.

On the chance that this book will go into a second edition, or result in a successor, readers are invited to send new examples of euphemisms, circumlocutions, and doubletalk to me, care of Crown Publishers, Inc., One Park Avenue, New York, New York 10016. All contributions will be appreciated, but those that include complete citations, with author, title, date of publication, and page number, will be especially appreciated. Contributors whose examples are included will be gratefully acknowledged by name. In case of duplicates, the one with the earliest postmark will be credited.

Brooklyn, N.Y.
April 1981

Hugh Rawson

INTRODUCTION
On the FOP Index & Other Rules of Life
in the Land of Euphemism

Mr. Milquetoast gets up from the table, explaining that he has to go to the *little boys' room* or *see a man about a dog*; a young woman announces that she is *enceinte*. A secretary complains that her boss is a pain in the *derrière*; an undertaker (or *mortician*) asks delicately where to ship the *loved one*. These are euphemisms—mild, agreeable, or roundabout words used in place of coarse, painful, or offensive ones. The term comes from the Greek *eu*, meaning "well" or "sounding good," and *phēmē*, "speech."

Many euphemisms are so delightfully ridiculous that everyone laughs at them. (Well, almost everyone: The people who call themselves the National Selected Morticians usually manage to keep from smiling.) Yet euphemisms have very serious reasons for being. They conceal the things people fear the most—death, the dead, the supernatural. They cover up the facts of life—of sex and reproduction and excretion—which inevitably remind even the most refined people that they are made of clay, or worse. They are beloved by individuals and institutions (governments, especially) who are anxious to present only the handsomest possible images of themselves to the world. And they are embedded so deeply in our language that few of us, even those who pride themselves on being plainspoken, ever get through a day without using them.

The same sophisticates who look down their noses at *little boys' room* and other euphemisms of that ilk will nevertheless say that they are going to the *bathroom* when no bath is intended; that Mary has been *sleeping* around even though she has been getting precious little shut-eye; that John has *passed away* or even *departed* (as if he'd just made the last train to Darien); and that Sam and Janet are *friends*, which sounds a lot better than "illicit lovers."

Thus, euphemisms are society's basic *lingua non franca*. As such, they are outward and visible signs of our inward anxieties, conflicts, fears, and shames. They are like radioactive isotopes. By tracing them, it is possible to see what has been (and is) going on in our language, our minds, and our culture.

Euphemisms can be divided into two general types—positive and negative. The positive ones inflate and magnify, making the euphemized items seem altogether grander and more important than they really are. The negative euphemisms deflate and diminish. They are defensive in nature, offsetting the power of tabooed terms and otherwise eradicating from the language everything that people prefer not to deal with directly.

Positive euphemisms include the many fancy occupational titles, which salve the egos of workers by elevating their job status: *custodian* for janitor (itself a euphemism for caretaker), *counsel* for lawyer, the many kinds of *engineer* (*exterminating engineer, mattress engineer, publicity engineer*, ad infinitum), *help* for servant (itself an old euphemism for slave), *hooker* and *working girl* for whore, and so forth. A common approach is to try to turn one's trade into a profession, usually in imitation of the medical profession. *Beautician* and the aforementioned *mortician* are

Introduction

the classic examples, but the same imitative instinct is responsible for social workers calling welfare recipients *clients*, for football coaches conducting *clinics*, and for undertakers referring to corpses as *cases* or even *patients*.

Other kinds of positive euphemisms include personal honorifics such as *colonel*, the *honorable*, and *major*, and the many institutional euphemisms, which convert madhouses into *mental hospitals*, colleges into *universities*, and small business establishments into *emporiums*, *parlors*, *salons*, and *shoppes*. The desire to improve one's surroundings also is evident in geographical place names, most prominently in the case of the distinctly nongreen *Greenland* (attributed to an early real estate developer named Eric the Red), but also in the designation of many small burgs as *cities*, and in the names of some cities, such as *Troy*, New York (*née* Vanderheyden's Ferry, its name-change in 1789 began a fad for adopting classical place names in the United States).

Negative, defensive euphemisms are extremely ancient. It was the Greeks, for example, who transformed the Furies into the *Eumenides* (the Kindly Ones). In many cultures, it is forbidden to pronounce the name of God (hence, pious Jews say *Adonai*) or of Satan (giving rise to the *deuce*, the *good man*, the *great fellow*, the generalized *Devil*, and many other roundabouts). The names of the dead, and of animals that are hunted or feared, may also be euphemized this way. The bear is called *grandfather* by many peoples and the tiger is alluded to as the *striped one*. The common motivation seems to be a confusion between the names of things and the things themselves: The name is viewed as an extension of the thing. Thus, to know the name is to give one power over the thing (as in the Rumpelstiltskin story). But such power may be dangerous: "Speak of the Devil and he appears." For mere mortals, then, the safest policy is to use another name, usually a flattering, euphemistic one, in place of the supernatural being's true name.

As strong as—or stronger than—the taboos against names are the taboos against particular words, especially the infamous *four-letter words*. (According to a recent Supreme Court decision, the set of *four-letter words* actually contains some words with as few as three and as many as 12 letters, but the logic of Supreme Court decisions is not always immediately apparent.) These words form part of the vocabulary of practically everyone above the age of six or seven. They are not slang terms, but legitimate Standard English of the oldest stock, and they are euphemized in many ways, typically by conversion into pseudo-Latin (e.g., *copulation*, *defecation*, *urination*), into slang (*make love*, *number two*, *pee*), or into socially acceptable dashes (*f——*, *s——*, *p——*, etc.). In the electronic media, the function of the dash is fulfilled by the *bleep* (sometimes pronounced *blip*), which has completed the circle and found its way into print.

The taboo against words frequently degenerates into mere prudery. At least—though the defensive principle is the same—the primitive (or *preliterate*) hunter's use of *grandfather* seems to operate on a more elemental level than the excessive modesty that has produced *abdomen* for belly, *afterpart* for ass, *bosom* for breast, *limb* for leg, *white meat* for breast (of a chicken), and so on.

When carried too far, which is what always seems to happen, positive and negative euphemisms tend finally to coalesce into an unappetizing mush of elegancies and genteelisms, in which the underlying terms are hardly worth the trouble of euphemizing, e.g., *ablutions* for washing, *bender* for knee, *dentures* for false teeth, *expectorate* for spit, *home* for house, *honorarium* for fee, *ill* for sick, *libation* for drink, *perspire* for sweat, *position* for job, etc., etc., etc.

All euphemisms, whether positive or negative, may be used either unconsciously or consciously. Unconscious euphemisms consist mainly of words that were developed as euphemisms, but so long ago that hardly anyone remembers the original motivation. Examples in this category include such now-standard terms as *cemetery* (from the Greek word for "sleeping place," it replaced the more deathly "graveyard"), and the names of various barnyard animals, including the *donkey* (the erstwhile ass), the *sire* (or studhorse), and the *rooster* (for cock, and one of many similar evasions, e.g., *haystack* for haycock, *weather vane* for weathercock, and Louisa May *Alcott*, whose father changed the family name from the nasty-sounding Alcox). Into this category, too, fall such watered-down swear words as *cripes, Jiminy Cricket, gee,* and *gosh,* all designed to avoid taking holy names in vain and now commonly used without much awareness of their original meaning, particularly by youngsters and by those who fill in the balloons in comic strips. Then there are the words for which no honest *Anglo-Saxon* (often a euphemism for "dirty") equivalents exist, e.g., *brassiere,* which has hardly anything to do with the French *bras* (arm) from which it derives, and *toilet,* from the diminutive of *toile* (cloth).

Conscious euphemisms constitute a much more complex category, which is hardly surprising, given the ingenuity, not to say the deviousness, of the human mind. This is not to imply that euphemisms cannot be employed more or less honestly as well as knowingly. For example, garbage men are upgraded routinely into *sanitation men,* but to say "Here come the sanitation men" is a comparatively venial sin. The meaning does come across intelligibly, and the listener understands that it is time to get out the garbage cans. By the same token, it is honest enough to offer a woman condolences upon "the loss of her husband," where *loss* stands for death. Not only are amenities preserved: By avoiding the troublesome term, the euphemism actually facilitates social discourse.

Conscious euphemisms also lead to social double-thinking, however. They form a kind of code. The euphemism stands for "something else," and everyone pretends that the "something else" doesn't exist. It is the essentially duplicitous nature of euphemisms that makes them so attractive to those people and institutions who have something to hide, who don't want to say what they are thinking, and who find it convenient to lie about what they are doing.

It is at this point, when speakers and writers seek not so much to avoid offense as to deceive, that we pass into the universe of dishonest euphemisms, where the conscious elements of circumlocution and doubletalk loom large. Here are the murky worlds of the CIA, the FBI, and the military, where murder is translated into *executive action,* an illegal break-in into a *black bag job,* and napalm into *soft* or *selective ordnance.* Here are the Wonderlands in which Alice would feel so much at home: advertising, where small becomes *medium* if not *large,* and politics, where gross errors are passed off as *misspeaking* and lies that won't wash anymore are called *inoperative.* Here, too, are our great industries: the prison business, where solitary confinement cells are disguised as *adjustment centers, quiet cells,* or *seclusion;* the atomic power business, where nuclear accidents become *core*

Introduction

rearrangements or simply *events*; the death business, where *remains* (not bodies) are *interred* (not buried) in *caskets* (not coffins); and, finally, of murder on its largest scale, where people are put into *protective custody* (imprisonment) in *concentration camps* (prison camps) as a first step toward achieving the *Final Solution* (genocide). George Orwell wrote in a famous essay ("Politics and the English Language," 1946) that "political language . . . is designed to make lies sound truthful and murder respectable, and to give an appearance of solidity to pure wind." His dictum applies equally through the full range of dishonest euphemisms.

Such doubletalk is doubly dangerous: Besides deceiving those on the receiving end, it helps the users fool themselves. As John W. Dean III has noted: "If . . . Richard Nixon had said to me, 'John, I want you to do a little crime for me. I want you to obstruct justice,' I would have told him he was crazy and disappeared from sight. No one thought about the Watergate coverup in those terms—at first, anyway. Rather, it was 'containing' Watergate or keeping the defendants 'on the reservation' or coming up with the right public relations 'scenario' and the like" (*New York Times*, 4/6/75). And as the Senate Intelligence Committee observed in 1975, after wading through a morass of euphemisms and circumlocutions in its investigation of American plots to kill foreign leaders: "'Assassinate,' 'murder,' and 'kill' are words many people do not want to speak or hear. They describe acts which should not even be proposed, let alone plotted. Failing to call dirty business by its rightful name may have increased the risk of dirty business being done." It is probably no coincidence that the conversations and internal memos of the Nixon White House were liberally studded with terms that had been popularized in the underworld and in the cloak-and-dagger business, where few, if any, holds are barred, e.g., *caper* (burglary), *covert operation* (burglary), *launder* (cleaning dirty money), *neutralize* (murder or, as used in the White House, character assassination), *plausible denial* (official lying), and so forth.

Euphemisms are in a constant state of flux. New ones are created almost daily. Many of them prove to be nonce terms—one-day wonders that are never repeated. Of those that are ratified through reuse as true euphemisms, some may last for generations, even centuries, while others fade away or develop into unconscious euphemisms, still used, but reflexively, without thought of their checkered origins. The ebb and flow of euphemisms is governed to a large extent by two basic rules: Gresham's Law of Language and the Law of Succession.

In monetary theory, where it originated, Gresham's Law can be summarized as "bad money drives out good"—meaning that debased or underweight coins will drive good, full-weight coins out of circulation. (By the by: Though Sir Thomas Gresham, 1519–1579, has gotten all the credit, the effect was noticed and explained by earlier monetary experts, including Nicolaus Koppernick, 1473–1543, who doubled as an astronomer and who is better known as Copernicus.) In the field of language, on the same principle, "bad" meanings or associations of words tend to drive competing "good" meanings out of circulation. Thus, *coition, copulation,* and *intercourse* once were general terms for, respectively, coming together, coupling, and communication, but after the words were drawn into service as euphemisms, their sexual meanings became dominant, so that the other senses are hardly ever encountered nowadays except in very special situations. The same thing happened to *crap* (formerly a general term for chaff, residue, or dregs), *feces* (also dregs, as of wine or salad oil), and *manure* (literally: "to work with the hands").

Gresham's Law remains very much in force, of course. Witness what has happened to *gay*, whose homosexual meaning has recently preempted all others. The law is by no means limited to euphemisms, and its application to other words helps explain why some euphemisms are formed. Thus, the incorrect and pejorative uses of "Jew" as a verb and adjective caused many people, Jews as well as Gentiles, to shift to *Hebrew* even though that term should, in theory, be reserved for the Jews of ancient times or their language. A similar example is "girl," whose pejorative meanings have recently been brought to the fore, with the result that anxiety-ridden men sometimes fall into the worse error of referring to their *lady* friends.

Gresham's Law is the engine that powers the second of the two great euphemistic principles: the Law of Succession. After a euphemism becomes tainted by association with its underlying "bad" word, people will tend to shun it. For example, the seemingly innocent *occupy* was virtually banned by polite society for most of the seventeenth and eighteenth centuries because of its use as a euphemism for engaging in sex. (A man might be said to *occupy* his wife or to go to an *occupying* house.) Once people begin to shun a term, it usually is necessary to develop a new euphemism to replace the one that has failed. Then the second will become tainted and a third will appear. In this way, chains of euphemisms evolve. Thus, "mad" has been euphemized successively as *crazy, insane, lunatic, mentally deranged*, and just plain *mental*. Then there are the poor and backward nations that have metamorphosed from *underdeveloped* to *developing* to *emergent*. (*Fledgling* nations never really took hold despite the imprimatur of Eleanor Roosevelt.) A new chain seems to be evolving from the FBI's *black bag job*, which has fallen into sufficient disrepute that agents who condone break-ins are more likely now to talk in terms of *surreptitious entries, technical trespasses, uncontested physical searches*, or *warrantless investigations*.

Extraordinary collections of euphemisms have formed around some topics over the years as a result of the continual creation of new terms, and it seems safe to say that the sizes of these collections reflect the strength of the underlying taboos. Nowhere is this more evident than in the case of the *private parts*, male and female, whose Anglo-Saxon names are rarely used in mixed company, except by those who are on intimate terms. Thus, the monumental *Slang and Its Analogues* (J. S. Farmer and W. E. Henley, 1890–94) lists some 650 synonyms for *vagina*, most of them euphemistic, and about half that number for *penis*. (These are just the English synonyms; for *vagina*, for example, Farmer and Henley include perhaps another 900 synonyms in other languages.) Other anatomical parts that have inspired more than their share of euphemisms include the *bosom, bottom, limb*, and *testicles*. All forms of sexual *intercourse* and the subjects of *defecation, urination*, and the *toilet* also are richly euphemistic, as are *menstruation* (well over 100 terms have been noted), all aspects of death and dying, or *passing away*, and disease (it used to be *TB* and the sexual, *social diseases* that were euphemized; now it is cancer, usually referred to in *obituaries*, or death notices, as a *long illness*).

The incidence of euphemisms may also reflect society's ambivalent feelings on certain subjects. Alcohol, for example, is responsible for a great many

Introduction

euphemisms: There are 356 synonyms for "drunk"—more than for any other term—in the appendixes to the *Dictionary of American Slang* (Harold Wentworth and Stuart Berg Flexner, 1976). The practice of punishing criminals with death (*capital punishment*) also makes many people uncomfortable, judging from the number of linguistic evasions for it, both in the United States, where the electric chair may be humorously downplayed as a *hot seat*, and in other countries, such as France, where the condemned are introduced to *Madame, la guillotine*. Meanwhile, the so-called victimless crime of prostitution has inspired an inordinate number of euphemisms, with some 70 listed in this book under *prostitute* (a sixteenth-century Latinate euphemism for "whore," which itself may have begun life as a euphemism for some now-forgotten word, the Old English *hōre* being cognate with the Latin *cara*, darling). The precarious position of *minorities* (a code term for blacks and/or Hispanics) and other oft-oppressed groups (e.g., homosexuals, servants, women) also is revealed by the variety of terms that have been devised to characterize them.

Just as the clustering of euphemisms around a given term or topic appears to reflect the strength of a particular taboo, so the unusual accumulation of euphemisms around an institution is strongly indicative of interior rot. Thus, the Spanish Inquisition featured an extensive vocabulary of words with double meanings (e.g., *auto-da-fé* for act of faith, and the *question* for torture). In our own time, the number of euphemisms that have collected around the CIA and its attempts at *assassination*, the FBI and its reliance on break-ins and *informants*, and the prison business and its noncorrectional *correctional facilities*, all tend to confirm one's darker suspicions. This is true, too, of the *Defense* (not War) *Department*, with its *enhanced radiation weapons* (neutron bombs) and its *reconnaissance in force* (search-and-destroy) missions. The military tradition, though, is very old. As long ago as ca. 250 B.C., a Macedonian general, Antigonus Gonatas, parlayed a "retreat" into a *strategic movement to the rear*. And, finally, there is politics, always a fertile source of doubletalk, but especially so during the Watergate period when euphemisms surfaced at a rate that is unlikely (one hopes) ever to be matched again: *Deep six, expletive deleted, inoperative, sign off,* and *stonewall* are only a few of the highpoints (or lowpoints, depending upon one's perspective) of this remarkably fecund period.

Watergate aside, it is usually assumed that most of our greatest euphemisms come from the Victorian era, but this is not quite correct. Many of the euphemisms that are associated most closely with the Victorians—*bosom* and *limb*, for instance—actually came into use prior to the start of Victoria's reign in 1837.

The beginning of the period of pre-Victorian prudery is hard to date—as are most developments in language. Normally, it is only possible to say, on the basis of a quotation from a book, play, poem, letter, newspaper, and so forth, that such-and-such word or phrase was being used in such-and-such way when the particular work was written. But there is no guarantee that the dictionary-maker—or compiler of euphemisms—has found the earliest example. Also, many words, especially slang words, may be used informally for a long time, perhaps centuries, before they are committed to writing. As a result, one can only say that fastidiousness in language became increasingly common from about 1750, and that this trend accelerated around the turn of the century, almost as if the incipient Victorians were frantically cleaning up their act in preparation for her ascent to the throne.

One of the first indications of the new niceness of the eighteenth century is the taint that was attached to "ass" after it became a euphemism for *arse* (the real term is now used cutely but quite mistakenly as a euphemism for the euphemism!). As early as 1751, polite ladies, whose equally polite grandmothers had thought it clever to say "arse," were shying clear of "ass" no matter what the occasion, with the result that a new euphemistic name had to be devised for the four-legged kind; hence, the appearance of *donkey*. The first *rooster* and the first *drumstick* (to avoid "leg") seem to date from the 1760s, while *darn* comes from the 1770s. By 1813, some farmers were speaking of the *bosom* of their plows, meaning the forward part of the moldboard, formerly called the "breast." And at about this time, too, begins the nineteenth-century sentimentalization of death, as recorded on tombstones of the period, which start to report that people, instead of dying, have *fallen asleep, gone to meet their Maker, passed over the river,* etc.

The two great landmarks in the development of pre-Victorian thought are the expurgations of the Bard and the Bible, with *The Family Shakespeare,* by the Bowdlers, appearing in 1807, and Noah Webster's version of the word of God ("with Amendments of the language"), coming out in 1833. The objective of the Bowdlers, as stated in the preface to the enlarged second edition of 1818, was to omit "those words and expressions . . . which cannot with propriety be read aloud in a family." (Note that "family" here has essentially the same meaning as when television executives speak of *family* time.) Though Dr. Thomas Bowdler has usually been given all the credit, the expurgation was primarily the work of his sister, Henrietta Maria. She has only herself to blame, however, for the lack of recognition: She didn't sign her name to the book probably because, as a maiden lady, she didn't want to admit publicly to understanding all the things she was censoring. As for Noah Webster, he carefully took out of the Bible every "whore," every "piss," and even every "stink," while making a great many other curious changes, such as *idolatries* for whoredom, *lewd deeds* for fornication (itself a Latinate evasion for an Anglo-Saxon word), and *nurse* for the apparently too animalistic "suck." In his introduction, Webster justified his rewrite of the King James Version of 1611, saying "Purity of mind is a Christian virtue that ought to be carefully guarded; and purity of language is one of the guards which protect this virtue."

The precise causes of this pre-Victorian linguistic revolution, whose legacy remains with us, are difficult to pinpoint, involving as they do a combination of religious revival, industrialization, an emerging middle class, increasing literacy, and an improvement in the status of women. Bench marks of change include the Great Awakening, the religious revival that shook New England in the late 1730s and soon spread to the rest of the colonies; the near-simultaneous development of Methodism in England; the beginnings of the factory system (Samuel Slater emigrated to America in 1789, bringing with him most of the secrets of the English textile industry); the invention of the steam-powered press (the *Times* of London installed two in 1814 that made 1,100 impressions per hour, a great technological advance); and, especially in the United States, a spirit of egalitarianism that extended to women and affected the language that men used

Introduction

in front of them. As Alexis de Tocqueville noted: "It has often been remarked that in Europe a certain degree of contempt lurks even in the flattery which men lavish upon women; although a European frequently affects to be the slave of a woman, it may be seen that he never sincerely thinks her his equal. In the United States men seldom compliment women, but they . . . constantly display an entire confidence in the understanding of a wife and a profound respect for her freedom . . . . their conduct to women always implies that they suppose them to be virtuous and refined; and such is the respect entertained for the moral freedom of the sex that in the presence of a woman the most guarded language is used lest her ear should be offended by an expression" (*Democracy in America*, 1835, 1840).

The ancient Egyptians called the deadhouse, where bodies were turned into mummies, the *beautiful house,* and the ways of expunging offensive expressions from language have not changed since. Simplest is to make a straight substitution, using a word that has happier connotations than the term one wishes to avoid. Frequently, a legitimate synonym will do. Thus, *agent, speculator,* and *thrifty* have better vibes than "spy," "gambler," and "tight," although the literal meanings, or denotations, of each pair of words are the same. On this level, all the euphemist has to do is select words with care. Other principles may be applied, however, a half dozen of which are basic to creating—and deciphering—euphemisms. They are:

Foreign languages sound finer. It is permissible for speakers and writers of English to express almost any thought they wish, as long as the more risqué parts of the discussion are rendered in another language, usually French or Latin. The versatility of French (and the influence of French culture) is evident in such diverse fields as love (*affair, amour, liaison*), war (*matériel, personnel, sortie, triage*), women's underwear (*brassiere, chemise, lingerie*), and dining (goat, cow, deer, and other animals with English names when they are alive and kicking are served up on the dinnertable as the more palatable *chevon, filet mignon,* and *venison*). *French* itself is a euphemistic prefix word for a variety of "wrong" and/or "sexy" things, such as the *French disease* (syphilis) and one of the methods of guarding against it, the *French letter* (condom). Latin is almost equally popular as a source of euphemisms, especially for the body's sexual and other functions. Thus, such words as *copulation, fellatio, masturbation, pudendum,* and *urination* are regarded as printable and even broadcastable by people (including United States Supreme Court justices) who become exercised at the sight and sound of their English counterparts Other languages have contributed. For example, the Dutch *boss* (master), the Spanish *cojones* (balls), and the Yiddish *tushie* (the ass). Not strictly speaking a foreign language is potty talk, a distinct idiom that has furnished many euphemisms, i.e., *number one, number two, pee, piddle,* and other relics of the nursery, often used by adults when speaking to one another as well as when addressing children.

Bad words are not so bad when abbreviated. Words that otherwise would create consternation if used in mixed company or in public are acceptable when reduced to their initial letters. Essentially, such abbreviations as *BS* and *SOB* work the same way as the dash in *f——:* Everyone knows what letters have been deleted, but no one is seriously offended because the taboo word has not been paraded in all its glory. Dean Acheson even got away with *snafu* when he was secretary of state, though the acronym did cause some comment among the British, not all of whom felt this to be a very diplomatic way of apologizing for an American—er—*foul up*. This acronym also is noteworthy for spawning a host of picturesque albeit short-lived descendants, including *fubar* (where *bar* stands for Beyond All Recognition), *janfu* (Joint Army-Navy), *tarfu* (Things Are Really), and *tuifu* (The Ultimate In). Abbreviations function as euphemisms in many fields, e. g., the child's *BM*, the advertiser's *BO*, the hypochondriac's *Big C*, and the various shortenings for offbeat sex, such as *AC/DC* for those who swing both ways, *bd* for bondage and discipline, and *S/M*.

Abstractions are not objectionable. The strength of particular taboos may be dissipated by casting ideas in the most general possible terms; also, abstractions, being quite opaque to the uninformed eye (and meaningless to the untrained ear) make ideal cover-up words. Often, it is only a matter of finding the lowest common denominator. Thus, *it, problem, situation,* and *thing* may refer to anything under the sun: the child who keeps playing with *it* and the girl who is said to be doing *it;* *problem* days and *problem* drinking; the *situation* at the Three Mile Island, Pennsylvania, nuclear power plant; an economic *thing* (slump, recession, or depression), *our thing* (i. e., the Cosa Nostra), or the Watergate *thing* (elaborated by the president himself into the *prething* and the *postthing*). The American tendency toward abstraction was noted early on by Tocqueville, who believed that democratic nations as a class were "addicted to generic terms and abstract expressions because these modes of speech enlarge thought and assist the operation of the mind by enabling it to include many objects in a small compass." The dark side of this is that abstractions are inherently fuzzy. As Tocqueville also noted: "An abstract term is like a box with a false bottom; you may put in what ideas you please, and take them out again without being observed" (*op. cit.*). Bureaucrats, engineers, scientists, and those who like to be regarded as scientists, are particularly good at generalizing details out of existence. They have produced such expressions as *aerodynamic personnel decelerator* for parachute, *energy release* for radiation release (as from a nuclear reactor), *episode* and *event* for disasters of different sorts and sizes, *impact attenuation device* for a crash cushion, and *Vertical Transportation Corps* for a group of elevator operators.

Indirection is better than direction. Topics and terms that are too touchy to be dealt with openly may be alluded to in a variety of ways, most often by mentioning one aspect of the subject, a circumstance involving it, a related subject, or even by saying what it is not. Thus, people really do come together in an *assembly center* and soldiers do stop fighting when they *break off contact with the enemy,* but these are indirect euphemisms for "prison" and "retreat," respectively. *Bite the dust* is a classic of this kind, and the adjective is used advisedly, since the expression appears in Homer's *Iliad,* circa 750 B. C. Many of the common anatomical euphemisms also depend on indirection—the general, locational, it's-somewhere-back-there allusions to the *behind* the *bottom,* and the *rear,* for example. A special category of anatomical euphemisms are those that conform to the Rule of the Displaced Referent, whereby "unmentionable" parts of the human body are euphemized by

Introduction

referring to nearby "mentionable" parts, e.g., *chest* for breasts; *fanny*, a word of unknown origin whose meaning has not always been restricted to the back end of a person; *tail*, which also has had frontal meanings (in Latin, *penis* means "tail"), and *thigh*, a biblical euphemism for the balls. Quaintest of the indirect euphemisms are those that are prefaced with a negative adjective, telling us what they are not, such as *unnatural, unthinkable,* and *unmentionable*. (The latter also appears as a noun in the plural; some women wear *upper unmentionables* and *lower unmentionables*.) An especially famous negative euphemism is the dread *love that dare not speak its name,* but the phrase was not totally dishonest in the beginning, since it dates to 1894 (from a poem by Oscar Wilde's young *friend,* Alfred, Lord Douglas), when "homosexual" was still so new a word as not to be known to many people, regardless of their *sexual orientation.*

Understatement reduces risks. Since a euphemism is, by definition, a mild, agreeable, or roundabout word or phrase, it follows logically that its real meaning is always worse than its apparent meaning. But this is not always obvious to the uninitiated, especially in constructions that acknowledge part of the truth while concealing the extent of its grimness. Thus, a nuclear reactor that is said to be *above critical* is actually out of control, *active defense* is attack, *area bombing* is terror bombing, *collateral damage* is civilian damage (as from nuclear bombs), and so on. The soft sell also is basic to such euphemisms as *companion, partner,* and *roommate,* all of which downplay "lover"; to *pro-choice* for pro-abortion, and to *senior citizen* for old person. The danger with understatement is that it may hide the true meaning completely. As a result, euphemists often erect signposts in front of the basic term, e.g., *close personal friend, constant companion, criminal conversation* (a legalism for adultery), *meaningful relationship,* etc. The signposts ensure that even dullards will get the message.

The longer the euphemism the better. As a rule, to which there are very few exceptions (*hit* for murder, for instance), euphemisms are longer than the words they replace. They have more letters, they have more syllables, and frequently, two or more words will be deployed in place of a single one. This is partly because the tabooed Anglo-Saxon words tend to be short and partly because it almost always takes more words to evade an idea than to state it directly and honestly. The effect is seen in euphemisms of every type. Thus, *Middle Eastern* dancing is what better "belly" dancers do; more advertisers agree that *medication* gives faster relief than "medicine"; the writers of financial reports eschew "drop" in favor of *adjustment downward,* and those poor souls who are required to give testimony under oath prefer *at this point in time* to "now." The list is practically endless. Until this very point in time, however, it was impossible for anyone to say exactly *how much* longer was *how much* better. That important question has now been resolved with the development of the Fog or Pomposity Index (FOP Index, for short).

The FOP Index compares the length of the euphemism or circumlocution to the word or phrase for which it stands, with an additional point being awarded for each additional letter, syllable, or word in the substitute expression. Thus, "medicine" has 8 letters and 3 syllables, while *medication* has 10 letters and an extra, fourth syllable, giving it a point count of 11. Dividing 8 into 11 produces a FOP Index of 1.4. By the same token, *adjustment downward* has a FOP Index of 5.75

compared to "drop" (18 letters, plus 4 extra syllables, plus 1 extra word, for a total of 23, divided by the 4 letters of the euphemized term).

Like most breakthroughs in the social (or soft) sciences, the FOP Index doesn't really tell you anything you didn't already know. Everyone (well, almost everyone) has always sensed that *medication* is on the pretentious side. The index, however, arms users with a number to back up their intuition, thus enabling them to crush opponents in debate. It can now be said authoritatively that *lower extremity* (FOP Index of 6.6) outdoes *limb* (1.3) as a euphemism for leg. In much the same way, *prostitute* (2.4) improves upon *harlot* (1.4) for whore. In another field: *Oval Office* (2.6) is better than *Presidency* (2.4) is better than "Nixon," but both pale in comparison to the 17.8 of former HEW Secretary Joe Califano's *Personal Assistant to the Secretary (Special Activities)*, who was a "cook." (Califano's *Personal Assistant*, illustrates a basic rule of bureaucracies: the longer the title, the lower the rank.) And so it goes: *Active defense* has a FOP Index of 2.5 for attack; *benign neglect* rates 2.3 for neglect (the "benign" being an example of a Meaningless Modifier); *categorical inaccuracy* is a whopping 10.3 compared to lie; *intestinal fortitude* is 6.5 for guts.

With quantification, the study of euphemisms has at last been put on a firm scientific footing. FOP Indexes have been included for a number of the entries in this dictionary and it is hoped that readers will enjoy working out indexes for themselves in other instances. As they proceed, given the nature of the terms for which euphemisms stand, they may also wish to keep in mind Shakespeare's advice (*Henry IV*, Part 2, 1600):

> 'Tis needful that the most immodest word
> Be looked upon and learned.

Euphemisms, circumlocutions, and doubletalk are printed in *italic* type except when discussed in a generic sense, in which case the terms are enclosed in quotation marks, and when used illustratively, in which case the style of the original source is followed. Thus, the first *abattoirs* were constructed in France, "abattoir" entered the English language as a euphemism, and "abattoirs have recently been erected in London." SMALL CAPS indicate a separate entry for that term; for example, see LINGERIE.

abattoir. A slaughterhouse. One of the great laws governing the formation (and detection) of euphemisms is that the unseemly is more palatable when couched in a foreign language, preferably Latin or its Romantic, fair-sounding descendant, French.

The first *abattoirs* were constructed in France, the word coming from *abattre*, to strike down. English writers reported their existence at least by 1820, according to the *Oxford English Dictionary*, and by 1866, the word had been taken into the language with the *Cyclopedia of Useful Arts* (I, 2) noting: "Abattoirs have recently been erected in London." The Victorians, as John Moore has pointed out, "seized gratefully upon 'abattoir' for slaughterhouse, 'lingerie' for the unmentionable undergarments, and 'nude' as a substitute for naked" (*You English Words*, 1962). See also LINGERIE, NUDE, and UNMENTIONABLE itself.

abdomen. The belly. Some people are so refined that they can't stomach "stomach," let alone "belly," so they say "abdomen," despite the example of Winston S. Churchill, who did *not* urge that the Nazis be attacked through the "soft abdomen" of Europe. See also MIDDLE EASTERN DANCING, STOMACHACHE, and TUMMY.

ablutions, perform one's. To wash, ceremonially. The phrase dates to the middle of the eighteenth century, when the seeds of Victorianism already were beginning to sprout.

above critical. Out of control; running away; melting down; in danger of blowing up. "The reactor began to run out of control—'above critical' in the parlance of the nuclear engineer" (John G. Fuller, *We Almost Lost Detroit*, 1975). A meltdown of the fuel in a nuclear reactor may also be characterized—again in the parlance of the nuclear engineer—as a *superprompt critical power excursion* (where "excursion" equals "runaway") or *prompt critical*, for short. See also BLIP, CORE REARRANGEMENT, ENERGY RELEASE, EVENT, INCIDENT, and SUNSHINE.

accident. An omnibus term for any of a variety of unspeakable happenings, ranging from the MESS that Fido makes on the Persian carpet to murder or ASSASSINATION. Thus the Senate Intelligence Committee reported in 1975 that the CIA offered $10,000 in 1960 to a Cuban agent for "arranging an accident" for Fidel Castro's brother, Raul. Other kinds of "accident" include "stroke," sometimes referred to as "an accident in the brain," and "pregnancy," a notoriously DELICATE subject, e.g.: "But, accidents do happen. So, could Midnight take her to one of those nice clinics where these accidents can be taken care of?" (New York *Village Voice*, 1/2/78). See also ANKLE, SPRAIN AN; CASUALTY, and THERAPEUTIC ACCIDENT.

accouchement. Lying in; childbirth; *parturition* (as the doctors say). "Meanwhile the skill and patience of the physician had brought about a happy *accouchement*" (James Joyce, *Ulysses*, 1922). The Frenchification (from *accoucher*, to put to bed) dates to around 1800 in Britain and it became popular in the United States after the Civil War.

Prior to *accouchement*, a woman is said (assuming one is speaking consistently) to be ENCEINTE.

account for. To kill. When soldiers are being awarded medals for doing a lot of killing, the citations tend to be phrased blandly rather than baldly. As John Keegan notes, "Citation writers, flinching from 'kill', deal largely in 'account for', 'dispatch', 'dispose of' . . ." (*The Face of Battle*, 1976). A typical citation, according to Keegan, might tell how Corporal So-and-so "worked his way round the flank of the machine-gun which was holding up the advance and then charged it, firing his carbine from the hip, so accounting for six of the enemy." See also BITE THE DUST, DISPATCH, DISPOSE, and the basic military CASUALTY.

AC/DC. Bisexual; a play on Alternating Current/Direct Current. See also BISEXUAL.

act of God. A disaster—but not necessarily one that is beyond human power to prevent, despite the effort to dump the blame on the Deity. "It is an odd thing that even the most scientifically sophisticated society known to history insists on building on faults, flood-plains, and evanescent beach fronts, and calls the inevitable disasters that occur 'acts of God'" (James K. Page, Jr., *Smithsonian*, 7/78). Note that "act of God" presumes an awe-ful deity in the Old Testament sense, a god known more by his punishments than his blessings, who is best approached gingerly and indirectly because of his quickness to dish out death and destruction to those who fail him. See also ADONAI.

action. A euphemism for violence in television and for sex in real life. In the first case, the euphemism partakes of the term's military sense ("action" as an engagement with the enemy) and its literary sense (the "action" or series of events that form the plot of a story or drama). The euphemistic meaning is dominant, however, when vice-presidents of program content ask for more "action-oriented" scripts. As Joseph Wambaugh, the writer, said on a 1977 NBC news special, "Violence in America": "We never use the word 'violence' in this industry—it's called action." As for the sexual "action": "I therefore denounced the idea of conjugal visits as inherently unfair; single prisoners needed and deserved action just as much as married prisoners did" (Eldridge Cleaver, *Soul on Ice*, 1968). See also EXECUTIVE ACTION and, for other examples of the unfortunately common association between violence and sex, DIE, F——, GUN, and OFF.

active defense. Offense; the circumlocution sounds better when one is getting ready to cross another nation's border. For example, on March 13, 1978, Israeli Minister Menachem Begin declared: "We should make use of active defenses in order to break the strength of the P.L.O." (*New York Times*, 3/14/78). And the next day, more than ten thousand Israeli troops advanced into Lebanon. See also DEFENSE, DEPARTMENT OF; INCURSION, and PREEMPTIVE STRIKE.

adjective/adjectival. Either term allows the reader to insert mentally the modifier of his or her choice into the prepared text; literary counterparts of the electronic BLEEP and BLIP. Thus, reporting on a tour of the London underworld, Charles Dickens sanitized the words of a notorious fence named Bark, who probably included "bloody" when he yelled: "If the adjective coves [rogues] in the kitchen was men, they'd come up now and do for you!" ("On Duty with Inspector Field," *Household Words*, 6/14/1851). And in our own time, that best-of-all-sportswriters, Red "Walter" Smith, produced this gem while fielding a quote from the otherwise unprintable Rogers Hornsby—and he made it look easy: "He [Leo Durocher] was an excellent shortstop on defense, but as Rogers Hornsby once remarked, 'You can shake a glove man out of that adjectival palm tree.' Rog happened to be in Florida when he spoke. In other climes you can shake glove men out of adjectival oaks, elms, and maples" (*New York Times*, 5/12/76). See also F—— and *the Shavian adjective* in RUDDY.

adjustment center. A solitary confinement cell in the psychologically disturbed language of prison administrators. ". . . some prisons are now called 'therapeutic correctional communities,' convicts are 'clients of the correctional system,' solitary confinement and punishment cells have become 'adjustment centers,' 'seclusion,' or, in Virginia, 'meditation'" (Jessica Mitford, *Kind and Usual Punishment: The Prison Business*, 1974). Still other kinds of solitary include the *quiet cell* (one such was reported in the Essex, New Jersey, County Jail in 1971), the *special housing unit* (at the Attica, New York, Correctional Facility), and such jawbreakers as *administrative confinement, administrative segregation*, and, nicest of all, *therapeutic segregation*. See also SECLUSION and the basic CORRECTIONAL FACILITY.

adjustment downward. A circumlocutory "drop," with a FOP Index of 5.75. The phrase is much favored by accountants, especially when preparing glossy annual reports on companies whose stock has dropped. See also RECESSION and TECHNICAL ADJUSTMENT.

adjustment of the front. American troops never "retreat"; see STRATEGIC MOVEMENT TO THE REAR.

administrative assistant. A secretary, especially in a company that is under the gun to prove that it doesn't discriminate against women, and so has created a new job classification to which they can be "promoted." See also ENGINEER and TRAFFIC EXPEDITER.

Adonai. The Hebrew circumlocution for God's real name, YHWH, i.e., Yahweh or, to Christians, Jehovah. "In the Hebrew Old Testament, the name of the deity is Yahweh. In reading the Old Testament aloud, however, pious Jews must pronounce the word Adonai" (Anatol Rapoport, *Semantics*, 1975).

Similar taboos against mentioning the name of God—or any other supernatural being, for that matter—are very common in other cultures. In most instances, the underlying fear seems to be that saying the being's name will cause it to appear. As a result, there are many circumlocutions for *not* mentioning the names of dead people (the ghosts might hear), evil spirits, feared animals, the angel of death. See also, for example, DEPARTED ONE, THE; DEVIL, THE; GOOD PEOPLE, THE; GOSH; GRANDFATHER; SUPREME BEING, and WEALTHY ONE, THE.

adorable. Commonly encountered in classified ads for houses; it translates as "small."

adult. A capacious closet of a word from whose roomy interior different meanings may be plucked, depending on need and circumstance. Technically meaning anyone who has matured—in civil law, fourteen for males and twelve for females—"adult" is used most often to make old people seem younger and to characterize, without describing, certain pleasures that older people prefer to reserve for themselves.

When applied to a home (e.g., the Moncie Home for Adults), the implication is that the residents are rather elderly, "home for adults" actually being a double-euphemism, akin to NURSING HOME (see HOME and RESIDENT). Then there are the *adult communities*, whose citizens are old, but not as old as those in *adult homes*, since *adult communities* are merely "retirement villages." Common age minimums for residence in *adult communities* are forty-eight and fifty-two.

"Adult" takes on an entirely different coloration when used to modify such words as "book," "entertainment," "film," and "novelty." Then, "adult" means "sex" (just as FAMILY signals the absence of same). Thus, the city of Boston, also known as the Athens of America, boasts an *adult entertainment zone*, also known as "the combat zone," where almost anything goes. (A Bicentennial attempt was made to change the district's name to the wonderfully euphemistic *Liberty Tree Neighborhood*, but this didn't take.) See also EROTICA and SEXUALLY EXPLICIT (or ORIENTED).

advisement, take under. To shelve, usually for good. "I'll take that under advisement" is a typical bureaucratic dodge for deferring action in the hope (not infrequently fulfilled) that the problem will go away of its own accord.

adviser. A soldier in educational guise; for example, one of the 15,000 Cuban *advisers* sent to Angola in 1975–76, or one of 3,000 Russian *advisers* discovered to be in Cuba in 1979. Or were they combat troops? It all depended on whose terminology was being used—just as it did in the world's most famous advisory operation, which began in 1954 when 200 American soldiers were sent to South Vietnam. As President John F. Kennedy said in a TV interview in September 1963: ". . . we can send our men out there as advisers, but they have to win it, the people of Vietnam" (quoted in Theodore C. Sorensen, *Kennedy*, 1965). See also ERA.

aerodynamic personnel decelerator. A parachute, with a FOP Index of 4.8. The *aerodynamic decelerator* for PERSONNEL is essentially the same as the "aerodynamic breaking system" (in the words of a Tass announcement) for bringing Russia's *Venera 9* probe to a soft landing on Venus in 1975. See also IMPACT ATTENUATION DEVICE and VENUSIAN.

affair. An essentially neutral word that can be used to cover dirty work of various kinds. For example, there is the illicit love *affair*, or intrigue (sometimes described as an EXTRAMARITAL or *premarital affair*, or further fancied up as an *affaire de coeur*); the *affair of honor*, which is a duel or MEETING; the man of *affairs*, or businessman, and the man with an *affair*. The last is the most euphemistic, being one of the blander terms for PENIS, as in "Her gallant . . . drew out his affair ready erected" (John Cleland, *Memoirs of a Woman of Pleasure*, 1749).

 The ordinary, everyday love *affair* or *affaire* (people actually have been known to conduct Frenchified *office affaires*) is of some venerability, with the oldest example in the *Oxford English Dictionary* dating from 1702. It took a distinguished British philosopher, Bishop George Berkeley, to sort out the euphemism: "In pure Dialect a vicious Man is a Man of Pleasure . . . a Lady is said to have an affair, a Gentleman to be a gallant, a Rogue in business to be one that knows the world" (*Alciphron, or the Minute Philosopher*, 1732).

 Today, "affair" seems to be holding its own, in face of stiff competition from semipsychological claptrap, such as INVOLVED WITH and RELATIONSHIP, e.g., from a nonliterary ad in the *New York Review of Books* (1/26/78):

> KENT STATE PROFESSOR/AUTHOR will respond enthusiastically to all applications received for a discreet and sincere affair to be arranged in Northeast Ohio or surrounding areas.

See also AMOUR, LIAISON, MATINEE, and SEXUAL VARIETY.

affirmative. Yes. "He answered in the affirmative," has a mush-mouth FOP Index of 3.8, compared to the straightforward, "He said yes." See also NEGATIVE and SIGN OFF.

age, of a certain. Old enough to be circumlocutory about it. The span of years covered by the phrase is imprecise, varying according to who is using it. As good a working definition as any comes from a book on the subject, *Women of a Certain Age* (1979), by Lillian B. Rubin, a sociologist in her "mid-years." The book discusses women aged thirty-five to fifty-four. See also MATURE.

agent. A spy who is on your side; an OPERATIVE, or SOURCE OF INFORMATION.

 Showing grace under pressure, Edmee Brooks, an Alsatian, recruited by French intelligence to infiltrate the German armed forces in World War II, drew the distinction nicely when a relative in Saxony, to whom she had gone for aid, called the Gestapo instead. "You are a spy," the terrified relative said. "You've got it wrong, dear," Ms. Brooks replied. "A spy works for the other side. I'm an agent." (*New York Times*, 8/28/75).

 The desirable attributes of an *agent*, as viewed by the CIA, were summarized in a cable, sent to the Congo in 1960, when plans were being made to assassinate Prime Minister Patrice Lumumba. The cable commended a particular *agent:*

He is indeed aware of the precepts of right and wrong, but if he is given an assignment which may be morally wrong in the eyes of the world, but necessary because his case officer ordered him to carry it out, then it is right, and he will dutifully undertake appropriate action for its execution without pangs of conscience. In a word, he can rationalize all actions. (Senate Intelligence Committee report on American assassination plots against foreign leaders, 11/75.) See also ASSASSINATION.

When suitably qualified, "agent" may have other meanings. For example, meter maids and meter men in New York City are called *parking enforcement agents;* this is another example of the near-universal movement to upgrade job titles (see ENGINEER) and to avoid typing them by sex ("agent" being neuter, of course). The FBI, meanwhile, has *special agents* (in effect, making each and every one of them into something "special"), a ploy that J. Edgar Hoover may have picked up from the Post Office, which had long employed "special agents" for particular or special purposes. Around the turn of the century, "agent" also was short for "road agent," or highwayman, while today, the term may be used to confer legitimacy upon underworld informers, or snitches. As the United States Supreme Court put it in a 1972 decision: "He did not know that Chin Poy was what the Government calls an 'underworld agent' and what [the] petitioner calls a 'stool pigeon' for the Bureau of Narcotics." See also FIELD ASSOCIATE, INFORMANT, and INVESTIGATOR.

air support. The official military term for what everyone else calls bombing; see ARMED RECONNAISSANCE.

The official position was stated succinctly and dramatically in 1973 by Col. David H. E. Opfer, air attaché at the United States embassy in Phnom Penh, Cambodia, when he complained to newsmen: "You always write it's bombing, bombing, bombing. It's not bombing. It's air support." For this contribution to semantic clarity, Colonel Opfer was honored the following year with one of the first Doublespeak Awards, presented by the Committee on Public Doublespeak of the National Council of Teachers of English. Among the other award winners that year was Ron (INOPERATIVE) Ziegler. Winners in later years have included CONSUMER COMMUNICATION CHANNEL, ENHANCED RADIATION WEAPON, EVENT, and VERTICAL TRANSPORTATION CORPS. For more about the language of military briefers, see CASUALTY and ORDNANCE.

Alaska sable/Alaska strawberries. (1) Skunk fur; (2) dried beans. "Alaska sable" is a nineteenth-century euphemism, designed to make skunk fur more attractive to ladies of fashion. "Alaska strawberries," from the same era, was for the benefit of local digestive tracts. See also GREENLAND and WELSH RAREBIT.

all the way. In a sexual sense, "all the way" is too far, the allusion being to what is also called COITION, INTERCOURSE, or a SCREW, depending on the circle in which one happens to be traveling at the moment. Note that the usually good connotations of the phrase in nonsexual contexts, where it indicates complete or unqualified support or agreement, are reversed in the sexual sense, which is in keeping with traditional attitudes on *that* subject. "The limits to acceptable female sexual behavior varied from family to family and from community to community, but one rule remained constant [until recently]: Unmarried women were not supposed to 'go all the way.' They were expected to remain virgins until they married" (Barry McCarthy, *What You Still Don't Know About Male Sexuality*, 1977). To go *all the way* is the same as to go *the whole route* or the LIMIT. See also GO.

alter. To castrate or spay, as in "It's time to have kitty altered." In the nineteenth century, even farmers used *alter*, as well as the similarly bland *change* and *arrange*, in preference to "castrate." See also BILATERAL ORCHIDECTOMY.

altogether. Naked; in one's BIRTHDAY SUIT. "Altogether" is an example of Reverse English, its euphemistic meaning, "without clothes," being almost precisely opposite its formal dictionary definition, "Completely . . . With everything included; all told." See also NUDE.

ambidextrous. The dexterity is sexual, both hetero- and homo-. To say that "Charlie is ambidextrous" is the same as saying "Charlie is AC/DC." Women are rarely, if ever, described as *ambidextrous*, though they are sometimes said (as are men) to be *versatile*. See also BISEXUAL.

amour. Illicit love; an AFFAIR, LIAISON, or RELATIONSHIP. Medieval "amours" were not necessarily dishonorable, but the neutral and good senses of the word faded in the seventeenth century as people with something to hide resorted increasingly to the French, e.g.: "Intrigue, Philotis, that's an old phrase; I have laid that word by: amour sounds better" (John Dryden, *Marriage à la Mode*, 1673). A petty or passing affair was at one time an *amourette*. See also PARAMOUR.

Anglo-Saxon. Dirty, as in "Harry used an Anglo-Saxon word." *Anglo-Saxon* is the only language in the world whose vocabulary consists entirely of FOUR-LETTER WORDS.

ankle, sprain an. To be seduced, pregnant, and unmarried; an old circumlocution for an exceedingly DELICATE condition, recorded by Capt. Francis Grose, aptly named compiler of *A Classical Dictionary of the Vulgar Tongue* (1796). Variations, working upward, include *stub a toe, break an ankle, break a leg*, to be *broken-kneed* or *broken-legged*, and, most daringly, to *break a leg above the knee*. Eric Partridge dates "break a leg" to circa 1670 in *A Dictionary of Slang and Unconventional English* (1970), and he notes that the French have a similar expression, e.g., *Elle a mal aux genoux* (She has a pain in her knees). "Broke her ankle" is still current in the United States for "a woman having gotten pregnant out of wedlock" but, confusingly, in some parts of the country the phrase may refer to "having had an abortion" (Robert A. Wilson, ed., *Playboy's Book of Forbidden Words*, 1972). See also ACCIDENT, EXPECTANT, and, for *stubbing one's toe* in yet another way, MENSTRUATE.

anticipating. Pregnant. As a rule, women who are *anticipating* do not actually have babies; rather, they bring forth *vital statistics* or BLESSED EVENTS. The gossip columnists, meanwhile, have given us the fatherly *anticipatering, heir conditioned,* and *infanticipating.* By the same treacly token, a newborn bastard is a *sinfant.* See also EXPECTANT and LOVE CHILD.

antipersonnel weapon. A people-killer—"personnel" being the military way of eliminating figuratively what the weapon eliminates literally (see PERSONNEL). The ultimate *antipersonnel weapon,* as we now understand these things, is the neutron bomb, aka ENHANCED RADIATION WEAPON. The army's Weteye nerve gas bombs, stored near Denver, where some were found in 1979 to be leaking, also have great promise. Technically, and militarily, the poison gas is a *chemical antipersonnel agent.* (The "Weteye" also is a euphemism, considering that the gas kills within seconds.)

Antipersonnel weapons began showing up in World War II, e.g.: "The antipersonnel mine . . . was dramatically introduced by the Germans in the fall of 1939. . . . Its chief feature was an arrangement whereby the mine, on being tripped, was boosted out of the ground to about the height of a man's waist before exploding. It was really a bomb, which sprayed a wide area with shrapnel" (*Reader's Digest,* 12/42). "Antipersonnel mines" have earned themselves such loving sobriquets as *Bouncing Betty, Hopping Sam,* and *Leaping Lena.* See also SELECTIVE ORDNANCE and the basic military CASUALTY.

antiperspirant. Antisweat. It is very doubtful that the horrid word "sweat" has ever appeared in any of the ads that promise relief from it. See also PERSPIRE.

anti-Semitic. Anti-Jewish. The euphemism has even been sanctioned more or less officially by Israeli Prime Minister Menachem Begin, i.e.: "One third of Mr. Begin's prepared text was devoted to what he termed anti-Semitic remarks in the Egyptian press, although Arabs, too, are Semites" (*New York Times,* 1/24/78). "Anti-Semitic" is preferred to "anti-Jewish" because "Jew" is a loaded word. See also ARAB and HEBREW.

apprehend. To arrest, to nab; police-ese.

appropriate. To steal. With a FOP Index of 2.8, "appropriate" may be further embellished to cover particular kinds of thefts by particular thieves, e.g., bank tellers who *misappropriate* and nations that *expropriate.* The similarity between *appropriating* and stealing was noted in 1864 by a correspondent for the *New York Herald,* William Conyngham, while marching through Georgia with the Union army of Gen. William Tecumseh Sherman: "To draw a line between stealing, and taking and appropriating . . . would puzzle the nicest casuist. Such little freaks as taking the last chicken, the last pound of meal, the last bit of bacon . . . from a poor woman and her flock of children, black or white not considered, came under the order of legitimate business" (Conyngham, *Sherman's March Through the South,* 1865).

For other ways of downplaying theft, see HOOK, INTERPRET THE MOOD OF, INVENTORY LEAKAGE, LIBERATE, SALVAGE, SCIENTIFIC AND LITERARY INVESTIGATION, SWAGGING, and UNAUTHORIZED USE OF A MOTOR VEHICLE.

Arab

Arab. Strange as it may seem, an old euphemism for "Jew." Credit for devising this euphemism is given by H. L. Mencken to Jack Conway (d. 1928), a *Variety* staffer, who enriched the language with *palooka, bellylaugh, S.A.* (for "sex appeal"), *high-hat, pushover,* BALONEY, *headache* (in the sense of "wife"), and the verbs *to click* (to succeed), *to scram* (Conway's claim to this one has been disputed), and *to laugh that off*. The Arab-for-Jew substitution was popular enough that by 1929 "Arab" was formally banned by the Keith booking office. (Other expressions that vaudevillians were told not to use included *hell with, cockeyed,* and *wop*.) "Arab" is only one of a number of similar euphemisms for "Jew." Among the others: *Joosh* (a Walter Winchell-ism), *Mexican,* and, oddest of all, HEBREW. Of course, Arabs and Jews are still conjoined in another term; see ANTI-SEMITIC.

area bombing. City bombing; also called "saturation bombing" or, more precisely, "terror bombing." "From 1942 to 1944 . . . the British carried on a sustained area bombing campaign with cities and their people candidly its primary targets" (Russell F. Weigley, *The American Way of War,* 1973).

Area bombing was pioneered during World War II by the British, who preferred to fly bombing missions during the night, when the enemy couldn't see them (and when they couldn't see their targets); the Americans, by contrast, flying daytime missions, popularized PRECISION BOMBING. Highlights of the *area bombing* campaign include Hamburg, fire-bombed at the end of July 1943 (42,000 dead), and Dresden, another fire-bombing, on the night of February 13–14, 1944 (no one knows how many dead; estimates of the total number of killed and wounded range from 250,000 to 400,000). See also SPECIFIED STRIKE ZONE.

armed reconnaissance. Bombing; the airborne equivalent of *reconnaissance in force* (search and destroy). Thus, speaking of air operations over North Vietnam, circa 1965: "Attacks were also permitted against certain broad categories of targets, such as vehicles, locomotives and barges, which were defined in Washington. In this type of attack, known as armed reconnaissance, the final selection of a specific target was left to the pilot" (*New York Times* edition of *The Pentagon Papers,* 1971). "Armed reconnaissance" is one of a series of evasions for "bombing" that flourished during the Vietnam ERA. See also AIR SUPPORT and PROTECTIVE REACTION.

arse. The ass. Some people say "arse" instead of "ass," thinking they are being cute and talking Cockney, but they are really speaking Standard English, since "ass," now commonly thought to be a bad word for a bad thing, began as a euphemism for the older "arse." In effect, the original term has become a euphemism for itself.

"Arse," traced back to about the year 1000 in the *Oxford English Dictionary,* was used without a great deal of shame by many writers for many years, e.g., from Geoffrey Chaucer's *The Miller's Tale* (ca. 1387–1400), in which a young man bestows a dreadfully misplaced kiss—in the dark:

> With his mouth he kiste hir naked ers
> Ful savourly, er he were war of this

Toward the end of the seventeenth century, polite people began to avoid the word. Samuel Johnson was bold enough to include it in full in his *Dictionary of the English Language* (1755), but other writers of the period frequently felt they had to shield readers from the full force of the expression with dashes or asterisks, a practice that is by no means obsolete, e.g., "I'm going to whip his ————," which was how the *New York Times* reported President Jimmy Carter's estimate of how he would handle a challenge by Sen. Edward M. Kennedy (D., Massachusetts) for the Democratic presidential nomination (6/14/79).

Just when people began dropping the "r" out of "arse" (the aural equivalent of a written euphemism) is not known, but "ass" already had acquired low connotations by 1751, when Capt. Francis Grose defined "Johnny Bum" as "A he or jack ass; so called by a lady that affects to be extremely polite and modest, who would not say . . . ass because it was indecent" (*A Classical Dictionary of the Vulgar Tongue*, 1st ed.). The sudden and mysterious appearance of DONKEY upon the lexicographical scene in the eighteenth century is another indication that the four-legged "ass" was being avoided by then because it sounded exactly like the r-less two-legged word. (N.B.: All this also goes to show how long it can take for some words to be recorded in even the greatest of dictionaries, since the *OED*'s oldest example of "ass" in the sense of "arse" comes only from 1860. Moreover, indirect evidence suggests that "ass" may be far older, perhaps dating back to Elizabethan times, if Joseph T. Shipley has guessed correctly about the antiquity of the closely related BOTTOM.)

As with other topics that are surrounded by especially strong taboos (see MENSTRUATE, PROSTITUTE, TOILET, and VAGINA, for example), there are a great many other euphemisms for the otherwise lowly ass. Among them:

afterpart
backseat, BACKSIDE, BEHIND, *body*, *bosom of the pants* (see BOSOM), BOTTOM,
    breech, BUTT/BUTTOCKS
caboose, *can*, *cheeks*, *crapper* (see CRAP)
DERRIÈRE, DUFF
face, FANNY, FUNDAMENT
GLUTEUS MAXIMUS
hereafter, *hind end*, *hinder parts*, *hiney*, *home base*, *hunkies*
kazoo, *keel*, KEISTER
latter end
nock (see KNOCK UP)
patellas, *poop*, POSTERIOR(S), PRAT
REAR, *rumble seat*, *rump*, *rumpus*
saddle (see SADDLEBLOCK ANESTHESIA), SEAT, *setdown*, SIT-ME-DOWN, *sit-upon*
    ("sit-upons," by this token, are trousers, or UNMENTIONABLES), *south side*,
    southern exposure, *squat* (see also "diddly-squat" in DIDDLY-POO and "hot
    squat" in HOT SEAT), *squatter*, *stern*, *Sunday face*
TAIL, TUSHIE
van
whatsis, and WHAT-YOU-MAY-CALL'EM.

artificial dentures. False teeth; see DENTURES.

assassination. A murder or upperclass HIT; the five-syllable word rationalizes the deed while sliding around it with soft-sounding sibilants.

"Yet, the evidence mounts in obscene detail that the murder—a word for which 'assassination' is only a euphemism—of Fidel Castro was a subject of frequent, pointed and practical discussion in the Kennedy Administration—and sometimes by the President himself" (Tom Wicker, *New York Times*, 6/3/75). Mr. Wicker proved to be wrong only in supposing that the discussions were "pointed." In its 1975 report on its investigation of United States assassination plots against the Cuban prime minister and other foreign leaders (President Rafael Leonidas Trujillo, of the Dominican Republic; Gen. René Schneider Chereau, of Chile; President Ngo Dinh Diem, of South Vietnam, and Prime Minister Patrice Emergy Lumumba, of the Congo), the Senate Intelligence Committee paid especial note of the use of euphemism and circumlocution whenever murder was discussed, quoting from an internal report of 1967 by the CIA inspector general on the subject of official assassination:

> The point is that of frequent resort to synecdoche—the mention of a part when the whole is to be understood, or vice versa. Thus, we encounter repeated references to phrases such as "disposing of Castro," which may be read in the narrow, literal sense of assassinating him, when it is intended that it be read in the broader figural sense of dislodging the Castro regime. Reversing the coin, we find people speaking vaguely of "doing something about Castro" when it is clear that what they have specifically in mind is killing him. In a situation wherein those speaking may not have actually meant what they seemed to say or may not have said what they actually meant, they should not be surprised if their oral shorthand is interpreted differently than was intended.

In this linguistic morass, high presidential advisers could maintain that their bosses never understood from conversations with the CIA that murder was intended (see PLAUSIBLE DENIAL), while lower-level CIA officers, pointing to the same verbiage, could assert—as did William Harvey, who spearheaded one of the plots to kill Castro—that they thought their murderous plans had been approved "at every appropriate level within and beyond the Agency." Moreover, though all the foreign leaders but Castro were killed, and though the senators were able to trace shipments of weapons to dissidents in the Dominican Republic and Chile, and of poisons to the Congo (see NONDISCERNIBLE MICRO-BIONOCULATOR), the Intelligence Committee found itself unable, even in these instances, to pin the blame directly on CIA AGENTS. The CIA's plots, it seemed, had never worked. Or the agency had backed off at the last minute, while other parties proceeded to do the killing. In other words, paradoxically, whenever the agency (according to the agency) really tried to kill someone, it failed, and whenever it didn't try to kill someone, the person died. Such consistent ineffectiveness is so rare that one wonders if we shouldn't take advantage of it and lower the global level of violence by having the CIA try harder to kill more people.

While swallowing the agency's story, the senators did condemn the idea of using *assassination* as an instrument of American policy. In particular, they cited the kind of loose talking that abets such thinking, saying, in a section headed "The Danger of Using 'Circumlocution' and 'Euphemism'":

> "Assassinate," "murder" and "kill" are words many people do not want to speak or hear. They describe acts which should not even be proposed, let alone plotted. Failing to call dirty business by its rightful name may have increased the risk of dirty business being done.

Putting the question in historical perspective, one of the committee members, Charles McC. Mathias (R., Maryland), questioned CIA director Richard Helms, as follows:

> SENATOR MATHIAS: Let me draw an example from history. When [Archbishop] Thomas [à] Becket was proving to be an annoyance, as Castro, the King [Henry II] said "who will rid me of this troublesome priest?" He didn't say, "go out and murder him." He said "who will rid me of this man," and let it go at that.
> MR. HELMS: That is a warming reference to the problem.
> SENATOR MATHIAS: You feel that spans the generations and the centuries?
> MR. HELMS: I think it does, sir.

Coincidentally, at about the time (A.D. 1170) of Becket's murder, the word "assassin" was coming into its own. The word is Arabic, meaning "hashish-eater," and originally was applied to a Moslem sect that flourished in Persia and Syria circa 1090–1255. Its members distinguished themselves for murdering their enemies and for eating hashish; hence their name. The conversion of "Assassin" into the generic "assassin" is a tribute to their effectiveness, which seems to have been substantially greater in their time than that of the CIA in ours.

For other kinds of more-or-less official murder (as opposed to the aforementioned, nongovernmental HIT), see ACCIDENT, AUTO-DA-FÉ, DISPATCH, ELIMINATE/ELIMINATION, EXECUTIVE ACTION, LIQUIDATE/LIQUIDATION, NEUTRALIZE/NEUTRALIZATION, NO RIGHT TO CORRESPONDENCE, SPECIAL TREATMENT, TERMINATE/TERMINATION, and WET AFFAIR. For the quieter, natural way to die, see PASS AWAY.

assault. A common journalistic euphemism for "rape"—a word that was barred for many years from newspapers in Britain and the United States. ". . . delicacy becomes absurdity when it produces such an anticlimax as is contained in *Pathological tests suggest that she had two blows on the head, was strangled and probably assaulted*" (H. W. Fowler, *A Dictionary of Modern English Usage*, rev. and ed. by Sir Ernest Gowers, 1965). Elaborations on the "assault" theme, all with the same meaning, include *brutal assault, criminal assault, felonious assault, improper assault,* and *indecent assault.* The sheer profusion of terms suggests an indecent interest in the subject. As noted in the *Columbia Journalism Review* (5–6/78):

> The news columns, too, have always depended heavily on sex to attract readers—in some publications it has been the major attraction—but . . the language has been devious. Women were never raped in

news reports; they were criminally assaulted. Men were never found guilty of sodomy; they were convicted of a statutory offense.

See also INTERFERE WITH and MOLEST.

assembly (or **relocation**) **center.** A prison camp, American style; specifically, one of the camps in which some 100,000 Japanese-Americans were held during World War II on the dubious assumption (not one was ever found guilty of sabotage) that they were more loyal to their country of origin than to the country in which they made their homes. See also CONCENTRATION CAMP and PROTECTIVE CUSTODY.

assignation. A meeting between lovers, usually secret. The fancy "assignation" perhaps derives from "assignation house," a nineteenth-century house in which rooms were let for short periods. See also HOUSE and MATINEE.

associated with. The executive form of "employed by," sometimes shortened to "with," as in "I'm with General Motors." In general, top dogs are *associated with* firms in particular CAPACITIES or POSITIONS for which they receive REMUNERATION, and when they leave, they RESIGN. Lower ranking PERSONNEL work at jobs for pay, and they are fired. See also HELP.

asylum. A madhouse. Originally a place of refuge, or sanctuary, from which debtors and criminals could not be removed without sacrilege, the meaning of "asylum" was gradually broadened, starting in the eighteenth century, to include institutions for the deaf, the dumb, the blind, the orphaned, and the mad, or lunatic (in effect, the "moonstruck," from Luna, Roman goddess of the moon). "Asylums" for the demented appeared on both sides of the Atlantic practically simultaneously. In 1828, Sir A. Halliday prepared a report, entitled *A General View of the Present State of Lunatics, and Lunatic Asylums, in Great Britain and Ireland.* Two years earlier, in the American hinterland, a petition was prepared for "the addition of a Lunatic Asylum" (Benjamin Drake and E. D. Mansfield, *Cincinnati in 1826*, 1827). See also MENTAL HOSPITAL.

athletic supporter. Not an ardent sports fan but a jockstrap, where "jock," like "john," is a quintessentially male name. See also JOHN and JOHN THOMAS.

at liberty. Out of work; the free-sounding euphemism makes it seem as though one is on vacation. See also FURLOUGH, the *gentleman at large* in GENTLEMAN, and the basic LET GO.

attack. Rape, archaic; see ASSAULT.

attendance teacher. A truant officer, new style. For some reason, truants are not called *attendance pupils*, although it would be entirely consistent to do so. See also TEACHER PRESENCE.

at this/that point in time. Now/then. "At this point in time" and "at that point in time" were used so often by erstwhile presidential COUNSEL John W. Dean III when testifying before the Senate Watergate Committee in the summer of 1973 that they came to sum up the tenor of the hearings in the public mind, much as "point of order" did for the Army-McCarthy hearings of 1954. The circumlocutions, known technically as periphrases, have relatively high FOP Indexes of 8.3 and 6.25, respectively. Though they inspired much merriment at the time, the stock phrases are not as laughable as they look on paper. In conversation generally—and in cross-examination particularly—they are immensely useful, enabling the speaker to fill the air with words while the mind races ahead to frame the substance of the reply. In this respect, "at this point in time" is merely a more articulate version of the humdrum *uh, um, er,* and YOU KNOW. For more testimonial talk, see INDICATE, NO RECALL (or MEMORY or RECOLLECTION) OF and THIGH.

attorney. Lawyer. They study law at law school rather than attorneying at attorney school, but most lawyers prefer to be called "attorney" even though this term, which actually refers to a legal agent—to someone who is authorized to act for another—is not as accurate as "lawyer," meaning someone who is entitled to practice the law. Evidently, the lawyers wish to escape the negative associations connected with the correct name of their profession. (When did you ever hear of a Philadelphia *attorney?*) See also COUNSEL.

au naturel. Naked, undressed. See also NUDE.

authentic reproduction. A reproduction, the "authentic" being pure doubletalk, signifying nothing. If something is "authentic," in the legitimate sense of that word, it isn't a "reproduction," and if it is a "reproduction," it isn't "authentic." The phrase is much used by furniture dealers and reproducers of art treasures. (May Nelson Rockefeller's soul rest in peace.) "From *Esquire* comes an ad passed on to me by Gould B. Hagler, of Atlanta; in it, The Bombay Company offers 'an authentic reproduction of a fine old English antique.' An authentic reproduction strikes me as not far removed from a genuine sham" (John Simon, *Esquire,* 12/5/78). See also RIGHT, NOT.

author. Writer; "author" sounds classier because of the ear's uncanny preference for Latinate words. Thus, an otherwise excellent organization for writers is known as the Authors Guild. To the ear, the *or* ending is the giveaway. See also REALTOR.

authoritarian. Totalitarian; a subtle distinction for justifying American support of foreign governments, no matter how unsavory, so long as they are friendly. Cataloging the reasons why the United States should aid and abet "moderate autocrats," such as the late Shah of Iran, as well as other totalitarian governments in what used to be known as the FREE WORLD, Jeane T. Kirkpatrick, professor of political science at Georgetown University, asserted in an article entitled "Dictatorships and Double Standards": ". . . the *facts* [are] that traditional authoritarian governments are less repressive than revolutionary ones, that they are more susceptible of liberalization, and that they are more compatible with U.S. interests" (*Commentary,* 11/79). The professor's fine distinction became of more than academic interest about a year later, when she was appointed American ambassador to the United Nations, and "authoritarian" suddenly materialized as a foreign policy watchword of the Reagan administration.

auto-da-fé. Literally, "act of faith," but in reality, a pious circumlocution for the execution of a sentence of the Holy Office of the Inquisition, most spectacularly by burning. In English, the Portuguese spelling is more common than the Spanish *auto-de-fé*, but it was in Spain that the Inquisition achieved its greatest notoriety. "Act of faith," which compares well in opacity with the modern FINAL SOLUTION, is merely one of a cluster of words and expressions that were given special meanings by the Inquisitors in their zeal to root out heresy. The bending of the meanings of words is symptomatic of a diseased institution (see ASSASSINATION for another modern parallel), with the angle of linguistic deflection indicating the seriousness of the cancer within. The Spanish Inquisition represented an advanced case. Consider:

The Inquisitors depended on torture (from the Latin *torquere*, to twist, the name of the inquisitor general, Tomás de Torquemada, being merely a happy coincidence), as few people would confess without torture, or the threat of it, to sins for which they could lose their property and their lives. The Inquisitors did not speak of "torture," however. Rather, they referred to this stage of their inquiry as *the question*.

The Inquisitors were forbidden from repeating tortures, a seemingly enlightened prohibition, which they broke regularly, particularly when victims lost consciousness, thus nullifying the effects of the torture. The Inquisitors got around the prohibition by pretending they had never stopped the torture. Thus, they talked of *continuing to put the question* or of *suspending* it for a time.

The Inquisitors conducted their operations in the *Casa Santa*. The name was the same wherever the building was located. It translates as "Holy House" or "Holy Office."

The Inquisitors were forbidden from committing murder or from shedding blood (priest-torturers gave one another immediate absolution when accidents occurred) and they could not even ask the state to execute the people they had condemned. Accordingly, one of the high points of the *auto-da-fé* came when the Church formally *abandoned* its victims to secular authority, *beseeching* the state to deal moderately with the poor souls, neither taking their lives nor shedding their blood. This pious entreaty was honored in the sense that burning or strangulation do not involve bloodletting, but everyone realized that the request for moderation was for God's ears only. Any secular official who heeded the letter of the Inquisitors' words, rather than their spirit, was likely to face *the question* himself.

The ultimate "act of faith," the public burning, was reserved for those who had committed the greatest crimes in the eyes of the Inquisitors and who also remained *obstinate*, i.e., they had refused to repent despite prolonged *questioning*. People who had fled to other countries were burned in effigy and the bodies of those who had had the good luck to die before being judged were disinterred and burned also. In the case of an especially grievous sinner, the faggots might be dampened in order to roast the victim slowly. Of course, repentance could be made at any time—even as the fire was being lit—and to those who repented, the Church offered *mercy* . . . in the form of strangulation before burning.

See also CAPITAL PUNISHMENT and INTERROGATION.

aversion therapy. The use of pain and/or fear to persuade a person to change his or her behavior; also called *behavior modification*. Typically, *aversion therapy* involves electric shocks or forced vomiting. The idea is that the "patient" will associate the pain with the undesirable behavior, come to regard that behavior pattern as repugnant, and then change it. The technique is used in many up-to-date CORRECTIONAL FACILITIES and MENTAL HOSPITALS. From the standpoint of a person who is forced to undergo it, *aversion therapy* is difficult to distinguish from "torture." And it doesn't always work. For example, from the summary of a 1964 British case: "Aversion therapy was conducted with a male homosexual who had a heart condition. The particular form of aversion therapy involved creation of nausea, by means of an emetic, accompanied by talking about his homosexuality. The second part of the therapy involved recovery from the nausea and talking about pleasant ideas and heterosexual fantasies, which was sometimes aided by lysergic acid. In this case, the patient died as a result of a heart attack brought on by the use of the emetic" (Martin S. Weinberg and Alan P. Bell, *Homosexuality; An Annotated Bibliography*, 1972, in Jonathan Katz, *Gay American History*, 1976). See also ADJUSTMENT CENTER, BRAINWASH, and STRESS-PRODUCING STIMULUS.

B

backside. The ass; a general reference to the entire back of the body when, in truth, a single portion is meant. The oldest "backside" in the *Oxford English Dictionary* comes from about 1500: "With an arrowe so broad, He shott him into the backe-syde" (Joseph Ritson, ed., *Robin Hood*, 1795). As recently as 1943–44, "backside" was considered sufficiently bawdy to be cited in a proceeding of the U.S. Post Office Department against that primeval playboy, *Esquire*. Today, however, the euphemism is thought so innocuous that even broadcasters and FAMILY newspapers can use it without anyone raising an eyebrow, e.g., from a 1977 Los Angeles KNBC-TV review of *The Act*: "After three hours, not only does the show need a new book, you need a new backside." See also ARSE.

ball. A happy-sounding FOUR-LETTER WORD substitutes for a rather coarser one, as in, from *What Really Happened to the Class of '65*: "'In the summers I'd go to the beach. Maybe I'd ball two or three fellows a day.'" (Michael Medved and David Wallechinsky, 1977). The copulatory "ball" may simply be a spin-off of "ball" in the good-time sense of "I had a ball last night." The word's sexual sense, however, is reinforced by the proximity of the anatomical ball, or TESTICLE. Thus, predating the antics of the class of '65 by some seventy-five years: "I ballocked that little girl" (anon., *My Secret Life*, ca. 1890). See also BOLLIXED UP and F——.

ball game, end of the. Death. In the words of astronaut Maj. Alfred M. Worden: "When you are out there 200,000 miles from earth, if something goes wrong, you know that's the end of the ball game" (*New York Times*, 8/14/71).

Life frequently is conceived of as a game (see GAME), so it is only natural that death should often be euphemized in game-playing terms. Among the expressions available for dead or dying gamesters:

> *cash in one's chips* (or *hand*)
> *drop the cue* (billiards)
> *go to the races*
> *is knocked out* (or *KO'd*)
> *jump the last hurdle*
> *out of the game* (or *running*)
> *pass* (or *hand*) *in one's checks* (or *chips*)
> *pegged out* (cribbage)
> *race is run* (or *ran the good race*)
> *shuffled* (*clean*) *out of the deck*
> *struck out*
> *take the last* (or *long*) *count*
> *throw for a loss*
> *throw in the sponge*
> *throw sixes*
> *throw up the cards*
> *trumped.*

See also PASS AWAY.

baloney/boloney. A byword for "nonsense" or "rubbish" as well as a euphemism for the decidedly stronger "bull (or horse) shit." For example, speaking of Federal Judge John J. Sirica's refusal to require Richard M. Nixon to testify at the Watergate COVER-UP trial, for fear that such a stand-up performance would kill the (then-ailing) former president, one of the principal defendants, John D. Ehrlichman, asserted that the judge's reasoning was "just pure—if you'll pardon the expression—baloney" (speech, Dutch Treat Club, New York City, 5/1/79).

On the face of it, "baloney" seems to derive from the bologna sausage, but the connection has never been proved, and attempts have been made to link it to other sources. Perhaps because English eat *polony* instead of baloney, Eric Partridge, whose opinion is not to be dismissed lightly in these matters, suggested the gypsy *peloné* (testicles) as the source (*A Dictionary of Slang and Unconventional English*, 1970). If Partridge is correct, the true euphemistic meaning of "That's a lot of baloney" actually is "That's all balls."

Credit for popularizing baloney-as-rubbish in the United States usually is given to former New York governor Al Smith, who talked of the "baloney dollar" after the 1934 devaluation. Smith, in turn, probably picked up the term from Jack Conway, a remarkably fecund wordsmith (see ARAB) and longtime *Variety* staffer. What inspired Conway is unknown. Perhaps "baloney" sprang full-blown from his Zeus-like brow. Or perhaps he got it from the lingo of prizefighting, where a "baloney" used to be a clumsy, unskilled fighter (a "palooka"), or from the Chicago stockyards, where an old bull, who was fit for making nothing else, was called a "bologna." See also BS, NUTS, and SHUCKS.

bang. To engage in sexual intercourse and, as a noun, the act thereof (see INTERCOURSE), perhaps from "bang" in the sense of "thrill" or "excitement," but more likely from the "bang" that is a loud hit or blow, somewhat in the sense of "Wham, bam, thank you ma'am." The association between sex and violence is strong; see also ACTION and the etymology of F——.

barnyard epithet. Bullshit—and the second most memorable euphemistic circumlocution coined by the *New York Times* (for the current number one, see OBSCENE, DEROGATORY, AND SCATOLOGICAL).

"Barnyard epithet" arose this way: On February 4, 1970, during the course of the trial of the Chicago Eight for conspiracy to disrupt the Democratic National Convention of 1968, one of the defendants, David Dellinger, exclaimed "Oh, bullshit!" upon hearing Chicago Deputy Police Chief James Riordan's version of Dellinger's actions some seventeen months before. The exclamation became news because Judge Julius Hoffman (who had ears like a rabbit; see WOMAN) later reprimanded Dellinger for using "that kind of language" and revoked his bail. Covering for the *Times* was Pulitzer Prize winner J. Anthony Lukas, who recalled subsequent events this way:

> Knowing the *Times'* sensitivity about such language, I called the National Desk and asked how they wanted to handle Mr. Dellinger's phrase. The editor on duty said he didn't think we could use it and suggested I just say "an obscenity." I objected, arguing that it wasn't, strictly speaking, an obscenity; that if we called it that most people would assume it was something much worse; and that since it was

central to the day's events we ought to tell our readers just what Mr. Dellinger had said. The editor thought for a minute and said, "Why don't we call it a barnyard epithet?" Everything considered, that seemed like the best solution, and that was the way it appeared in the *Times* the next morning. (Hillier Krieghbaum, *Pressures on the Press*, 1972)

Variations on the "barnyard epithet" theme, also used at different times by the *Times*, include *barnyard vulgarity* (one was attributed to White House Press Secretary Jody Powell on 3/23/77), *henhouse epithet* (chickenshit, presumably, let fly by South Dakota Senator James G. Abourezk, 1/2/79), and *cow-pasture vulgarism* (used by a defense attorney to characterize the government's Abscam investigation, 8/20/80). For more about cleaning up the barnyard, see BS and ROOSTER.

bastard. It's an epithet now, and has been one for many centuries, but its etymology suggests that it started life as a euphemism. The word comes from the Old French *fils de bast*, packsaddle child, where the *bast*, or packsaddle, often was used as a bed by mule drivers. Its synonym, "bantling," seems to have parallel etymology, being rooted in the German *bank*, bench, with the implication that the child was begotten on a bench rather than in a bed.

Though somewhat less-heavily tabooed than formerly, "bastard" is not yet entirely out of the linguistic woods. It is sometimes euphemized as *B.* and *b——*, and when a miniseries called "The Bastard" was prepared by a consortium of television stations in 1978, 10 of the 93 broadcasters diffidently dropped that title in favor of "The Kent Family Chronicles," the subtitle of the John Jakes novel from which the series was adapted. See also BLANKET, BORN ON THE WRONG SIDE OF THE; LOVE CHILD, and SOB.

bathroom. A generalization for "toilet," as in a TV commercial, "Does your husband care about bathroom tissue?" (WOR, NYC, 8/8/78). "Bathroom" reaches its euphemistic height in connection with visits to the bathless *bathrooms* of public buildings. From a column of advice for those fortunate few who had tickets to attend the King Tut exhibit at New York's Metropolitan Museum of Art: "Be prepared not to have to go to the bathroom, since once you leave the exhibit you can't get back in . . ." (*Brooklyn* [NY] *Phoenix*, 1/11/79). See also TOILET.

bd (also **B&D** or **B/D**). Bondage and discipline, in classified ads of a very personal nature. See also S/M and, for an example of "bd" in use, the classified ad in FRENCH.

beautician. A person who works in a beauty parlor; especially a hairdresser. "Beautician" is kissing kin to MORTICIAN, both descending from "physician." The earliest known example of "beautician" comes from a Cleveland, Ohio, telephone directory of 1924. The sonorous appelation seems to have caught on quickly, since, by 1926, newspapers from as far away as Scotland were commenting upon it, e.g., "The immense growth of 'beauty parlors' in the United States has added to the American language the word 'beautician'" (*Glasgow Herald*, 6/12/26). The establishment in which the *beautician* works also is something of a euphemism: Before there were *beauty parlors* and *beauty shoppes*, there were *hairdressing parlors*, *rooms*, and *salons*. All these euphemisms, however, pale before the seventeenth-century English dressers of female coiffures who called themselves *woman-surgeons*. See also COSMETICIAN/COSMETOLOGIST, PARLOR, SALON, and SHOPPE.

begorra(h). An Anglo-Irish euphemism for "by God." It is the functional equivalent of "bejab(b)ers," or "by Jesus." See also GOLLY and GOSH.

behind. The ass; the general, locational it's-somewhere-back-there reference is what is known technically as a topographical euphemism.

In 1882–88, when volume B of the *Oxford English Dictionary* was being prepared, "behind" was considered colloquial and vulgar, and was so labeled. And as recently as 1943–44, "behind" was cited (along with such other filth as BACKSIDE and "bawdyhouse") in a Post Office suit to prevent *Esquire* from sullying the nation's mails. Today, however, "behind" has been overtaken by other words, and it is regarded as such a mild term (comparable to FANNY or TUSHIE) that even the *New York Times*, justly famed for avoiding anything OBSCENE, DEROGATORY, AND SCATOLOGICAL, has found it fit to print—and on its front page yet, e.g., quoting an assistant New York City police chief: "The feeling right now is, 'Cover your behind and forget about taking chances. . . .'" (10/27/76).

The oldest anatomical "behind" in the *OED* comes from 1786 and actually refers to an article of clothing: "Two young ladies . . . with new Hats on their heads, new Bosoms [see BOSOM], and new Behinds in a band-box" (*Lounger*, no. 54). More typical is King George IV's utterance, from about 1830: "Go and do my bidding—tell him he lies, and kick his behind in my name!" (*Saturday Review*, 2/18/1862). But prior to the Civil War, the anatomical meaning was not always the first one that came to mind. Thus, Americans were able to use this as the alternate title for the catcher of a baseball team, e.g., "The first nine of the Gotham Club are:——— Burns, behind; T. G. Van Cott, pitcher" (*Porter's Spirit of the Times*, 1857). Would you believe: Johnny Bench, Behind? Accepted variations on the "behind" theme include *hind end, hind part, hinder part(s), hindhead,* and *hiney.* See also ARSE and CYA.

Bell Telephone Hour. Torture time, circa Vietnam ERA. The euphemism comes from the field telephones, whose wiring was used to deliver shocks to the GENITALS or breasts of suspected Viet Cong. Domestically, telephones also have been used this way; for example at the Tucker State Farm (i.e., prison) in Arkansas, where the arrangement was known as the Tucker Telephone. See also INTERROGATION and STATE FARM.

bench, the. Here come de judge; this topographical euphemism elevates people by identifying them in terms of the positions they occupy. "As for magistrates acquiescing in or relishing the term *the bench*—surely language is too important a matter to be left in the hands of magistrates" (John Simon, *Esquire*, 4/25/78). See also OVAL OFFICE.

bender. A drunken spree, perhaps from "bender," a hard drinker (? one who bends his elbow a lot, lifting mug to lips), or a nineteenth-century human knee, particularly a female one, and particularly in Boston, home of the bean, the cod, and the bluenose. "Young ladies are not allowed to cross their benders in school" (Henry Wadsworth Longfellow, *Kavanagh*, 1849). See also HIGH and LIMB.

benign neglect. Neglect; the "benign," which is just so much eyewash, gives the expression a FOP Index of 2.3. The most famous "benign neglect" of our time occurred in a memo that Daniel Patrick Moynihan wrote on March 2, 1970, to President Richard M. Nixon. Moynihan, then serving as Nixon's urban affairs adviser, suggested: "The time may have come when the issue of race could benefit from a period of 'benign neglect.'" Moynihan took the phrase from the earl of Durham, who had recommended to Queen Victoria in 1839 that Canada be given the right to govern herself, since she had done so well on her own "through a period of benign neglect." Moynihan's memorandum was leaked to the press, presumably by someone in the administration who hoped it would embarrass him, which it should have done. Of course, Moynihan has a real flare for words, and he was a runner-up for the 1976 Doublespeak Award, given by the Committee on Public Doublespeak of the National Council of Teachers of English. His near-winner was the statement he made in 1975 when resigning as chief U.S. delegate to the United Nations. Denying that he was resigning in order to run for the U.S. Senate, he told a national TV audience ("Face the Nation"): "I would consider it dishonorable to leave this post and run for any office, and I hope it would be understood that if I do, the people, the voters to whom I would present myself in such circumstances, would consider me as having said in advance that I am a man of no personal honor to have done so." And despite this rather clear warning, the voters of New York elected him.

    See CONSUMER COMMUNICATION CHANNEL for the 1976 Doublespeak Award winner as well as, for another form of not-so-benign *benign neglect*, TRIAGE.

beverage host. A bartender at Florida's Walt Disney World. "Thus a bartender, rare species that he is in these precincts, is a 'Beverage Host'" (Robert Craft, *New York Review of Books*, 5/16/74). "Beverage host" is only the latest of many efforts to replace the blunt "bartender." Among them: *bar clerk, bartarian, mixer, mixologist, server,* and *tapster.* Consistent with this, cocktail waitresses in other bars in other places are sometimes known as *beverage attendants.* See also HIGH, REFRESHMENT, and SALOON.

B-girl. Some people say the "B" stands for "bar"; others think it refers to "putting the bee" on someone to buy a drink, and still others believe it means "bad." Or it could even stand for all three combined, since *B-girls* are prostitutes or floozies who congregate in bars, where they often receive commissions on the drinks they persuade customers to buy. "I seem to meet nothing but B-girls out here" (Budd Schulberg, *What Makes Sammy Run?*, 1941). See also PROSTITUTE and the *B-girl's* cousin, the *V-girl*, OR VICTORY GIRL.

bilateral orchidectomy. From the root, "orchid," one might easily suppose this to be a horticultural expression, perhaps something to do with pruning—and, as it happens, pruning is involved, this being the proper surgeon's way of alluding to an operation otherwise known as "castration."

    The orchid plant is so-called on account of the bulbous shape of its roots, the Latin *orchis* coming from the Greek word for "testicle." It was because of this "sexy" etymology that the eminent Victorian critic and writer John Ruskin (1819–1900), campaigned to have the plant's name changed to "Wreathewort."

The failure of Ruskin's noble effort may reflect declining educational standards, his objections to "orchid" not being immediately apparent to those with little Latin and less Greek. See also ALTER, FIX, MUTILATED, and TESTICLES.

birthday suit. Without a suit or other clothes, naked, NUDE. People have been going about in invisible *birthday suits* at least since 1771, when Winifred Jenkins told Mrs. Mary Jones how she and a housemaid had been surprised by Sir George Coon while they "bathed in our birth-day soot" (Tobias Smollett, *Humphrey Clinker*). Variations of the period included *birthday attire, birthday clothes, birthday finery,* and *birthday gear.*

birthparents. A new euphemism for unwed parents; specifically, those who have given up their bastard, or LOVE CHILD, for adoption. An organization in the field calls itself Concerned United Birthparents—CUB, for short.

bisexual. Homosexual; often used in self-reference by people who have not fully come to grips with their SEXUAL ORIENTATION. For example, from the account of a National Football League player, who later came all the way out of the closet: "'Bisexual' is a term Stiles and I would use about ourselves at that time. . . . That is a way of putting it, I guess, that's intended to make it more acceptable, maybe even to other football players. The word 'bisexual' also fits the swinger's image—and most everybody can go along with that" (David Kopay and Perry Deane Young, *The David Kopay Story*, 1977).

This usage is not at all new. For example, in *Autobiography of an Androgyne* (1918), the pseudonymous Earl Lind told of New York City's "Paresis Hall," a favorite gathering place in the 1890s of male transvestites: ". . . the 'Hall's' distinctive clientele were bitterly hated, and finally scattered by the police, merely because of their cogenital bisexuality. The sexually full-fledged were crying for blood. . . . Bisexuals must be crushed—right or wrong!" (Jonathan Katz, *Gay American History*, 1976).

One reason for using "bisexual" in the nineteenth century was that "homosexual" was still a very new word; see LOVE THAT DARE NOT SPEAK ITS NAME, THE. And for other modern forms of *bisexuality,* continue with AC/DC, AMBIDEXTROUS, and GREEK ARTS.

bite the dust. To die in combat; the phrase sounds trite only because it has been used so many times over so many centuries.

The great Achilles speaks: "Not all these too many Achaians would have bitten the dust, by enemy hands, when I was away in my anger" (*The Iliad of Homer*, ca. 750 B.C., trans. Richmond Lattimore, 1951). Variations include *bite the ground, bite the sand,* and the modern, slangy *kiss the dust.* Homer himself also could be more vivid. Again, from Lattimore's very faithful translation: ". . . let many companions about him go down headlong into the dust, teeth gripping the ground soil."

For other military deaths, see ACCOUNT FOR, BUY THE FARM, CASUALTY, EXPENDABLE, FALL/FALLEN, GO WEST, and WASTE. For dying in general, continue with PASS AWAY.

black. More a state of mind than a color, "black" applies to any of an infinite variety of skin hues, ranging from an off-white that is whiter than the skin of many so-called whites, to a black that is, indeed, magnificently black. The stretching of "black" to cover such a wide spectrum has caused a great deal of confusion in the minds of a great many people, including those who staff the U.S. Census Bureau. According to a *New York Times* Op Ed page analysis of the guidebook that was prepared to assist census takers in classifying write-in entries in the 1980 census:

> If you list your race as "coffee," or "chocolate," the guidebook says you are "black." But if you write that you are "brown," then you are "white." . . . If you write in "Oriental," you are considered Japanese. But if you write in "Yellow," you are classified as "Other." If you write in "Brazilian," the guidebook says you are "white" (this will be news to Pelé). If you're black and prefer to be white, simply write in "American," since that, according to the guidebook, means "white." So does 'South African.'" (7/24/76)

It would be easy to poke fun at the bureaucrats who devised these guidelines, presumably while sober, but perhaps they should be thanked instead for demonstrating the irrationality of racial classifications by carrying them to their illogical extreme. See also CAUCASIAN, MINORITY, NEGRO, and POOR; for more Census-ese, continue with LOW-INCOME.

black bag job. An illegal break-in by a government employee, typically an FBI AGENT or a CIA OPERATOR, usually for the purpose of photographing or stealing DOCUMENTS (papers) but occasionally to install a HIGHLY CONFIDENTIAL SOURCE (a bug); often abbreviated to *bag job;* also called a SURREPTITIOUS ENTRY, TECHNICAL TRESPASS, or WARRANTLESS INVESTIGATION.

The FBI is thought to have conducted the first *black bag jobs* in 1942, when the pressure of World War II seemed to justify the lawless activity. The phrase probably refers to the small bag, similar to a doctor's bag, in which the agent carried a kit of burglar's tools. As is usually the case with wartime precedents, the end of the war did not bring an end to the practice, and many FBI agents were glad to receive the criminal assignments, as they carried $150 bonuses when successfully completed. The bonuses were known as *MVP Awards* (for "Most Valuable Player"). Supposedly discontinued (except at foreign embassies) in 1966, on the orders of FBI director J. Edgar Hoover, *black bag jobs* were still being conducted in 1973 and perhaps as late as 1975. For the later break-ins, there were semantic changes, with supervisors in the field requesting approval for an investigation employing an "unorthodox" or "unusual" technique, and promising "full security" (*Time,* 7/5/76). According to an unnamed FBI official, quoted by *Time,* approval by headquarters was usually qualified in these terms: "As long as full security is assured, go ahead." This, the official explained, meant "Go ahead, but if you're caught, it's your ass." And, after a break-in, an agent might discreetly report that "a highly placed sensitive source of known reliability was contacted and furnished items of personality" (*New York Times,* 9/23/80).

"Black bag job" probably is obsolete today as a term if not as a practice: The new bureaucratic euphemism is reported to be *uncontested physical search* (*Wall Street Journal,* 1/18/80). For the classic justification for conducting *black bag jobs* and similar unlawful activities, see ILLEGAL; for a *black bag job* that boomeranged on the authorizer, despite his circumlocutary approval, see COVERT OPERATION.

blame. Damn. "'He's my tick and I'll do what I blame please with him, or die'" (Mark Twain, *The Adventures of Tom Sawyer*, 1876). See also DAD.

blanket, born on the wrong side of the. Bastardy. "'Frank Kennedy,' he said, 'was a gentleman, though on the wrong side of the blanket'" (Sir Walter Scott, *Guy Mannering; or The Astrologer*, 1815). By the same token, "blanket love" also was a euphemism for what the *Oxford English Dictionary* terms "illicit amours." See also AMOUR, BASTARD, and LOVE CHILD.

blazes. A euphemistic expletive for "hell," as in "What in blazes is going wrong?" (*Best of Saturday Night Live*, WNBC-TV, 11/14/79). "Blazes" was especially popular in the nineteenth century when it appeared regularly in such combinations as *hot as blazes, cool as blazes, blue as blazes, black as blazes,* and *by blazes.* See also HECK.

bleeder. British for "a superlative," or "bloody" fool. For more about the British fear of blood, see RUDDY.

bleep. The electronic sound, made when a censor erases an unbroadcastable word from a television tape, has been converted to print in order to save the eyes as well as the ears from any possible embarrassment. As former New York Yankee manager Billy Martin is unlikely to have said, following his ejection from a baseball game: "'You know what the ironic part of this bleeping game is? . . . I'll get fined $250 and the bleeping umpire blows five calls at second base'" (*New York Post*, 7/2/76). See also ADJECTIVE/ADJECTIVAL, the related BLIP, and the grander CHARACTERIZATION OMITTED (or DELETED).

blessed event. The birth of a babe (also called a *bundle from heaven*). The euphemistic twist to the expression seems to have been the inspiration of radio and newspaper journalist Walter Winchell, who also used it as a verb, as in "Stop the presses: So-and-so is going to blessed event." Progeny of "blessed event" include *blessed he-vent, blessed she-vent,* and sometimes, alas, *blasted event.* All these and many other coy evasions, such as *little newcomer* and *little stranger* reflect a reluctance to talk plainly about pregnancy and birth that is nearly as strong as the refusal to discuss dying and death. See also ANTICIPATING and PASS AWAY.

blip. (1) A dirty word; (2) an explosion, specifically, one at a nuclear power plant.

In the first case, "blip" is an alternate pronunciation of BLEEP. For example: "The blips you hear are four-letter words which our broadcasting code forbids us to use" (WCBS-TV, "Sixty Minutes," 10/7/78). See also FOUR-LETTER WORDS.

In the second, explosive case, when the members of the Nuclear Regulatory Commission gathered together to discuss the SITUATION at the Three Mile Island nuclear power plant: ". . . the commissioners were concerned about a percentage problem: if three percent of the bubble was oxygen, what percent oxygen would have to accumulate for it to combine with the hydrogen to cause a 'blip'—an explosion that might, at worst, make a small part of Pennsylvania uninhabitable because of radioactivity for decades" (*Smithsonian*, 7/79). See also ABOVE CRITICAL and, for more about the NRC and Three Mile Island, EVENT.

BM. A second-order euphemism, the abbreviation standing for "bowel movement," itself a euphemism. See also DEFECATE/DEFECATION.

BO. Along Broadway, the initials stand for "Box Office," but along Madison Avenue, this is the soap huckster's abbreviation for "body odor," itself a euphemism for "bad smell" or "stink." A dread condition that was first revealed to the public in the 1930s, *BO* is to the carcass as HALITOSIS is to the mouth. "Do you ever ask yourself about Body-Odour?" (Dorothy Sayers, *Murder Must Advertise*, 1933). Descendants of "BO" include *CO* (canine odor) and *DO* (dog odor). See also FRAGRANCE and PERSPIRE.

body briefer. A chic corset with a built-in brassiere; a corselet.
    Most women today would die before purchasing a girdle, which is merely a sawed-off corset, let alone the complete thing. Instead, the new woman who wishes to make herself seem slimmer than she really is buys a *body briefer* (also called a *body shaper* or *body hugger*). But names aside, resemblance to a corset is strong, as advertising copy makes clear, e.g., ". . . body briefer with soft contour cups, firm control panty to whittle away inches even before you lose pounds" (Macy's flyer, rec'd 1/9/79). See also BRASSIERE, FOUNDATION GARMENT, and LINGERIE.

body count. Dead person count. "Body" has served as euphemistic shorthand for "dead body" since at least the thirteenth century, but it took the Vietnam War to elevate the *body count* into an index of military progress. ". . . weekly casualty stories reported the number of Americans killed, wounded, or missing, and the number of South Vietnamese killed, but the casualties on the other side were impersonally described as 'the Communist death toll' or the 'body count'" (*Columbia Journalism Review*, 1–2/79). See also CASUALTY and NEUTRALIZE/NEUTRALIZATION.

bollixed up. Balled up. "You're getting your cues all bollixed up" (Jerome Weidman, *I Can Get It For You Wholesale!*, 1937). "Bollix," also spelled "bolax" and "bolex," is a variant of "bollock" (or "ballock"), which means "little ball," and which is an extremely old word for "testicle," recorded in the plural "beallucas," as early as A.D. 1000. "Ballock" descends from "ball" in the same way that *buttock* comes from BUTT. Remember the song that innocent schoolchildren sing about "Bollocky Bill the Sailor"? The tradition is that he had big ones. "Balled up," meanwhile, is by today's standards merely a euphemism for "fucked up." See also BALL and TESTICLES.

bonding. The behavioral psychologist's way of squeezing the love out of "love."

    . people associated with infants inevitably find themselves drawn
    into answering their signals and providing for their needs. Given

attraction, attachment soon follows. And, with further intimacy, attachment develops into affection. The currently popular technical term for this is 'bonding.' Its perennial affection is love. (Janet Flannery Jackson and Joseph Jackson, *Infant Culture*, 1978)

bordello. Literally, a little house, such as a cabin or hut, but in practice a fancy name for a whorehouse. See also HOUSE.

bosom aka **bazoom.** The breasts. Technically, only the singular is required: "Bosom I saw, both full, throat warbling" (James Joyce, *Ulysses*, 1922). Modern euphemizers, however, perhaps less certain than Joyce of what they are doing, tend to double their bets with the plural, as in: "What you react to, first, are the artsy drawings, in color, of a man (well-hung) and a woman (slender but with bosoms) going through a 30-page sexual exhibition" (review of *The Joy of Sex, New Times*, 2/22/74).

An extremely old word of uncertain origin (perhaps related to the Sanskrit *bhasman*, blowing), "bosom" has signified "breast" since at least the year 1000. Originally, the term was androgynous. Thus, "wife of his bosom" was a more common expression than "husband of her bosom," though both are used in the Bible (King James Version, 1611). "Bosom" seems to have taken hold as a euphemism for female breasts during the first third of the nineteenth century when incipient Victorians were cleaning up their language in preparation for Her ascent to the throne in 1837. Not only did "breasts" become *bosoms*, but "breast knots" became *bosom knots*, while "breastpins" turned into *bosom pins*, and the "bubby blossom" (or "flower") became the *bosom blossom*. Even men, who had worn "breast plates" back in the bolder days of chivalry, were fitted out with *shirt bosoms*. By the 1860s, women were padding themselves with false *palpitating bosoms*, or PALPITATORS. In addition, "bosom" replaced "breast" in some nonanatomical contexts. Thus, the forward part of the moldboard of a plow originally was called the "breast," but as early as 1813, some fastidious farmers had adopted the new terminology, e.g., "This degree of roundness and fulness in the bosom [of the plough] is necessary on heavy ground" (Arthur Young, *General View of the Agriculture of the County of Essex*). "Breast" was not entirely eliminated, however. It still was preferred when the choice was between it and something even "worse." Thus, Noah Webster euphemized "teat" as "breast" when he bowdlerized the Bible in 1833. In the Bible, according to Webster, such passages as "They shall lament for the teats" (Isaiah, XXXII, 12), became "They shall lament for the breasts." (See PECULIAR MEMBERS for more about the pre-Victorian period generally and for Webster in particular.)

"Bosom" remains the politest of the many terms that have been used over the years to describe women's breasts. Most of the words relate to form, function, or size. Among them:

apples, beausome (a beautiful bosom)
big brown eyes, boobs, (not from "bosom," but from the Elizabethan "bubbies,"
   by way of "boobies"), *bumps,* BUST, BUXOM
CHEST

diddies (an eighteenth-century corruption of "titties"), droopers (or super-
droopers), DUCKYS
ENDOWED/ENDOWMENT
globes, grapefruits
headlights (after automobiles of the 1940s)
jugs (from "jugs of milk," and not to be confused with "double-jugs," old and
now-obsolete British slang for the BUTTOCKS)
kettledrums (or Cupid's kettledrums, eighteenth and nineteenth centuries), knobs,
knockers (perhaps from the height and shape of old-fashioned door-
knockers; see also KNOCK UP)
lungs
MAMMARY GLANDS (or, less technically, milk bottles and milkers), marshmallows,
mosob ("bosom" spelled backward; see also ENOB), molehills, melons (or
watermelons)
ninnies (from "ninny" in the sense of "child"?)
PHYSIQUE, pointers, pumps
teacups, titties (see TITTIE), tonsils, TNT (Two Nifty Tits), twins
warts, and, on a fowl, WHITE MEAT.

boss. Master. "Boss" comes from the Dutch baas, meaning "master," but American servants of the early nineteenth century found it possible to say the foreign word, where the English one stuck in their throats, e.g.: "No one, in this republican country, will use the term master or mistress; 'employers,' and the Dutch word 'boss,' are used instead" (Isaac Holmes, An Account of the United States of America, Derived from Actual Observation, 1823). Naturally, the egalitarian servants didn't like to be called "servants" either; for more on that topic, see DOMESTIC, HELP, and SERVANT itself.

Though not popularized as a substitute for "master" until after the Revolution, "boss" was used in the colonies from as early as 1645. In the related adjectival senses of best, first-class, or excellent, "boss" also is older than most hipsters probably suspect. Thus, in The Adventures of Huckleberry Finn (Mark Twain, 1884), the king congratulates his fellow con man in these terms: "Good land, duke, lemme hug you! It's the most dazzling idea 'at ever a man struck. . . . Oh, this is the boss dodge, ther' ain't no mistake 'bout it."

Finally, "boss" may also be used as an attack word—as a dysphemism as well as a euphemism. For example, newspapers commonly will describe the leader of the Communist party in, say Italy, as a boss, though they would never call the boss of, say, the British Conservative party, anything but a leader. See also CZAR.

botheration. Damnation; similar alternatives include tarnation and thunderation. See also DARN and THUNDER.

bottom. The ass; as with BACKSIDE, BEHIND, and REAR, the general directional reference has a specific euphemistic meaning. Thus, in the case of Commodore Cornelius Vanderbilt (1794–1877): "He was a bellowing rube partial to pinching housemaids' bottoms, yet more than once he burst into tears and sobbed, 'Oh, Goddamnit! I've been a-swearing again!'" (David E. Koskoff, Saturday Review, 7/22/78).

"Bottom," from the Indo-European *bhund*, to place solidly, has acquired its anatomical meaning rather recently, judging from the *Oxford English Dictionary*, whose oldest example of the word in the sense of "The sitting part of a man" (N.B.: not "woman"), comes from *Zoönomia* (1794), by Erasmus Darwin, grandfather of Charles. The lack of earlier examples is one reason for thinking the British "bum" is not a mere contraction of "bottom," since "bum" itself goes back at least to the fourteenth century; (see TRAMP). While "bottom" may not be quite *that* old, it is certain people were using it anatomically for at least a couple of generations before Darwin committed this sense to paper. It may even go back to Elizabethan times. As Joseph T. Shipley points out in *In Praise of English* (1977), it hardly seems coincidental that the weaver who is transformed into an ass in Shakespeare's *A Midsummer Night's Dream* (1594) is named Nick Bottom.

Naturally, "bottom" itself has been euphemized. Thus, England is populated by *Higginbothams, Longbothams,* and *Sidebothams* (pronounced "Siddybotaams"), etc. Even the near-anagram, "beetoteetom," caused Gerty MacDowell to turn crimson when madcap Cissy Caffrey said it out loud—especially as a gentleman named Bloom happened to be nearby (James Joyce, *Ulysses,* 1922).

During the eighteenth and nineteenth centuries, before the anatomical meaning became dominant, "bottom" was popularized as a synonym for "endurance" or "grit" by sportsmen who used it to describe the spirit of their racehorses and pugilists ("bruisers," as they were often called). The British of this period also liked to think that the men in their army had a great deal of "bottom," e.g.: "For solidity, bottom, and a courage that never wavers, they [British troops] are incomparable" (Robert H. Patterson, *Essays in History and Art,* 1862). "Bottom" in this sense was replaced by yet another euphemism—PLUCK.

boy. Now usually a fighting word, "boy" was once a common euphemism, e.g., "These Western boys (every man living beyond the Missouri is a Boy, just as every woman is a Lady)" (W. H. Dixon, *New America,* 1867). It continues as a euphemism, but mainly during time of war or the immediate threat thereof. Then, "boys" or "American boys" may be employed in place of "soldiers" or "troops" in order to build up sympathy on the home front for the "fighting men" in the field. Typically, the call is to "get the boys home by Christmas." However, the palm in this category goes to Sen. Burton K. Wheeler (D., Montana), a Progressive gone Isolationist, who opposed the Lend-Lease program to aid Britain, asserting in January 1941 that it "will plow under every fourth American boy." See also LADY and MAN.

brainwash. The popular term softens the nasty business of drastically changing a person's beliefs and behavior by breaking down the victim's self-image, precipitating an identity crisis, and then substituting a new set of values for the old. A fairly straight translation of the Chinese term for "thought reform" or "ideological reprogramming," "brainwash" dawned on the Western consciousness soon after the Chinese Communists began consolidating their victory of 1949 by using the technique on large numbers of their fellow citizens. See also AVERSION THERAPY and INTERROGATION.

brassiere. The garment for supporting the breasts has noticeably little to do with the *bras* (French for "arm") from which it has been derived. In Old French, a *bracière* was an arm protector, and in modern French, *brassière* has carried such non-bust-like meanings as "shoulder strap" (as of a knapsack) and, in the plural, "leading strings" (for infants)—all of which are far cries from what are known informally in the garment district today as *boobytraps* or *bust-buckets*. Of course, the full "brassiere" is hardly ever seen anymore, not even in advertisements, which invariably use the clipped euphemism "bra" or—Rudy Gernreich's contradiction in terms—the "No Bra Bra." The reason (linguistically) for this is that the original, euphemistic "brassiere" has been around long enough to have acquired overly sexy connotations. "Bra," which seems to have come in about 1930, is light, airy, and acceptable, as in the popular ditty circa 1940:

> Now you ought to see Ma—
> In her peek-a-boo bra.
> She looks only sweet sixteen.

As for the basic "brassiere": Women have been wearing this garment, or similar items, for some thousands of years; Roman mosaics depict women in outfits that could pass for bikinis on the Riviera today. However, the first "brassiere" by that name did not appear until the twentieth century. Otto Titzling is reported to have designed one in 1912 as supports for Swanhilda Olafsen, a very large opera singer. Clearly, though, the *brassiere* was an idea whose time had come, as the great change in women's fashions, usually associated with World War I, to freer, looser clothing already was beginning. In fact, the *brassiere* also seems to have been invented independently by Mary Phelps Jacob, an American heiress, later better known as Caresse Crosby. As a young debutante, Caresse rebelled against being encased in an armored corset. She made her first *brassiere* one night, just before going to a dance, with the aid of two pocket handkerchiefs, some ribbon, some thread, and a French maid named Marie. She also did something that Titzling failed to do: She filed a patent application for a "brassière" on February 12, 1914, and the patent was granted to her on November 3 of that year. As a descendant of Robert Fulton, of steamboat fame, Caresse certainly had inventive genes. Still, one can't help wondering in her case, not to speak of Titzling's, about the extent to which people's lives may be influenced by their names. See also BOSOM, BUST, GAY DECEIVERS, LINGERIE, and PALPITATORS.

break off contact with the enemy. To run away from the fight, to retreat. See also STRATEGIC MOVEMENT TO THE REAR.

break wind. The polite form of "fart," which IS a FOUR-LETTER WORD. The phrase dates to at least the sixteenth century. Thus, from a translation by Sir John Harington (1561–1612) of a Latin verse by Sir (or "Saint," depending on one's persuasion) Thomas More: "To break a little wind, sometimes ones life doth save/ For want of vent behind, some folke their ruine have."

Where Chaucer and other early English writers used "fart" unashamedly, as in, from *The Miller's Tale* (ca. 1387–1400), "This Nicholas anon leet fle a fart/As greet as it had been a thonder-dent," later generations were more reticent, e.g., "Now they are always in a sweat, and never speak, but they f--t" (Thomas Gray, *Works in Prose and Verse, 1740* [1884]). The most recent example of "fart" in the *Oxford English Dictionary* is from 1825, shortly before the official onset of the Victorian era. The rest is silence, or nearly so, as people began to have doubts even about the propriety of "breaking wind." Thus, H. Montgomery Hyde reports in *A History of Pornography* (1966) that "the great English Greek scholar Dr. Gilbert Murray always insisted upon translating the verb 'to break wind' as 'to blow one's nose.'" Of course, Dr. Murray had plenty of company, including the anonymous editor who rewrote one of the classic nursery rhymes, so that it reads:

> Little Robin Redbreast,
> Sat upon a rail;
> Niddle noddle went his head,
> Wiggle waggle went his tail.

But according to the earliest-known version of this verse (from William S. Baring-Gould and Ceil Baring-Gould, *The Annotated Mother Goose,* 1962):

> Little Robin red breast,
> Sitting on a pole,
> Niddle, Noddle,
> Went his head,
> And Poop went his Hole.

Where "poop," according to Nathan Bailey's *English Dictionary* (1721) equals "to break Wind backwards softly." See also MADE A TRUMPET OF HIS ASS and the *petard* in PETER.

brief illness. Suicide on the obituary page, where self-murder is hardly ever mentioned. "The daily faithful know what it means when they see, instead of 'suicide,' death due to a 'brief illness'" (Rinker Buck, MORE, 9/77).

As former obit writer for the *Berkshire Eagle,* of Pittsfield, Massachusetts, Mr. Buck wrote with some authority. Such delicacy, however, is by no means confined to western Massachusetts. Surveying other publications, MORE found that the *Dallas Morning News* did not mention "suicide" without permission from the family of the DECEASED, while the *Philadelphia Inquirer* did not run any obits at all on people who committed suicide unless required to by the prominence of the individuals. By these standards, *Time* magazine's famed circumlocution, "died by his own hand," is relatively explicit. See also ILL/ILLNESS, LONG ILLNESS, and OBITUARY.

broad-beamed. Fat-assed. "Captain Morton is . . . bowlegged and broad-beamed (for which the crew would substitute 'lard-assed')" (Thomas Heggen, *Mr. Roberts,* 1946). See also ARSE and PORTLY.

BS. The abbreviation helps clean up "bullshit," also euphemized as *bull, bullpeep, bullish,* and BUSHWA, and all with the general meaning of bunk, nonsense, rubbish, or BALONEY. Related abbreviations include *CS* (where "C" equals

CHICKEN), TS (where "S" sometimes equals "situation"), *SOL* (where "OL" equals "out of luck"), and *SOS* (depending on context, either "same old shit" or, if in an army mess hall when chipped beef is served on toast, "shit on a shingle"). A *BS artist*, meanwhile, is an expert at throwing it.

"BS" may also be described euphemistically as *bullshoot*, in which case the act is *bullshooting*, and the person is a *bullshooter* (see SHOOT). Nor does this exhaust the euphemistic riches of "BS," as demonstrated by the following: "At one time, oilfield workers vulgarly referred to the sludge that befouls the bottoms of oil tanks as 'bullshit.' This was gradually abbreviated to 'B.S.', which the industry's trade journal primly translated into 'basic sediment'" (Gary Jennings, *Personalities of Language*, 1965).

The oldest "bullshit" in the *Oxford English Dictionary* (1972) is from a letter by Wyndham Lewis, circa 1915, in which he reports that "Eliot has sent me Bullshit and the Ballad for Big Louise. They are excellent bits of scholarly ribaldry." About the same time, "BS" was recorded as college slang by Robert Bolwell, who carefully defined the meaning of the initials as *"bovine excrescence*, nonsense, 'hot air'" (*Dialect Notes*, vol. IV, Part III, 1915). However, both phrase and initialed euphemism probably were in use many years before. The short form, "bull," dates to at least 1850 in the sense of talking nonsense, and, in *You English Words* (1961), John Moore tells of finding an 1893 dictionary of words from Worcestershire that contained the suspicious-looking "bull-squitter," defined as "Much talk or fuss about a little matter."

Besides the basic *S* that comes from the *B*, there are many other euphemisms for the produce of other animals. For example, sheep excrete *buttons*, while buffalo, camels, and cows shit *chips* of different sorts, i.e., "white flats" and "round browns." Cows also make *cowslip, cow pies, heifer dust, meadow dressing*, and *prairie pancakes*. Horses, meanwhile, turn out *horse apples, road apples*, and *biscuits*. See also DEFECATE/DEFECATION and POPPYCOCK.

buff. Naked. "Buff," the color, comes from "buffalo," the animal, whose hide, a dull, whitish yellow, is not dissimilar in appearance to human hide. As a byword for lack of clothes, "buff" surfaced circa 1600, and it has remained popular to the present day. See also NUDE.

burleycue. An aural euphemism for burlesque; the cutesy mispronunciation supposedly softens the sounds of the bumps in the night. It has even been used in a book title: *Burleycue*, by Bernard Sobel (1931). See also ECDYSIAST, EXOTIC, and, for more about aural euphemisms, HOOR and the *cony* in RABBIT.

bushwa; also **bushwah, booshwa, booshwah, boushwa, or boushwah.** They all add up to the same thing: bullshit. "Looks to me like it's all bushwa" (John Dos Passos, *Three Soldiers*, 1922). Though probably just a mispronunciation of the word for which it stands, imaginative etymologies have been proposed for "bushwa," i.e., that it comes from *bourgeois* or even *bois de vache* (cow's wood), the euphemistic name for the buffalo chips, or bits of dried dung, used by the pioneers on the prairies for their fires. See also BS.

business. An omnibus term: In American slang, "business" may refer to the PENIS, the VAGINA, or to sexual INTERCOURSE. A *business girl*, meanwhile, is the

British counterpart of the American WORKING GIRL, or whore. Most commonly, "business" is a euphemism for what children and other small animals do when they RELIEVE themselves, e.g., ". . . there they were. Drake with his arm around little Nelson's shoulder, leading him down the path to keep him company while he did his 'business'" (John Le Carré, *The Honorable Schoolboy*, 1977). See also IT.

bust. The breasts; the general term for the upper, front part of the body—the head, shoulders, and breast, if one is talking about a statue—has a much narrower meaning when one is speaking euphemistically about a real, live woman, e.g., "I do not approve of any dress which shows the bust" (Miss Cleveland, *Pall Mall Gazette*, 3/13/1886). In addition to the basic "bust," the late nineteenth and early twentieth centuries featured *bust bodices* and *bust improvers*, which functioned somewhat like BRASSIERES; *bust extenders*, which obscured the shapes of *bustlines* with ruffles, and *bust forms*, which made *busts* seem larger and/or shaplier. See also BOSOM.

butt/buttocks. The ass. The four-letter "butt" is printable and otherwise usable where the three-letter word would offend (some people), e.g., ". . . kiss my royal Irish butt" (Edwin O'Connor, *The Last Hurrah*, TV movie version, 1977).
   "Butt," meaning the thicker end of something, was once considered Standard English for "ass." The earliest example in the *Oxford English Dictionary* comes from the fifteenth century, but the word seems to be much older, since "buttock," which is probably a diminutive of it, can be traced back to the thirteenth century. By Victorian times, the human "butt" (as contrasted with the tree butt, the butter butt, and so forth) was regarded, according to *OED*, as chiefly dialectal and colloquial in the United States, e.g., "The buttocks. The word is used in the West in such phrases as 'I fell on my butt,' 'He kick'd my butt'" (J. R. Bartlett, *Dictionary of Americanisms*, 1859).
   The full "buttocks," meanwhile, may also be used euphemistically, as in "That Texas oil worker who was charged in Federal court with having repeatedly slapped some airline attendants [see FLIGHT ATTENDANT] on the buttocks pleaded guilty in Miami" (*New York Times*, 2/24/77). In this case, the euphemistic effect was enhanced by an FBI AGENT who testified discreetly about "the rear anatomy" (see REAR) that was slapped. As if this were not enough, the culprit's name—*mirable dictu*—was Bumbard. See also ARSE and, for the lowdown on "bum," BOTTOM.

buxom. Overweight; especially having large breasts. "When we call a girl *buxom* we mean that she is fat" (Wilfred Funk, *Word Origins and Their Romantic Stories*, 1950). See also BOSOM and PLUMP.

buy the farm. To die. Explaining to his colonel why a medical evacuation helicopter had to be sent to his position after it was hit by FRIENDLY FIRE in the early morning hours of February 18, 1970, an American army lieutenant in Vietnam pleaded by radio: "Sir, the only thing I can tell you is that two of my people have bought the farm, and if I don't get it, two more will" (C. D. B. Bryan, *Friendly Fire*, 1976). The metaphor fits well with others for a grave, e.g., *future home, long home, narrow home,* and, for burial, *becoming a landowner*. See also BITE THE DUST and SPACE.

C, The Big. Cancer, a disease so dreaded that it is often not named. See also LONG ILLNESS.

Reviewing a novel, *The Discovery:* "Parry's title refers to a cure for 'the Big C,' cancer" (*Publishers Weekly*, 7/17/78). Linguistically, as well as medically, cancer has taken over where tuberculosis left off; see TB.

call girl. A whore; specifically, one who makes connections with her customers by phone; a COURTESAN. Compared to the ordinary WORKING GIRL of the street, the *call girl* generally leads a better, safer life, while catering to a better-heeled clientele, e.g.: "John, these are the finest call girls in the country. . . . They are not dumb broads, but girls who can be trained and programmed. I have spoken with the madam in Baltimore, and we have been assured their services at the convention" (John W. Dean III, *Blind Ambition*, 1976, quoting G. Gordon Liddy, on the occasion of his presentation to U.S. Attorney General John N. Mitchell, on January 27, 1972, of a million-dollar, intelligence-gathering plan—a sawed-off version of which led to the Watergate CAPER).

It is commonly assumed that the "call" in "call girl" represents Alexander Graham Bell's contribution to the world's oldest profession, but this probably isn't right, although the telephone *is* involved. Instead, the term apparently comes from the older *call house*, a brothel, or HOUSE, in which "girls" are "on call." See also PROSTITUTE.

calls (or **needs**) **of nature.** The periodic requirement that the body discharge waste materials. "The calls of Nature are permitted and Clerical Staff may use the garden below the second gate" (*Tailor & Cutter*, 1852). In our own informal age, the expression "I have to pay a call" is another way of announcing that one has to go to the TOILET.

camisole. In normal life, a loose-fitting garment, a jacket for men or a short negligee for women, but in MENTAL and other hospitals, a straitjacket; sometimes glorified as an *ambulatory camisole*. "The use of the straitjacket, called the 'camisole,' is now permitted only on written permission of a physician" (*New York Times*, 5/28/73).

canola. Rapeseed. The healthy-sounding name (modeled after "granola"?) has been proposed by Canadian processors, who are apparently ashamed of their product, although its name derives from the innocent Latin *rapum* (turnip) not *rapere* (to seize). See also MOLEST and PARSON-IN-THE-PULPIT.

capability. Ability, with a FOP Index of 1.6. "Capability" is favored by bureaucrats and other artful dodgers, especially when acquiring new powers, such as a first-strike *capability*, because of its overtones of contingency, which suggest to innocent bystanders that the new potential may never be realized.

Unfortunately, this is not always so. For example: "Late in the fall of 1971 . . . the co-ordinates for Watergate were fixed even if no brain as yet had made the calculation. The White House retained the Plumbers' 'capability' . . ." (*New York Review of Books*, 4/4/74). And on the international scene: "In early 1961, McGeorge Bundy [National Security Adviser to the president] was informed of a CIA project described as the development of a capability to assassinate. Bundy raised no objection and . . . may have been more affirmative" (report on assassination plots against foreign leaders by the Senate Intelligence Committee, 11/75). See also AFFIRMATIVE, EXECUTIVE ACTION, and PLUMBER.

capacity. A voluminous synonym for a high-class job. No manager with a proper sense of his or her own importance would ever be caught saying, "As senior vice president I supervised such-and-such." Rather, the proper boardroom style is: "In my capacity as senior vice president, I supervised . . ." The *capacity*, then, is strictly excess, except for the purpose of emphasizing the highness of the muck-a-muck. There is also a certain human tendency to confuse oneself with one's job (and sometimes, even, with the job one hopes to have). This results in such sentences as "I am considering offering my capacity for state-wide leadership" (Rep. Hugh Carey. D., New York, as quoted in Edwin Newman, *Strictly Speaking*, 1974). And the people of New York not only elected but reelected Carey's *capacity* as governor. See also POSITION.

Cape Cod turkey. Dried salt codfish, sometimes further disguised with a sauce; a humorous euphemism, comparable to ALASKA STRAWBERRIES (dried beans), *Irish apricots* (potatoes, naturally), or WELSH RAREBIT (cheese on toast). In the nineteenth century, when the Hudson River teemed with sturgeon, and poor people could not afford much meat, the flesh of this fish was known as *Albany beef*. For other euphemisms that swim, see ROCK LOBSTER and SEA SQUAB.

caper. A lighthearted euphemism for dirty business, ranging from the overthrow of a foreign government to a domestic burglary; a COVERT OPERATION.

Thus, trying to clean up some of the dirty linen in the CIA's closet, Ray S. Cline, a former deputy director of the agency, said of CIA-aided coups in Iran in 1953 and Guatemala in 1954: "The tragedy is that the concept of what CIA was intended to be eventually became gravely distorted as a result of the Iranian and Guatemalan capers" (*Secrets, Spies, and Scholars: Blueprint of the Essential CIA*, 1978). On the home front, meanwhile, President Nixon's men often passed off the Watergate burglary as a *caper*. For instance, H. R. Haldeman, the president's chief of staff, warned his boss on June 30, 1972, just thirteen days after the break-in at the offices of the Democratic National Committee: "You run the risk of more stuff, valid or invalid, surfacing on the Watergate-caper type of thing" (White House tape, not released until 5/17/74). See the related HANKY-PANKY and, for more about the Watergate *caper*, continue with CONTAIN, COVER-UP, PLUMBER, and SIGN OFF.

capital punishment. The death penalty. The phrase sounds rather innocuous. If taken literally, it could mean nothing more than a box on the ears. The "capital" comes from the Latin *caput*, head, while "punishment" ordinarily implies a chastisement that one survives. For the varieties of *capital punishment,* see AUTO-DA-FÉ, EXECUTE, HOT SEAT, MADAME, NECKTIE PARTY (or SOCIABLE), and SHOT. For the wisdom of Nancy (Mrs. Ronald) Reagan on the *capital punishment* question, continue with CONSUMER COMMUNICATION CHANNEL.

care of, take. To kill; a classic example of Reverse English, in which the figurative meaning of the phrase has been twisted 180 degrees from the actual meaning, with its connotations of affection, benevolence, and concern.

At the murder trial of W. A. (Tony) Boyle, former head of the United Mine Workers of America, ". . . the state's key witness testified that he had heard Mr. Boyle give the order in 1969 to 'take care of' Joseph A. Yablonski" (*New York Times,* 4/9/74). Mr. Yablonski, an insurgent candidate for the union presidency, was *taken care of* by being shot to death, along with his wife and daughter.

For other specimens of Reverse English, see FAIR TRADE and JOB ACTION.

carnal knowledge. Sexual intercourse. "Carnal," from the Latin word for "flesh," is a signpost word, erected so that even dullards will understand that "knowledge" in this instance is being used in the good, old-fashioned biblical sense; see KNOW. It should surprise no one to discover that the branch, or body, of learning called *carnal knowledge* has been pursued studiously, even avidly, for some centuries. For example, speaking of the early New Englanders, who were not always as Puritanical in deed as word, John Josselyn reported in *An Account of Two Voyages to New England* (1674) that the figure of an Indian, cut from red cloth, was used to shame a woman for "suffering an Indian to have carnal knowledge of her." (*Suffer* here is something of a euphemism, too, since even in the word's older, pre-painful sense of merely "allowing" or "enduring," it implies more patience and passivity than the woman who earned the red Indian badge probably had.)

And it wasn't so long ago that the film *Carnal Knowledge* ran into trouble on account of its title: ". . . *Variety* reports that newspapers in 14 cities have balked at carrying ads for the Nichols-Feiffer film. . . . There was no objection to the artwork . . . or to the copy . . . the papers just didn't like the title" (*New Republic,* 9/18/71). See also F—— and INTERCOURSE.

cash advance. A debt; especially, a small loan with a high rate of interest to a bank credit-card customer. "Cash advance" has a nicer jingle to it.

casket. The bronze-handled word for coffin. From the standpoint of the undertakers (FUNERAL DIRECTORS), who push the word and the object, "casket" has several advantages over the plainer "coffin": (1) the mere mention of "coffin" inevitably conjures up grim thoughts, while casket, being also "a small box, or chest, as for jewels," seems one step further removed from the final, fatal condition; (2) "casket" makes the happy suggestion that its contents (the REMAINS) are at least as valuable as the container itself, and (3) the undertaker enjoys a higher markup on the more opulent *casket.*

"Casket" seems to have been an American invention, made about the middle of the last century, probably through a discreet shortening of *burial casket.* Almost from the time the euphemism was introduced, some people protested it. As early as 1863, for instance, Nathaniel Hawthorne railed: "'Caskets!'—a vile modern phrase which compels a person of sense and good taste to shrink more disgustedly than ever before from the idea of being buried at all" (*Our Old Home*).

All this was in vain, of course, as undertakers (and, to be fair, most of their customers) have continued to call coffins anything but. Other terms include the understated, nondescriptive *box*, the hopeful *eternity box*, the airtight (all the better to preserve the body) *burial case*, and the gentle *slumber cot* (see SLUMBER COT/ROBE/ROOM). Slang terms tend to be funnier, but the humor is of the gallows variety, e.g., *bone box, cold meat box, crate, pine overcoat, six-foot bungalow, wooden kimono, wooden overcoat,* and *wooden suit*. (The modern "wooden" terms replace the *wooden doublets* and *wooden surtouts* of yore.) In a completely different field, but illustrative of the same kind of thinking, the people who bring us atomic power have spent a great deal of time figuring out ways to store radioactive wastes in—what else?—*caskets*. See also FUNERAL HOME/PARLOR, INTERMENT, PASS AWAY, and SELECTION ROOM.

casualty. Victim. Until a century or so ago, "casualties" were accidents or losses (e.g., "casualty insurance"), but now they are people: dead ones, wounded ones, and, in the military, also missing ones and captives. An opaque term that conceals the horrors of death and disfigurement, "casualty" is much loved by professional soldiers, who tend to compensate for the bloodiness of their work by describing it in the blandest possible terms. (See AIR SUPPORT, ORDNANCE, and PERSONNEL in this connection.) The oldest "casualty" in the military sense in the *Oxford English Dictionary* comes from as recently as 1898. An early user was Winston Spencer Churchill: "In spite of more than a hundred casualties, the advance never checked for an instant" (*London to Ladysmith*, 1900). As the Churchillian example implies, "casualty" is ideal for reducing the results of war to dry statistics. For instance: There were 33,769 American *casualties* in the Revolutionary War and 210,291 in the Vietnam CONFLICT.

On etymological grounds, "casualty" may seem at first glance to be appropriate enough. It comes from the Latin *casus*, accident, and violence often does seem to occur in an accidental, random manner, even on battlefields where it is better organized than in civilian life. The bloodless "casualty," however, actually is a perversion on this level, too, since it evades responsibility by attributing to accident, or chance, events that are really the fault of humans—on the battlefield and elsewhere. For example: "And so it could be said that I was—if I—that I was one of the casualties, or maybe the last casualty, in Vietnam" (Richard M. Nixon, TV interview with David Frost, 5/19/77).

See also ACCIDENT, BITE THE DUST, COLLATERAL DAMAGE, and POST TRAUMATIC NEUROSIS.

categorical inaccuracy. A lie; usually used when making denials. For example, following his nomination for the vice-presidency, Gerald R. Ford spiked rumors that he had been a patient of a New York City psychotherapist by declaring: "That's a categorical inaccuracy" (*New York Times*, 10/17/73). See also TERMINOLOGICAL INEXACTITUDE.

cat house. A brothel, especially a cheap one. "Cat house" comes from "cat," a very old word for "whore," e.g., from a poem of 1401: "Be ware of Cristis curse, and of cattis tailis." And for more about the old "tailis," see the modern TAIL.

Caucasian. White. Now restricted mainly to police blotters ("Two Caucasian males were apprehended on the corner of Nevins and Dean"), the euphemism had a much wider application in the era of SEPARATE-BUT-EQUAL facilities, e.g., "Members of the Caucasian race only served here." The Caucasian-white equation was established in 1781 by Johann Friedrich Blumenbach, who divided all humanity into five races on the basis of skull measurements, with one skull from the South Caucasus giving its name to the type because of its supposedly typical white measurements. For more on the confusing question of racial classification, see BLACK.

caught or **caught out.** To be made pregnant; like KNOCKED UP, seldom encountered in the present tense. The usage is not, as one might think, limited to the lower classes, e.g.: "The pride of giving life to an immortal soul is very fine . . . perfectly furious as I was to be caught" (Queen Victoria, letter, 6/15/1858, in *Dearest Child*, 1964). See also EXPECTANT.

caught (or **taken**) **short.** To be in somewhat desperate straits on account of the need to empty the bladder or bowels at an awkward time. "I was caught a bit short . . . had the trots" (*Pennies from Heaven*, WNET, NYC, 3/15/79). By extension, "taken short" may also refer to the soiling of one's underwear. See also DEFECATE/DEFECATION and PEE.

cemetery. A graveyard; the euphemism is betrayed by its origin, the original Greek *koimeterion*, meaning a "dormitory" or "sleeping place" (see SLEEP).
   "Cemetery" was applied first by early Christian writers to the Roman catacombs, later to consecrated churchyards, and still later to non-church-related burying grounds. If "cemetery" seems to be a relatively honest, straightforward word today, that is just because we have grown used to it—and it looks good in comparison to some of the newer terms that have been floated by graveyard developers. Among the floaters: *burial-abbey* and *burial-cloister; garden of honor* (for veterans and their wives); *garden of memories* (in the great Forest Lawn Memorial Park of Southern California, the most expensive section, open only to property-holders who possess a Golden Key, is called the *Gardens of Memory*); *love glade;* MEMORIAL PARK; *mausoleum* (an old word for a fancy tomb that is having something of a revival as rising land prices make it more profitable for graveyard developers to build up instead of digging down); *mortarium,* and *necropolis* (from the Greek for "city of the dead"). Another special kind of graveyard is the *columbarium* or *cinerarium,* which is not a place to see a special kind of 3-D movie, but a site for INURNMENT of CREMAINS (ashes). In the language of slang, too, there are many circumlocutions for "graveyard" (whistling past it, in effect). For example: *bone orchard, boneyard, future home, God's acre* (or *field*), *Hell's half-acre, last home* (or *abode*), *marble city* (or *orchard*), *permanent rest camp, skeleton park, Stiffville,* and *underground jungle.*
   For more about the graveyard business today, see (in addition to the aforementioned MEMORIAL PARK) INTERMENT, MONUMENT, PERPETUAL CARE, PRE-NEED, and SPACE. For the great, pre-Victorian shift in graveyard styles, see PASS AWAY.

chamber. A discreet shortening of "chamber pot," as in, from a discussion of the conditions in which slaves lived on Southern plantations, "There are seldom or never any conveniences in the way of chambers" (J. Hume Simons, *The Planter's Guide and Daily Book of Medicine,* 1849). See also CONVENIENCE and UTENSIL.

chapel. An undertaker's establishment; long forms include *funeral chapel, memorial chapel,* and *mortuary chapel.*

The death business, like so many other businesses, seems to be consolidating as it expands. Thus, many *chapels* are parts of the same organization, forming what might be called "chapelchains." For example, in the New York area, Walter B. Cooke, Inc., (10 *chapels*); Frank E. Campbell, "The Funeral Chapel," Inc.,; Riverside Memorial Chapel, Inc. (five *chapels*), and Universal Funeral Chapel, Inc., are all controlled by anonymously named Service Corporation International, of Houston, Texas, which itself is part of an international chapelchain with some 170—er—locations. See also FUNERAL DIRECTOR, FUNERAL HOME/PARLOR, and MORTUARY.

characterization omitted, or **deleted.** Presidential expurgations. Both phrases appeared with titillating frequency in the 1,308 pages of transcripts of White House conversations that President Richard M. Nixon made public at the end of April 1974. For example, there was the president's thumbnail opinion of the LATE Sen. Robert F. Kennedy (D., New York): "Bobby was a ruthless (characterization omitted)" (tape of 2/28/73, *The White House Transcripts,* 1974). In this instance, "characterization omitted" merely represented a slight bow to public proprieties, similar to a TV censor's BLEEP, but the effect of the presidential expurgations was not always so innocent; see EXPLETIVE DELETED.

character line. A wrinkle, as in "Matilda is starting to get character lines." The euphemism is unusually apt, since "character" derives from a Greek verb meaning "to engrave" or "make furrows in."

chemise. A slip—and yet another Frenchified undergarment; see LINGERIE for more details.

In olden times, "chemise" was applied in English (as it still is in French) to the linen underthings of men as well as women. During the nineteenth century, as "lingerie" itself was coming into fashion, "chemise" gradually became restricted to feminine garments, replacing "smock" and "shift." From Leigh Hunt's *Autobiography* (1850), via the *Oxford English Dictionary:* "That harmless expression [shift] . . . has been set aside in favour of the French word 'chemise'." From "chemise," in turn, we get "shimmy," which is used corruptly in place of "chemise" and (also corruptly, some would say) to describe what the *chemise* does when worn by a dancing girl, i.e., the *shimmy shake.* Automobiles, too, are said to *shimmy* when they wobble, but that is another, far less fascinating matter. See also LINGERIE and SNOWING DOWN SOUTH, IT'S.

chest. The breasts. ". . . she was so angry at her swinging breasts that she wanted to cry; no matter how nice he was he couldn't fail to notice her 'chest'" (John O'Hara, *Appointment in Samarra,* 1934). Persons with large *chests* are

chevon

sometimes said to be *chesty* or, more formally, to have *amply* (or *well-*) *endowed chests*. See also BOSOM and ENDOW/ENDOWMENT.

chevon. Goat meat; the U.S. Department of Agriculture has allowed meat-packers to use the French label since 1971. The precedent of the official sanction is ominous. As meat prices continue to rise, it may not be long before horse begins appearing in the nation's butcher shops, and when it does, the meat-packers probably will be allowed to call it *cheval*. See also FILET MIGNON and FRAGRANT MEAT.

chicken. Chicken shit; also euphemized as *chicken——* and CS (which is to "chicken" as BS is to "bull"). In the military, for instance, a unit in which the commander insists on small-minded attention to unnecessary details may be described as "a *chicken* outfit." Or a recruit may complain: "Having to polish the back of your belt buckle is a lot of CS." Civilians also have been known to use such expressions. Thus, the discreetly cleaned-up remarks of former New York Knick basketball player Phil Jackson on the subject of former teammate and (now) former coach Willis Reed: "He's intimidating. When a guy calls time out, and you have to go to the bench and face him, and he calls you 'Chicken——,' you'd better have your act together" (*New York Times Magazine,* 10/16/77). See also CRAP, DEFECATE/DEFECATION, and, for more about the use and abuse of dashes, F——.

city. Town. European cities usually are important, populous places, but when Americans began naming their burgs, they were much more liberal with the "city" designation. Occasionally, this may simply have been the result of over-optimism, but the root cause seems to be the human desire to make one's surroundings appear as grand as possible. "It is strange that the name of city should be given to an unfinished log-house, but such is the case in Texas: every individual possessing three hundred acres of land, calls his lot a city" (Capt. Frederick Marryat, *Narrative of the Travels and Adventures of Monsieur Violet in California,* etc., 1843). The Texans weren't alone in their pretensions, and the result today is such thriving metropolises as Pell City, Alaska (1970 population of 5,602); Yreka City, California (pop. 5,394); Garden City, Georgia (pop. 5,790); and Central City, Kentucky (pop. 5,450). See also GREENLAND and UNIVERSITY.

clarify. To eat one's words. For example, there was the remarkable performance of Gen. George S. Brown, chairman of the Joint Chiefs of Staff, who was required to hold a special news conference on October 18, 1976, to clarify previous comments on Israel, Britain, and Iran. The general's comments had been to the effect that the shah had "visions of the Persian Empire," that Britain and its military forces were a "pathetic" sight, and—most impolitic of all—that Israel, just in military terms, had "to be considered a burden" on the United States. The last remark was "clarified" or, as the general also said, put in "proper perspective," by the declaration that "United States policy toward Israel over the years has been clear: we are fully committed to the security and survival of the state of Israel. I believe in that policy wholeheartedly." Another definition of "clarify" is "to eat crow." See also MISSPEAK.

clean bomb. A dirty bomb that is clean only in comparison to the worst bombs (or DEVICES) that can be built. "The development, for example, of a 'clean' hydrogen bomb—one in which the area of serious contamination resulting from an explosion can be reduced from thousands to only tens of square miles—can radically change our concepts of nuclear defense and warfare" (*New York Times Magazine*, 12/9/56). See also ENHANCED RADIATION WEAPON and TACTICAL NUCLEAR WEAPON.

cleaning person. A cleaning woman; formerly a cleaning lady, DOMESTIC, HELP, MAID, or SERVANT. "Then there was the white radical feminist, about to meet with the black female militant about a strike of hospital workers; the radical feminist gave her black female cleaning person the day off" (John Leonard, *New York Times*, 8/18/76). See also PERSON.

client. A catchall term for covering up a variety of less-speakable relationships. Thus, welfare recipients have metamorphosed into the *clients* of social workers, convicts into the *clients* of prison administrators, patients into the *clients* of psychoanalysts. For social workers, in particular, "client" has an important rub-off effect: To the extent that it dignifies the people they deal with, it increases their own prestige, putting them in the same class as lawyers, who have long had "clients" instead of "customers." See also PATRON and WELFARE.

clinic. Shamelessly imitating the medical profession, practitioners in a host of other fields have latched on to "clinic" to describe their own operations. For example, a "collision clinic" is a body and fender shop in "Floridian," an American dialect first described by Robert Craft, who viewed its appearance as a symptom of the general deterioration of language and culture in the peninsula. ". . . Floridian is now euphemistically and compulsively alliterative. Thus a garage is a 'Collision Clinic,' a furniture store a 'Gallery' selling not tables and chairs but 'Concepts' (though without explaining how one *sits* on a concept)" (*New York Review of Books*, 5/16/74). In defense of Floridian, it should be noted that as long ago as 1937 a *car clinic* was sighted in Wrexham, North Wales (H. L. Mencken, *The American Language, Supplement One*, 1945). Other kinds of "clinics" include *auto clinic, baseball clinic, coaches clinic, decorator clinic, football clinic, home remodeling clinic, legal clinic, marriage clinic, tax clinic, teachers clinic,* and *writers clinic.* For more about the influence of medicine in other fields, see CONSULTANT.

cloakroom or **cloaks.** A common British euphemism for (euphemisms all) a LAVATORY, REST ROOM, or TOILET; not to be confused with a "checkroom," which is where Americans put their cloaks, overcoats, and parcels. "Cloakrooms" with running water seem to be a relatively recent invention, but the general idea is old: When our medieval ancestors went to the castle *garderobe*, they did not—as the name of the place implies—merely hang up their clothes. It is possible, too, that "cloakroom" has been influenced by "closet" (see EASE and WC), and perhaps even by "cloaca," the Latin word for sewer, which did time as a euphemism for PRIVY. "Cloaca," in turn, comes from "Cloacina," the Roman goddess of disposal. In the nineteenth century, an especially fancy privy might be hailed as a "Temple of Cloacina," but the short form was more common, e.g., "To every house . . . a cloaca" (Frederick Marryat, *Olla Podrida*, 1840).

club. A bar, dressed up as a fraternal organization in order to evade local liquor laws. Thus, as Calvin Trillin reports, thirsty guests of the Ramada Inn in Topeka, Kansas, must become "members" of Le Flambeau Club before they can get a drink at the hostelry's Le Flambeau Bar (*The New Yorker*, 8/7/78). See also DONATION and TEMPERANCE.

cohabitor. Legal Latin for a person who is living in sin (i.e., in a sexual RELATIONSHIP) with another person, not necessarily of the opposite sex. "Unmarried couples, known in the law as 'cohabitors' but otherwise rather awkwardly left without a label, are beginning to take an interest in buying cooperative apartments" (*New York Times*, 9/4/77). The verb is "cohabit" and the noun is "cohabitation." The latter once had the specific meaning of INTER-COURSE. Contemporary *cohabitors* will be glad to know that this sense is entirely obsolete, in view of the danger attached to it, i.e., "The death of Galeas happened by immoderate cohabitacion" (Sir Geoffrey Fentron, *The Historie of Guicciardini*, trans. 1579). See also FRIEND.

coition or **coitus.** Sexual intercourse; a safe, scientific, Latinate retreat. The actual meaning of the Latin is appropriately, and euphemistically, vague. Both "coition" and "coitus" derive from *coire*, where *co* equals "together" and *ire* is "to go." They may be translated as "going together" or, with greater felicity perhaps, "coming together."

Of the two, "coition" is the older in English, dating to the sixteenth century. Before it became a euphemism, it had other, nonsexual meanings. For instance, back in the sixteenth and seventeenth centuries, people spoke of the "coition" (or "coming together") of magnets, and of the "coition" (or "conjunction") of planets. The word's sexual sense seems to date from the first half of the seventeenth century. Thus, Sir Thomas Browne, despite having a wife, children, and an apparently happy family life, could write: "I would be content . . . that there were any way to perpetuate the world without this triviall and vulgar way of coition" (*Religio Medici*, 1643). In conformance to Gresham's Law (bad meanings drive out good), the sexual sense eventually took over, making the other, older meanings of "coition" obsolete. The same thing happened to COPULATE and INTERCOURSE.

cojones. The balls, aka TESTICLES; from the Spanish *cojon*, for the same item in the singular. "Cojones," like "balls," also may be used figuratively for "guts," aka INTESTINAL FORTITUDE. For example: "It takes more cojones to be a sportsman where death is a closer party to the game" (Ernest Hemingway, *Death in the Afternoon*, 1932). A very similar, though obsolete, term is "cullion," a French cousin of "cojones." (Both go back to the Latin *culleus*, a bag.) Thus, referring to an old method of taking oaths: "I wolde I had thy coillons in myn hond/In stede of relikes or seintuarie [holy objects]" (Geoffrey Chaucer, *The Pardoner's Tale*, ca. 1387–1400). See also THIGH.

collateral damage. Civilian damage, in the language of nuclear-war gamesters. "A primary factor that would influence thinking in governments and among the people in Western Europe is 'collateral damage,' a euphemism for civilian casualties and destruction of nonmilitary structures and facilities" (*New York Times*, 12/6/79). See also CASUALTY, EXCHANGE, and STRUCTURE.

colonel. Lacking inherited titles to distinguish themselves from their fellow citizens, Americans have had to make do with a variety of euphemistic honorifics, of which "colonel" is perhaps the most common after HONORABLE itself.

As a title of esteem rather than an actual military rank, "colonel" goes back at least to the eighteenth century. In 1744, noting the prevalence of *colonels* in the Hudson valley, Alexander Hamilton (a Scottish physician, not the other one, who wasn't born yet) explained: "It is a common saying here that a man has no title to that dignity unless he has killed a rattlesnake" (Albert Bushnell Hart, ed., *Hamilton's Itinerarium. . . . From May to September, 1744*, 1907). Two years later, Edward Kimber, an English traveler, reported: "Whenever you travel in Maryland (as also in Virginia and Carolina) your ears are constantly astonished by the number of *colonels*, *majors*, and *captains* that you hear mentioned; in short, the whole country seems at first to you a retreat of heroes" (*London Magazine*, 7/1746). For a time, MAJOR was an especially popular rank in the South, and it was the usual title awarded to those who served as railroad conductors. The greater profusion of *colonels*, though, stemmed from the practice of state governors, north and south, to bestow this rank upon all comers. In 1942, a legislator in Virginia even introduced a bill to enable any citizen of the state to purchase an official colonel's commission for the sum of one dollar (providing that the citizen was adult, male, and white). Of the hordes of state *colonels*, those from Kentucky have long been the most famous. As early as 1825, according to H. L. Mencken's *The American Language, Supplement One* (1945), the Chief Justice of the United States, John Marshall, penned the following:

> In the blue grass region
> A paradox was born:
> The corn was full of kernels
> And the *colonels* full of corn.

colored. A traditional euphemism for "Negro" in the North and for "nigger" or NIGRA in the South; as "coloured," the official designation in the Republic of South Africa for people of mixed ancestry, i.e., black or brown with some trace of CAUCASIAN. See also NEGRO and SEPARATE DEVELOPMENT.

combat emplacement evacuator. A shovel, in the army; also known as a *digging instrument* or *entrenching tool*.

come. To experience sexual orgasm. Now the most common nonclinical term, "come" started out as a euphemism, being essentially a bland, generalized allusion to a specific, intense event. Though it did not become popular until the twentieth century, the sexual sense of the word has been dated to before 1650 in the 1972 supplement of the *Oxford English Dictionary*, where the oldest example happens to refer to a timeless problem: "Then off he came, & blusht for shame soe soone that he had endit" (*Walking in Meadow Green* in *Bishop Percy's Loose Songs*).

comfort station

And from our own time comes, so to speak, the remarkable word palindrome (word by word, it reads the same backward as forward), created by Gerard Benson in *The New Statesman:*

> "Come, shall I stroke your 'whatever' darling? I am so randy."
> "So am I darling. Whatever your stroke, I shall come."
> (Willard R. Espy, *An Almanac of Words at Play*, 1975)

Where people today "come," earlier generations were said to DIE or *spend.* Thus, Capt. Francis Grose explained that "to make a coffee-house of a woman's **** [his asterisks]" was "to go in and out and spend nothing" (*A Classical Dictionary of the Vulgar Tongue*, 1796). And sometimes, instead of "coming," people did just the reverse. Thus, Fanny Hill overheard Polly say (ellipses in the original): "Oh! . . . oh! . . . I can't bear it . . . It is too much . . . I die . . . I am going . . ." (John Cleland, *Memoirs of a Woman of Pleasure*, 1749).

During most of the nineteenth century, the dominant term was "spend"; for example, the index of *My Secret Life* (anon., ca. 1890) includes "spending," but not "coming," even though the latter occasionally crops up in the text, and in virtually the same breathless breath as the other, e.g., "'I'm coming love, are you?' 'Aha—yes . . . I'm spend—ing!'" Probably, "spend" isn't entirely extinct. As recently as the mid-1950s, Springmaid used the term in an off-color ad showing an American Indian male in a sheet-hammock, obviously in a state of postcoital bliss, and with a BUXOM squaw nearby, bearing the caption, "A buck well-spent on a Springmaid sheet." There is no doubt, however, that "come" comes quicker to most people's minds today, and the shift away from "spend" seems to be psychologically significant—though in just what way is hard to say. In general, "come" certainly appears to be a healthier, more positive term than "spend," with its debilitating suggestion that the body's precious fluids are being used up. The change in orgasmic nomenclature may also have helped relax society's attitudes toward MASTURBATION, as reflected in the slow trend away from *self-abuse* and *self-pollution* to today's liberated SELF-(or MUTUAL) PLEASURING. See also COITION, INTERCOURSE, and PREORGASMIC.

comfort station. A public toilet. "Comfort station" (and "comfort room") have been with us since circa 1900. The oldest example of a FACILITY of this kind in *A Dictionary of American English* (1942) comes from a report in the *New York Evening Post* of June 30, 1904, of "The excavation for the public comfort station in Chatham Square." Not until 1978 did New Yorkers take the next logical step, responding to the DOG DIRT/LITTER/WASTE crisis by erecting the city's "first 'canine comfort station' complete with tile walls and shingle roof . . . in front of the Manhattan Plaza housing development" (*New York Times*, 8/1/78). See also REST ROOM and TOILET.

commission. A bribe, in international business. Typically, a manufacturer in one country will pay a *commission* to a public official or private influence-peddler in a foreign country in order to sell its wares to or in the recipient's nation. The size of the *commission* usually varies according to the size of the order. For example, Lockheed Aircraft Corp. agreed to pay its Japanese CONSULTANT, Mr. Yoshio Kodama, a *commission* of $4 million if any major Japanese airline ordered 3 to 6

TriStar passenger planes, plus $120,000 each for TriStars 7 through 15, plus $60,000 for every TriStar beyond that. Thus, a *commission* differs from a flat, general-purpose bribe, or CONTRIBUTION, whose objective, frequently unstated, may be essentially defensive, intended only to maintain the existing business climate.

With all due respect to the Japanese, the biggest *commission* scandal of recent years occurred in the Netherlands in 1976, after Lockheed disclosed that it had paid $1.1 million in the early 1960s to Prince Bernhard. Though the prince denied receiving the money, the surrounding details were sufficiently sordid—including Bernhard's request in 1974 for "sales commissions" of $4 million to $6 million on prospective plane purchases by the Dutch government—for him to be required to resign virtually all his official and business posts.

"Commission" takes on another strange meaning in straight-laced Arab countries, such as Saudi Arabia, where Moslem law forbids interest on loans: There, oil-rich lenders receive instead of "interest" a *commission*—at the going interest rate, naturally. See also DONATION, KICKBACK, and QUESTIONABLE.

commode. A somewhat old-fashioned toilet, still occasionally encountered, as in Pauline Kael's observation that Jane Fonda played one scene in *Fun with Dick and Jane* on a "commode," apparently for no other reason than to keep the audience from dozing off (*The New Yorker*, 2/28/77). In the nineteenth century, before flush toilets were in widespread use, "commode" meant the small cabinet or chair that enclosed a chamber pot, or CHAMBER, and in the eighteenth century, a "commode" was a bawd, or procuress. Thus, "commode," the French word for "convenient," acquired virtually the same complex of euphemistic meanings as CONVENIENCE. See also TOILET.

community. Establishment, as in the intelligence *community* or the defense *community*. "The intelligence community is made up by and large of people who lie under oath, who plan assassinations" (Frank Mankiewicz to Dick Cavett, WNET-TV, NYC, 12/21/78). See also ASSASSINATION.

companion. A person who is not married to the person with whom he or she is living; a FRIEND; often but not always a "mistress," since the androgynous "companion" applies to men as well as to women, and to homo- as well as to hetero-RELATIONSHIPS.

"Companion" frequently is accompanied by such modifiers as "constant," "devoted," "frequent," "longtime," and "traveling." In the world of euphemisms, these are known as signpost words. This is because their only function is to draw attention to the euphemism that follows, so that everyone is sure to get the point, even those who are slightly inattentive. For example: "Miss Helen Dunlop, the Senator's long-time secretary and traveling companion, told the authorities last month that Mr. Long told her that night that he had eaten candy that tasted bitter and that he feared he had been poisoned" (*New York Times*, 5/5/73). In this case, an autopsy of former Sen. Edward V. Long (D., Missouri) revealed no candy and no poison; just the remains of an undigested apple. Meanwhile, an autopsy of "traveling companion" includes the findings that (1) Mr. Long's widow had filed a $3.25 million suit against her husband's *traveling companion,* charging alienation of affections, and (2) the widow had received just $10 in the Senator's will, while the *traveling companion* was made executrix of his large estate. See also COHABITOR, PARTNER, and ROOMMATE.

company. In the intelligence COMMUNITY, the informal name for the Central Intelligence Agency. This follows the example of the older British Secret Intelligence Service, known fondly to its employees as "The Firm," or "The Old Firm," while trading on the organizational acronym, "Cia" being the abbreviation for "company" in Spanish. Outside the so-called intelligence community, "company" has many of the overtones of COMPANION, e.g., ". . . one of his main functions is . . . to provide company. The company is preferably blond, and under 25. . . . and will be paid $500 apiece for their services . . ." (*New York* magazine, 5/26/75). See also SERVICE.

As a verb, the sexual use of "company" and the longer "accompany" goes back some ways, e.g., from William Caxton's *Geffroi de la Tour* (1483): "Thamar that had company with her husbondes fader." "Accompany," meantime, is labeled specifically as a euphemism in the monumental *Slang and Its Analogues* (J. S. Farmer and W. E. Henley, 1890–1904), which includes, among other examples, this, from Roger Coke's *Elements of Power and Subjection* (1660): "We teach that upon Festival and Fasting times, every man forbear to accompany his wife." See also INTERCOURSE.

concentration camp. A prison camp. Although now popularly associated with Nazi Germany, the institution of the "concentration camp" dates to at least 1901 when Lord Kitchner began locking up women and children in them during the Boer War in South Africa. His plan was to lay waste to the entire countryside outside the camps, but it didn't work. Instead, he just relieved the Boers of the burden of taking care of their families.

At about the same time, the United States was pursuing a similar policy, which it called "reconcentration," in the Philippines. There, the idea was to separate the populace from the nationalist guerrillas led by Emilio Aguinaldo. With noncombatants "reconcentrated" into certain localities and kept under guard, anyone found outside the designated areas was assumed to be a guerrilla and could be shot on sight. The United States seems to have learned this tactic from the Spanish, who had adopted a policy of *reconcentrado,* or reconcentration, in an effort to repress the rebellion in Cuba, starting in 1895, that American JINGOS blew up into the Spanish-American War of 1898. *Reconcentrado* involved removing peasants and agricultural workers from farms and locking them up in *concentration camps,* with results that should have surprised no one, i.e., "Starvation of thousands of non-combatants through reconcentration" was reported. (*Westminster Gazette,* 4/6/1898). The tactic is essentially the same as that used in Vietnam, except that then the talk was in terms of creating SPECIFIED STRIKE ZONES and GENERATING refugees from the countryside in order to attrit the Viet Cong's population base. See also ASSEMBLY (or RELOCATION) CENTER, CORRECTIONAL FACILITY, DETENTION, PROTECTIVE CUSTODY, and WATER CURE.

confidant. Technically, only a person entrusted with private affairs, commonly love affairs, but euphemistically, a lover; the feminine form is *confidante,* as in the

New York Times headline: "Kay Summersby Morgan Dies; Eisenhower Confidante in War" (1/21/75). Ms. Morgan's posthumously published memoirs were entitled *Past Forgetting: My Love Affair with Dwight D. Eisenhower*. See also AFFAIR and FRIEND.

confidence course. What the U.S. Army used to call an "obstacle course."

confidential source. An informer; a live spy as opposed to an inanimate, electronic, HIGHLY CONFIDENTIAL (or SENSITIVE) SOURCE. The FBI, for example, has been helped by friendly journalists who thus became *confidential sources* (the CIA would call the same people *assets*). For many years, the bureau also had a high-ranking *confidential source* in that dangerously radical organization, the American Civil Liberties Union. (The FBI carefully filed away some 10,000 pages of material on the ACLU in its own *do not file files*; see also FILE.) The "confidential" is especially deceptive: It is supposed to make the *source* feel secure, the implication being that the FBI, the local prosecutor, or whoever, will not tell anyone who is doing the spying. But this is not so. All a judge has to do is ask, and the minions of the law will name their *sources*. Journalists, by contrast, tend to be more protective toward their HIGHLY (or USUALLY) RELIABLE SOURCES, and their plain, ordinary *sources*, too, and judges have been known to send journalists to jail on this account. See also INFORMANT and SOURCE OF INFORMATION.

conflict. War, as in the Korean *conflict*, which seemed like a war to most people, lasting three years and causing 157,530 American CASUALTIES. Since the war was never officially declared to be one, however, the Veterans Administration now counts 5,841,000 veterans of the "Korean Conflict" (*The World Almanac and Book of Facts*, 1981). As an extension of "war" by other means, "conflict" has a FOP Index of 3.0. See also ERA and POLICE ACTION.

confound. Damn; a somewhat old-fashioned euphemism in a free-speaking age, occasionally encountered in the present tense, as in "Confound you!" but more often in the past, e.g., "Sir, you are a confounded liar and a cheat." Similar (though it stems from "concern") and even more antique is "consarn," as in "I've always heard tell that there were two kinds of old maids—old maids an' consarned old maids" (Mary E. Wilkins, *A Humble Romance and Other Stories*, 1887). See also DARN.

congress. Sexual intercourse; the general term for an assembly or gathering of persons served as a euphemism for the more intimate kind of meeting from the sixteenth through the nineteenth centuries, e.g., ". . . I picked up a fresh, agreeable young girl called Alice Gibbs. . . . and had a very agreeable congress" (Frederick A. Pottle, ed., [James] *Boswell's London Journal, 1762–1763*, 1950). Occasionally, the term was dolled up as *amorous congress* or even *sexual congress*, a construction that has borne the test of time, e.g., "I found only one abrupt verb for sexually congressing a woman . . ." (Kurt Vonnegut, Jr., reviewing the *Random House Dictionary*, 1967, from *Welcome to the Monkey House*, 1970). See also INTERCOURSE.

conjugal. A good, clean, nonsexy adjective, whose dictionary definition

connection

("Pertaining to marriage or the relation of husband and wife; connubial") hardly explains the furor—and lawsuits—occasioned when either husband or wife are deprived of their *conjugal rights*. The vacuous formal definition was given body by United States District Judge Vincent P. Biunno, when ruling against a suit by two New Jersey convicts, who asserted that the state's refusal to grant them home furloughs or *conjugal* visits amounted to unconstitutionally cruel and unusual punishment. Said the judge: "The term conjugal visits is to be taken as a euphemism for sexual intercourse" (*New York Post*, 7/24/74). See also ACTION and INTERCOURSE.

connection. A somewhat old-fashioned form of sexual intercourse; a RELATIONSHIP. For example, James Boswell, distressed by an unexpected visit of "Signor Gonorrhoea," confronted the source of his infection, an actress known to history only as Mrs. Lewis (and to his journals as Louisa) in these terms: "Madam, I have had no connection with any woman but you these two months" (1/20/1763, Frederick A. Pottle, ed., *Boswell's London Journal, 1762–1763*, 1950).

The euphemistic "connection" is by no means limited to the so-called civilized nations. Just as prudish are the Nupe, of West Africa: "Nupe lacks any native word for sexual intercourse; instead, its speakers use a word of Arabic derivation that means 'to connect'" (Peter Farb, *Word Play: What Happens When People Talk*, 1974). See also CRIMINAL CONVERSATION, INTERCOURSE, and Noah Webster's use of *carnal connection* in PECULIAR MEMBERS.

consultant. An adviser. Originally—going back to the seventeenth century—a "consultant" was the person who asked a question of an oracle rather than the person who posed as one. During the nineteenth century, however, consulting physicians began to appear as *consultants*, and since then, trading on the prestige of the medical profession, practically everyone under the sun has adopted the term. (See also CLINIC in this connection.) Private detectives (also called INVESTIGATORS) were among the first to adopt the medical term. Conan Doyle referred to "our London consultant" as early as 1893. Then there are the ubiquitous business and management *consultants*, the engineering *consultants*, and the teachers who spend more time as *consultants* than as teachers. More picturesque, and a whole lot rarer, are *mortuary consultant* (H. L. Mencken passed along a report of one in Boston, circa 1935) and *chimney consultant*, as in: "Sort of a latter-day chimney sweep is Richard Bruno, a chimney consultant . . . whose concern cares for many fireplaces in Manhattan and in Westchester County" (*New York Times*, 11/3/76). A *moving consultant*, meanwhile, is the fellow from the furniture movers who tries to estimate in advance how much you'll be taking.

"Consultant" also makes a wonderful rug for sweeping dirt under. For example, E. Howard Hunt, Jr., the Watergate PLUMBER, was officially a *consultant* to the White House. Other, even more complicated forms of consultantship occur in international business, where "consultant" is a cover for an influence-peddler. Thus, Lockheed Aircraft Corp.'s principal *consultant* in Japan was Mr. Yoshio Kodama, who was recognized unofficially as that nation's most important *kurumaku*, or wire-puller. (The term comes from the Kabuki theater, where its literal meaning, "black curtain," suggests the way in which Mr. Kodama manipulated events from behind the scenes.) In the Netherlands, a similar role was played by Prince Bernhard (see COMMISSION).

consumer communication channel. This sterling example of bureaucratic nonlanguage formed a key element of the State Department announcement that won the 1976 Doublespeak Award of the Committee on Public Doublespeak of the National Council of Teachers of English. The announcement, chosen not so much for its duplicity as its sheer impenetrability, told of the department's plans to appoint a consumer affairs coordinator, who would "review existing mechanisms of consumer input, thruput and output, and seek ways of improving these linkages via the 'consumer communication channel.'"

Also-rans in the 1976 Doublespeak Award contest included Ugandan President Idi Amin for calling his secret police "The State Research Bureau"; Nancy Reagan, wife of Ronald (ILLEGAL) Reagan, who explained on a TV show that she favored CAPITAL PUNISHMENT "Because it saves lives," and Sen. Daniel Patrick Moynihan (D., New York), for BENIGN NEGLECT. See also AIR SUPPORT.

contain. To obstruct justice; specifically and historically, the White House conspiracy to COVER UP the Watergate scandal. John W. Dean III explained the psychology of the terminology this way:

> If Bob Haldeman or John Ehrlichman or even Richard Nixon had said to me, "John, I want you to do a little crime for me. I want you to obstruct justice," I would have told him he was crazy and disappeared from sight. No one thought about the Watergate coverup in those terms—at first, anyway. Rather it was "containing" Watergate or keeping the defendants "on the reservation" or coming up with the right public relations "scenario" and the like. No one was motivated to get involved in a criminal conspiracy to obstruct justice—but under the law that is what occurred." (*New York Times*, 4/6/75)

To be sure, Nixon has never managed to see it this way. As he insisted in a televised interview with David Frost on May 4, 1977: "I was trying to contain it politically. And that's a very different motive from the motive of attempting to cover up criminal activities of an individual." For another notable Nixonian legal opinion, see ILLEGAL.

contribution. A bribe or payoff, made by a corporation, out of company funds, to a politician.

The parties to such transactions like to pretend they don't know what they are doing, and they muffle their deeds accordingly in euphemistic language. The extent of this sham was revealed clearly in an analysis by John Brooks in *The New Yorker* (8/9/76) of the philanthropical operations of Gulf Oil Corp., which dispensed more than $12 million in *contributions*, at home and abroad, during the 1960–73 period. Thus, Gulf's guilty awareness of the true nature of what it was doing can be inferred from knowing: (1) the *contributions* were made in cash; (2) the cash was obtained by channeling corporate funds through the bank account of a subsidiary in the Bahamas (see LAUNDER); (3) the existence of the account—and of the political payments themselves—was kept secret from those Gulf executives who were thought to be "Boy Scouts"; (4) the Gulf official in charge of the Bahamas account regularly tore up records of deposits and withdrawals and flushed them down a toilet; (5) the payments, though usually handed over at meetings at airports or in the offices of the recipients, occasionally were made in such exotic locales as behind the barn of a New Mexico ranch or in the men's WASHROOM of an Indianapolis motel. Meanwhile, what the "political figures" on the receiving end really thought about the *contributions* can be inferred from: (1) No one ever blinked an eye at receiving large amounts of cash or ventured to ask if the *contributions* actually came from individuals rather than from corporate funds; and (2) almost every one of the *contributions* was requested, if not urgently demanded, by the recipient. See also COMMISSION and KICKBACK.

convalescent hospital. An old age, rest, or nursing home. "Many of the 'rest homes' of the 1950s, with their broad verandas sporting rows of rocking chairs, have been replaced by 'convalescent hospitals'—air-conditioned, cinderblock edifices whose windows are sealed shut. The word *convalescent* implies recovery, yet few who enter leave by the same door" (*New Age*, 11/77). See also HOME and NURSING HOME.

convenience. A toilet—sometimes, especially in Britain, a "public convenience" or, humorously dismissing someone else's attempt at humor, "Henny Youngman would have thrown that one down the porcelain convenience" ("B. C.," *New York Post*, 8/8/75). The euphemistic uses of "convenience" parallel those of COMMODE. Thus, before indoor plumbing came into fashion, "convenience" referred to any of a variety of handy articles, from a chamber pot (see CHAMBER); to a spittoon (aka CUSPIDOR); to a wife, mistress, or harlot (the latter might also be described as a *convenient*). Back in the seventeenth and eighteenth centuries, it was not impossible for a *convenient* to make use of a *convenience*, e.g., "A convenience to spit in appeared on one side of her chair" (Tobias Smollett, *Roderick Random*, 1748). Meanwhile, in the nineteenth century, the plural *conveniences* also was one of the many euphemisms for the UNMENTIONABLES that covered the LIMBS of gentlemen. See also TOILET.

conversation. Sexual intercourse. The euphemism goes back aways, e.g., "The men hath conuersacyon with the wymen, who that they ben or who they fyrst mete" (*First English Book on America*, ca. 1511). Today, the term usually is reserved for *conversations* that shouldn't have taken place; see CRIMINAL CONVERSATION.

cony. An aural euphemism for "cunny." See also RABBIT.

copulate/copulation. Sexual intercourse; thus, from a scene within the sacred precincts of Plato's Retreat, a New York City club for the *swinging* set: "An orange plastic ball zips through the air, occasionally caroming off . . . one of the swimmers. Two giggling women start to push a third into the water. . . . It is normal poolside fun, except that everyone is naked and three couples are copulating in the water" (*Time*, 1/16/78).
    "Copulate" and "copulation" originally referred to coupling in a nonsexual way, but by the fifteenth century people were beginning to speak of "carnal copulacyon." In accordance with Gresham's Law, whereby "bad" meanings of words drive out "good" ones, the sexual sense gradually became dominant (as it did with the related COITION), making it ever more difficult for teachers to give lessons on the "copulative" verbs without reducing classrooms to snickers. Any

teacher who can get through this lesson unscathed may advance to "lay-lie", see LIE/LIE WITH. And for more about the varieties of *copulation*, continue with INTERCOURSE.

cordless massager. A term used by those who wish to order a vibrator but are too shy to ask for one by name. The picture accompanying an ad for a *cordless massager* in *House and Garden* (9/77) showed the gadget being used on a foot, but the advertising copy was suggestive of other possibilities: "Battery-operated massager brings satisfying relaxation. Deep gentle penetrating vibrations . . ." This particular brand of *cordless massager* came in four models: 4½-inches long, 7 inches, 10 inches, and 12 inches.

Technically, a *cordless massager* is a kind of semiautomatic *dildo*, a word that enjoyed something of a vogue as a euphemism several centuries ago, when it was commonly used in ballads, with more than one meaning in mind, e.g., from William Shakespeare's *The Winter's Tale* (1610–11):

> He has the prettiest love songs for maids so with-
> out bawdry, which is strange, with such delicate
> burdens of dildos and fadings, "jump her and thump her."

The origin of "dildo" itself is somewhat mysterious. The name of the instrument bears a suspicious resemblance to the name of the dildo bush or tree, an exotic plant that is rather thin and grows straight up, 10 or 12 feet high. It seems more likely, however, that the term is a corruption of "diddle" or perhaps an Italian import, from *diletto*, delight. (The Italians themselves call the gadget a *passatempo*, or pass the time, while the French have termed it variously a *godemiché*, from the Latin for "enjoy myself"; a *bientateur*, or do-gooder, and *consolateur*, which should require no explanation.) By whatever name, the antecedents of the dildo or *cordless massager* are decently lost in the mists of time. From the Bible (Ezekiel, XVI, 17): "Thou has also taken thy fair jewels of my gold and silver, which I had given thee, and madest to thyself images of men, and didst commit whoredom with them" (King James Version, 1611).

See also FRIG, MARITAL AID, and, for more about "whoredom," Noah Webster's handling of that term in PECULIAR MEMBERS.

core rearrangement. In the nuclear power biz, the opaque way of describing the explosive destruction of the core of a reactor. "The reaction could be self-propagating, producing a 'core rearrangement'—destruction of the reactor core" (Norman Metzger, *Energy: The Continuing Crisis*, 1977) See also ABOVE CRITICAL.

correctional facility. A prison—and the key euphemism in a sweeping change in jailhouse nomenclature to softer, more "professional-sounding" jargon. Thus, New York's famous Sing Sing (established in the 1820s as, of all things, Mount Pleasant) has been known officially since 1970 as the State Correctional Facility at Ossining. But the Empire State is by no means out in front of the other forty-nine. As long ago as 1952, the old National Prison Association, the organization of people whose trade it is to lock other people up, changed its name to the American Correctional Association. This and the other semantic changes have not affected the underlying reality, of course. As was noted in 1972 in *The Official Report of the New York State Special Commission on Attica:*

> Effective July 8, 1970 . . . there were no more prisons; in their places, instead, stood six maximum security 'correctional facilities.' The prison wardens became 'institutional superintendents' . . . and the old-line prison guards awakened that morning to find themselves suddenly 'correctional officers.' No one's job or essential duties changed, only his title. Certainly the institutions themselves did not change. . . To a man spending 14 to 16 hours a day in a cell being 'rehabilitated,' it was scarcely any comfort and no reassurance to learn that he was suddenly 'an inmate in a correctional facility' instead of a convict in a prison. (Jessica Mitford, *Kind and Usual Punishment: The Prison Business*, 1974) See also FACILITY.

Not all prisons are called *correctional facilities.* There are still some STATE FARMS as well as such oddities as the California Men's Colony in San Luis Obispo (the nearby county jail masquerades as the Sheriff's Facility). And the prisoners, besides being called INMATES in correctional newspeak, are also known as CLIENTS and RESIDENTS—unless they are political prisoners, in which case they are DETAINEES or INTERNS, and their prisons are CONCENTRATION CAMPS, *detention centers,* and (in the United States, during World War II) ASSEMBLY CENTERS. Particularly bad RESIDENTS usually are housed in the *maximum security dormitories* (cellblocks) of SECURE FACILITIES. When they act up, they may be put into ADJUSTMENT CENTERS (solitary confinement) or SECLUSION (same thing). Sometimes they are tortured; see the *Tucker telephone* in BELL TELEPHONE HOUR as well as the aboveboard AVERSION THERAPY.

cosmetician/cosmetologist. Not, as one might be forgiven for assuming, a practitioner of what is known variously as *cosmetic* or *aesthetic* (i.e., plastic) surgery, but a worker in a beauty parlor; a BEAUTICIAN.

counsel. A lawyer—or someone, such as a public relations *counsel,* who is trying very hard to enhance the prestige of his or her business. Among themselves, lawyers go a few steps further, commonly addressing one another as *distinguished counsel* or *learned counsel.* Not even the boldest press agent has yet dared do this. It is a form of grooming behavior—you massage my ego and I'll massage yours—that lawyers have perfected to an unmatched degree.

Nowhere is the preference for "counsel" more apparent than in the White House, where the president's official lawyer is his *counsel:*

> P—Why don't we just say . . . "He is the White House Counsel and, therefore, his appearance before any judicial group is on a different basis from anybody else . . . with his unique position of being a top member of the President's staff but also the Counsel. There is a lawyer, Counsel—not lawyer, Counsel—but the responsibility of the Counsel for confidentiality." (Richard M. Nixon, 3/27/73, *The White House Transcripts,* 1974)

See also ATTORNEY, ENGINEER, and PUBLIC RELATIONS.

courtesan. A medium-priced whore—and a word that has been working its way down the social ladder for the past four or five centuries.

Originally, a "courtesan" was simply "a woman of the court," but the association with high-class prostitution developed early, which says something about life at the top in medieval times. The oldest example of the word in the *Oxford English Dictionary* comes from 1549, and already the reference is to those who "keepe Courtisanes." By the start of the seventeenth century, the following distinction was made: "Your whore is for euery rascall, but your Curtizan is for your Courtier" (Edward Sharpham, *The Fleire*, 1607). As time went on, *courtesans* began taking on commoners, too, though still retaining some traces of their formal social standing. Thus, during the Victorian era, the label was reserved for the most-refined whores—of the sort frequently patronized by the anonymous author of *My Secret Life* (ca. 1890), e.g.: "Beyond a voluptuous grace natural to her, she had not at first the facile ways of a French courtesan, they came later on." Today, the term has become further cheapened, so that anyone who doesn't actually walk the streets may class as a "courtesan." From a report on the world of big-city prostitutes: "They call themselves 'working girls,' or, if they are call girls, 'courtesans'" (*New York Times*, 8/9/71). See also CALL GIRL, WORKING GIRL, and the basic PROSTITUTE.

cover. To engage in sexual intercourse; said of male animals, especially stallions, when they are, as the saying goes, standing at stud. See also SERVICE and SIRE.

cover one's feet. An ancient and now-obsolete Hebrew euphemism for the relieving of the bowels, e.g.: "And he came to the sheep-cotes by the way, where was a cave; and Saul went in to cover his feet" (I Samuel, XXIV, 3, King James Version, 1611). See also EASE.

cover story. A lie, often a long and involved one, compounded partially out of truths, making the tale easier for the teller to remember and more difficult for the hearer to disprove; a LEGEND. Originally a cloak-and-dagger term, "cover story" dates at least to World War II. Thus, speaking of the Office of Strategic Services, the wartime predecessor of the CIA: "When an agent's training was completed and his mission in Germany or German-occupied territory decided upon, this OSS branch [the authentication bureau] would be given the outline of what was known as an agent's 'cover story.' A cover story is a biography in fiction. It was up to the authentication bureau to make that fiction look like fact" (Stewart Alsop and Thomas Braden, *Sub Rosa—The O.S.S. and American Espionage*, 1946).

Since World War II, "cover stories" have been prepared for domestic as well as foreign consumption. For example, after the U-2 piloted by Francis Gary Powers was brought down over Russia (see OVERFLIGHT) on May 1, 1960, the United States announced that one of its weather observation planes was missing—a *cover story* that was shot down, too, when Soviet Premier Nikita Khrushchev announced four days later that the Russians had Powers, "alive and kicking." For many Americans of that innocent era, the U-2 *cover story* was the first convincing demonstration that sometimes the Russians told the truth, while their own government lied.

Though "cover story" is a relatively new phrase, the basic "cover," in the sense of something that hides, conceals, or disguises, is several centuries old, e.g.: "Wicked men have divers covers for their lewdnesse" (Jeremiah Burroughs, *An Exposition of Hosea*, 1643).

See also EMBROIDER THE TRUTH, SCENARIO, STORY, and WHITE LIE.

cover-up. Not necessarily a Watergate term: In the National Basketball Association, for instance, to "cover up" is to play an illegal zone defense. As Willis Reed, then captain of the New York Knickerbockers, explained after a win over the Houston Rockets: "When someone got caught out of position, we zoned it until he got back. I mean we covered up, not zoned" (Leonard Lewin, *New York Post*, 11/1/73).

Among the Watergaters, "cover-up" also was used when referring to the illegal zone defense (or conspiracy) that was set up when some members of the team were caught out of position in the offices of the Democratic National Committee (see CAPER). As President Richard M. Nixon himself said, in a slip that Freud would have admired:

> That is, because of—because of our—and that is—we are attempting, the position is to withhold information and to cover up—this is totally true—you could say this is totally untrue. (3/30/73, *The White House Transcripts*, 1974)

See also CONTAIN and STONEWALL.

covert operation. A break-in, burglary, or other underhanded action, such as murder or the toppling of a foreign government, and one of the leading examples, along with CAPER, which is a synonym of "covert operation" in all of its nefarious senses, of how the language of the intelligence COMMUNITY has slopped over into domestic politics.

On the foreign front, referring to the overthrow of Premier Mohammed Mossadegh in Iran: "In 1953 . . . a covert operation so successful that it became widely known all over the world was carried out in Iran" (Ray S. Cline, *Secrets, Spies, and Scholars: Blueprint of the Essential CIA*, 1978). Though generally applauded in the 1950s and 1960s, the CIA's *covert operations* have subsequently received such a bad press (see ASSASSINATION) that they are now usually referred to as *special activities* instead.

On the home front, meanwhile, one of the more famous *covert operations* of recent times was set in motion on August 11, 1971, when Egil "Bud" Krogh and David R. Young, co-chairmen of the PLUMBERS, addressed a memo to John D. (DEEP SIX) Ehrlichman, in which they recommended that "a covert operation be undertaken to examine all the medical files still held by [Daniel "Pentagon Papers"] Ellsberg's psychoanalyst covering the two-year period in which he was undergoing analysis." Ehrlichman approved the memo in virtually the same terms as used in FBI headquarters for authorizing BLACK BAG JOBS, initialing it and noting, "If done under your assurance that it is not traceable." As a result, the *covert operation*, or break-in, at the offices of Dr. Lewis Fielding, of Beverly Hills, California, was carried out over the following Labor Day weekend. Unfortunately for Ehrlichman, it proved to be traceable, and he eventually went to jail. For more about the *covert operation* at Fielding's place, see NEUTRALIZE/NEUTRALIZATION.

cow brute. One of a herd of euphemisms for "bull," a sexually potent word that many Americans have tried to avoid saying over the years, e. g., "I was not fooling with a two-year-old cow brute" (J. M. Hunter, ed., *The Trail Drivers of Texas*, 1920).

It is sometimes thought that *cow brute* and other de-sexualized synonyms, such as *cow creature, male cow,* and *gentleman cow,* are purely regional curiosities, retained only in such cultural backwaters as the Ozarks, but this is not so. As recently as 1933, no less than forty-two bullish euphemisms were current in the New England states. As recorded in the *Linguistic Atlas of New England* (Hans Kurath, ed., 1939–43), they were, in order of popularity: *gentleman cow, male, toro, sire, animal, gentleman ox, critter* (or *creature*), *gentleman, beast, male animal, male cow, he cow, top cow, roarer, masculine, bison, he animal, seed ox, short horn, he critter, the he, top ox, he ox, male ox, kooter, cow critter, he creature, old man, top steer, gentleman heifer, master, male beast, brute, male critter, man cow, cow man, bullock, cow topper, doctor, bullit, paddy,* and *bungy.*

Nor does this exhaust the possibilities: *buttermilk cow, cow's husband, duke, he thing, surly,* and *bullette* (a young bull or baby calf) also are included in *The American Thesaurus of Slang* (Lester V. Berrey and Melvin Van den Bark, 1953).

While the prejudice against "bull" is terribly widespread, it is, admittedly, in the isolated Ozarks that the taboo has been developed into a high art form, being extended there to other words in which the "sexy" one appears. Thus, Vance Randolph reported in "Verbal Modesty in the Ozarks":

> It was only a few years ago that two women in Scott county, Arkansas, raised a great clamor for the arrest of a man who had mentioned a *bull-calf* in their presence. Even such words as *bull-frog, bull-fiddle* and *bull-snake* must be used with considerable caution, and a preacher at Pineville, Mo., recently told his flock that Pharaoh's daughter found the infant Moses in the *flags:* he didn't like to say *bull-rushes."* (*Dialect Notes,* vol. VI, Part 1, 1928)

The bull is only one of a number of male animals whose name has been euphemized for strictly sexual reasons. See also GENTLEMAN, ROOSTER, SIRE, and SLUT.

crap. "Crap" is to "shit" as SCREW is to "fuck"—a newer term, considered coarse but not as coarse as its synonym and, so, something of a euphemism for it. Thus, writers could get away with "crap" back when editors were usually editing out "shit," in its literal sense, e. g., "There didn't look like there was anything in the park except dog crap," as well as figuratively, e. g., "all that David Copperfield kind of crap . . ." (both from J. D. Salinger, *The Catcher in the Rye,* 1951).

"Crap" was used in the sense of the chaff, residue, or dregs of something from at least the fifteenth century, but it appears not to have acquired its modern odiferous meaning until the eighteenth or nineteenth. "Crapping ken" (where "ken" = "house") and, on occasion, "cropping ken" were used in the sense of PRIVY as far back as the seventeenth century (variants included *crapping casa, crapping case,* and *crapping castle*), but Capt. Francis Grose did not include any excremental meanings for "crap" in the 1796 edition of *A Classical Dictionary of the Vulgar Tongue*—and he probably would have, had he known them. He *did* include "crap" in the sense of "money" (a parallel to Francis Bacon's MUCK), and "crapped" for "hanged," as well as the marginally stronger "sh-t sack," for "a dastardly fellow," and "sh-t-ng through the teeth," for "vomiting." Meantime, the *Lexicon Balatronicum* of 1811, a revision of Grose's work by an otherwise anonymous "Member of the Whip Club," omitted "crap" altogether, and the oldest citation for the word in its pure, unadulterated sense in the *Oxford English Dictionary*'s 1972 supplement comes from as recently as 1898. The popularization of "crap" in this sense may have been aided by confluence with the name of the eminent sanitary engineer, Thomas Crapper (1837–1910), who invented the valve for automatically shutting off the water after flushing a TOILET. Not surprisingly, the newer meanings of "crap" have proved strong enough to drive out the older ones. Thus, no one ever talks anymore about the "crap" or "settlings" at the bottom of a beer barrel. Even dice players usually speak of shooting craps, plural, thus preventing any possible misunderstanding. Of course, "crap" itself may also be euphemized as *frap* or even CRUD. The change in meaning of "crap" parallels similar shifts in FECES, FERTILIZER, and MANURE. See also DEFECATE/DEFECATION.

cremains. Human ashes; an unctuous combination of "cremated" and REMAINS that supposedly softens the sorrow of the bereaved while enhancing the professional image of the furnace-stoker. ". . . in the special language of death, the mortician did not say 'ashes'; he referred to them as 'cremains'" (Lynn Caine, *Widow*, 1974).

Cremains are produced in the *cremation chamber* or *vault* (as opposed to "retort") of a *crematorium* (a late Victorian word, dating to circa 1880) by means of "calcination—the *kindlier* heat" (Jessica Mitford, *The American Way of Death*, 1963). See also INURNMENT and MORTICIAN.

criminal conversation. Adultery, in British common law and in the laws of some of the states in the United States; frequently abbreviated to "crim. con." in Britain, where the "con." may also be construed as "connexion" (see CONNECTION). The "conversation," of course, is a euphemism for nonspoken INTERCOURSE; see CONVERSATION.

The subject of *criminal conversation* usually arises when someone is suing someone else (a correspondent) for having an AFFAIR with his wife. A formal definition comes from the anonymous "A Member of the Whip Club," who revised Capt. Francis Grose's *A Classical Dictionary of the Vulgar Tongue* and reissued it as the *Lexicon Balatronicum* in 1811:

> CRIM. CON. MONEY. Damages directed by a jury to be paid by a convicted adulterer to the injured husband, for criminal conversation with his wife.

A famous suit for *crim. con.* money involved James Thomas Brudenell, seventh earl of Cardigan, who led the charge of the Light Brigade at Balaclava in 1854. A notorious womanizer, Cardigan was accused in 1843 of adultery with Lady Frances, wife of Lord William Paget, who asserted that he'd been damaged to the tune of £15,000. Paget was supported by the testimony of Frederick Winter, a private detective, who had managed to post himself beneath a sofa in a drawing room adjoining the one in which the adultery allegedly took place. (This forward position was not without peril: At one point the couple perched on Winter's sofa, and he was in some danger of being raked by Cardigan's spurs, the latter being attired, still, in full-dress uniform.) Winter told the court that the breathing of the couple subsequently became "hard like persons distressed for breath after running," and that he had no doubt, from what he had heard and seen, that a "criminal connection had taken place between the parties," not once but twice. Despite this evidence, the jury let Cardigan off, apparently because Paget himself was shown to be such a blackguard that they sympathized with Lady Frances and had no wish to see Lord William enjoy all that *crim. con.* money (Donald Thomas, *Charge! Hurrah! Hurrah! A Life of Cardigan of Balaclava,* 1974). See also EXTRA-MARITAL.

criminal (or **illegal**) **operation.** Abortion back when "abortion" couldn't be mentioned in polite society, especially not in FAMILY newspapers, and when the operation was against the law. "Criminal operation" seems to have been used mainly in the United States, "illegal operation" in Great Britain. (British newspapers also used to avoid "abortion" with the completely opaque *producing a certain state.*) See also ILLEGAL and MISCARRIAGE.

cripes. Christ; one of many euphemisms for the holy name. Among the others: *cricky, cracky, Christmas, Christopher Columbus, criminey,* JIMINY CRICKET, and, most elegantly, *G. Rover Cripes.* See also GEE.

cross over. To die; "cross" is synonymous as a euphemism with "pass" (as in PASS AWAY), and it appears in various phrases, all with a deathly meaning, such as *cross over the range, cross the bar,* and *cross the border.* Samuel Eliot Morison used the construction to excellent effect in describing the death of John Quincy Adams on July 4, 1826: "He lingered until the tide turned, and crossed the bar at sunset" (*The Oxford History of the American People,* 1965). Still more remarkable, for being unself-conscious, are the dying words of Gen. Thomas J. ("Stonewall") Jackson, CSA, on May 10, 1863, eight days after having been mistakenly shot by his own troops at the Battle of Chancellorsville: "Let us cross over the river and rest under the shade of the trees." See also FRIENDLY FIRE and REST.

crower. A cock. "I'm going to have the Plymouth Rock crower killed" (Mary E. Freeman, *Six Trees,* 1903). For more about the *crower* and why he got this name, see ROOSTER.

crud. A general term for a number of nasty things (e.g., an intestinal upset that features vomiting and/or diarrhea, dried semen; venereal disease, usually syphilis) that also functions as a euphemism for "crap," as in "I'll beat the living crud out of you" (*West Side Story,* film, 1961). See also CRAP and the *Cairo Crud* in MONTE-ZUMA'S REVENGE.

cull. The general term for selecting or picking later acquired the sense of tossing out or removing that which is inferior and, as a noun, "a cull," the rejected object itself. "Cull" is especially favored in agricultural and GAME MANAGEMENT circles to the word it sounds so much alike, "kill," as in "The battery boys 'cull' (or liquidate) their hens when they've laid for about a year" (*Listener,* 3/27/69). See also HARVEST, LIQUIDATE, SACRIFICE, SELECT OUT, and TRIAGE.

culturally deprived. Poor and, frequently, also black. ". . . what used to be called a 'slum' is now delicately referred to as 'a culturally deprived environment'" (William Safire, *Safire's Political Dictionary*, 1978). See also DISADVANTAGED and POOR.

cunnilingus. A relatively new word for an old practice—and one of the greatest examples of the cleansing power of an otherwise dead language, the Latin being printable in many places where the English is not. The Latin, as it happens, is quite straightforward (to Latin-speakers), the term deriving from *lingere*, to lick, and *cunnus*, which means "female pudenda" or, in the vernacular, "cunt." (And that last word is not slang, but legitimate, Standard English; see VAGINA.)

"Cunnilingus" seems to be a late-Victorian invention, with the oldest example in the 1972 supplement to the *Oxford English Dictionary* coming from Havelock Ellis's *Studies in the Psychology of Sex*, of 1897. Ten years earlier, "the obscene act of cunnilinging" was mentioned in J. R. Smither's translation of *Forberg's Manual of Classical Erotology*. During this period, the anonymous author of *My Secret Life* (ca. 1890) also discussed "female cunilingers," but this was exceptional: He was more apt to refer to *gamahuching*. See also FELLATIO and SOIXANTE-NEUF.

curiosa. Pornography. The generalized "curiosa," actually meaning "curiosities" or "oddities," is one of the euphemisms used by literate booksellers to describe their dirtier wares. "Curious" also has been used this way. Thus, playing the two off against each other: "She's not . . . the type to pore over literary curiosa unless . . . they were curious in the specialised sense" (Ngaio Marsh, *Final Curtain*, 1947). See also EROTICA.

cushion for flotation. A life preserver on an airplane; see PERSONAL FLOTATION DEVICE and WATER LANDING.

cuspidor. A spittoon; the more ornate word is preferred by those who choose to EXPECTORATE instead of spit. He whose task it is to empty the contents of the receptacle, and to keep it polished, is, naturally, the *cuspidorian*.

cuss. Damn. "Cuss" is a euphemistic variant of "curse," itself a generalized euphemistic substitute for the more specific "damn." For example: "Not keering a tinker's cuss what meeting house you sleep in Sundays" (C. F. Browne, *Artemus Ward: His Book*, 1862). See also DARN and SWAN.

custodian. A cleaned-up JANITOR, frequently found in schools; a SUPERINTEN-DENT. "Custodian" improves upon "janitor," just as JANITOR improves upon "caretaker," "furnace-stoker," and "floor-sweeper." Variations include *custodian-engineer* and, of all things, *engineer-custodian*. The switch to "custodian" has had a ripple effect: "One of the amusing sequels of the shift in terminology from *janitor* to *custodian* in one American university was that the title of the head of the research library had, in turn, to be changed from *Custodian* to *Director*, since there was some danger of confusing him with the janitor of the place" (Albert H. Marchwardt, *American English*, 1958). The janitorial *custodian* should not be confused with the *custodial office*. who is really a *correctional officer*, or prison guard. See also CORRECTIONAL FACILITY and ENGINEER.

C.Y.A. The abbreviation, especially popular among bureaucrats in Washington, D.C., and elsewhere, for "Cover [or Covering] Your Ass." Occasionally, for the benefit of those with especially tender sensibilities, the initials also are interpreted to mean "Cover Your Aft [end]." See also ARSE and BEHIND.

czar. Politically, it is hard to imagine anything less appetizing than a "czar" but, speaking of the American predilection for "half-hearted planning" by energy *czars*, John Kenneth Galbraith explains: ". . . the use of the word czar. . . . is in accordance with a bipartisan convention of some years standing in Washington which holds that czar has a more democratic connotation than planner" (*New York Review of Books*, 9/29/79). See also BOSS.

dad. A euphemistic form of "God," especially useful in forming such mild oaths as *dadblame, dadblast, dadburn, dadang, dadfetch,* and *dadgun,* where the BLAME, *blast, burn,* etc. all stand for "damn." For example: "Dad fetch it! This comes of playing hookey and doing everything a feller's told not to do'" (Mark Twain, *The Adventures of Tom Sawyer,* 1876). See also DOGGONE and EGAD.

dang. Damn, with "dang" itself sometimes being euphemized as *ding.* "Dang" has a countrified ring, which makes it sound obsolete, but it isn't: "Sure they'll drill holes in wood but the danged things 'walk' all over the place so that you can't put the hole where you want it" (Leichtung ad, *Natural History,* 10/78). See also DARN.

darky or **darkey** or **dark.** Black; the term dates to the colonial period, with the oldest example in *A Dictionary of American English* (Mitford M. Mathews, ed., 1951) coming from a song of 1775: "The women ran, the darkeys too; and all the bells, they tolled." It remained current at least through 1915 (e.g., "The Darktown Strutters Ball"), but fell into disfavor soon thereafter. H. L. Mencken reports that the *Baltimore Afro-American* launched a crusade in 1936 against "My Old Kentucky Home" because it contains the word. N.B.: In Britain, a *dark gentleman* may be a native of India. See also NATIVE and NEGRO.

darn. Damn. A euphemism of uncertain origin, it appears first in the 1770s in New England. Some authorities (led by Noah Webster, no less) have held it to come from the Middle English *dern* (secret), while others have argued that it is a corruption of "eternal" (as in "eternal damnation"), via *tarnal* and *tarnation,* both of which also surfaced as euphemisms for "damn" and "damnation" at about the same time as "darn." (Later developments included *darnation, goldarn,* and *gosh darn;* see GOLLY and GOSH.) Whatever the source, the euphemistic nature of "darn" was immediately recognized, e.g.: "In New England prophane swearing (and everything *'similar to the like* of that') is so far from polite as to be criminal, and many of the lower class of people use, instead of it, what I suppose they deem to be *justifiable* substitutions such as *darn* it, for d———n it" (*Pennsylvania Magazine,* 6/20/1781).

   While the Puritan blue laws may have helped inspire *darn, tarnal,* and the rest, as the preceding example suggests, the sudden appearance of so many euphemisms at about the same time also suggests another cause—in this case, the simultaneous rise of a new middle class and the blossoming of pre-Victorian prudery.

   Of course, "darn" is only the most popular of a great many euphemisms for "damn." Among the others, many of which are encountered most often in the past tense: BLAMED, *blast, blowed* (as in "I'll be blowed"), *bother,* BOTHERATION, *D.,* DANG, *dear* ("Oh dear me!"); DEUCE (also a euphemism for Satan); *ding; dog* ("I'll be dogged!" or "Dog my cats!"), *drat, jiggered, switched,* and THUNDER. See also DOGGONE, GEE, and HECK.

deceased. Dead; the dead person. This is probably the most popular way of not saying "dead." It also is used frequently in lieu of the dead person's name, e.g., "Don't you think the deceased would prefer the mahogany model?" (See DEPARTED for more about the taboo against naming the names of the dead.)

"Deceased" amounts to a verbal flinch—a quick blink of the eye to escape a gruesome sight. It has a FOP Index of 2.25. Even in the original Latin, it is a euphemism, deriving ultimately from *decedere*, which has the bland meaning of "to go away" or "to depart" (*de-*, away + *cedere*, to go). Strictly speaking, which isn't often done nowadays, "deceased" is a legal term (although not as legal as *decedent*), applying only to people. As such, it is the counterpart of DEMISE, which originally related to the transfer of property and property rights. John O'Hara, whose ear for language was notoriously fine, embedded "deceased" perfectly in its proper context at the tragic conclusion of *Appointment in Samarra* (1934): "Fortunately deceased had seen fit to vent his rage and smash the clock in the front part of the car, which readily enabled the deputy coroner to fix the time of death at about eleven P.M. . . ." The euphemistic blink usually is more noticeable, as in the following defense of public propriety by the Reverend William Sloane Coffin, Jr.: "If The New York Times wants to 'do a number' on Nelson Rockefeller [i.e., by trying to find out exactly when and how he died], why don't they have the courage to take him on as a public figure rather than as a private person now deceased?" (letter to the *New York Times*, 2/16/79).

The *deceased* may also be described politely as the *defunct*, the *late lamented* (see LATE), the LOVED ONE, and the REMAINS. Slang expressions tend to be more macabre, as well as more picturesque. Among them: *backed* (not used much since the nineteenth century but of sufficient ingenuity to warrant revival; as explained by Capt. Francis Grose in *A Classicial Dictionary of the Vulgar Tongue*, 1796: "He wishes to have the senior, or old square toes, backed: he longs to have his father on six men's shoulders; that is, carrying to the grave."); *cold meat* (in which case the hearse, or PROFESSIONAL CAR, becomes a *cold meat cart* and the CASKET a *cold meat box*); *crowbait; food for worms; morgue-aged property,* and *napoo* (a relic of World War I and the AEF, from the French *il n'y a plus*, there is no more). For the many ways in which people become *deceased*, without actually "dying," see PASS AWAY.

decision-making. Deciding, with a FOP Index of 2.1. The use of "decision-making" elevates the status of the *decision-maker*.

deed. Copulation. Originally, the operative phrase was "with the deed," as in, from a translation from the French, of 1585: "The Adulterer being found with the deed." At about the same time, though, William Shakespeare used the word in the modern way, with Berowne describing Rosaline in *Love's Labor's Lost* (1593?) as "A whitely wanton . . . one that will do the deed/Though Argus were her eunuch and her guard." Today, in seeking to clarify their use of the euphemism, people sometimes reveal their true feelings about sex, calling it *the dirty deed*. See also COPULATE/COPULATION and INTERCOURSE.

deep six. To destroy evidence—what John W. Dean III, President Nixon's COUNSEL, said he was advised to do by John D. Ehrlichman, the president's chief domestic affairs adviser, with papers found in the White House safe of E. How-

defecate/defecation

ard Hunt, Jr., the PLUMBER. "I asked him what he meant by 'deep six.' He leaned back in his chair and said: 'You drive across the [Potomac] river at night, don't you? Well, when you cross over the river on your way home, just toss the briefcase into the river'" (testimony to the Senate Watergate Committee, 6/25/73). Before becoming a euphemism for a criminal act, "deep six" (for six fathoms' depth) was a relatively innocent naval expression for jettisoning, e.g., "Give that gear the deep six" (Cary Grant, as a submarine captain, *Destination Tokyo*, film, 1941). "Deep six" also was another term for a grave, or SPACE. See also SANITIZE.

defecate/defecation. The words are long, Latinate, and "printable," but they're not ordinarily used by ordinary people, e.g., "'The only big words I use were taught me in the police academy, Roscoe,' said Baxter. 'Words like hemorrhage and defecation'" (Joseph Wambaugh, *Onionfield*, 1976). Compared to the word that Baxter would have learned as a boy, i.e., shit, "defecation" has a FOP Index of 3.25.

"Defecate/defecation" appear to be products of the nineteenth century, with the *Oxford English Dictionary*'s first example of "defecation" in the modern sense coming from 1830, seven years before Victoria became queen. (See PASS AWAY, PECULIAR MEMBERS, and ROOSTER for more about the euphemistically important pre-Victorian period.) Originally, "to defecate" was "to purify," both literally, as by removing the sediment (also called the CRAP) from a liquid, or figuratively, as by cleansing the mind or soul of guilt. Today, one hardly ever comes across such sentences as, "Consider the defecated nature of that pure and divine body" (Thomas Taylor, *Two Orations of the Emperor Julian*, trans. 1793).

Besides the classical Latinate "defecate" and "defecation," there are many other euphemistic expressions for the act and its result, with those for the act often overlapping with the large set of euphemisms for PEE. See, for example: BUSINESS, CALLS (or NEEDS) OF NATURE, CAUGHT (or TAKEN) SHORT, COVER ONE'S FEET, DUTY, EASE, ELIMINATE/ELIMINATION, GO, *make* (see MAKE [or PASS] WATER), NUMBER ONE AND/OR TWO, POWDER MY NOSE, RELIEVE, *sit on the* THRONE (see TOILET), and *squat* (see the "diddly-squat" in DIDDLY-POO).

As for the results, the euphemistic synonyms fall roughly into three categories: those relating mainly to people, those relating mainly to animals, and those relating to agriculture. For example:

People: BM, CRAP, *dead soldier*, ("pay a visit to the old soldier's home" is another form of POWDER MY NOSE), DIDDLY-POO (basic potty talk; see WEE WEE), *doo doo*, DUMP, FECES, *honey* (deposited in a *honey bucket*), NIGHT SOIL, STOOL, and *(body) wax*.

Animals: ACCIDENT, BS, BUSHWA, *button* (from a sheep), *chip* (as in *buffalo chip, prairie chip*, etc.), DOG DIRT/LITTER/WASTE, DROPPINGS, *heifer dust, horse apple, meadow dressing*, MESS, NUISANCE, POPPYCOCK, SHY-POKE (the name of a bird), WASTE, and WHITE DIELECTRIC MATERIAL.

Agriculture: FERTILIZER, MANURE, MUCK, *(organic) plant food, poudrette* (a nineteenth-century term for the contents of privies, from the French *poudre*, powder), and the latter's fair-sounding companion, *urette*.

Of course, many of the above, as well as some others, also can be used euphemistically as interjections. See also, for example, BALONEY, BARNYARD

EPITHET, BS, BUSHWA, CHICKEN, CRAP, HORSEFEATHERS, MERDE, NUTS, PISH/ PSHAW, SHUCKS, and SUGAR.

Defense, Department of. In the beginning—i.e., in 1789, when George Washington was putting together his first cabinet—there was the War Department, later (1798) supplemented by a separate Navy Department. This arrangement lasted until 1947, when the "Department of Defense" was created as the umbrella for the Departments of the Army (erstwhile "War"), Navy, and Air Force. Naturally, the nonaggressive *Defense Department* was formed just as the Cold War was, as the saying goes, heating up—and just as the development of nuclear weapons was giving the ultimate lie to the notion of effective "defense" (see LIMITED WAR for details). In complete consistence with this new nomenclature, the United States has not fought any "wars" since the *Defense Department* was established—merely the Korean POLICE ACTION and the Vietnam CONFLICT. See also ACTIVE DEFENSE, FLYING FORTRESS, and PREVENTIVE ACTION/DETENTION/ WAR.

delicate. A dainty reference to a "sensitive" subject: If a woman is in a *delicate* (or *certain* or INTERESTING) *condition* or *state of health,* she is pregnant. "Delicate" flourished in America as a euphemism for pregnancy in the years following the Civil War (aka WAR BETWEEN THE STATES), according to H. L. Mencken (*The American Language,* 1936). The British also leaned on it: "Mrs. Micawber, being in a delicate state of health, was overcome by it" (Charles Dickens, *David Copperfield,* 1850). See also EXPECTANT/EXPECTING.

deliver. The proper military term for "drop," when the falling objects come from airplanes. Thus, deciphering the language of U.S. military briefers in Vietnam: "Planes do not drop bombs, they 'deliver ordnance'" (Sydney H. Schanberg, *New York Times Magazine,* 11/12/72). See also ORDNANCE.

"Deliver" is an extremely convenient word. It dulls the sense of what is happening by dispensing with the suggestion of the physical impact of bombs upon people that is inherent in "drop." At the same time, it plants the idea that bombing is an exact business, akin to delivering mail or milk. (Bombers also travel on *milk runs.*) The latter aspect was especially important to United States briefers, who wanted the world to know that American bombs always were deposited neatly on military targets and never on hospitals, schools, churches, homes. The technique of seeming to hit nothing but military targets is known as PRECISION BOMBING.

Given the military precedent, one winces at hearing doctors and public officials speak of the delivery of health care. As California Governor Edmund G. (Jerry) Brown, Jr., has pointed out: "Now, health—I am healthy or unhealthy. I can care for you or I can't. But how to 'deliver health care' is a very complex metaphor that uses something from heavy industry to go over into spiritual reality" (*Thoughts,* 1976). See also CASUALTY and HEALTH CARE.

deluxe. A sumptuous euphemism for first class, especially treasured by manufacturers who want to avoid assigning numbers to their different models, since this would result in such ignominious, hard-to-sell labels as "second class," "third class," and so on. Plymouth, for example, came out with a *deluxe* model in 1949, and Ezra Pound used the term at the end of World War II, while confined in a United States Army stockade in Italy: "Before the deluxe car carried him over the precipice" (*Pisan Cantos*). Travel agents and hotelkeepers also found "deluxe" to be a useful addition to their vocabularies, with the result that other once-honest terms have become euphemisms. See also FIRST CLASS.

demise. Death. "Demise" referred originally (and still does, technically) to the transfer of rights or an estate, usually the sovereignty or property of a monarch, and usually, but not necessarily, by death. Thus, the diarist John Evelyn could note in 1689, "That King James . . . had by demise abdicated himself and wholly vacated his right." The king in this case, James II, of Great Britain and Ireland, was still very much alive and would remain so until 1701. He had, however, fled to France and been replaced on the throne by William and Mary.

Today, "demise" frequently is used when referring to the doings of nonroyal people, e.g., "Following the *demise* of her husband, Clara left on a round-the-world trip." While the *demise* may have made the trip possible, the main purpose of the term in such constructions is merely to avoid mentioning "death." See also BITE THE DUST, DECEASED, and PASS AWAY.

demi-vierge. The French helps obscure the action, which is hot and heavy, the reference being to a woman whose amorous engagements are such that only on the thinnest of physiological technicalities can she still be called a virgin. Once especially common among Roman Catholics, the *demi-vierge* is an endangered species, now that most American RC's have parted company with the pope on the question of using artificial means of birth control. See also PET.

democracy. Benevolent (?) dictatorship. A special award for the best foreign example of Doublespeak for 1979 was given by the Committee on Public Doublespeak of the National Council of Teachers of English to the incoming president of Brazil, Joao Baptista Figueiredo, who announced after the election: "I intend to open this country up to democracy and anyone who is against that I will jail, I will crush." See also PEOPLE'S REPUBLIC and, for the chief domestic Doublespeak winner in 1979, EVENT.

dentures. False teeth; sometimes further embellished as *artificial dentures*. The Latinate *dentures* presumably makes their owner feel better about having to take them out at night. See also PROSTHESIS.

Nancy Mitford, in her famous essay "The English Aristocracy," in which she introduced the concepts of U (upper-class speech) and non-U to the English-speaking world, held that *"dentures . . . and glasses for spectacles amount almost to non-U indicators"* (*Noblesse Oblige*, 1956). What happens, according to Ms. Mitford, is that the poor non-U speaker continuously betrays his or her non-U-ness by a fatal tropism toward artificially refined and elegant language. For examples, see HOME, ILL, and SERVIETTE. Americans may take pride in knowing that the essence of Ms. Mitford's discussion of U-ness was anticipated by nearly 120 years by their own James Fenimore Cooper. See also SABBATH.

departed. Dead, as in *the departed, the dear departed,* and *the departed one.* "Beth . . . sat making a winding-sheet, while the dear-departed lay in the domino-box" (Louisa May Alcott, *Little Women,* 1871). For more about winding-sheets, continue with SLUMBER ROBE, and for a curious gnarl on the Alcott family tree, see ROOSTER.

"Departed" frequently is used in lieu of the dead person's name, which is tabooed in this as well as other, more exotic cultures. Speaking of the Australian aborigines for example: "The name of a dead person was not mentioned, for to do so would bring back the spirit which the name represented. . . . after Dawudi, the great artist of Milingimbi, died, I could not mention his name directly to his brother, Djawa, but was obliged to refer to him as *bunakaka wawa,* 'the departed one'" (Louis A. Allen, *Time Before Morning,* 1975). A similar aborigine allusion, also mentioned by Allen, is *one gone.*

The fear of naming certain names is so widespread as to be almost universal; see ADONAI; DEVIL, THE, and GRANDFATHER, for instance. In our own culture, the strength of the taboo against mentioning the name of a dead person is suggested by the profusion of alternate ways that have been devised for getting the message across without saying it; see DECEASED for examples. About the only time the dead person's name is mentioned by choice is at the FUNERAL HOME (or PARLOR), when the relatives are present, in which case the MORTICIAN or FUNERAL DIRECTOR will say "This is where we plan to put Mr. Doe," instead of "This is where we plan to put the corpse." See also PASS AWAY.

derrière. The French, feminine equivalent of the Latin, usually masculine GLUTEUS MAXIMUS, the ass. "They snuggle close to your waist and hips, and hug your derrière" (ad for Gloria Vanderbilt jeans, WCBS-TV, NYC, 9/6/79). Not all *derrières* are so fashionable. For example, one of the heroines of "The Rock Rain Bow," a 1978 ABC-TV production, spoke of "putting my derrière on the line." Then there are the SWINGING derrières, as in the following classified:

> HARTFORD REBELLIOUS LADY WITH VERY SPANKABLE round-
> ed derriere enjoys reasonable bondage and discipline at the hands of an
> intell masculine partner. (*Ace,* undated, ca. 1976)

"Derrière" has been used as a euphemism for the ANGLO-SAXON word since at least the eighteenth century. The earliest example in the 1972 supplement to the *Oxford English Dictionary* comes from a letter that was written in 1747. Naturally, being British, it has to do with spanking: "*S'il fait le fier* .   I shall give him several spanks upon his *derriere.*" See also ARSE and POSTERIOR(S).

detainee. A prisoner; a person in DETENTION. As a rule, *detainees* are held for political rather than criminal reasons, e.g., from the Republic of South Africa: ". . . Mr. [Steven] Biko was the 45th political detainee to die in the hands of the security police . . ." (*New York Times,* 9/20/77). See also INTERN.

detention. Imprisonment without trial, usually for political reasons. The prison or other enclosure (football stadiums and other buildings occasionally are pressed into service) in which the DETAINEES are confined, usually is described as a *detention camp, detention center,* or *detention facility.* In politically advanced countries, the term may be gussied up . . . as *New York Post* columnist James A. Wechsler discovered when he got a look at his FBI dossier: "My file reveals that from June 1942 until February 1945, I was on the FBI director's list of Americans targeted for 'custodial detention,' . . ." (*New York Post*, 1/4/77). See also CONCENTRATION CAMP, INTERN, PREVENTIVE DETENTION, and PROTECTIVE CUSTODY

deuce. The Devil, Satan. "The deuce we are!" (Owen Johnson, *Stover at Yale*, 1931). And in a variant spelling from *Tom Thumb's Pretty Song Book*, (ca. 1744):

> The Wheelbarrow broke
> And give my Wife a fall,
> The duce take
> Wheelbarrow, Wife & all.

"Deuce" doubles as a euphemism for "damn"; see DARN as well as DEVIL, THE.

develop/developer/development. Real estate terms for, in order: (1) to ruin the land, or whatever is standing on it; (2) the person who does the ruining; and (3) the generally ticky-tacky result of the operation.

Real estate has been "developed" at least since the nineteenth century, and the euphemism has long been recognized as such, e.g.: "Hogarth's house in Chiswick . . . will probably be purchased by a builder who will do what is called develop the property; we all know pretty well what that means" (*Times* [London], 11/6/01).

"Developers" and "development" tend to proceed inexorably, as well as execrably, and without regard for national boundaries: "The push to explore and exploit the remotest corners of the earth cannot be stopped easily, if at all, especially now that mankind is becoming uneasily aware of the planet's finite resources. The process is usually called development and most people welcome it. Small tribal societies are thus seen 'standing in the way of development' and it is felt that they must adapt or face extinction" (David Maybury-Lewis, *New York Times*, 3/15/74). See also DEVELOPING and REALTOR.

developing. As applied to countries: poor, backward, or primitive. "Developing" is a third-order euphemism. It replaced UNDERDEVELOPED, which was marginally kinder than *undeveloped*, which, in turn, was gentler than the original "poor," "backward," or "primitive." This illustrates the Principle of Succession: In time, euphemisms tend to become tainted by the "bad" meanings of the words for which they stand, with the result that new euphemisms must continually be created to replace old ones. Already, "developing" seems to be on the way out, but it is not yet clear what its successor will be. The technical "LDC" (Lesser-Developed Country) is a good bet, though EMERGENT and EMERGING are still waiting in the wings.

For the domestic equivalent of the international "developing," see DISADVANTAGED.

device. A bomb, ordinarily a nuclear one, as in such phrases as *low yield thermonuclear device* or *five-megaton device* (where "megaton" helps diminish the explosive effect of "one million tons of TNT"). Talking about the way people talk at the headquarters for American bomb-makers in Los Alamos, New Mexico: "An explosion, however large, was a 'shot.' The word 'bomb' was almost never used. A bomb was a 'device' or a 'gadget.' Language could hide what the sky could not. The Los Alamos Scientific Laboratory was 'the Ranch.' Often, it was simply called 'the Hill.' An implosion bomb was made with 'ploot'" (John McPhee, *The Curve of Binding Energy*, 1974). See also GADGET, SPECIAL NUCLEAR MATERIALS, and, for a certifiably mad bomb-maker whose language paralleled that of the certifiably sane ones in Los Alamos, see UNIT.

Devil, the. Satan. There are (or are said to be) many devils—Beelzebub, Belial, Mephistopheles, et al.—but the generic term usually is used for Satan, on the theory that it is safer not to mention his real name. As the saying goes: Speak of the *Devil* and he appears.

"He's full of the Old Scratch, but . . . I ain't got the heart to lash him, somehow" (Aunt Polly, in Mark Twain's *The Adventures of Tom Sawyer*, 1876). Of course, "Old Scratch" (from the Old Norse *scratle*, a wizard, goblin, or monster) is only one of many possibilities for the faint of heart. "If you are in Scotland, you call him Clootie or Auld Hornie; in Germany, Meister Peter; in the Shetlands, da black tief; in England, Old Nick; in New England, the Deuce [see DEUCE] or The Old Boy Himself" (Maria Leach, ed., *Funk & Wagnalls Dictionary of Folklore, Mythology, and Legend*, 1972). Still other alternatives include *The Adversary, The Archfiend* (also *The Fiend* or *Foul Fiend*), *The Black One, The Evil One, the good man, the great fellow, the old gentleman, Old Harry,* and *The Tempter.* As an interjection, too, "Satan" is euphemized as "the dickens," e.g., "I cannot tell what the dickens his name is . . ." (William Shakespeare, *The Merry Wives of Windsor*, 1599?). The taboo against naming Satan is carried all the way to its illogical conclusion by the Yezidis, a religious sect of Iran, Armenia, and the Caucasus, who call their devil "Peacock" because that word, in their language, sounds least like his real name. For similar supernatural euphemisms and circumlocutions, see ADONAI, DEPARTED, and GRANDFATHER.

diddly-poo. Diddly-shit, the "poo" being an example of children's potty talk carried over into the adult world (see also WEE WEE). "Diddly-poo" turns up in the oddest places . . . such as the convention of the Associated Press Managing Editors Association, where one hard-bitten newspaper executive opined: "A lot of our guys are small town editors who don't know diddly-poo about Washington or Watergate" (*[MORE]*, 12/73). A variation is *diddly-squat*, where the "squat" is a simple phonetic substitution. See also DEFECATE/DEFECATION and POOPER-SCOOPER.

die. To experience sexual orgasm; a predecessor of the modern COME. "Die" was much favored by poets, who made many plays on it. For example, from the works of John Donne (pre-1631):

> Wee can dye by it, if not
> live by love.
>
> (*The Canonization*)

ding-a-ling

> Wee dye but once, and who lov'd
> last did die.
>
> *(The Paradox)*

And from Alexander Pope's *The Rape of the Lock* (1712–14):

> Nor feared the Chief th' unequal
> fight to try,
> Who sought no more than on his
> foe to die.

The metaphor remains current (*re* the lyric in the pop hit "Annie's Song": "Come, let me love you . . . Let me die in your arms"). "Die" epitomizes the set of associations between sex, death, and violence. See also ACTION, GUN, OFF, and WEAPON, as well as, for nonsexual dying, PASS AWAY.

ding-a-ling. The PENIS; adult potty talk. "Lines such as 'I like to play with my ding-a-ling' . . . are intended as deliberate stimulation to self and mutual masturbation" (*Daily Telegraph* [London], 11/17/72). "Ding-a-ling" is only the most infantile of a series of related "D" sounds that may be used to signify "penis," e.g., *dicky, dingus, dong, doodad, doodle* (see TIMBERDOODLE), *doohickey,* and *doojigger.* For more about potty talk, see WEE WEE.

direct mail. Unsolicited mail or, descending one more notch toward reality, junk mail. Obviously, *direct mail* has a happier ring to the people in the business, e.g., the members of the Direct Mail-Marketing Association, especially when they are lobbying in Congress for favorable postal rates for junk mail.

directory assistance. The telephone company used to call it "information."

disadvantaged. Poor. Sometimes fancied up into *culturally disadvantaged* or *socially disadvantaged,* this is basically the domestic equivalent of the international DEVELOPING. "Poor children have disappeared, if not from the slums, then at least from the language. First, they became 'deprived,' then 'disadvantaged,' and finally 'culturally disadvantaged,' as though they lacked nothing more serious than a free pass to Lincoln Center" (Grace Hechinger, *Wall Street Journal,* 10/27/71). See also CULTURALLY DEPRIVED, LOW-INCOME, POOR, and UNDER-PRIVILEGED.

discharge. Cannons are "fired" as well as "discharged"—and so are people. In both cases, the longer, less active word softens the action in much the same way as DELIVER does for "drop." As Charles Dillon (Casey) Stengel told the Subcommittee on Antitrust and Monopoly of the Senate Judiciary Committee on July 9, 1958: "I became a major league manager in several cities and was discharged. We call it discharged because there was no question I had to leave." See also LET GO.

disinvestment. Mealymouthed banker's code for the more vivid "redlining," itself financial jargon for the refusal to give mortgages or write insurance policies in city neighborhoods (usually demarcated by zip codes) that have changed, or are in the process of changing, racially and economically (white to nonwhite and middleclass to DISADVANTAGED). Reporting on hearings of the Senate Banking Committee: ". . . both industry and government witnesses steered away from using the term redlining, preferring to talk about 'disinvestment,' an Orwellian term meaning the same thing" (*New Republic*, 6/21/75).

dispatch. To kill. Almost from the time the word came into the English language in the early sixteenth century, it has been used both in the sense of sending someone or something (as a message) off, posthaste, and in the sense of sending someone off, permanently. The Japanese use the same circumlocution. *Hara-kiri*, the ritual form of suicide in which a greatly dishonored or disgraced person disembowels himself and is then beheaded by someone else, translates as "happy-dispatch." See also DECEASED, DISPOSE, HIT, and KAMIKAZE.

dispose. To kill, to *get rid of*, or to ACCOUNT FOR. "Dispose" is so opaque that it is easy to misinterpret: See the CIA inspector general's comments on the question of "disposing of Castro" in ASSASSINATION. "Dispose" also has euphemistic meanings in reverse; see INDISPOSED/INDISPOSITION.

document. A piece of paper that has been sanctified by a bureaucrat. The term appears in various combinations. Thus, an organization that wishes to get rid of most of its old papers may establish a *document retention program*, while a Mexican who slips illegally into the United States is known (today) as an UNDOCU-MENTED PERSON.

dog dirt/litter/waste. By any other name, dog shit smells the same. ". . . the Dog Control Committee of the Carl Schurz Park Association has organized to try to solve the 'dog dirt' problem in their park" (*New York Times*, 2/1/76). This problem also was attacked by Section 1310 of the New York State Public Health Law, which went into effect on August 1, 1978, and which was variously described, depending on what day you read the *Times*, as the "'canine waste' law" (7/23/78), or the "'Canine Litter Law'" (8/1/78). This law required people to clean up after their pets (POOPER-SCOOPERS were sold for the purpose), with the threat of a $100 fine per offense. And the threat worked—for several months at least. London has a similar law on the books, with a fine for permitting a dog to "foul the footpaths," but the English love their animals so much that it, too, is rarely enforced. See also ACCIDENT, COMFORT STATION, DROPPINGS, MESS, NUISANCE, and WASTE.

doggone. Goddam, itself a euphemistic spelling of the eschatological "God damn." "Doggone" seems to be a genuine mid-nineteenth-century Americanism, but no one is sure of its immediate antecedents. One theory is that it comes from the Scotch *dagone* (gone to the dogs); another is that it is a compression of "dog on it" (similar to the older "pox on it"). Also suspicious is the fact that "God" spelled backward is "dog." The most likely explanation, however, is that this is just another example of the tropism that English speakers have toward "D" sounds when devising ways to water down their oaths and imprecations, e.g., DAD, DANG, and DARN. See also ADONAI, GEE, GOSH, and HECK.

domestic. A diplomatic condensation of "domestic servant," the "servant" part having become anathema in the early nineteenth century through overuse as a euphemism for "slave." (See SERVANT.) "Domestic" is less common in Britain than the United States, judging from Graham Greene's *The End of the Affair* (film, 1955):

> "We've been able to make contact with the domestic."
> "The what?"
> "The maid, sir."

Note that the verb "domesticate," as commonly applied to plants and animals, carries the same euphemistic connotations as "domestic," when applied to humans, e.g., "More than nearly any other animal, the raccoon has managed to coexist with man without becoming domesticated, i.e., enslaved" (*Smithsonian*, 8/79). See also HELP and MAID.

donation. A universally abused word. For example, in the United States, *donations* are requested by organizations and businesses that have legal reasons for not wanting to charge "fees" for the goods or services they provide. Thus, a museum may ask for a *donation* instead of charging for admission, and a bar that is operating as a CLUB may also ask for *donations* for drinks. Meanwhile, in Ireland, where it was long illegal to sell contraceptives, a *donation* is what clients of family planning centers were asked to leave in return for the goods. Even as far away as India, it is reported that "many prestigious educational institutions in Kerala collect a sum of money as a bribe from every one who seeks admission to them. But a bribe to an institution is called a donation and by calling it that bribing has become a nonobjectionable practice" (George John, "The Land of Euphemism," *Indian Express* [Bombay], 8/3/79). Of course, American colleges and institutions never, never use "donation" in this manner. See also COMMISSION.

donkey. Ass. The beast's original name (from the Latin *asinus*) was contaminated by the development of "ass" as a euphemism for *arse*. "Donkey" first appeared on the scene in the eighteenth century, but no one is quite sure where it came from. An imaginative etymology was proposed by Capt. Francis Grose in *A Classical Dictionary of the Vulgar Tongue* (1796), i.e., "DONKEY, DONKEY DICK. A he, or jack ass: called donkey, perhaps, from the Spanish or don-like gravity of that animal, intitled also the king of Spain's trumpeter." A likelier explanation is that the word is a familiar form of Duncan, one of the personal names (Dicky, Jenny, Neddy were others) commonly bestowed by farmers upon their asses. By the middle of the nineteenth century, if not before, "donkey" was the word that most nice people used most of the time, except in Ireland, where "ass" was kept, and in Scotland, where the ass was called "cuddie," perhaps from another personal name, Cuthbert. In the case of male donkeys, the "ass" might also be obscured to varying degrees by calling them *jackasses, jassacks, jacks*, or, quaintest of all, *John Donkeys*, e.g., "Some one passed the road with a long-eared animal, politely called a John Donkey" (Harden E. Taliaferro, *Fisher's River [North Carolina] Scenes and Characters*, 1859).

See also ARSE, BOTTOM, and, for the richly euphemistic subject of animal names, begin with ROOSTER.

doubtless. A case of Reverse English: The word's literal meaning—"without a doubt" or "unquestionably"—is bent 180 degrees when writers use it to dress up unproved statements. Henry A. Barnes, onetime transportation commissioner of New York City (and inventor of the kitty-corner pedestrian crossing called the Barnes Dance) defined "doubtless" as "unverified" in a glossary of bureaucratese. See also UNDOUBTEDLY.

droppings. Animal dung, aka shit; the verbal action covers up a noun, a common euphemistic technique. (See FERTILIZER for another such.) Indicative of what is happening to the landscape, especially in cities, is the fact that the term is rarely, if ever, encountered in the singular form. See also DOG DIRT/LITTER/WASTE.

drumstick. The notorious taboo against "leg" was so strong that fowls on the dinnertable began sprouting "drumsticks" about the same time all the diners became equipped with "limbs." Like so many of the euphemisms commonly associated with the Victorian era (see ROOSTER, for example), this one actually predates Victoria's ascension in 1837 by several generations, with the oldest example in the *Oxford English Dictionary* of a "drumstick" for eating, rather than for banging on a drum, coming from 1764, i.e., "She always helps me herself to the tough drumsticks of turkies" (Samuel Foote, *The Mayor of Garrett*). It was in the United States, however, that the taboo against "leg" reached its grandest proportions. Besides "drumstick," Americans used a variety of other euphemisms for the legs of birds, including *dark meat*, JOINT, and *lower limb*. Still more picturesquely, an excessively polite person at the dinnertable might ask for "the trotter of a chicken" (Richard Mead Bache, *Vulgarisms and Other Errors of Speech*, 1869). See also LIMB, WHITE MEAT, and, for meat-eating in general, FILET MIGNON.

duckys. The breasts of a woman. ". . . wishing my self (specially an Evening) in my Sweethearts Armes whose pritty Duckys I trust shortly to kysse" (Henry VIII to Anne Boleyn, ca. 1533). See also BOSOM.

duff. The ass, as in "Congress needs to get off its duff" (Governor William G. Milliken, R., Michigan,, WCBS-TV, 11:00 P.M. news, 8/27/78). "Duff" is probably of military origin; a shortening, possibly, of the "duffel bag" on which soldiers sit while waiting for something to happen. "Duff" might also be related to "doughboy," since "duff" was a not uncommon pronunciation of "dough" (like "enough" or "rough") in the nineteenth century. See also ARSE.

dump. A defecation; short for "dump a load of a shit." "Every time you take a dump or a leak in a standard john, you flush five gallons of water out with your piddle" (*Last Whole Earth Catalog*, 1972). See also JOHN, LEAK, and PIDDLE, as well as DEFECATE/DEFECATION.

Dutch treat. Not a treat, since each person is paying his or her own way. "Dutch treat" probably is the most common of the many uses to which "Dutch" has been put ever since the seventeenth century, when the Dutch contested the English for control of the seas, and the English tried to get back at their rivals by using

duty

"Dutch" to mean "inferior," e.g., *Dutch bargain* (a one-sided bargain, i.e., no bargain at all), *Dutch courage* (false courage, induced by brandy or other spirits), and *Dutch wife* or *husband* (a bed bolster). For more about the English view of their neighbors, see FRENCH.

duty. The act of urinating and/or defecating, frequently encountered in the phrase, "do one's duty," but not only, as one might think, in connection with the doings of children, e.g., "The lamb ran away and stood in the middle of the field doing duties at an adjacent haystack" (A. J. Cronin, *The Stars Look Down*, 1935). See also DEFECATE/DEFECATION and URINATE/URINATION.

E

earth closet. A toilet; specifically, a water closet without water—and with various disadvantages, to wit: ". . . the earth-closet, which, because it must of necessity be kept dry, is unsuited to durable comfort for those who experience difficulty in separating their natural functions and therefore [is] a poor place to read" (Reginald Reynolds, *Cleanliness and Godliness*, 1946). See also TOILET and WC.

earth-sheltered. Below ground; said especially of a house that is built there. "Why the term 'earth-sheltered' rather than 'underground' . . . advocates of this unique brand of architecture recognize that for many people, the very word 'underground' triggers near-visceral impressions of dark, damp, claustrophobic, even frightening space" (*Smithsonian*, 2/79).

ease. *To do one's ease, to ease nature, to ease oneself*—all are somewhat old-fashioned but not-yet-entirely extinct expressions for the discharge of excrement. For example, illustrating the customs of the ancient Hebrews (Deuteronomy, XXIII, 13, King James Version, 1611):

> And thou shalt have a paddle upon thy weapon: and it shalt be when thou wilt ease thyself abroad, thou shalt dig therewith, and shalt turn back, and cover that which cometh from thee . . .

From the action, the term was extended to cover the place of performance. Hence: *closet of ease, house of ease,* and *seat of ease.* In the words of that well-known cleric, Jonathan Swift ("Strephon and Chloe," 1731):

> Had you but through a cranny spied
> On house of ease your future bride.

Because the English of the seventeenth and eighteenth centuries were not as fastidious as the Hebrews of the Bible about where and how they *eased* themselves, a remarkable secondary euphemism, *sir-reverence*, was created. This expression, which may be translated as "save reverence" or "saving your reverence," was used in such contexts as "Watch out—don't step in the sir-reverence," or, an actual example: "His face . . . and his Necke, were all besmeared with the soft sirreuerence, so he stunk" (Robert Greene, *Ned Browne, Life and Complete Works*, 1592). The origin of this euphemism was explained in the following manner by Capt. Francis Grose in *A Classical Dictionary of the Vulgar Tongue* (1796):

> REVERENCE. An ancient custom, which obliges any person easing himself near the highway or foot-path, on the word *reverence* being given him by a passenger, to take off his hat [and hold it] with his teeth, and without moving it from his station to throw it over his head, by which it frequently falls into the excrement: this was considered as a punishment for the breach of delicacy. A person refusing to obey this law, might be pushed backwards.

See also COVER ONE'S FEET, DEFECATE/DEFECATION, and TOILET.

eat-in kitchen. Real estate-ese for "no dining room." See also REALTOR.

ecdysiast. A stripteaser—and one of the relatively few euphemisms (INTESTINAL FORTITUDE is another) that can be attributed with confidence to a particular individual. This one was devised in 1940 by H. L. Mencken, at the request of a practitioner of the art, Miss Georgia Sothern, who felt public objections to her profession would vanish if it was called by "a new and more palatable" name. Relating stripteasing to "the associated zoölogical phenomenon of molting," Mencken told La Sothern that "the word *moltician* comes to mind, but it must be rejected because of its likeness to *mortician*. A resort to the scientific name for molting, which is *ecdysis*, produces both *ecdysist* and *ecdysiast*" (Mencken, *The American Language, Supplement One*, 1945). The new name quickly caught on, and it continues to be the euphemism-of-choice, despite various misguided efforts to improve upon it (*ecdysiste*) and to compete with it (*strippeuse* and *stripteuse*, neither of which should be confused with *scripteuse*, which is, or was, circa 1943, a woman scriptwriter). See also BURLEYCUE and EXOTIC.

economical. Frugal. See also THRIFTY.

eff. A euphemistic "fuck," having all the versatility of the word for which it stands. For example: "I have already had several abusive phone calls, telling me to eff off back to effing Russia, you effing, corksacking limey effer. This is because I suggested some time ago . . . that America would be better off for a bit of socialized medicine" (Anthony Burgess, *New York Times Magazine*, 10/29/72). See also F——.

effluent. A mellifluent pollutant, typically smoke, sewage, or other outflow of industrial waste; called a "residual effluent" if it remains too long in one place. "Radiation doses from airborne effluents of a coal-fired [power] plant may be greater than those from a nuclear plant" (subhead, *Science*, 12/8/78). See also LANDFILL.

egad. A somewhat archaic euphemistic oath that survives in some circles—and on some blocks. From Sesame Street for instance: "Egad! It sounds like a job for Sherlock Hemlock, who sees all" (Betty Lou, *Sherlock Hemlock and the Great Twiddlebug Mystery or The Mystery of the Terrible Mess in My Friend's Front Yard*, 1972). The substitution of "Gad" for "God" is common. Near relations to "egad" include *Gadsbodikins, Gads me, Gads my life, Gadsprecious*, and GADZOOKS. See also ADONAI, GOSH, and ODDS BODKINS.

egress. Exit. P. T. Barnum (1810–1891) is said to have made room for new customers in his American Museum by posting a sign, "This way to the egress," thereby keeping the hoi polloi moving along until, suddenly, they found themselves on the outside. In the parlance of the time, they had been "humbugged." One would not have expected "egress" to have outlived this usage, but as recently as 1976 the sign, "Not an Accredited Egress," was spotted over the doorway in the Ritz-Carlton Hotel in Boston.

Attempts have been made to separate the meanings of "egress" and "exit," but they are not totally convincing. Consider the following, from a rulebook of the Occupational Safety and Health Administration, which defined an exit as "that portion of a means of egress which is separated from all other spaces of the building or structure by construction or equipment as required in this subpart to provide a protected way of travel to the exit discharge." By contrast, a "means of egress," according to the safety and health people, is "a continuous and unobstructed way of exit travel from any point in a building or structure to a public way and consists of three separate and distinct parts: the way of exit access, the exit and the way of exit discharge." For these definitions, the Occupational Safety and Health Administration received one of the 1977 Doublespeak Awards of the Committee on Public Doublespeak of the National Council of Teachers of English. For other 1977 winners, see ENHANCED RADIATION WEAPON and VERTICAL TRANSPORTATION CORPS.

eliminate/elimination. The Latinate words are doubly euphemistic, covering the expulsion of waste matter from the body as well as the wasting, or murder, of people. In the first, less-objectionable sense, Skylab astronaut Joseph P. Kerwin's self-checklist went like this: "How's my sleeping? Eating? Drinking? Eliminating?" (Henry S. F. Cooper, Jr., *A House in Space*, 1974). As for murder, "eliminate/ elimination" may be used synonymously with TERMINATE/TERMINATION. Thus, speaking of a suspected double agent, who had reportedly been injected with morphine, shot twice in the head, and whose weighted body had then been dropped into the sea, a former Green Beret could admit: "He was my agent and it was my responsibility to eliminate him with extreme prejudice" (*New York Times*, 4/4/71). And on a grander level, Allen Dulles, when head of the CIA, appears to have talked openly of giving "thorough consideration" to the "elimination" of Fidel Castro (Senate Intelligence Committee report on American plots to kill foreign leaders, 11/77). See also ASSASSINATION, DEFECATE/DEFECATION, and WASTE.

embroider the truth. To lie, ornamentally. The circumlocution acknowledges what every good liar knows, i.e., the best lies are composed largely of truths. See also COVER STORY and WHITE LIE.

emergent (or **emerging**) **nation.** A poor or backward nation; a DEVELOPING nation. An alternative is "fledgling nation," attributed to Eleanor Roosevelt. But it never really flew. See also UNDERDEVELOPED.

emporium. A grandiloquency for a store or other business establishment. Originally, a place, usually a town or city, where merchandise from a wide area was gathered for trade, "emporium" later was applied pompously to stores and shops, and in our own time, the term has sunk all the way to the pits, e.g.: "The 'weaker' sex will take over once again out at Jimmy Kilshaw's grapple emporium Tuesday night when Nell Stewart, comely Jacksonville, Fla., miss, meets Dottie Dotson, of Houston, Tex., in the weekly main event" (*Baton-Rouge* [LA] *State-Times*, 2/23/47).

So beloved is the "orium" ending that it has been picked up in other ways. "Lubritorium" has made it into the dictionaries as a place where automobiles are lubricated, i.e., greased. And in fair Brooklyn, a thriving business (with three branches) is the Corsetorium. See also PARLOR.

enceinte. Pregnant; a sterling example of the sometimes desperate lunge into another language to avoid plain mention in English of sexually charged matters. ". . . women who are enceinte, or have been recently confined . . . frequently give long accounts of things that never happened although at ordinary times absolutely truthful and worthy of credence" (Hans Gross, *Criminal Investigation*, Norman Kendal, ed., 1934).

"Enceinte" comes via the French from Latin, probably from *inciens*, being with young, though some have argued for *in*, not, plus *cinctus*, girdled, i.e., "girdle loosened." A popular nineteenth-century allusion to the DELICATE condition, "enceinte" is considerably older. It seems to have been used first as a legal term. The oldest example in the *Oxford English Dictionary* is from 1599 and the last will of one G. Taylard: "Yf my wife be pryvyment insented wt a manchilde." Here, and in other early references, "pryvyment insent" translates as "pregnant but not discernibly so." Today, nearly four centuries later, pregnant persons who are not yet showing may announce their condition to the world by putting on T-shirts with the message, *"Je suis enceinte."* In the words of a Saks Fifth Avenue ad: *"'Je suis enciente'* announces to the world what I already know about me" (*New York Times*, 2/9/76). A variation is the shirt that says *"le bébé"* up top and has an arrow pointing down below.

Females of other species also may become *enceinte*. Thus, an AP dispatch of September 21, 1933, referred to a "scheme to raise livestock prices by slaughtering pigs and enceinte sows" (from H. L. Mencken, *The American Language*, 1936). For more about pregnancy, see EXPECTANT/EXPECTING.

encore. A repeat or rerun; TV talk.

endowed/endowment. The essentially financial terms (from the Latin *dotare*, dowry) become euphemisms for other kinds of riches when used to describe the human body. Usually, the context is feminine and the reference is to large breasts, e.g., in the words of *Playboy*'s West Coast photography editor, Marilyn Grabowski (whose surname bears thinking about in the context): "Most men look at a girl's endowments and that suffices" (*New York Times*, 2/26/77). Women may also be "well" or "amply endowed"—as may men, though the meaning then is that they are well HUNG. In the poignant words of a classified from Texas: "HOUSTON VERY PASSIONATE WIDOW wants to meet well-endowed men for dates and fun and games" (*Ace*, undated, ca. 1976). See also BOSOM and FUN.

energy release. Radiation release, as from a nuclear reactor. "There was still no realistic estimate as to exactly how many people would be killed, maimed, or come down with leukemia if an 'energy release' hit a populated area" (John G. Fuller, *We Almost Lost Detroit*, 1975). It is not necessary for a reactor actually to blow up in order to have an *energy release*, but if one ever does, it is likely that the people who are responsible will try to muffle the blast by describing it as a *disruptive* or *explosive energy release*—the result of a *superprompt critical power excursion* that led to a *containment-breeching incident*. See also ABOVE CRITICAL and EVENT.

engineer. A vastly popular title for elevating the status of occupations of all sorts, "engineer" has been reported in more than 2,000 combinations. In general, the term should be interpreted as a euphemism for "man" (or PERSON), as in *advertising* *engineer, cost engineer, patent engineer,* or *sales engineer.* For many years, *Engineering News-Record,* a trade magazine for real engineers, delighted in keeping tabs of spurious breeds of "engineer" as they surfaced. The remarkable versatility of the title is evident from the following very partial list of examples, many but not all of which were reported by H. L. Mencken in *The American Language* (1936) and its first supplement (1945): *automobile engineer* (a mechanic), *casement window engineer, crowd control engineer* (a four-footed member of the police Canine Corps in Birmingham, Alabama, circa 1963), *custodian-engineer* (also *engineer-custodian,* see CUSTODIAN), *dansant engineer* (an agent for nightclub dancers and musicians), *dry cleaning engineer, educational engineer* (a school principal), *exterminating engineer* (rat and roach killer), *footwear maintenance engineer* (a bootblack), *human engineer* (a kind of psychoanalyst), *mattress engineer* (one of *ENR's* favorites, this was a bedding manufacturer who later metamorphosed into the even finer *sleep engineer*), *publicity engineer* (see PUBLICITOR), *recreation engineer, sanitary engineer* (a professionalization of SANITATION MAN), *racial engineer* (an "uplifter"; Mencken), *vision engineer* (an optician), *wardrobe engineer* (a person who tells you what clothes to buy, a 1980 variant being *taste technician*), and *window cleaning engineer.*

Even the engineer who runs a locomotive is something of a euphemism. The dubious nature of the American term was recognized in the nineteenth century by John R. Bartlett, whose *Dictionary of Americanisms* (1860) included this entry: "Engineer, the engine-driver on our railroads is thus magniloquently designated." "Engine-driver" is still the title for this job among the British who, as a seafaring nation, naturally reserve the high-sounding "engineer" for those in charge of marine engines.

For more about the great and continuing effort to upgrade job titles, see, in addition to those entries already cited in passing: ADMINISTRATIVE ASSISTANT, AGENT, BEAUTICIAN, BEVERAGE HOST, COUNSEL, CUSTODIAN, ECDYSIAST, FIRE FIGHTER, FUNERAL DIRECTOR, INVESTIGATOR, MARKETING, OFFICER, PERSONAL ASSISTANT TO THE SECRETARY (SPECIAL ACTIVITIES), PROSTITUTE, REALTOR, REPRESENTATIVE, SERVANT, TECHNICIAN, and VERTICAL TRANSPORTATION CORPS.

English guidance or **arts** or **culture.** Sadism and/or masochism. "BOW YOUR HEAD! The Mistress is now accepting slaves for English guidance" (personal ad, *Screw,* 8/2/76). According to classified ads on the subject, *English guidance* seems to feature (though it is by no means limited to) whips, canes, riding crops, and hairbrushes, which are applied to what the English, in such situations, call the DERRIÈRE or POSTERIORS. See also FRENCH and S/M.

enhanced radiation (or **radiation enhancement**) **weapon.** A neutron bomb. The terminological enhancement won the 1977 Doublespeak Award of the Committee on Public Doublespeak of the National Council of Teachers of English. It was selected, the committee explained, because it concealed so well the true effects of the bomb, i.e.: "The body convulses, limbs shake, the nervous system fails so that all automatic body functions, even breathing, are affected. Death comes within 48 hours." The beauty part is that the bomb does all this to people while sparing most of the buildings and other valuable property in the vicinity. Thus, the *enhanced radiation weapon* classes as a CLEAN BOMB.

Running a close second for the 1977 Doublespeak Award was the CIA's

"Society for Investigation of Human Ecology," an agency conduit for funding research on human behavior modification. See also EGRESS and, for more about the good work of the English teachers, continue with AIR SUPPORT.

enob. The penis, from "bone" spelled backward. See also PENIS and note the *mosob* in BOSOM.

episode. A disaster, or the immediate threat of one. For example, in November 1975, Pittsburgh, Pennsylvania, underwent a five-day "air pollution episode," during which the "coefficient of haze" across the Monongahela River from U.S. Steel's Clairton Coke Works reached 7.8, on a scale where "8" indicates "imminent and substantial endangerment" to human health. The Environmental Protection Agency later estimated that "the pollution episode" probably caused 14 deaths. In reply, U.S. Steel said the EPA was engaging in "scare tactics" (*New York Times*, 5/1/76). See also EVENT and INCIDENT.

equipment. Airline-ese for "airplane," typically encountered in loudspeaker announcements in the form of "There will be a slight delay in the departure of Flight 707 while we have a change of equipment." The point, of course, is to avoid implying that anything ever goes wrong with an "airplane." See also the "late arrival of equipment" in WATER LANDING.

era. War; specifically, the one in Vietnam; an INVOLVEMENT. "Era" is the official governmental euphemism for this war, which the United States does not recognize as a war, since Congress never got around to declaring it to be one. Thus, as of April 1980, the Veterans Administration carried on its books a total of 8,965,000 veterans of the "Vietnam era" (*World Almanac and Book of Facts*, 1981). During this *era*, which lasted longer than any war in the nation's history, the United States suffered 210,291 CASUALTIES, nearly as many as the combined total of the Revolutionary War, the War of 1812, the Mexican War, the Spanish-American War, and the Korean War. Of course, the Korean War wasn't really a war either; see POLICE ACTION.

erotica. Pornography (whose root, "porne," is Greek for "harlot"). Cousins include *esoterica* and *exotica*. See also ADULT, CURIOSA, FACETIAE, and SEXUALLY EXPLICIT (or ORIENTED).

erratum. Error. No one likes to have to admit publicly to making mistakes, but there are times when this simply has to be done, and in those cases, the confession is easier if cloaked in Latin. Book publishers, for example, do not issue "error slips," but *erratum slips*—or if, horrors, more than one mistake has been made—*errata slips*. See also CLARIFY and THERAPEUTIC ACCIDENT.

erroneous report. A lie. ". . . the Department of Defense man . . . had no trouble when asked if the Pentagon had lied to the Senate about the bombing of Cambodia. Spokesman Jerry W. Friedheim replied that the Pentagon hadn't lied, it had merely submitted an erroneous report. This is pure Pentagon Doublespeak" (Israel Shenker, "Zieglerrata," *New Republic*, 4/13/74). This particular *erroneous report* had omitted any mention of 3,630 B-52 air raids made over Cambodia, a neutral nation in the Vietnam CONFLICT, during a 14-month period in 1969–70. The raids were kept secret by means of a "special security reporting" procedure, which featured the burning of records of the Cambodian raids and, in order to account for the fuel and bombs expended, the creation of fictitious reports of fictitious raids in South Vietnam. Among other things, this concealment made it possible for President Richard M. Nixon to justify the invasion of Cambodia in April 1970, by saying the North Vietnamese had been operating in "privileged sanctuaries" across the border, even though the United States had been bombing away at those "sanctuaries" for quite some time. See also PROTECTIVE REACTION and WHITE LIE.

escalate. To increase the level of something, especially the violence of a war. The increment of increase is an *escalation*, a *graduated escalation*, or, sometimes, a *measured response.*

"Escalate" became a vogue word in the Vietnam ERA, but it predates it. For example: ". . . by 1960 . . . the predominant feeling among the critics of massive retaliation was always that limited nuclear war would billow up quickly (in the jargon, 'escalate') into full nuclear war" (Arthur M. Schlesinger, Jr., *A Thousand Days*, 1965). Or as President John F. Kennedy said on the morning of October 27, 1962, when he and his advisers were trying to decide whether or not to attempt to solve the Cuban missile crisis with a PREEMPTIVE STRIKE: "It isn't the first step that concerns me, but both sides escalating to the fourth or fifth step—and we don't go to the sixth because there is no one around to do so" (Robert F. Kennedy, *Thirteen Days*, 1969).

During Vietnam, the question of *escalation* was intrinsic to most SCENARIOS. Thus, Assistant Secretary of Defense John T. McNaughton warned the secretary, Robert S. McNamara, in a memo on January 19, 1966: "The situation . . . requires a willingness to escalate the war if the enemy miscalculates, misinterpreting our willingness to compromise as implying we are on the run" (*The Pentagon Papers*, 1971). It was also McNaughton who memorably characterized pauses in the bombing of North Vietnam as a "ratchet," rather like "the device which raises the net on a tennis court, backing off tension between each phase of increasing it." See also GAME, LIMITED WAR, OPTION, and QUARANTINE.

estate. A grave site. From the opening of a letter, prepared by the Matthews Memorial Bronze Company (quoted in Jessica Mitford, *The American Way of Death*, 1963):

> Dear Friend,
>   The other day, we and our maintenance crews were out working the section of the cemetery, where your family estate is located. . . . One of the workmen commented that an unmarked grave is a sad thing.

See also CEMETERY and MEMORIAL PARK.

ethnic. White, but not Wasp; "ethnic" is shorthand for *ethnic group, ethnic minority,* or, plainest, *white ethnic.* Regardless of the exact form, "ethnic" usually signals racism, or *ethnic purity,* and the different kinds of *ethnics* all contrast with MINORITY group, a common code phrase for "black and/or Hispanic."

Eumenides

"The former 'ethnics', a polite term for Jews, Italians, and other lesser breeds just inside the law" (*Times Literary Supplement* [London], 11/17/61). "For years—ever since the triumph of Franklin D. Roosevelt—the Democratic power base in the big cities had been an alliance of the workingmen in their unions, the minority ethnic communities and the Negroes" (Theodore H. White, *The Making of the President 1964*, 1965). See also MIDDLE CLASS.

Eumenides or **the Kindly Ones.** The ancient Greek euphemism, popularized by Aeschylus in his play of this name, for the Erinyes or the Furies.

event. A neutral word that becomes a euphemism when used to soft-pedal "disaster."

"Event" is especially beloved in the nuclear power business, where "accidents" must be reported to the government but "events" need not be. Thus, if a truck carrying nuclear wastes runs off the road, this is likely to be passed off as a *transportation event* (kissing kin to the *unscheduled descent* that occurs when a crane accidentally drops fuel rods into a reactor core). And in California, where the Diablo Canyon nuclear plant was built unfortunately close to the San Simeon-Hosgri fault, power company officials resort to such mind-numbing phrases as "the excitations produced by the larger potential Hosgri event" (read: "earthquake"). On an administrative level, the tropism of the nuclear-minded to "event" is best demonstrated by the opening sentence of the transcript of one of the hairier meetings of the U.S. Nuclear Regulatory Commission:

As the Three Mile Island situation developed beginning on Wednesday, March 28 [1979], the Commissioners met to discuss the nature of the event.

The commissioners had many things to worry about, up to and including the possibility of an explosion (a BLIP or "energetic displacement," in nuclear-ese), and they played a key role in helping the nuclear power industry win the 1979 Doublespeak Award of the Committee on Public Doublespeak of the National Council of Teachers of English. Beautiful features of the industry's "lexicon of jargon and euphemism," according to committee chairman William Lutz, include such comforting phrases as *abnormal evolution, normal aberration,* and *plant transient* to describe the *event-in-progress* at Three Mile Island; the use of *rapid oxidation* in place of "fire"; and the discreet admission that plutonium had *taken up residence* in the reactor vessel instead of "contaminating" it.

For other 1979 Doublespeak winners, see DEMOCRACY and FAIR; for more about the nuclear power business, see ABOVE CRITICAL, and for more about the many synonyms for "event," continue with INCIDENT.

excellent. Not so good. Army officers who receive *excellent* ratings on their efficiency reports had better start shopping around for new careers as *excellent* probably puts them in the bottom 20 percent of their group. The six army rating categories are: 1. Outstanding; 2. Superior; 3. Excellent; 4. Effective; 5. Marginal; 6. Inadequate. The other services have similarly inflated ranking systems. The navy, for example, has a "Top" grade—with four subdivisions—followed by "Typically effective," with two subdivisions. In the air force, "Meets standard" is the third of six categories, and an officer who gets this rating has, in effect, been given the kiss of death. The marines also have an *excellent* category; it is midway between "Above average" and "outstanding," which is the top category. See also FAIR.

exceptional. Disturbed, handicapped, retarded. On the mental side: "Children who failed to acquire skills expected at their age used to be called 'dull.' Later they were called 'retarded.' Now they are called 'exceptional'" (Anatol Rapoport, *Semantics*, 1975). See also MENTAL, SLOW, and SPECIAL.

excess. To fire someone, not for cause but to cut costs; usually encountered in the past tense, e.g.: "A good friend of mine, a brilliant teacher and first-rate literary critic, was 'excessed' from New York College in early August because he first arrived at the college two years ago, and the rules of seniority must be served" (*New Republic*, 10/2/76). "Excessive" synonyms include *displace* and SUR-PLUS. See also the British REDUNDANCY and the basic American LET GO.

exchange. War; specifically the nuclear holocaust that would be labeled World War III by any who survived it; sometimes called an *all-out strategic exchange*. The amiable "exchange" usually is used when thinking about the UNTHINKABLE, e.g.: "When that day comes, and there is a massive exchange, then that is the end, because you are talking about . . . 150 million casualties in the first eighteen hours" (John F. Kennedy, quoted by Arthur M. Schlesinger, Jr., *A Thousand Days*, 1965). See also CASUALTY, LIMITED WAR, STRATEGIC, and TACTICAL NUCLEAR WEAPON.

execute. To murder. "Execute" is preferred by terrorists because it lends an aura of legality to their killings. Such nuances are thought to be especially important when, as is frequently the case, the victim is a helpless captive. For example, "The Irish Republican Army said today . . . police constable William Turbitt, who was kidnapped in a bloody IRA ambush . . . was 'executed' because he was part of the 'British war machine'" (*New York Post*, 6/19/78). See also CAPITAL PUNISHMENT, HIT, and KILL.

executive action. A CIA euphemism for getting rid of people, especially the leaders of foreign countries, and especially by murder. (The killing, or NEUTRAL-IZATION, of a low-level enemy AGENT also would class as an *executive action*, as would a coup in which a foreign leader was removed though not killed.) The phrase was linked especially to foreign leaders through the 1975 investigation of the Senate Intelligence Committee into American plots to kill five of them, though the committee report made clear the broader application of the euphemism:

> Assassination capability (Executive action)—In addition to these five cases, the Committee has received evidence that ranking Government officials discussed, and may have authorized, the establishment within the CIA of a generalized assassination capability. During these discussions, the concept of assassination was not affirmatively disavowed.

Later, David Wise reported in *The American Police State: The Government Against the People* (1976) that the CIA assassination unit was piquantly called the Health

ex gratia

Alteration Committee—very nearly as clever a title as Idi Amin's STATE RESEARCH BUREAU. See also ACTION, ASSASSINATION, CAPABILITY, WET AFFAIR, and the similarly bland *executive measures* in FINAL SOLUTION, THE.

ex gratia. It translates as "out of kindness" or "as a favor," and it is a convenient dodge for people who are morally but not (yet) legally required to pay damages to others. Thus, explaining the reasons for making a $3 million *ex gratia* payment to the Bikinians who had been kicked off their atoll in 1946 so that the United States could test atomic bombs there, Harry Brown, of the Interior Department, said, "That's a payment saying thank you for the hardships they've undergone, the sacrifices they've endured in giving up their island for international peace" (*New York Times*, 4/6/75). For international peace?

Similar to an *ex gratia payment* is the "condolence award" made during the Vietnam ERA to the families of South Vietnamese who were killed by American troops by mistake. The standard *condolence award* was $34. More generous was the "missing person gratuity" awarded by the United States to the wife of a Vietnamese who had been working for the Green Berets and was apparently murdered by them (see ELIMINATE/ELIMINATION). The *missing person gratuity* was $6,472. See also GESTURE OF GOODWILL.

exotic. A stripteaser, or that which pertains to the profession of disrobing in public. "'Exotic dancer—' 'A euphemism for stripper'" (R. Hardwick, *The Plotters*, 1965). An *exotic* is one step this side of *exotica*, i.e., EROTICA. See also ECDYSIAST.

expectant/expecting. Pregnant. The terms usually are encountered in feminine contexts, as in "I hear that Amanda is expectant," or from a TV ad for Preparation H, "When you're expecting, check with your doctor before using any medicine" (6/22/78). Masculine objects, however, are not unknown, e.g., *Expectant Fathers*, by Sam Bittman and Sue R. Zalk, a book that first saw the light of day in 1978. In fact, it seems likely that "expectant" was first applied to fathers-to-be in the legitimate sense of "having expectations," with its development as a euphemism for pregnancy coming slightly later. The oldest male "expectant" in the *Oxford English Dictionary* (1972 supplement) is from 1861, while the first fully pregnant female "expectant" doesn't crop up until 1882. Today, as the birthrate declines, pregnancy is becoming rare enough to be fashionable—and also mentionable. Nevertheless, many of the nineteenth-century euphemisms for this DELICATE condition linger on. See also ACCIDENT; ANKLE, SPRAIN AN; ANTICIPATING; CAUGHT (or CAUGHT OUT); ENCEINTE; FAMILY WAY, IN A; INTERESTING CONDITION, KNOCK UP; THAT WAY; WITH CHILD, and YOU-KNOW-WHAT.

expectorate. To spit. "As Tom wended to school after breakfast, he was the envy of every boy he met because the gap in his upper row of teeth enabled him to expectorate in a new and admirable way" (Mark Twain, *The Adventures of Tom Sawyer*, 1876). Just as boys love to learn to wrap their tongues around the word "expectorate" while they are teaching themselves to spit, so, when they are a little older, word and deed will be similarly conjoined in OSCULATE. See also CUSPIDOR.

expendable. Military-ese for those who are about to die. Before 1900, "expendable" was considered a rare word, and one that applied more to property and provisions than to men's lives; it took the twentieth century to give it a new meaning. A key work on the subject is W. L. White's *They Were Expendable* (1942). As far back as the eighteenth century, however, the similar "expended" was used by sailors in the sense of "killed." This was an allusion "to the gunner's accounts, wherein the articles consumed are charged under the title of expended" (Capt. Francis Grose, *A Classical Dictionary of the Vulgar Tongue,* 1796). See also BITE THE DUST, CASUALTY, and WASTE.

experience. An opaque word for masking almost anything from private pleasure to public pain. Thus, in what is usually construed as the pleasurable side, "experience" translates as "sex" when a MASSAGE PARLOR advertises a "$50 Experience" or when a sex therapist talks about the *group experience* or *prostitute experience.* Harvard MBA's generally have something else on their minds when they refer to the *career experience,* which is a "job" to someone who has a POSITION. Then there is the kind of catchall "experience" that H. R. "Bob" Haldeman had as chief of staff to President Richard M. Nixon: "Few men in all history have had the privilege of being raised as high as I was; and few have had the tragedy of being brought as low. It has been an enriching experience . . ." (Haldeman with Joseph D. DiMona, *The Ends of Power,* 1978).

expire. To die; the longer, softer, Latinate word (FOP Index of 2.3) lingers on the lips, delaying and evading the awful moment; its primary meaning, "to breathe out," has been extended to include the unstated thought that this breath is the last one. "Expire" is the formal, somewhat technical equivalent of PASS AWAY, and it is preferred by professionals who deal with death at first hand, e.g.: "The word 'death' is seldom heard in hospital wards. Whether from a sense of delicacy or for greater exactness, 'to cease breathing' or 'to expire' are the usual expressions. Upon inquiry, a nurse will say that 'So-and-So did not live' in preference to 'he died'" (*American Speech,* 4/27). See also NO MAYDAY and NOT DOING WELL.

expletive deleted. Along with CHARACTERIZATION OMITTED, the most famous excision from the transcripts of the White House conversations about the Watergate affair. While preserving public decorum, the phrase also helped the conspirators maintain the fabric of the COVER-UP. For example, the White House version of President Richard M. Nixon's conversation with H. R. "Bob" Haldeman and John W. Dean III on March 21, 1973 (the meeting that Dean opened with his "cancer-on-the-presidency" speech), contained an especially deceptive "expletive deleted." It occurred during the course of a discussion about paying $120,000 to buy the silence of Watergate burglar E. Howard Hunt, Jr., about all the "seamy things" (Hunt's words, according to Dean) that he had done as a PLUMBER. Quoth Nixon:

> (Expletive deleted), get it. In a way that—who is going to talk to him? Colson? He is the one who is supposed to know him?

extramarital

On the basis of this rendering, the president's lawyers argued that he had not solved what was usually called "the Hunt problem" (see PROBLEM) by authorizing the payment of hush money. Nixon, they asserted, was merely exploring the available OPTIONS. This interpretation seemed forced to some people, but others—probably still a majority—were willing to give the president the benefit of every possible doubt. When members of the House Judiciary Committee got to play the actual tapes, however, they heard the president say, "Well, for Christ's sakes, get it." With the expletive in, Nixon's words sounded much more like a direct order, and some committee members were so angry about the whitewashed White House transcript that they leaked the real text to the press. Special Prosecutor Leon Jaworski agreed with their interpretation. After listening to the tape, he told Nixon's chief of staff, Alexander Haig, Jr., that "I'm afraid the President engaged in criminal conduct" (Barry Sussman, *The Great Cover-Up*, 1974, and Jaworski, *The Right and the Power*, 1976).

Watergate and Nixon have come and gone, but "expletive deleted" lingers on. Thus, reporting on the latest (last??) fight of baseball manager Billy Martin, the *New York Times* quoted Joe Cooper, a marshmallow salesman Martin had decked in a hotel lobby in Bloomington, Minnesota:

> "Billy said, 'They were both [expletive deleted] and you're an [expletive deleted] too for saying it.'" (10/31/79)

See also ADJECTIVE/ADJECTIVAL, BLEEP, and BLIP.

extramarital. Adulterous, as in *extramarital affairs*, *extramarital relations*, and *extramarital relationships* (note that all tend to come in the plural). The Latin takes much of the edge off the violation of the seventh commandment. Would you believe: "Thou shalt not commit extramarital affairs"? Deep-thinkers have recognized the euphemistic quality of "extramarital" for at least the last fifty years, e.g.: "We, however, wish to appeal to reason, and we must therefore employ dull neutral phrases, such as 'extra-marital sexual relations'" (Bertrand Russell, *Marriage and Morals*, 1929). See also AFFAIR, FORNICATE/FORNICATION, OPEN MARRIAGE, RELATIONSHIP, and SWINGING.

extremity. An arm or a leg, usually the latter, but with a FOP Index of 4.0 in either case. ". . . even medical students too often in their histories call legs and arms extremities somewhat to the confusion of those who read hospital notes and are compelled to study out which extremities are meant" (Dr. Charles W. Burr, *Annals of Medical History*, IX, 1927, from Allen Walker Read, *American Speech*, 12/34). See also LIMB.

F

f——; also f___, f——k, ————. It hardly takes a genius to figure out that this is the most distinguished of the FOUR-LETTER WORDS—that the meaning is neither "fair" nor "foul," neither "fink" nor "funk," but simply "fuck." Yet the blanks continue to be more printable than the letters for which they stand, especially in FAMILY magazines and newspapers, which exclude whatever is OBSCENE, DEROGATORY, AND SCATOLOGICAL. For example, "Leff's response: 'F——k him, although maybe I shouldn't say that in a family magazine'" (*New York* magazine, 2/13/78). Books, by contrast, tend to be more ADULT. (They can afford to be; society gives more leeway to books than other media because relatively few people read them.) Thus, Mario Puzo could use all the right ("wrong"?) letters in *Fool's Die*, but when his book was reviewed in *The Washington Post Book World* (9/24/78), cold water was dashed on such otherwise inflaming quotations as "he f——ed broads as devotedly as a heroin addict taking a fix," and "[seeing her] energy pills made me think she needed them to make love to me because she was f——ing other people." (The euphemistic opposition between what she does with the "me" and what she does with those "other people" also is worthy of consideration; see MAKE LOVE.)

From the sheer transparency of the dashes, it is obvious that the dasher-outers are more concerned with the imprint of the word upon the page than with the imprint of the thought upon the mind. It is the actual configuration of the letters before the eye that arouses an emotional response, one whose intensity has only recently begun to diminish through familiarity with the sight. As contrasted with ordinary euphemisms, which attempt to improve reality (SANITATION MAN for garbage man, for instance), or even to repress it (SLEEP for death), the dashes for the letters of "fuck" are straight substitutions and, as such, are closer kin to such substitutes for tabooed words as ADONAI, DARN, and DEPARTED. This is true, too, of other dashed euphemisms, such as c——t, p——, d——, and G—— D——, as well as aural euphemisms for f——, such as *fork*, FRIG, *fug*, and *fratting* (see FRATERNIZE).

The origins of "fuck" are surprisingly mysterious. One suggestion is that it is an acronym, used in medieval rape and sodomy cases, for the phrase "for unnatural carnal knowledge." However, neither acronym nor phrase has ever been found in any court record, and it seems likely that this explanation is merely the wishful thinking of some frustrated lexicographer. The oldest examples of the word's use come from Scottish writings of the early sixteenth century. For instance, Sir David Lindsay employed it thusly in *Satyre* (1535): "Bischops . . . may fuck thair fill and by vnmaryit." Attempts have been made—but without success—to link "fuck" to the German *ficken*, which has the same meaning. It would be especially nice to be able to prove the German connection because *ficken* originally meant "knock," and this would make a neat psychological parallel with the modern KNOCK UP. The Latin *pungere*, to prick, and *pugil*, a boxer, both of which have the root *pug*, to thrust or strike, are presumed to be cognates of "fuck." As Allen Walker Read has pointed out, this makes *"pugilist, pugnacious, puncture, appoint,* etc.   . cousins of our nastiest word" ("An Obscenity Symbol," *American Speech,* 12/34). The link to "pugilist," *et al.,* also is in keeping with the common conjunction of violent and sexual meanings within the same word; see ACTION, for example.

Whatever its genesis, "fuck" soon became *the* taboo term, replacing such now-forgotten beauties as *jape, sard,* OCCUPY, and *swive,* the last of which was what people did in Chaucer's time ("Thus swyved was this carpenteris wyf." *The Miller's Tale,* ca. 1387–1400) and, even later, as in "The Mock Song" (1680), attributed to John Wilmot, second earl of Rochester:

> I swive as well as others do,
> I'm young, not yet deform'd
> My tender Heart, sincere, and true,
> Deserves not to be scorned.

By Rochester's time, however, "swive" already was going out of fashion, except as a learned euphemism, while "fuck" was well on its way to becoming the-word-that-couldn't-be-printed. From the middle of the seventeenth century to the middle of the twentieth, it hardly ever appears except in underground literature. It was not included by Samuel Johnson in his *Dictionary of the English Language* (1755), though the good doctor seems to have been familiar enough with the word. At least, it is reported on the actor David Garrick's authority that "when it was asked what was the greatest pleasure, Johnson answered ********" (from Read, *op. cit.*). Capt. Francis Grose *did* include the term in his *A Classical Dictionary of the Vulgar Tongue* (1785), but discreetly, in the form of "TO F——K" and "DUCK F–CK–R." (The latter was defined as "The man who has care of the poultry on board a ship of war.") And in the next, Victorian century, "fuck" was one of the two most conspicuous omissions (the other was "cunt") from the monumental *Oxford English Dictionary* (vol. F being prepared in 1893–97).

Not until after World War I, which had a liberating influence on language as well as on clothes (see BRASSIERE and PANTIES), did the word appear in above-ground literature. James Joyce made the breakthrough in *Ulysses* (1922) when Private Carr shouted, "I'll wring the neck of any bugger says a word against my fucking king." And almost 200 pages later, he used the word again, this time in the even more shocking literal sense, in Molly Bloom's final soliloquy: ". . . I'll let him know that if that's what he wanted that his wife is fucked yes and damn well fucked yes and damn well fucked up to the neck nearly not by him 5 or 6 times handrunning . . ." And it was, of course, for language of this sort that *Ulysses* was banned in the United States until 1933.

In fact, the precedent established by *Ulysses* was not really confirmed until after the world had had a chance to experience the liberating influence of yet another global conflict. (Progress in semantics is sometimes costly in other ways.) In the United States, the great change seems to have occurred about 1950. Whereas Norman Mailer resorted to the euphemistic *fug* in *The Naked and the Dead* (1948), James Jones used "fuck" in *From Here to Eternity* (1951). Which is not to imply that Jones wrote with complete freedom. Speaking of the editing of that book: ". . . in the 859 pages, *fuck* was reduced from 258 mentions to a mere 50, and *cunt* and *prick,* which appeared many times in the original manuscript, were eliminated by the cleansers" (Edward Sagarin, *The Anatomy of Dirty Words,*

1962). The taboos were tumbling down, however. By 1959 (in the United States) and 1960 (in England), it became legal to publish D. H. Lawrence's *Lady Chatterley's Lover* (1928) and, not long afterward, even dictionary-makers stopped pretending that the word didn't exist. The *Penguin Dictionary* listed it in 1965, the *American Heritage Dictionary* in 1969, and the *Oxford English Dictionary*, finally, in its 1972 supplement.

Still, "fuck" retains much of its old power and even the most sophisticated publications will genuflect to it when rendering spoken English into type. For example, consider how *The New Yorker*, which is supposedly not written and edited "for the old lady in Dubuque," handled an exchange between a future mayor of New York City and a campaign heckler:

> A member of the Progressive Labor Party stuck a megaphone in [Edward I.] Koch's ear and shouted "War criminal! War criminal!"
> Koch replied, "**** off!"
> Shocked, the young man asked, "Can I repeat that?"
> Koch said, "Sure," and the young man announced through his megaphone, "Congressman Koch just told me to **** off!" (Ken Auletta, 9/10/79)

See also INTERCOURSE, MOTHER, and, for background on the other great omission from the *Oxford English Dictionary*, VAGINA.

fabrication. A long-winded, Latinized lie. The word, which originally referred to the process of making something, has been tarnished by the later sense of making up something. "Fabrication" has a FOP Index of 4.7. See also WHITE LIE.

facetiae. A euphemism among learned bookmen for pornography. Originally, and innocently, "facetiae" were merely witty, refined, or facetious sayings, considered collectively. Thus, from a 1657 book on rhetoric: "The merry and pleasant sayings incident hereunto are called Facetiae." The word seems to have taken its turn for the worse during the nineteenth century. "He puts to the end of his catalogue . . . two pages that he calls 'Facetiae' . . . indecent books, indeed" (Henry Mayhew, *London Labour and the London Poor*, 1851). See also EROTICA.

facility. (1) A toilet; (2) a building.

The generalized "facility" has several advantages. In the case of "toilet," it simply blots out the embarrassment. Meanwhile, in the larger structural sense, "facility" also is preferred by those who realize that they will seem to be more profound if fewer people understand what they say. Thus, "sports facility" is preferred to "sports arena" or "stadium," either of which present a much clearer picture of what is meant, while "ancillary facility," which is how a soldier might describe a "bomb shelter," is very hard to beat. "Facility" also has other attractions. As opposed to "building," it is a Latinate term, and the tropism of double-talkers toward that language is well known. A still subtler advantage of "facility" is that it also means "ease of performance," "ability," and "dexterity." Thus, "facility" implants the idea that someone may actually be accomplishing something in the building concerned. See also STRUCTURE, TOILET, and the specialized CORRECTIONAL FACILITY.

fair. The dictionary definition of "moderately satisfactory or acceptable; passably good," is belied by the word's actual meaning in performance ratings of various kinds. Consider the financial stability ratings in *A Shopper's Guide to Health Insurance,* issued by the Pennsylvania Insurance Department: "Stability ratings are graded as follows: 0—no recommendations; 1—fair; 2—good; 3—very good; 4—excellent. The guide recommends avoiding companies whose rating is not 3 or 4" (*New York Times,* 1/3/74). Still more rococo—it received an honorable mention when the Committee on Public Doublespeak of the National Council of Teachers of English handed out its Doublespeak Awards in 1979—there was the effort of A. J. Spano, a Colorado state representative, to improve air quality in Denver, which ranks as the second-dirtiest city in the nation in this respect. Spano's idea, incorporated in a bill, which was approved by legislative committee, was to change federal pollution standards so that hazardous would be redefined as "poor," dangerous as "acceptable," very unhealthy as "fair," unhealthful as "good," and moderate as "very good." See also EXCELLENT, FIRST CLASS and, for the main 1979 Doublespeak Award winner, EVENT.

fair trade. Fixed price; restraint of trade. This is another good example of Reverse English, or the power of the euphemism to imply exactly the opposite of its actual meaning. For the unknowing consumer, *fair trade* has comforting overtones of "free trade," though neither fairness nor trade are involved; rather, it is a tactic of manufacturers to avoid price competition by requiring wholesalers and retailers to sell goods at set prices, without discounts or special sales. "The Corning Glass Works announced today that it was discontinuing so-called 'fair trade' price fixing arrangements that have come under attack by consumer advocates" (AP, 4/7/75). As a euphemism, "fair trade" fits hand-in-glove with FREE ENTERPRISE.

fall/fallen. To die, especially in combat; to be dead. When applied to soldiers who "drop down" on the battlefield, "fall" actually is a euphemistic shortening of "fall dead." The expression probably originated soon after the first soldier *fell.* As Aias said of Achilles after Patroklos was killed: ". . . I think he has not yet heard the ghastly news, how his beloved companion has fallen" (*The Iliad of Homer,* ca. 750 B.C., trans. Richmond Lattimore, 1951). See also BITE THE DUST.

fallen woman. A woman who is not married and who is not a virgin; in the nineteenth century, one of the polite terms for a whore, or PROSTITUTE. The *fall* of the *fallen woman* was metaphoric (In Adam's fall, We did sin all), as well as literal. Her status and expectations were described most succinctly by that eminent authority on promiscuity, George Gordon Lord Byron: "The once fall'n woman must for ever fall" (*Marino Faliero, Doge of Venice,* 1820). One hardly ever hears about *fallen women* nowadays in the United States, the expression having grown obsolete as society came to agree that it was better to be chased than chaste. It lingers on as a colloquialism for becoming pregnant in Britain, where a woman might say, "We were married nearly a year before I fell." For a similar *fall,* see ANKLE, SPRAIN AN.

family. No sex; as distinguished from ADULT. "Most newspapers still use the cliché 'a family newspaper' to describe themselves, although the kind of family to which they are presumably dedicated disappeared during the sixties, except at certain levels. Broadcasting shares this dedication. . . . In both media, 'family' applied to 'newspaper' or 'entertainment' means 'no sex'" (John Tebbel, *The Media in America*, 1974).

Of course, the publishers of *family* newspapers and the TV broadcasters of Family Time shows are just tippytoeing along in the giant footsteps of Henrietta Maria Bowdler and her brother Thomas, whose expurgated edition of Shakespeare, called *The Family Shakespeare* (what else?), made their own family name synonymous with censorship of the most ridiculous kind. As Thomas explained in the preface to the enlarged, second edition of their work, published in 1818: ". . .nothing is added to the original text; but those words and expressions are omitted which cannot with propriety be read aloud in a family." Because his name appeared as editor of the 1818 edition, Thomas has usually been given all the credit for the squeamishness that made bowdlerism a household word. Recent researches, however, suggest that the true culprit was Henrietta Maria, who produced the first edition of *The Family Shakespeare* in 1807, but didn't sign it. Probably, as a maiden lady, she didn't want to admit publicly to knowing the meanings of all the words she had excised.

For more about taking the bite out of the Bard, see LIE/LIE WITH, and for the comparable job that Noah Webster did on the Bible, continue with PECULIAR MEMBERS.

family jewels. The balls or TESTICLES, which are precious and must be protected, not only because of the progeny that descends from them but because of the pain that occurs when they are injured. In the CIA, the phrase gained another euphemistic meaning when it was used in 1973 by "a wag" (ex-director William Colby's characterization) to describe the agency's most embarrassing (i.e., illegal) secrets, such as its domestic MAIL COVER (i.e., mail opening) and SURVEILLANCE programs. Colby maintained that he himself referred to the *family jewels* as "our skeletons in the closet" (*Honorable Men*, 1978). See also ROCKS and SHMO.

family way, in a. Pregnant. This and WITH CHILD were two euphemisms cited by Johnny Carson on "The Tonight Show" for "pregnant," a word that he noted "couldn't be used on TV ten years ago" (WNBC-TV, 11/19/74). See also EXPECTANT/EXPECTING.

fancy. A precious, euphemistic building block. Thus, over the years, *fancy house* has meant whorehouse, while *fancy woman* and *fancy girl* have stood at different times for sweetheart, mistress, and whore (or PROSTITUTE). The history of *fancy man* is even more tangled, having been applied to gigolos, to sweethearts generally, to pimps, and to homosexuals. Speaking about the last, David W. Maurer has this enlightening note about the mores of seafaring folk (*American Speech*, 10/42): "The 'fancy men' are homosexuals, usually passive, of whom there are always several on any windjammer even in these days and who cater to the desires of the officers (and often the men) in return for money, special privileges, etc." In rhyming slang, a *fancy man* might also be known as a *nancy*. See also GAY

fanny

fanny. The buttocks or ass. As Sally Quinn, who is what *Time* used to call a "newshen," has said: "If a senator is putting his hand on my fanny and telling me how he's going to vote on impeaching President Nixon, I'm not so sure I'm going to remove his hand no matter how demeaning it is" (*Media People* magazine, mailing, rec'd 11/29/79).

The blossoming of "fanny" in the public prints is a comparatively new phenomenon. As recently as 1929, it was considered so impolite as to be included in a list of words forbidden to vaudevillians traveling the Keith circuit. Other words and expressions on this list included: to hell with, cockeye, wop, ARAB, pushover, dammit, belly (see ABDOMEN), and lousy (H. L. Mencken, *The American Language, Supplement One*, 1945). In recent years, however, it has even been sighted on the front page of such a respectable FAMILY newspaper as the *New York Times*, i.e., on August 2, 1974, when one New York City official was reported to have told a colleague, in the course of a telephone call to London, to "get his fanny back here." (This message was said to have been delivered "in thundering tones," and, on the next day, the language was characterized in an editorial as "colorful"—all of which makes one suspect the original quotation was only euphemistically correct.)

The origin of "fanny" is a minor lexicographical mystery. "Parking her fanny in here," from Hecht and MacArthur's *Front Page* (1928), is the oldest example of the word in this sense in both the *Oxford English Dictionary* (1972 supplement) and the *Dictionary of American Slang* (1975), but it surely was in widespread use before this, or the Keith censors wouldn't have been so ready to ban it in 1929. Several etymologies have been proposed. One school of thought holds that the term commemorates a particular Fanny with a very large one. (In this connection, note that Fanny Rose Shore is now known as Dinah Shore, while the usual diminutive of Frances is Fran or Franny, with the general shift away from "Fanny" almost certainly reflecting the increasing taint of the anatomical connotation.) Another possibility is that the anatomical "fanny" derives from the punishment sometimes administered to it, i.e., "to fan," in the sense of "to spank."

More likely, though equally unproved, is that the human "fanny" comes from the nautical "fantail"—the overhanging stern of some ships. There is a strong convergence here, since people also have TAILS, while both ships and people are said to have *poops* and *sterns*. Finally, the authority on British slang, Eric Partridge, noting that "fanny" also meant "the female *pudenda*" from 1860, and perhaps much earlier, suggests that this kind of "fanny" also may go back to a particular individual—to one of the most famous of them all, as it happens: Fanny Hill, heroine of John Cleland's *Memoirs of a Woman of Pleasure* (1749). "Fanny" in this sense may sound odd to American ears, but it is by no means the only word to have managed to carry both meanings; see KEISTER, TAIL, and, for more about the many words for the *fanny*, the basic ARSE.

fatigue. "Battle fatigue" is World War II's enervated version of World War I's "shell shock," and "mental fatigue" closely resembles "mental depression," as in: "Six days earlier, Eagleton [Thomas E., D., Missouri] had revealed that he had undergone electric shock treatment for mental fatigue in the 1960's" (Bob Woodward and Carl Bernstein, *All the President's Men*, 1974). Then there is the original *fatigué*, which is not only acceptable but "smart" in places where plain

English would never do, e.g., from an ad for a woman's T-shirt with *"Je suis fatigué"* emblazoned across the chest: "'I'm tired!' says the tee—so much more expressive in French, isn't it?" (Lillian Vernon catalog). See also MENTAL and POSTTRAUMATIC NEUROSIS.

favors. To enjoy the favor of a woman's company is one thing, but to enjoy her *favors* is quite another, since the word that in the singular may refer to a "little gift or remembrance given as a token of esteem, affection or hospitality," becomes in the plural a euphemism for some form of sexual INTERCOURSE or SERVICE. Careful writers have been making use of "favors" for many years. Thus, speaking of the Flathead Indians: "Chastity is particularly esteemed, and no woman will barter her favors, even with the whites, upon any mercenary consideration" (*Alexander Henry's Journal*, 1811). It is a pleasure to be able to report that the high standards of the Flatheads continue to apply in Washington, D.C. Thus, speaking of Elizabeth Ray and Rep. Wayne L. Hays (D., Ohio): "Mr. Hays today admitted having a relationship with the woman, but denied that she had been hired [at $14,000 a year] for her sexual favors" (*New York Times*, 5/26/76).

"Favors" of this sort are a literary convention. It is very unlikely that anyone, whether a white trader or a congressman, has ever asked a PERSON for her "favors," as such. It is quite possible, however, that our forefathers occasionally entreated our foremothers for "the last favor." As Moll Flanders reports: "However, though he took these freedoms with me, it did not go to that which they call the last favour . . ." (Daniel Defoe, *Moll Flanders*, 1722). See also RELATIONSHIP.

feces. Normal people do not normally use this word, and when they do, it is as a euphemism for "shit." It is even possible, and correct, to retreat one step farther into the Latin, inserting an "a," to make "faeces." "Feces" originally meant "dregs" (or CRAP) and the earliest examples of the word's use in English (ca. 1465) deal with the "feces" of wine, salad oil, etc. The term began to be used for excrement in the seventeenth century and now, of course, the "bad" meaning has driven out the "good" one, so this is its only meaning. See also DEFECATE/DEFECATION.

fellatio. A relatively new and printable term for an old and unprintable act, the sucking or licking of the PENIS—"corksacking," as Anthony Burgess euphemized it in EFF. "Fellatio," deriving from the Latin *fellare*, to suck, and so, through the root *fe*, to suckle, is related to such relatively innocuous words as "fecund," "fetus," "filial," and FEMALE. The oldest example of "fellatio" in the 1972 supplement to the *Oxford English Dictionary* comes from H. Havelock Ellis's *Studies in the Psychology of Sex* (1897), a work that also supplies—by a not-so-remarkable coincidence—the oldest, CUNNILINGUS. Previously, going all the way back to 1887, other writers had used *fellation*, for the act, and *fellator* and *fellatrix* for those who perform it, male and female, respectively. The proper adjective is "fellatory" and the verb is "fellate," as in "Lazily she fellated him while he combed her lovely hair" (John Updike, *Couples*, 1969). See also SOIXANTE-NEUF.

female. One of two (with LADY) main euphemisms in nineteenth-century America for WOMAN. Thus, when Emma Willard, pioneer of education for women, began founding schools, the operative word was always "female," as in the Middlebury (Vermont) Female Seminary (1814) and the Waterford (New York) Female Academy (1819). But gradually things changed, as they always do, and "female" began to acquire some of the base sexual associations of the word it had replaced. By 1861, the pendulum had swung so far that when Vassar Female College was established, the editor of *Godey's Lady's Book,* Mrs. Sarah Josepha Hale, protested loudly. She argued that "female" was not in good taste because "many writers employ the word as a noun, which, when applied to women, is improper and sounds unpleasantly, as referring to an animal. To illustrate: almost every newspaper we open, or book we read, will have sentences like these: 'A man and two *females* were seen,' etc. . . . 'The *females* were much alarmed.'. . . . It is inelegant as well as absurd." Mrs. Hale won the day; the offending "female" was expunged from Vassar College (just as well, now that males are admitted) and her argument was generally accepted. At the end of the century, the *Oxford English Dictionary* noted that "female" as a synonym for "woman" was "now commonly avoided by good writers, except with contemptuous implication." Today, "female" still seems irredeemably biological (N.B.: *female complaint,* not "women's complaint"), and so is still avoided except when constructing classified ads, e.g.: "Female, 32, attractive, sensitive, warm, alive, seeks intelligent, sincere, stable male . . . 138297." Even in this context, however, "female" appears less often than "woman." For example, in a randomly selected issue of the *New York Review of Books* (2/3/77), references to feminine gender in the personal ads broke down this way: woman, 22; female, 9; lady, 4; blonde, 1; femme, 1; girl, 1; person, 1; one, 1.

Aside from its essential sexual aspect, another strike against "female" in the minds of some liberated PERSONS is that the word implies by its formation that "females" are in some way derived from, or subordinate to, "males." But this is a mistake. "Female" does not come from its "obvious" root any more than "woman" comes from its apparent source. Rather, "female" derives from the French *femelle,* which, in turn, comes from the Latin *femella,* the diminutive of *femina,* meaning "woman" (literally, "one who suckles"). The present spelling of "female" is the result of a fourteenth-century confusion with the sound-alike "male," which actually has an entirely different Latin ancestor, *masculus.* See also MALE.

fertilizer. MANURE; a second-order euphemism, MANURE itself standing for something worse, i.e., shit.

There is a famous story about Harry S. Truman, which may be apocryphal but which has the ring of truth:

"I grew up on a farm," the president is said to have said, "and I know that farming means manure, manure, and more manure." At which a friend of the president's wife leaned over to her, saying "Really, Bess, you should teach Harry to say 'fertilizer,' not 'manure.'" Mrs. Truman shook her head sadly. "Good Lord," she replied, "Do you know that it has taken me thirty years to get him to say 'manure'?"

"Fertilizer," which is sometimes further dolled up as *plant food* (or even *organic plant food*), did not come into its present meaning until the nineteenth century. Originally, the word applied only to the person or other agency that enriched the soil, perhaps even, in a sentence that was composed as late as 1872 but which only an irreverent writer would produce today, the Lord himself: "The march of

Jehovah, the Fertiliser, may be traced by the abundance which he creates" (Charles Haddon Spurgeon, *The Treasury of David*). The extension of the word's meaning, from the action of fertilizing to include the material, is standard euphemistic operating technique; see DROPPINGS and MANURE.

festival seating. General admission; unreserved seating. It was holders of *festival seating* tickets who stampeded while trying to get into a rock concert in Cincinnati, Ohio, in 1979, killing eleven people and injuring at least eight more.

fib. A lie or to lie. Deriving perhaps from "fable," the "fib" implies that the lie is trivial or childish, except, of course, when the word is being used euphemistically, e.g., "I do not say he lyes neither: no, I am too well bred for that: but his Lordship fibbs most abominably" (John Dryden, *Amphitryon, or The Two Sosias*, 1690). Keeping company with John Dryden is William Safire, who reports: "Newspapers, magazines, and broadcasters harped on news management as soon as the worst of the [1962 Cuban] missile crisis was over, with much justification. There had been some fibbing in high places. Assistant Defense Secretary Arthur Sylvester later talked about the 'government's right, if necessary, to lie' . . ." (*Safire's Political Dictionary*, 1978). See also WHITE LIE.

field associate. A police officer assigned to spy on other police, a shoofly. "In New York City, in 1971, one of the more drastic measures employed by [Police Commissioner Patrick] Murphy and his anticorruption coordinator, William McCarthy, was to ply the ranks with internal spies, otherwise known as 'field associates'" (*Washington Post Book World*, 2/12/78). See also AGENT and OFFICER.

file. Forget. "Let's put that in the circular file" (i.e., wastebasket) translates as "Let's forget it." Naturally, since "file" means "forget," it follows that "do not file" must mean "remember." Note the FBI's "do not file files" in CONFIDENTIAL SOURCE.

filet mignon. The foods we eat almost always seem tastier when served with French names. In part, this is due to the general euphemistic rule that "French is always finer." (See ABATTOIR for more on this topic.) Also, in the case of meat dishes, the foreign term makes the meal more palatable by blurring the diner's mental image of the creature being consumed. As semanticist-turned-senator, S. (for "Sam") I. Hayakawa (R., California) has pointed out: "finest quality filet mignon" is just another way of saying "first-class piece of dead cow."

"Filet mignon" is but one of a number of similar conversions in the names of animals, from English, when the animals are on the hoof, to French, when the same animals appear on the plate. Thus, a live calf becomes dead veal (*veau*), a steer becomes beef (*boeuf*), a deer becomes VENISON (*venaison*), a goat becomes CHEVON, a pig becomes pork (*porc*), and a sheep becomes mutton (*mouton*). The elegant "filet mignon," a somewhat unhappy combination of the French words for "thick slice" (*filet*) and "delicate" or "dainty" (the *mignon*), is a relatively new entrant into English: The earliest example of it in the 1972 supplement to the *Oxford English Dictionary* comes from *The Four Million*, a 1906 collection of short stories by William Sydney Porter (O. Henry).

For more about eating meat, see DRUMSTICK, FRAGRANT MEAT, FRY, JOINT,

fille de joie

PENGUIN, PRAIRIE OYSTERS, RABBIT, SALISBURY STEAK, SWEETBREAD, VARIETY MEATS, and WHITE MEAT. Fish-eaters should consult CAPE COD TURKEY.

fille de joie. A whore. "Bill Novak and Norman MacArthur . . . bought their 1881 Neo-Grec style house seven years ago when it was a rooming house with two *filles de joie*" (*Park Slope* [Brooklyn, NY] *Civic News*, 4/77). *Filles de joie* may also be said to live and work in a *maison, maison de joie*, or *maison close* (closed house). See also HOUSE and PROSTITUTE.

Final Solution, the. The best known of the opaque Nazi allusions to the program for exterminating Europe's Jews during World War II. Besides "Final Solution" (*Endlösung*), the Nazis also used "evacuation" (*Aussiedlung*), "special treatment" (*Sonderbehandlung*), and "resettlement" (*Umsiedlung*) in the same way.

Just when "Final Solution" became a euphemism for mass murder is not known. The term was used as early as September 1938 by Franz Stuckart, who had drafted the Nuremberg Laws of 1935. He wrote that the decisions embodied in these laws, which stripped German Jews of their citizenship and placed many restrictions upon them, would "lose their importance as the 'Final Solution' of the Jewish problem is approached." At this date, Stuckart probably was referring to the purging of the Reich of Jews by deportation rather than by killing. After the war began, however, the genocidal meaning was attached to the phrase. Probably, the original version of what became known as the "Führer Order on the Final Solution" was issued verbally to Hermann Göring, Reinhard Heydrich, and Heinrich Himmler, who passed it down the line. This apparently occurred as plans were being made to attack Russia on June 22, 1941. During May, the army and the S.S. reached an agreement allowing the invading forces to be accompanied by the *Einsatzgruppen*, roving units charged with taking "executive measures affecting the civilian population." The "executive measures" (euphemistically comparable to the later, American EXECUTIVE ACTION) involved the summary execution of 11 categories of people: Russian officials, "fanatical" Communists, etc., with "Category Number 10" including "All Jews." Adolf Eichmann seems to have understood the euphemism as early as May 20, 1941, when a memo from his office advised German consulates that Jewish emigration from Belgium and France was banned because "the final solution of the Jewish question" was in sight. And by July 31, 1941, when Göring wrote Heydrich, who was in charge of the *Einsatzgruppen*, saying "I request, furthermore, that you send me an overall plan . . . for the implementation of the desired final solution of the Jewish question," it seems quite likely that Heydrich knew exactly what Göring had in mind (quotes from Nora Levin, *The Holocaust*, 1968).

See also LIQUIDATE/LIQUIDATION, PROTECTIVE CUSTODY, and SPECIAL TREATMENT.

fire fighter. A fireman—and a rarity among genderless job designations for appealing to men as well as to women. The women like it because it desexualizes the occupation, e.g.: "Terms incorporating gender reference should be avoided. Use fire fighter instead of fireman, business executive instead of businessman, letter carrier instead of mailman" (*The Bulletin*, American Society of Newspaper Editors, 9/76). Meanwhile, the firemen, who are among the staunchest resisters to admitting women into their occupation, also prefer "fire fighter." Presumably, they hope to put themselves on a par with police in salary negotiations by stressing the warlike, dangerous nature of their work. Hence, most of the "firemen" in the United States and Canada belong to the International Association of Fire Fighters. See also ENGINEER and PERSON.

first class. A euphemism in the travel business for second class.

"First class" became second class in fact, though not in name, following the creation of DELUXE. For example, British Airways advertised tours to Egypt in the winter of 1975–76 that provided for stays in Cairo at any of three *deluxe* hotels or two *first-class* hotels. The *first-class* hotels naturally were cheaper. Naturally, too, such a displacement has ripple effects throughout the classification system, with *second class* in name becoming third class in fact, and so forth. See also FAIR, LARGE, and TOURIST.

fix. A neutral word for concealing various unmentionable operations, such as neutering ("Has kitty been fixed?"); bribery ("The legislature's been fixed again."); tampering of various kinds (*fixing* a race, say, by *fixing* a horse), and even killing, e.g., "McDonald got up and said, 'I'll fix you, Fiddler Neary.' He drew a weapon" (*Chicago Tribune*, 9/25/1875). See also ALTER and HIT.

flight attendant. While airlines also employ stewards, most *flight attendants* are women, and they are what used to be known as "stewardesses." The union in the field is the Association of Flight Attendants. The adoption of the neuter "flight attendant" is part of the current, sweeping desexualization of job titles (see PERSON), but the stewardesses had another, specific gripe, this title often being shortened to "stew," an old word for "brothel," where a girl who says "Fly me" really means it. See also STEW.

Flying Fortress. The B-17, of World War II fame. It was designed for long-range bombing missions and was strictly an offensive weapon for striking the enemy behind his lines. "In 1936 the Army agreed to buy thirteen such planes, which it designated the B-17 and called the Flying Fortress, in politically expedient but ironic suggestion that the purpose was thoroughly defensive" (Russell F. Weigley, *The American Way of War*, 1973).

The role of the *Flying Fortress* was to carry out daylight PRECISION BOMBING. See also DEFENSE, DEPARTMENT OF and the *strategic bombing* in STRATEGIC.

fornicate/fornication. Whether as a verb or a noun, the technical, Latinate terms for voluntary sexual intercourse between people who are not married to each other serve also as euphemisms for the prototypical FOUR-LETTER WORD. Thus, the anonymous author of *My Secret Life* (ca. 1890) describes the pictures owned by a London whore (or GAY woman) back in the days when the world had not yet been blessed with color photography: "She had . . . a selection of thoroughly good, coloured, cock rousing lithographs of fornication." In our own time, the greater acceptability of the Latin was well illustrated by public reaction to the famous Jimmy Carter interview in *Playboy* (11/76). Where many of the bluenoses wrinkled theirs at Carter's use of SCREW and SHACK UP, hardly anyone

fouled up

objected to the future president's remark that, as governor of Georgia, "I didn't run around breaking down people's doors to see if they were fornicating."

"Fornication" is distinguished for having an unusually piquant etymology: It comes from *fornix*, the Latin word for "arch" or "vault." The Roman brothels, it seems, were built underground, with arched ceilings. Because of this, *fornix* acquired the additional meaning of "brothel"; "to frequent brothels" became *fornicari*, and the noun, for the act, followed naturally. See also EXTRAMARITAL, F——, INTERCOURSE, and, for Noah Webster's euphemism for "fornication," PECULIAR MEMBERS.

fouled up. Fucked up. See also SNAFU.

foundation garment. A corset, corselet, or girdle, sometimes abbreviated to "foundation," as in "Abraham and Straus Semi-annual Foundations Sale June 4 to July 4" (flyer, 1978). See also BODY BRIEFER.

four-letter word. A "dirty" word, usually an ANGLO-SAXON one; a MONOSYL-LABLE. "The obscene 'four-letter words' of the English language are not cant or slang or dialect, but belong to the oldest and best established element in the English vocabulary. They are not even substandard, for they form part of the linguistic equipment of speakers of standard English" (Allen Walker Read, "An Obscenity Symbol," *American Speech*, 12/34). "'Four-letter words' (itself a euphemistic expression to skirt having to use other words) are more strictly taboo than any others in the English language" (Peter Farb, *Word Play: What Happens When People Talk*, 1974).

The phrase, "four-letter word" is dated to 1929 by Eric Partridge, who links it to the furor over the appearance the previous year of *Lady Chatterley's Lover* by D. H. Lawrence (*A Dictionary of Slang and Unconventional English*, 1970). It may have been preceded, and even inspired, by *four-letter man*, which was a euphemism of World War I for a very objectionable or obnoxious person (i.e., a "shit"). Later, around 1930, "four-letter man" also came to mean "homosexual" (from "homo"). See also THREE-LETTER MAN.

Authorities are divided as to the exact number of four-letter words, with different lists varying according to the fastidiousness of the list-maker. For example, "guts" has four letters, and some have believed it revolting enough to deserve euphemizing (see INTESTINAL FORTITUDE and PLUCK). "Yale" also has four letters and, believe it or not, a Harvard lyricist had a song censored in 1961 for daring to include the line "Yale is a four-letter word." Still, "guts" and even "Yale" seem lily-livered in comparison to some of the other *four-letter words* that may possibly come to the reader's mind. In fact, all the true *four-letter words* deal with the most intimate parts of the human body, and the excretory and sexual functions thereof. Partridge (*op. cit.*) gives the following list: arse, ball(s), cock, cunt, fart, fuck, piss, quim, shit, and twat. Of these, the greatest is generally conceded to be "fuck"; it was, in fact, the subject of Allan Walker Read's "The Obscenity Symbol," although not once in the course of the entertaining, erudite, 15-page article did he actually use that word. (This was 1934, remember.)

The determination of just which words constitute the group of *four-letter words* was complicated immensely in 1978 when Supreme Court Justice John Paul

Stevens, in framing a 5–4 opinion upholding the Federal Communication Commission's authority to ban seven words from the airwaves, referred to "contemporary attitudes about four-letter words" even though three of the words at issue were either longer or shorter. For the benefit of those who read about this decision but couldn't tell what the fuss was all about, since their local newspapers wouldn't print the dirty seven, which had been aired by WBAI in New York City on October 30, 1973, they were: "cunt," "fuck," "piss," "shit," and the non-four-letter words, "cocksucker" (see FELLATIO), "motherfucker" (see MOTHER), and "tit" (see TITTIE).

On a more profound level, the ultimate obscenity is none of the above *three- to twelve-letter words*, but the banning of the very phrase "four-letter words," apparently because of the unspeakable thoughts that these seemingly innocuous words aroused in some extremely sensitive minds. Thus, Cole Porter wrote in "Anything Goes" (1934) that "Good authors too/Who once used better words/ Now only use four-letter words," but when this song was featured in a duet medley by Mary Martin and Nöel Coward, on a CBS telecast on October 22, 1955, the operative line was changed to "Now only use three-letter words." And just what the audience was supposed to make of this—one of the stranger euphemisms of our time—only the CBS censor knows.

For more about the nature of taboos surrounding the *four-letter words*, see the short history of F——.

foxy. Sexy, as "Lulu is a foxy little chick," or "I have a date with a foxy lady tonight." (See SEX.) The basic "fox," meaning an attractive, desirable girl is Black English, popularized during 1963 by the boxer, Muhammad Ali, then known as Cassius Clay (Harold Wentworth and Stuart Berg Flexner, *Dictionary of American Slang*, 1975). "Foxy" was certified officially as a euphemism in 1976 by the Advertising Acceptability Department of the *New York Times*, which caused the ads for the Labor of Love Company's "exclusive New York Times Crossword Puzzle T-shirt" to be changed so that the caption for a picture of a man, filling out a puzzle on the well-filled-out T-shirt of a woman, read "What's another word for foxy?" instead of the original "What's another word for sexy?" (*MORE*, 10/76).

Answer: Stimulating.

fragrance. Once upon a rather long time ago (ca. A.D. 700–1200), people did not always wrinkle their noses at "stink." Originally, that word was used to characterize sweet smells as well as foul ones. Thus, a rose might be said to have "a good stink." However, as usually happens when words bear both "good" and "bad" meanings, the bad ones took over, with the result that "stink" became practically unmentionable. (Noah Webster omitted every "stink" in the Bible when he rewrote it in 1833; see PECULIAR MEMBERS for details.) To replace "stink" in the original, neutral sense, people first used "smell," but this, too, became contaminated, and so they turned to "odor," which, in its turn, acquired noxious connotations; see BO. Almost certainly, the same thing eventually will happen to "fragrance," despite its present, firm entrenchment as a byword for ye olde "good stink." Perfume-makers, for example, have a trade association called the Fragrance Foundation, which occasionally blossoms forth with such sweet-

fragrant

smelling ideas as "The Five Fragrance Ages and Stages of Woman." (In case you don't know, they are Pre-teen, Teen, Young Adult, Middle Age, and Matron, with the last being a euphemism for "old.")

fragrant. More-or-less rhyming slang for those who are too embarrassed to say "pregnant." See also EXPECTANT/EXPECTING.

fragrant meat. A Chinese hot dog (the kind that is man's best friend). "Last November . . . Taiwan's first full-size restaurant offering 'fragrant meat,' the standard euphemism, opened on a major thoroughfare" (*New York Times*, 4/22/73).

Eating dog is ancient Chinese custom. Recipes for dog flank and liver were found in tomb of honorable lady of Marquis of Tai, died circa 160 B.C. Not all modern Chinese dog-lovers love to eat dog, however, and many protested when Chin Ting Restaurant openly advertised delicacy, previously available only from back-alley stalls. Because of furor, "fragrant meat" was removed from restaurant's outside sign, but inside it was still served—as the *Times* reported—smoked, "red-cooked," or in a clear soup with herbs. See also FILET MIGNON.

frank. A euphemism among swingers and a circumlocution among diplomats. Among the former, it stands for openness in sexual talk, e.g.: "The booze had had its effect and we became franker and franker. We admitting our fantasy about making it together with [another couple]. Martha and Sal admitted that they had been in that scene already" (*Forum*, 12/76). By contrast, diplomats (on official business, at any rate) use "frank" to avoid admitting publicly that they are at loggerheads, e.g.: "The communique [following the meeting of President Tito of Yugoslavia and Soviet party leader Brezhnev] spoke of a 'cordial, friendly and frank' atmosphere. In the Communist lexicon the word 'frank' was the tipoff to continuing differences" (*New York Times*, 6/11/72). A common variant is "full and frank," which has even been sighted on the domestic scene, as in "The White House spokesman, John W. Hushen, told newsmen afterward that the meeting included a 'full and frank' discussion of the full range of C.I.A. activities" (*New York Times*, 9/21/74). And it goes almost without saying that the meeting, between Secretary of State Kissinger and congressional leaders, was neither full nor frank, as the secretary neglected to mention the CIA's subsidization of strikers as part of the program to overthrow ("destabilize") the elected government of Chile. See also SERIOUS AND CANDID.

In a sexual sense, the open meaning of "frank" once applied to actions that spoke even louder than words, e.g., from Alexander Pope's *Epistle to a Lady* (1735):

> See Sin in State, majestically drunk;
> Proud as a Peeress, prouder as a Punk;
> Chaste to her Husband, frank to all beside,
> A teeming Mistress, but a barren Bride.

"Punk," by the way, meant PROSTITUTE in Pope's time. Fortunately for him, and for literature, he did not have to reckon with libel laws as they are now being reinterpreted by the Burger Supreme Court, since he probably had a real person in mind when he tossed off these lines: Lady Godolphin, daughter of the duke of Marlborough. See also SWINGING.

fraternize. Originally an all-male word for a close, brotherly association (the Latin *frater* means "brother"), the te.m takes on distinctly non-brotherly connotations when military commanders tell their troops not to *fraternize* with the local population or, in today's sexually integrated armies, with one another. It has, in fact, become a euphemism for sexual INTERCOURSE and has long been perceived by the troops as such. During the years just after World War II, the official "fraternization" also evolved various unofficial abbreviations: *fratting* for dating the former enemy; *frat* and *piece of frat* for the former enemy herself, and *fratter* for the soldier doing the *fratting*. The sexual implications remained strong in the short-forms, making "fratting" essentially a euphemism for another participle with a strong "f" sound; see F———.

free enterprise. Private enterprise. While the phrase has an open, competitive, equitable sound to it, cynics maintain that "free enterprise" amounts to "freedom to cheat." It would be easier to dismiss them as socialistic spoilsports if it were not for the advice of Adam Smith: "People of the same trade seldom meet together, even for merriment and diversion but the conversation ends in a conspiracy against the public, or in some contrivance to raise prices" (*The Wealth of Nations*, 1776). See also FAIR TRADE and SPECULATE.

free gift. This is what banks traditionally offer for new deposits and the redundancy should set antennae quivering, since a true "gift" does not require any elaboration about its being "free." In fact, if the recipient withdraws the deposit before a certain minimum period has expired, the bank gets back the value of the *free gift*—or more—by reducing the amount of interest paid on the account. In this sense, the *free gift* actually is an "Indian gift." See also DONATION.

Free World. Any ally of the United States, no matter how unfree. "Free World" was popularized during the 1950s, when the globe seemed to be divided more neatly into halves than it does today. The expression is now somewhat archaic, due partly to the emergence of more nonaligned "third world" nations and partly to its being applied too often to such bastions of democracy as Portugal under Salazar, Spain under Franco, Greece under various colonels, Taiwan under Chiang, the Dominican Republic under Trujillo, Haiti under Duvalier, South Korea under Rhee and Park, South Vietnam under Diem and Thieu, the Philippines under Marcos, Iran under the shah, and so forth and so on. As Arthur M. Schlesinger, Jr., has said: "There was often not much that was 'free' about many of the states that made up what we used to call the Free World" (*Today's Education*, 9/10/74). See also AUTHORITARIAN and WORLD SERIES.

French—culture, disease, kiss, leave, letter, pill, postcard, pox, way. Over the years, English speakers have attached many meanings to "French," and almost all of them reduce ultimately to some form of "wrong," or "sexy," or—most often—some evil combination of the two. For example:

"French" is a euphemism for "profanity," when someone says "Pardon my *French*," or "Excuse my *French*." And since at least the eighteenth century, *French novels*, *French prints*, and, of course, *French postcards* have had a reputation for raciness if not downright dirtiness. (The French have been known to purchase what they call *American* postcards, but that is another matter.) Then there is *French*

French

leave, which is what people take when they duck out of a party without saying goodbye to the hostess—or go AWOL from the military. (Strangely, the French expression for "to slip away" is *filet à l'anglaise.*) To do one's visitors *the French courtesy* is (or "was"—the custom is believed to be obsolete) to show special favor to one's guests by receiving them while sitting upon one's close STOOL, as French lords were wont to do.

Today, most commonly, "French" connotes "perversion," in the sense of oral-genital sex. (See SOIXANTE-NEUF.) This kind of "French" apparently dates to World War I and reflects the impression that France made upon the boys of the AEF. It appears in such combinations as *to French* (someone), *French job, French kiss* (also used, confusingly, for an openmouthed kiss in which the tongue or tongues come into play), and *French way.* In the more-or-less underground classifieds, *French culture* is distinguished from ENGLISH CULTURE (the subdivision of S/M that relies upon the cane or riding crop), GREEK CULTURE (anal INTERCOURSE), and ROMAN CULTURE (group sex, an orgy). The various terms often are abbreviated to *French* (or *fr*), *English, Greek* (*gr*), and *Roman.* Not infrequently, cultural differences dissolve within a single, very hot, melting pot:

> HORNY BLUE EYED DIVORCEE 24, seeks bi gals, married or sgl select males or cpls. Clean discreet and can travel. Love fr gr roman mild bd [bondage and discipline] or sm in fact love it all. (*Ace,* undated, ca. 1976)

Then there is syphilis, which was known for many years as the *French disease, French gout,* or *French pox,* with *French pox* being recorded as early as 1503, while the modern name comes from a literary production of 1530, entitled *Syphilis: Or, a Poetical History of the French Disease.* Not translated into English until 1686, the poetical history is the story of an unfortunate shepherd named Syphilis, who suffered from this SOCIAL DISEASE. The origin of the disease itself is a matter of dispute (it may have been brought back from the New World to the Old by Columbus's crews) and this uncertainty is reflected in the terminology: The complaint also has been called the *Italian disease,* the *Neapolitan disease,* the *Polish disease,* the *Spanish disease,* the *Canton disease* (in China), the *Chinese disease* (in Japan), and even (in France) the *English disease.*

For those who want to be sure of avoiding the *French disease* (as well as pregnancy), there is always the *French letter,* or condom. Again, the French return the favor, calling the same article *une capote anglaise,* a *capote* being a hooded cloak. Casanova, an enlightened lover (he was one of the first to use condoms to protect his partners "from anxiety" as well as himself from disease) called them *redingotes d'Angleterre* (English overcoats). At other times and places, they have been called *Spanish, Italian,* and even *American letters.*

Once more, the origin of the basic item, the condom, is something of a mystery. According to a *Tatler* of 1709: "A Gentleman of this House [Wills Coffee-House] . . . observ'd by the Surgeons with much Envy; for he has invented an Engine for the Prevention of Harms by Love-Adventures, and has . . . by giving his Engine his own Name, made it obscene to speak of him more" (Shirley Green, *The Curious History of Contraception,* 1971). Later research has turned up no independent evidence that Condom, rumored to be either a doctor or a colonel, ever existed, and the word was used generically before the *Tatler* piece appeared, so perhaps Condom, the man, never was. Whatever the truth of this matter, the name certainly did become too "obscene to speak," and the editors of the great *Oxford English Dictionary* could not even bring themselves to write it until 1972, when "condom" belatedly appeared in the revised supplement. In the intervening centuries, not having a proper word available, gentlemen who used such things had to speak of *French letters*, or of *purses* that were carried in a *bishop* (an extra-large condom), or of donning their *armour*. As noted in an old limerick:

> There was a young man of Cape Horn,
> Who wished he had never been born.
> And he wouldn't have been
> If his father had seen
> That the bloody French letter was torn.

Finally, in the event of a tear in the *French letter* a woman might wish to induce an abortion by means of *French Lunar Pills, French Renovating Pills*, or even *Portuguese Female Pills*. Thus, a January 1845 ad in the *Boston Daily Times* explained that "Dr. Peter's French Renovating Pills" were "a blessing to mothers . . . and although very mild and prompt in their operations, pregnant females should not use them, as they inevitably produce a miscarriage" (from James C. Mohr, *Abortion in America: The Origins and Evolution of National Policy, 1800–1900*). See also MISCARRIAGE.

friend. A lover; a COMPANION of either sex; frequently a COHABITOR or PARTNER; a PARAMOUR. "He hath got his friend with child" (William Shakespeare, *Measure for Measure*, 1604). "Miss [Shirley] MacLaine is trying to remedy the script shortage with the help of Pete Hamill, her friend and writer in residence" (*New York Times*, 4/18/76).

friendly fire. No matter what the military says, the "fire" is not "friendly" when it hits you. The contradiction in terms was epitomized in *Friendly Fire* (1976) by C. D. B. Bryan, who investigated the circumstances of the death in 1970 of Michael Mullen, a young soldier in Vietnam. Mullen was killed by a piece of shrapnel when an artillery shell hit a tree over the foxhole in which he was sleeping. The cannon, it turned out, had been aimed too low: An officer working from elevations on a map had forgotten to take the additional height of the trees into account when computing the shell's trajectory. Thus, Mullen became, in army terminology, a "nonhostile" casualty of a "defensive" round of "friendly artillery fire." For this, he was awarded a Bronze Star. Posthumously. Officially, his kind of death was designated by the Military Assistance Command in Vietnam as a "Misadventure." See also BUY THE FARM.

The phenomenon of death by *friendly fire* is by no means new. Ever since men with weapons have been bunched together in armies, soldiers have run the risk of being accidentally killed or wounded by their companions. As John Keegan notes in *The Face of Battle* (1976), "there are numerous authentic accounts of losses by 'friendly' fire—or even 'friendly' swordcuts—at Waterloo." See also CASUALTY, ORDNANCE, and, for what is probably the most famous death by *friendly fire*, CROSS OVER.

frig. An old euphemism for "masturbate" that evolved into a euphemism for "fuck." Probably deriving from the Latin *fricare*, to rub, the original, aboveground meaning of "frig" was "to move about restlessly," "to rub," or "to chafe" (*Oxford English Dictionary*). By the end of the sixteenth century, the general term for rubbing was being used for the particular action. Thus, in an age that was even more liberated than our own, John Wilmot, the bawdy second earl of Rochester, who lived a merry life but a short one (1647–1680), could address the following verse to one of the ladies of the court:

> *On Cary Frazier* (ca. 1677)
> Her Father gave her dildoes six;
> Her mother made 'em up a score
> But she loves not but living pricks,
> And swears by God she'll frig no more.

The change in the euphemism's meaning apparently occurred around the turn of this century. For example, Frank Harris, recalling his youthful struggles to improve his athletic prowess, circa 1868, was still using the term in the older sense, e.g.: "I soon noticed that if I frigged myself the night before, I could not [high] jump so well, the consequence being that I restrained myself, and never frigged save on Sunday, and soon managed to omit the practice three Sundays out of four" (*My Life and Loves*, 1925). The anonymous but immensely authoritative author of *My Secret Life* (ca. 1890) also used "frig" in its masturbatory sense. Meanwhile, the earliest example of the modern meaning in the *OED*'s 1972 supplement comes from a letter that James Joyce wrote in 1905: "Cosgrave says it's unfair for you to frig the one idea about love, which he had before he met you." Even after laws were relaxed to permit "fuck" to be printed, the euphemistic "frig" continued to see service. Thus, *The American Thesaurus of Slang* (Lester V. Berry and Melvin Van Den Bark, 1953), which does include "fuck," also defines "the four F's" as "find 'em, fool 'em, frig 'em, and forget 'em." See also CORDLESS MASSAGER, EFF, F——, and MASTURBATION.

fry. A testicle or other internal part of an animal (such as the PLUCK) that is about to be fried and eaten; usually encountered in the plural, e.g., "The products of lambs' castration are called lamb's fries" (Frederick T. Elworthy, *The West Somerset Word Book*, 1886). See also FILET MIGNON, PRAIRIE OYSTERS, and TESTICLES.

fudge. An interjection for "stuff and nonsense" that sometimes serves as a euphemism for "fuck," as in "Oh fudge!" It is a fit companion to SUGAR.

fun. A general-purpose substitute for something worse—sex, for instance. "Miss Hamblin said that she asked Representative Howe what he was doing and he told her, 'Looking for a little fun'" (UPI, 7/7/76). In this case, Mr. Allan Howe, Democrat of Utah, did not have any *fun*, since Ms. Margaret Hamblin turned out to be a police decoy posing as a PROSTITUTE. Here, the prospective customer's search for *fun* is the counterpart to the prostitute's opening line: "WANNA GO OUT?"

fundament. The ass or anus (i. e., asshole). "Fundament" is being used here in the sense of the bottom, foundation, or seat of the body. The expression can be traced to medieval times, e.g.: "He . . . with a spere smote the noble knyght in to the foundament soo that his bowels comen oute there" (William Caxton, *The Chronicles of England*, 1480). See also ARSE, BOTTOM, and SEAT.

funeral director. An undertaker; the person who operates a FUNERAL HOME or memorial CHAPEL.

Undertakers have come a long way. In England, in the eighteenth and early nineteenth centuries, they were known commonly as *carrion hunters, death hunters,* and *cold cooks.* (The *funeral home* then was a *cold cookshop.*) Even "undertaker" is something of a euphemism; "taker-under" would be more precise. As a general term for someone who takes on some job, challenge, or enterprise, "undertaker" has been applied in a wide variety of fields; book publishers, for instance, were once known as "undertakers." The first funeral "undertaker" to be recorded in the *Oxford English Dictionary* comes from 1698. Previously, funerals usually were stage-managed by the family rather than by outsiders. The new calling was not especially dignified, as indicated by the following couplet from Edward Young's *Love of Fame* (1728):

> While rival undertakers hover round,
> And with his spade the sexton marks the ground.

In the United States, meanwhile, development of the undertaking trade lagged behind that of England. (The Americans have since made up for lost time.) At the start of the nineteenth century, even in such a citadel of culture as Charleston, South Carolina, hardly anyone knew what an undertaker was. As a tourist of the period reported: "A few months before the yellow fever raged in that city, in 1807, an undertaker made his appearance, which was so great a novelty to the inhabitants that he was obliged to explain what was meant by the term undertaker in an advertisement" (John Lambert, *Travels Through Lower Canada and the United States of North America,* 1810).

Toward the end of the nineteenth century, American undertakers began to get their act together. (The Civil War had given business a big boost, with CASKET, a somewhat earlier invention, catching on, circa 1863.) By the 1880s, some of the more forward-looking ones were calling themselves "funeral directors." Thus, from a trade publication, *Sunnyside* (now *Casket and Sunnyside*), of 1885: "Funeral directors are members of an exalted, almost sacred calling . . . the Executive Council believed that a cut in prices would be suicidal, and notified the manufacturers that better goods, rather than lower prices, were needed."

Starting about 1925, the undertakers began campaigning to have Rotary and the *Yellow Pages* list them as "funeral directors." In this, they have been successful, as a glance at any telephone classified section will show. For example, in that for Manhattan, New York (1979–80), the entries for "undertaker" and "mortician" are followed by the note "See 'Funeral Directors.'"

Other terms for "undertaker" have been used at different times with varying degrees of success, including *counselor* and *funeral counselor, mortuary consultant* (see MORTUARY and CONSULTANT), and *sanitarian.* If "funeral director" is ever replaced—and, given the continual flux in titles of this sort, chances are it will

funeral home/parlor

be—the most probable successor is *funeral service practitioner,* which was proposed in 1959 by the Commission on Mortuary Education as a replacement for "embalmer" and "funeral director." The beauty part of *f.s.p.* is the "practitioner," which appeals to the long-standing, deep-felt wish of undertakers to have their trade regarded as a profession akin to, if not on a par with, medicine. This desire has been articulated in many ways over the years. Undertakers have referred to themselves as *Dr. So-and-So* and as *embalming surgeons;* they have embalmed *cases* and *patients,* rather than cadavers or corpses, and they have done their work in *operating rooms* and *parlors.* Some are even reported to have transported dead bodies in *ambulances* and *invalid coaches* instead of hearses (see PROFESSIONAL CAR). And, of course, it was the desire to emulate physicians that spawned MORTICIAN, a famous euphemism that seems to have failed, partly because it was cheapened by success. Meanwhile, waiting in the wings, on the chance that "funeral service practitioner" will not catch on, are *grief therapist* and *thanatologist* (see THANATOLOGY).

funeral home/parlor. An undertaker's place of business, especially when under the same roof as his residence; a MORTUARY; a deadhouse.

The oldest "funeral parlor" in the 1972 supplement to the *Oxford English Dictionary* comes only from 1927. In the case of "funeral home," we have it on the authority of the *Tishomingo* [OK] *Capital-Democrat* (6/10/48) that "the Chapman Funeral Home, established by Russell's father, has been operating under the same name for 50 years." Both terms probably go back at least to the closing decades of the nineteenth century, which seems to have been a period of great ferment in this particular field, with FUNERAL DIRECTOR and MORTICIAN also surfacing during it.

Today, the operation of deadhouses is no longer a cottage industry but big business, with many of the old-line *funeral homes* and *funeral parlors* having been replaced by *funeral directors* and chains of funeral and mortuary CHAPELS. Still, *funeral homes* are not only surviving, thank you, but actually breaking new ground (if you'll pardon the expression). For example, there is the Pointe Coupee Funeral Home, of New Roads, Louisiana, which in late 1976 opened a drive-up window, seven feet by five feet, through which grief-stricken motorists could view the DECEASED in an open coffin, bathed in the light of a small blue neon cross. Drivers could even sign the mourners register without getting out of their cars.

The funeral business is based upon death, but that is the last word that anyone in the trade wants to mention. To avoid even the slightest suggestion that it might possibly have taken place, a host of euphemisms and circumlocutions have been devised. For example, the well-spoken undertaker will say:

> *Baby* or *infant,* not stillborn.
> CASKET, not coffin.
> *Case, patient,* or *Mr. Smith*—anything but corpse or dead person.
> CEMETERY or MEMORIAL PARK, not graveyard.
> CREMAINS, not ashes.
> DECEASED or DEPARTED, not dead or dead person.
> ESTATE, not grave plot.
> INTERMENT, not burial.
> INURNMENT, not potting.

LOVED ONE, not corpse.
Memory picture, not last look.
MONUMENT, not tombstone.
Mortuary couch or *preparation couch*, not embalming table.
OBITUARY, not death notice.
Operating or *preparation room*, not embalming room or cellar.
PASS AWAY, not die.
PROFESSIONAL CAR or *coach*, not hearse.
Reposing room or *slumber room*, not laying-out room (see REPOSE).
Service, not funeral (in which instance, the undertaker may be called a Doctor of Services).
SLUMBER ROBE, not shroud.
SPACE, not grave.
Vital statistics form, not death certificate.

Of course, the operators of *funeral homes* and *parlors* are by no means the only business people to have traded on the positive connotations of those terms; see HOME and PARLOR.

furlough. In civilian life, a layoff from work. The civilian usage trades on the happy associations of the word in its military sense, where it means a leave of absence—in effect, a holiday from work. "Many of the pilots now being laid off . . . are experiencing their second 'furlough,' the airline euphemism for layoffs, in two years" (*New York Times*, 12/24/73). See also AT LIBERTY and LEAVE.

gadget. An atomic bomb, in the patois of Los Alamos, New Mexico, where they are made. The in-word has even appeared as the title of a suspense novel involving such a weapon—*Gadget* (Nicholas Freeling, 1977). In other contexts, the versatile "gadget" has also been made to stand for "girl" and for "penis," and it is of additional interest for being a relatively new word. The earliest citation for "gadget" in the *Oxford English Dictionary* (1972 supplement) comes from as recently as 1886. The term seems to have originated among seamen, who applied it to any small contrivance, fitting, or mechanism whose real name they did not know or had momentarily forgotten. It may come from the French *gâchette*, also applied to various mechanical items. See also DEVICE, DING-A-LING, and THING.

gadzooks. The "gad" is a euphemistic pronunciation of "god"; the "zooks" probably derives from the "hooks," or nails, used in the crucifixion of Christ. See also EGAD, ODDS BODKINS, and ZOUNDS.

gal/guy Friday. A lighthearted code phrase for a secretary-servant, general factotum, and gofer; an ADMINISTRATIVE ASSISTANT.

> Gal/Guy Fri. . . . $195–210 Some sten. 6 Mos–1 year experience. Learn Fashion advertising and magazine layout. Good benefits. Fantastic future. (*New York Times*, 9/25/77).

The "Friday" part of the "gal/guy Fri" construction comes from Robinson Crusoe's Man Friday. The "guy" is much newer; the usual request was just for a *gal Fri* before equal opportunity laws forced advertisers and employers to at least pretend to open all jobs to all persons of either sex. "Guy" itself, as a general term for "man" or "fellow," seems to be a nineteenth-century Americanism. It may have developed from the older English "guy," meaning someone of grotesque appearance, and possibly was influenced by the Yiddish *goy* (Gentile). The grotesque "guy," in turn, derived from the effigies of Guy Fawkes, burned annually on November 5 to commemorate the foiling in 1605 of his Gunpowder Plot to blow up the Houses of Parliament. As for the "gal" of the "gal/guy Fri," this slangy mispronunciation of "girl," dating from around 1795, can be used affectionately, referring to a young or pleasant woman or to a sweetheart. However, it is—or used to be—a dangerous word to use because of its implications that the girl is of the lower classes. As Bergen Evans and Cornelia Evans have noted: "Sal, of 'My Gal, Sal' was the madam of a sporting house in Evansville, Indiana" (*A Dictionary of Contemporary American Usage*, 1957). And as Tom Sawyer quickly replied, when Huck Finn asked him the name of the "gal" he intended to marry: "'It ain't a gal at all—it's a girl'" (Mark Twain, *The Adventures of Tom Sawyer*, 1876). See also SERVANT.

gallantry. "Gallantry" is out of fashion now, except among soldiers who occasionally display it under fire, but at one time the chivalrous word was a byword for sexual intrigue. For example, succinctly explaining the conditions surrounding the initial success of the protagonist of *Don Juan* (1819), George Gordon Lord Byron explained:

> What men call gallantry, and gods adultery,
> Is much more common where the climate's sultry.

Byron was referring to Spain, of course, but *gallantry* knew no national boundaries. Thus, Capt. Francis Grose defined the word "pray" in this manner: "She prays with her knees upwards; said of a woman much given to gallantry and intrigue" (*A Classical Dictionary of the Vulgar Tongue*, 1796).

"Gallantry" derived from "gallant," a word for fine-looking men, women, and ships that came to include those gentlemen who spent excessive amounts of time chasing ladies. By the turn of the last century, the usage was fading. A possible survival in the modern era is "gallivant," i.e., to gad about, looking for diversion, especially with the opposite sex. But "gallivant," the verb, may also come from the noun "gallivant," an early nineteenth-century slang term for a "nest of whores" (Eric Partridge, *A Dictionary of Slang and Unconventional English*, 1970).

game. Whether games imitate life or life imitates games is a matter of debate, but the use of "game," "game plan," and a host of other game-playing metaphors as euphemisms and circumlocutions for nonsporting activities is indisputable. Such analogies are especially common in politics, war, and love. Politics first:

> On the assumption that the proposed undertaking by Hunt and Liddy would be carried out and would be successful, I would appreciate receiving from you by about Wednesday a game plan as to how and when you believe the materials should be used. (Memo from John D. Ehrlichman to Charles W. Colson, 8/27/71)

"Game plan," a legitimate expression for a football coach, is popular, pseudo-macho doubletalk for "plan" in nonsporting contexts. (The *game plan* in the above instance was the White House plot to smear Daniel Ellsberg; see COVERT OPERATION.) Of course, the chief gamester in this, the Nixon Administration, was the president himself. He used "game plan" frequently in private conversation, usually as a verb, e.g., "We have to game-plan this" (William Safire, *Safire's Political Dictionary*, 1978). The president also was a great advocate of *hardball* tactics, which is playing the *game* of politics with few if any holds barred, and he switched easily into other sports, preparing for an all-out effort in maintaining the Watergate COVER-UP with the remark, ". . . I mean the—this is a full court press, isn't it?" Appendix 35, *The White House Transcripts*, 1974).

In the main, American politicians seem to have been a relatively sedentary breed, drawing their game-playing metaphors from the card table, e.g., Harry Truman's *Fair Deal*, FDR's *New Deal*, and Teddy Roosevelt's *Square Deal*. In the nineteenth century, a great American original, Col. David (Davy) Crockett said in his *Life of Martin Van Buren* (1835): "Statesmen are gamesters, and the people are the cards they play with. . . . the way they cut and shuffle is a surprise to all beginners." And so it goes, back into the mists of time. The oldest citation in the *Oxford English Dictionary* for "game" in the sense of "A proceeding, scheme, intrigue, undertaking," is from a song, called "The Story of Genesis and Exodus," from about the year 1250: "Ysmael pleide hard gamen." And one can't help but suspect that the gamen Ysmael pleide was *hardball*.

War, like politics, has been long thought of as a game: "War's a game which were their subjects wise/Kings would not play at" (William Cowper, "The Winter Morning Walk," *The Task*, 1785). However, it remained for the Prussians (who else?) to formalize the war-game equation with the invention (ca. 1824) of *kriegspiel*, the war game for training people to fight real ones. Practice at war-gaming, in turn, has helped the global politicians learn to regard nations as inanimate objects (e.g., the domino theory that all of Southeast Asia automatically would become Communist following South Vietnam's fall); to justify air raids ("The bombing campaign is one of the two trump cards in the hands of the President . ." (memo from the chairman of the Joint Chiefs of Staff to the secretary of defense, 10/14/66, *The Pentagon Papers*, 1971); to think of weapons systems as bargaining *chips* in arms limitation treaties; to play off one country against another, as in 1978's China *card*, where closer ties with China were viewed as a means of putting more pressure on the USSR, and—generally—to think the UNTHINKABLE in ever greater detail. If the indoctrination is good enough, even the soldiers in the field may come to think of what they're doing as a game, e.g.: "He refers to those years [in World War II] as the time he was on 'the first team' in the 'South Pacific playground' where tracers arced out 'like a touchdown pass' and the artillery fired 'orange blobs—just like a football'" (William Arens, quoting professional football coach Mike Holovak, *Natural History*, 10/75). What with all the romance of the *game* of war, it has to be added that one of the most famous remarks along these lines—the duke of Wellington's oft-quoted statement that "the Battle of Waterloo was won on the playing fields of Eton"—probably was never said by him. The epigram appeared first in French, three years after the duke's death, and in its original version did not mention the "playing fields" at all (Elizabeth Longford, *Wellington: The Years of the Sword*, 1969).

Then there is the *game* of love, or sex, also known as The Mating Game. Here, the euphemism does not always guarantee protection for the user. Thus, Earl L. Butz, agriculture secretary, jumped headfirst into boiling water in 1974, with a joke that quoted an Italian woman as justifying her dissent from the pope's ban on artificial means of birth control by saying, "He no play-a da game, he no make-a da rules." (For the last words on Butz, who seems to have had a political death wish, see OBSCENE, DEROGATORY, AND SCATOLOGICAL.) The virile James Boswell was on safer ground, confiding to his journal for January 12, 1763, the details of his first night with Louisa, a young actress: "Proud of my godlike vigour, I soon resumed the noble game. . . . Five times was I fairly lost in supreme rapture. Louisa . . . declared I was a prodigy, and asked me if this was not extraordinary for human nature. I said twice as much might be, but this was not, although in my own mind I was somewhat proud of my performance" (Frederick A. Pottle, ed., *Boswell's London Journal, 1762–1763*, 1950). P.S. Boswell was twenty-two. If he were living today, he might have said he "scored" in this *game*; as it was, he later had cause to rue the CONNECTION.

Finally, there is the ultimate game, which is life itself (with all due respect to Stephen Potter, who defined "lifesmanship" as the application of the principles of gamesmanship to the smaller world of life). In the words of Ralph Waldo

Emerson: "Play out the game, act well your part, and if the gods have blundered, we will not" (*Journals*, 1856). Of course, this is pretty much a restatement of Saint Paul's advice: "Know ye not, that they which run in a race, run all, but one receiveth the prize? So run, that ye may obtain" (I Corinthians, IX, 24, King James Version, 1611). Still another, more informal version of this thought was encapsulated in the title of a song that became a hit in Georgia in 1976, about the time Bible-belting Jimmy Carter was being elected president: "Drop Kick Me, Jesus, Through the Goal Posts of Life." There are a few dyspeptic souls, however, who don't go along with the life-as-a-game analogy. Consider Holden Caulfield's meditation on the subject of life as a *game*:

> Game, my ass. Some game. If you get on the side where all the hot-shots are, then it's a game all right—I'll admit that. But if you get on the *other* side, where there aren't any hot-shots, then what's the game about it? Nothing. No game. (J. D. Salinger, *The Catcher in the Rye*, 1951)

game management. Killing animals; hunting. Modern *game management* is a highly rationalized business, with an appropriate storehouse of bloodless words; see CULL and HARVEST.

garçon. A man; specifically, a waiter in an expensive French restaurant. "Garçon," meaning "boy," is a conspicuous exception to the rule against using that word anymore. The French makes it OK. See also BOY and MAN.

garden of honor. A graveyard for veterans and their families, and sometimes a come-on in the cemetery-sales racket, as in: ". . . military personnel and veterans were promised burial in a 'Veterans' Garden of Honor' complete with flags, a 'magnificent' fountain, and an eternal flame" (*Consumer Reports*, 3/75). In this case, "free" burial plots were being used by Richmond Memorial Parks, Inc., and Margel Sales Corp., both of Virginia, as bait to persuade people to purchase more expensive resting accommodations. The two firms pleaded nolo contendere to ten counts of mail fraud and were fined $10,000 apiece, while their joint sales manager was fined $1,000 and given a two-year suspended prison sentence. See also CEMETERY and MEMORIAL PARK.

gay. Homosexual; a code word, once used primarily among *gays*, that has not only come out of the closet but managed to preempt all other meanings of the term. Thus, so-called straight people hardly ever talk anymore about having "a gay old time" at "gay parties" for fear of being misunderstood. In return for losing such innocent uses of "gay," we have gained such barbarities as "'Post' Won't Say Who Died in D.C. Gay Fire," referring to a conflagration in a theater catering to homosexuals that claimed nine lives (*MORE*, 12/77).

"Gay," ironically, does not have the happiest of histories. In the sense of "addicted to social pleasures," it was used early as a euphemism for a "loose or immoral life" (*Oxford English Dictionary*). Thus, when a "lady" remarked in *Lady of Pleasure* (1637) that "gay men have a privilege," it seems that only heterosexual privileges and pleasures were contemplated. Proceeding from euphemism to slang, "gay" came to imply "whore." For example, some time toward the middle of the nineteenth century, the anonymous author of *My Secret Life* (ca. 1890), reported on one of his encounters in this way: ". . . I saw a woman walking along Pall-Mall dressed in the nicest and neatest way. I could scarcely make up my mind whether she was gay or not, but at length saw the quiet invitation in her eye, and slightly nodding in reply, followed her to a house in B**y Street, St. James." The *gay women* of this era also were said to lead the *gay life*, to work in *gay houses*, to be *gay in the arse* (another way of saying a woman was "loose"), and to *gay it* (either sex might *gay it*, this simply meaning "to copulate").

In the prevailing homosexual sense, the earliest *OED* example is from a slang dictionary of 1935: "Geycat . . . a homosexual boy." ("Gay-cat" had other meanings long before this; to hoboes, it meant a newcomer to the road and, in underworld argot, it referred to an apprentice who felt out jobs for the pros.) It usually is assumed that use of the simple "gay" in the modern manner dates just to the 1950s, but this is not so. For example, when Cary Grant (a euphemism for Archibald Alexander Leach) is asked what he is doing wearing Katharine Hepburn's peignoir, he jumps up and down and shouts: "Because I went gay all of a sudden" (*Bringing Up Baby*, film, 1938). Meanwhile, Eric Partridge lists "gay boy" as Australian slang for "homosexual" since about 1925 and suggests that "gay" may have been used a long time before this by homosexuals among themselves (*A Dictionary of Slang and Unconventional English*, 1970). Indeed, it seems likely that the word was adopted by the males who inhabited the homosexual underworld that flourished—complete with houses of male prostitution, drag balls, etc.— alongside the heterosexual *gay* underworld in most major cities, from the mid-nineteenth century if not before. Thus, John Saul, a male PROSTITUTE who played a leading role in the Cleveland Street Scandal of 1889 (it involved Post Office boys in a male brothel in London's West End), apparently used the word both ways. On the witness stand, Saul testified that he once earned part of his living by "cleaning out the houses of the gay people," by which he seems to have meant "the gay ladies on the beat," not homosexuals (H. Montgomery Hyde, *The Cleveland Street Scandal*, 1976). In a deposition to the police, however, Saul also referred to his male friends as "gay," and he is credited with the earliest known use of the word in its currently dominant sense by Philip Howard, in *New Words for Old: A Survey of Misused, Vogue & Cliche Words* (1977).

The rise of "gay," supplanting such earlier terms as *fag*, *fairy*, *fancy man* (see FANCY), *homo*, *queer*, and THREE-LETTER MAN, is a fairly new phenomenon. As recently as 1961, Billy Lee Brammer's novel of Texas politics could be entitled *The Gay Place*, without anyone—non-gays, at least—giving the word a second thought; in 1978, when the novel was reissued, the old title helped show how much "gay's" meaning had changed—and in how short a time.

See also BISEXUAL; GREEK ARTS; LOVE THAT DARE NOT SPEAK ITS NAME, THE; MALE, and QUEEN.

gay deceivers. Not a pair of policemen in drag but a padded brassiere designed to make a woman's breasts appear larger and more shapely. For women to use the term was only fair play; traditionally, a *gay deceiver* was the somewhat euphemistic description for a deceitful rake; see the earlier meanings of GAY. *Gay deceivers* in the feminine sense, commonly encountered in the 1940s and 1950s, when sweaters and girls with lots to fill them were in fashion, became rarer in the sixties, as did bras generally. See also BRASSIERE and PALPITATORS.

G. D. God damn. The abbreviation mitigates the oath, supposedly. ". . . that's what George is. A bog. . . . A fen. . . .A G.D. swamp. Ha, ha, ha, HA! . . ." (Edward Albee, *Who's Afraid of Virginia Woolf*, 1962). See also GOSH.

gee. Jesus. The oldest citation for "gee" in the *Oxford English Dictionary* (1972 supplement) comes from as recently as 1895: "Gee rod! how we will thump'em!" (Stephen Crane, *The Red Badge of Courage*). Other "gee" substitutes for "Jesus" include *gee-hollikins, gee-my-knee, geewhilliker(s), geewhillikins* (possibly the progenitor of "gee"), *geewhittaker(s), gee whiz* (perhaps from "gee ziz"), and *geewizard*, as well as such sound-alikes as *Jee, Jeez, jeepers(-creepers)*, JIMINY CRICKET, and JINGO. Many attempts also have been made to mitigate the sinfulness of the oath by extending the holy name, e.g., *holy jumping Jesus, holy jumping mother of Jesus, Jesus Christ and his brother Harry, Jesus H. Christ, Jesus H. Particular Christ*, and *Jesus Christ on a Bicycle*. See also CRIPES, GOSH, MARRY, and, for background on avoiding the name of God, ADONAI.

generate/generation. As a verb, to create but not necessarily to procreate. During the Vietnam ERA, there was much talk of *generating* refugees:

> In 1967 the AID representatives in the First Corps asked the U.S. military command to stop 'generating' refugees because they had neither the food nor the logistical capacity to feed the people already removed from their land. The military command agreed, but rather than stop its bombing raids or its search-and-destroy operations, it merely stopped warning the civilians that their villages would be destroyed. (Frances FitzGerald, *Fire in the Lake*, 1972)

As for the noun, "generation," it usually does stand for "procreation," especially in such phrases as *act of generation, members of generation*, and *organs of generation*, e.g.: "*Masochism* appears when the afflicted person allows himself to be ill-treated by his partner, in order to be sexually excited or to attain the full enjoyment of the act of generation" (Hans Gross, *Criminal Investigation*, Norman Kendal, ed., 1934). The basic circumlocution is particularly deceptive in view of the precautions that most people take most of the time to avoid generating a new generation. It is also old. Geoffrey Chaucer referred to the "werk of generacion" in his translation of Boethius's *The Consolation of Philosophy* (ca. 1374). See also F——, MEMBER, and ORGAN.

genitals. The external sexual organs, aka PRIVATE PARTS. For those who prefer to retreat further into fake Latin, the word becomes "genitalia." The real Latin *genitalis* (of generation) comes from the past participle of *gignere* (to beget), which makes "genitals" a misnomer when begetting is not the purpose of the exercise. See also PENIS, TESTICLES, and VAGINA.

gentleman. Man; male. Though its career is not as checkered as that of LADY, the gentle term has been used to paper over a wide variety of low, impolite, indecent, rascally, and altogether ungentlemanly conditions, creatures, and occupations. Following is a selection of these usages, most of them now obsolete due to the egalitarian, nongentlemanly spirit of our own age.

First, and perhaps least euphemistic, is the "gentleman" that is routinely extended to practically anything that is male and walks on two legs. In this category are *gentleman-caller, gentleman-lodger, gentleman-tailor, gentleman-volunteer,* and *gentleman-waiter*—among many others. Other, more picturesque "gentlemen" included the policeman, who was known as the *gentleman in blue* (or *of the short staff*); the soldier, who was the *gentleman in red* (before the British realized what good targets redcoats made and changed their uniforms); the *gentleman of fortune,* who was a pirate; the *gentleman of the road,* who was either a highwayman, gypsy, or traveling salesman; and the *gentleman's master,* who was definitely a highwayman because he made real gentlemen obey his command to "Stand and Deliver." Then there is the *gentleman at large,* originally a court attendant with no specific duties, who later became a person out of work (i. e., AT LIBERTY); the *gentleman's gentleman,* who was a valet (the French "valet," in turn, being a nicefied way of saying "servant"); the *gentleman of the back (door),* a sodomist; and the simple *gentleman,* who was a smuggler, as in "Watch the wall, my darling, while the Gentlemen go by!" (Rudyard Kipling, *Puck of Pook's Hill,* 1906).

The *old gentleman* or the *(old) gentleman in black* is Satan, who is not usually called by his real name for fear that he will hear it and come (see DEVIL, THE). A *gentleman of the three ins* was a person who was "In debt, in gaol, and in danger of remaining there for life; or, in gaol, indicted, and in danger of being hanged in chains" (Capt. Francis Grose, *A Classical Dictionary of the Vulgar Tongue,* 1796). This contrasted with a *gentleman of the three outs,* who was "without money, without wit, and without manners" (Grose, *op. cit.*), or "out of pocket, out of elbows, and out of credit" (Edward G. E. L. Bulwer-Lytton, *Paul Clifford,* 1830).

Finally, "gentleman" also has been awarded to various creatures that aren't necessarily male and that sometimes have four—or more—legs. The *gentleman that* (or *who*) *pays the rent* was a pig, in England, where a *gentleman's companion* was a body louse, and a *gentleman in brown,* a bedbug. In the United States, the turkey cock has been called a *gentleman turkey* and the bull has been dignified as a *gentleman cow. Gentlemen hounds* and *gentlemen sheep* also have been sighted by sharp-eyed lexicographers. This is the same kind of fastidiousness that was responsible for turning the ancient ass into the familiar DONKEY and the original cock into the contemporary ROOSTER.

See also COW BRUTE, LADIES/GENTLEMEN, and MAN.

George/Godfrey. Two given names for "God." Dating from the sixteenth century, "George" may actually derive from Saint George, but it is usually used in contexts where a true oath-sayer would say "God," e. g., "'By George, he *has* got something to tell . . .'" (Mark Twain, *The Adventures of Tom Sawyer,* 1876). "Godfrey," meanwhile, is a simple, euphemistic extension of "God," dating to around the turn of this century, and probably used most frequently by sailors who say they are steering "by guess and by Godfrey" when they are proceeding without a set course or the aid of landmarks. See also GOSH.

gesture of goodwill. A payment that one is required to make. Thus, I. G. Farben, the German combine, having already lost a suit to one of the people who had been a slave laborer for the company during World War II, tried to evade its responsibility by insisting that reparations to survivors be considered a "gesture of goodwill," not the "discharge of an obligation" (*New York Times Book Review,* 12/9/79). A *gesture of goodwill* is essentially the same as an EX GRATIA payment.

glands. The testicles; also called *sex glands* or *interstitial glands*. "Glands," from the Latin *glans*, acorn, was favored in the 1920s and 1930s by newspapers that didn't dare print "testicles." Women have glands, too—MAMMARY GLANDS. See also TESTICLES.

glow. Sweat. "Horses sweat, men perspire, women glow" (old saying, ca. Queen Victoria). See also PERSPIRE.

gluteus maximus. The ass; technically only the largest of the three muscles (*g. medius* and *minimus* are the others) that form the buttock of a person, but often used as a fancy euphemism for the entire affair. Generally, the Latin "gluteus maximus" is reserved for men, while women are awarded the French DERRIÈRE.

go. One of the most versatile words in the English language, "go" naturally has many euphemistic applications. For example, "to go" may mean, depending on the context, either to relieve oneself, as in "Mama, I have to go now," or to die, as in "I'm afraid he's about to go." In the latter case, it is also possible to *go* with flourishes, such as *go to a better world, go the way of all flesh,* GO WEST, etc. After *going* in this way, one is usually said to be *gone* ("I'm afraid he's gone now"). Other kinds of euphemistic "go's" include:

> *go all the way* (or *the limit* or *the whole route*), for sexual INTERCOURSE; see ALL THE WAY.
> *go down,* usually for oral-genital sex (CUNNILINGUS or FELLATIO) but also, confusingly, a euphemism in some parts of the country for conventional COPULATION.
> *go down like a submarine,* for someone who submerges sexually with especial speed and enthusiasm.
> *go out,* for an engagement with a whore; see WANNA GO OUT?

Finally, there is the very basic "go on," elegantly illustrated by George Gordon Lord Byron in *Don Juan* (1819), when the beauteous Julia berates her suspicious husband:

> Ungrateful, perjured, barbarous
> > Don Alfonso,
> How dare you think your lady would
> > go on so?

Strong words but—alas—even as Julia speaks, sixteen-year-old Juan is hiding in her bed, and as the reader knows from a previous verse, the lady is not as innocent as she pretends:

> A little she strove, and much
> > repented
> And whispering, "I will ne'er consent"—
> > consented.

goddam or **goddem.** A euphemistic "God Damn"; also, from the fifteenth century, an Englishman (to a Frenchman). Or to a Frenchwoman—say, Joan of Arc, who commonly referred to the English as the "Goddems." English soldiers of the period gained the sobriquet by their frequent use of the expression. See also DOGGONE, GOSH, and SOB.

golden age/years. Old age; the "golden years" variant probably is a half-breed ("hybrid," if you prefer), compounded of "golden age" and SUNSET YEARS.

The myth that the golden years are the best years is rooted in the concept of the Golden Age as the first and best of the ages of the world. The Golden Age was supposed to be a time of innocence and happiness, when truth and justice prevailed. Spears and swords had not yet been invented, perpetual spring reigned, and the rivers flowed with milk and wine. Thus, the euphemism completes a metaphorical circle, returning the oldster to the infancy of the species—another example of ontogeny recapitulating phylogeny.

"Golden age" appears to have been a product of the golden 1950s. The first example in the 1972 supplement to the *Oxford English Dictionary* is from 1961. Of course, the base metal beneath the gilding was recognized by some people from the start: "The brochure writers and the publicists talk of the 'golden years' and of 'senior citizens.' But these are euphemisms to ease the conscience of the callous. America tends to make people miserable when they are old and there are not enough phrases in the dictionary to gloss over the ugly reality" (Michael Harrington, *The Other America*, 1962). See also MASTER, MATURE, and SENIOR CITIZEN.

golly. A euphemistic deformation of "God," often encountered in the form of "By Golly!"

People have been exclaiming "Golly" since at least the eighteenth century; an early variant was "goles," e.g., "Why then, by goles, I will tell you—I hate you" (Henry Fielding, *Virgin Unmasked*, 1734). The "golly," in turn, has helped produce a raft of other euphemistic expletives, such as *goldamn, goldang, goldarn, golly gee,* and *golly Moses.* See also DARN, G.D., GEE, and GOSH.

good grief. Good God—as in the famous line in Charles Schultz's *Peanuts* comic strip, "Good grief, Charlie Brown." Functional equivalents include *good gosh, good gracious, good gracious to Betsy, good gravy,* and *goodness sakes alive.* See also GOSH and GREAT SCOTT.

good people, the. Fairies, gnomes, leprechauns, goblins, and other little people. These are not especially malevolent spirits. They often help mortals accomplish their tasks, give them valuable presents, and warn them of danger. Still, they love to play tricks on people, and they have a disturbing fondness for human babies—sometimes stealing them and leaving fairy babies in their places. Because they are what they are, most people have felt it wise to propitiate them with gifts and, of course, never to say anything bad about them.

> In medieval Europe, the common folk believed themselves constantly beset by supernatural pests, but took care never to risk offending them with a bad name. In Scotland, for instance, they were always *daoine sithe,* 'the little men of peace,' and in Spain *las estantiguas,* 'the venerable ones.' In India to this day the native fiends and imps are called *punya-janas,* 'the good people.' (Gary Jennings, *Personalities of Language,* 1965)

Some animals, either because they are dreaded, revered, or desired, also are commonly approached indirectly and euphemistically; see GRANDFATHER. Of course, the short, *good people* should not be confused with LITTLE PEOPLE.

gosh. Along with GOLLY, probably the most common of the many euphemisms still used for "God," e.g., ". . . 'Oh gosh,' murmured the darling close-eyed girl, biting her lip as . . ." (Maxwell Kenton, aka Terry Southern, *Candy,* 1965).

"Gosh" seems to be a product of the eighteenth century, with the oldest example in the *Oxford English Dictionary* coming from 1757. However, it was preceded by the similar *gosse,* recorded as "by gosse," circa 1553. Like DARN, GEE, and GOLLY, "gosh" has been developed into many picturesque combinations, such as *gosh-almighty, gosh-all-fishhooks, gosh-all-hemlock, gosh-all-Potomac, gosh-awful, gosh-dang, gosh-durn, goshwalader, by-guess-and-gosh,* and *ohmigosh.*

For the root reason for avoiding "God," see ADONAI, and for other ways of swearing without actually taking the sacred name in vain, continue with BEGORRA(H), DAD, DOGGONE, EGAD, GADZOOKS, G.D., GEORGE/GODFREY, GODDAM, GOOD GRIEF, GREAT SCOTT, JOVE, LAW, ODDS BODKINS, and ZOUNDS.

go west. To die, or PASS AWAY. The phrase "gone west" was popularized in World War I as a euphemism for "dead," but the association between the West, where the sun sets, and death is extremely ancient. The Celtic Otherworld was in the West, and "occident," the word we have inherited from the Romans for "the West" (as opposed to "the Orient") comes from *occidere,* to fall down—or to die. J. R. R. Tolkien drew on this association when he concluded the trilogy of *The Lord of the Rings* (1956) with Bilbo and Frodo going to the Grey Havens, where they boarded a white ship, and "went out into the High Sea and passed on into the West . . ." The same idea is echoed banally in the euphemism of old age as the SUNSET YEARS. See also BITE THE DUST, GO, and HAPPY HUNTING GROUNDS, GONE TO THE.

grandfather. A common euphemism among many peoples (and not only PRELITERATE ones) for any of a number of animals. "Depending on where you live, the euphemism grandfather may mean the bear, the tiger, the elephant, or the alligator" (Maria Leach, ed., *Funk & Wagnalls Standard Dictionary of Folklore, Mythology and Legend,* 1972). The bear, for example, is *grandfather* to the Ural-Altaic peoples of Siberia; to those who live near the Baltic Sea; and to the Tête de Boule Indians in Quebec. And this is only one of many euphemisms for the bear. "The Russian linguist A. A. Reformatsky notes the variety of euphemisms for 'bear' among Russian commercial hunters. Actually even the common word *miedvied* is an old euphemism; its literal meaning is 'honey eater.' Eventually secondary euphemisms developed: *khoziain* (landlord or boss), *lomaka* (he who breaks things, like bones maybe), *mokhnach* (the shaggy one), *liesnik* (the forest dweller) or simply *on* (he)" (Anatol Rapoport, *Semantics,* 1970). Other euphemisms for "bear" include *Little Old Man, Dear Uncle, Wise One, Beautiful Honey-Paw,* and *Broad Foot.* In Lappland, the bear is often referred to as *the old man in the fur coat.*

The set of euphemisms is ancient as well as widespread; speakers of Indo-European languages have almost always used them. "The name of the bear was likewise subject to a hunter's taboo; the animal could not be mentioned by his real name on the hunt. The southern Indo-European languages have the original form *rhso- (Latin *ursus*, Greek *arktos*), but all the northern languages have a substitute term: in Slavic he is the 'honey-eater,' in Germanic the 'brown one' . . ." (*The American Heritage Dictionary of the English Language*, 1969).

There are several intertwined and to some extent competing reasons for using euphemisms in place of the true names of animals that are feared, revered, or desired. The euphemistic or metaphoric name may be intended to flatter or propitiate the animal or, conversely, and not so flatteringly, it may be intended to deceive, the idea being that the animal won't realize hunters are talking about it if its true name is not mentioned. On another level, there is the deep-seated human belief that words are extensions of the objects for which they stand, and hence, that to name an object is to establish contact with the object named. (This principle applies to beings and things of all kinds, not just to animals; see ADONAI; DEVIL, THE, and GOOD PEOPLE, THE.) Because words are thought to have this quality, people in many cultures will not speak the real name of another person, especially not a king or a dead person (see DEPARTED). To speak the name of a dead person may raise a ghost; to say the true name of the bear may make him appear when he is not wanted. This belief in the magical power of words to affect the course of events helps explain the universal use of curses and blessings, of spells and of prayers. For other euphemisms for other animals, see STRIPED ONE.

Great Scott. Good God. Other kinds of "Great's," all with the same euphemistic meaning and all dating from the ultrapolite nineteenth century, include *Great Caesar, Great Caesar's Ghost, Great Grief, Great Guns, Great Horn Spoon, Great Shakes*, and *Great Sun*. Like CRIPES, JOVE, and other "oaths" of this ilk, "Great Scott" survives mainly in the comics, e.g., "Great Scott! Ya mean this is the year 2430?" (Robert C. Dille, *The World of Buck Rogers*, 1978). See also GOSH.

Greek arts/culture/way. The code in personal ads for anal intercourse, heterosexual as well as homosexual; frequently abbreviated to a space-saving *Greek* or *gr*. The association of the Greeks with homosexuality—pederasty in particular—goes back to ancient times. Thus, Herodotus (ca. 480 B.C.– ca. 425 B.C.) reflected on the cultural adaptations of the Persians: ". . . they have taken the dress of the Medes, considering it superior to their own; and in war they wear the Egyptian breast-plate. As soon as they hear of any luxury, they instantly make it their own, and hence, among other novelties, from the Greeks, they learnt to go to bed with boys" (*The Histories*). See also BISEXUAL, the "horny blue eyed divorcee" in FRENCH, and Oscar Wilde's citation of Plato in LOVE THAT DARE NOT SPEAK ITS NAME, THE.

Greenland. This has to be the world's most deceptive name for a piece of real estate; it wins hands down over such competitors as *Scranton* (née Skunk's Misery) Pennsylvania; New York City's *Clinton* district (formerly Hell's Kitchen); *Paradise* (replacing Hog) Island in the Bahamas; and *Hill 937* (the official designation for Hamburger Hill) in Vietnam. *Greenland*, though frequently colored green by mapmakers, is anything but. Some 60 percent of the island is covered by glaciers;

the rest alternates between barren rock and arctic prairie (40 percent). True, when Eric the Red explored the island in 981–84, the climate was somewhat warmer than now, and the land presumably somewhat greener. Still, the Norsemen who followed him took one look and concluded that only a shrewd real estate operator would have picked this name. As Ari Thorgilsson put it in the *Islendingabok*, a history compiled in the early twelfth century:

> The country which was called Gronland was discovered and settled from Iceland. Erik the Red was the name of the man from Breidafiord who went there and took possession of the land at the place since called Eriksfiord. He called the country Gronland, saying people would desire to go there if the country had a good name.

With this, Mr. Thorgilsson touched upon a basic human trait—the drive to dress up one's surroundings with fair-sounding names. This is why—in New York City, for example—Sixth Avenue was rebaptized the *Avenue of the Americas;* why the Lower East Side was reincarnated as the *East Village;* why Punkiesberg, the solid Dutch name of a Brooklyn neighborhood was discarded in favor of *Cobble Hill;* and why the adjacent neighborhood, North Gowanus, became *Boerum Hill*. This is why proper Bostonians tried to convert their city's ADULT entertainment (or "combat") zone into the *Liberty Tree Neighborhood;* why the Central African Republic became the *Central African Empire;* and why, on January 5, 1789, the good citizens of Vanderheyden's Ferry, New York, inaugurated the age of classical place names in the United States by voting to change the name of their town to *Troy*. This is also why, in the truly classical world, the Romans changed the name of a Greek colony in Italy from Malowenta (which meant "rich in sheep," but which the Romans misinterpreted in Latin as Maleuentum, or "ill-come") to the more auspicious *Beneuentum* ("welcome"), and why the Greeks referred to the cold and treacherous Black Sea as the Euxine, or HOSPITABLE SEA. In a general sense, too, this is why apartment houses are blessed with names like Castle *Arms* and Haddon *Hall;* why auto camps are MOTELS; why hotels are called HOUSES, and why houses are called HOMES. It is why small towns pretend to be CITIES; why normal schools become *colleges;* why colleges parade as UNIVERSITIES, and why, finally, stores and shops advertise themselves as EMPORIUMS, PARLORS, SALONS, and SHOPPES.

greens. Sex; INTERCOURSE. "Why not go after the girl? . . . She's not getting what I believe is vulgarly called her greens" (*May We Borrow Your Husband*, 1967, by—most appropriately—Graham Greene). Eric Partridge suggests that "greens," from circa 1850, may come from "garden" (sometimes, more fancifully, "garden of Eden"), a much older, circa sixteenth century, euphemism for the VAGINA (*A Dictionary of Slang and Unconventional English*, 1970).

growth stock. When the market is going down, a *growth stock* "is a stock the bank trust departments hold too much of" (*Barron's*, 2/12/73). See also RECESSION.

guidance counselor. A redundancy. What does a "counselor" do but offer "guidance"? The addition of "guidance" gives the title a FOP Index of 2.2. See also ENGINEER.

gun. The penis. A traditional punishment in the U.S. Marine Corps for a recruit who makes the grievous mistake of referring to his "rifle" as a "gun" is to require him to walk the area, holding his rifle in one hand and his penis in the other, while reciting the quaint quatrain:

> This is my rifle,
> This is my gun.
> This is for shooting,
> This is for fun.

The penis-as-gun is a classic example of the intimate associations that people make between sex and violence (see ACTION). Of course, "guns" of both types go BANG and both may cause someone to DIE. The modern "gun" seems to have taken over the historic role of "pistol," which stood for "penis" as far back as the sixteenth century. Thus, Shakespeare's *Henry IV*, Part 2 (1598) is loaded with puns on the name of Pistol, e.g., Falstaff speaking: "Here, Pistol, I charge you with a cup of sack. Do you discharge upon mine hostess." Before the invention of gunpowder elevated the penis into a firearm, it was regarded as a pointed weapon. See also PENIS and TOOL.

H

hairpiece. A wig; also called a TOUPEE or, especially in theatrical circles, a *rug*. "A hairpiece by any other name is still a cover-up" (ad for Thomas hair transplants, New York *Village Voice*, 8/21/78). A store that specializes in hairpieces is known, at its fanciest, as a *hairitorium*. In Brooklyn, *the* Hairitorium is located at 227 Duffield Street.

hair rinse. Hair dye. See also BEAUTICIAN.

Halifax. Hell, as in "Go to Halifax!" The expression dates to the seventeenth century and probably refers to Halifax, England, where judges practiced what was known as "Halifax Law," the guiding principle of which was purported to be "Hang first, try afterward." Other euphemistic but hellish locations to "go to" include *Guinea, Jericho,* and *Putney.* See also HECK.

halitosis. Scientific bad breath. "What else can ruin romance so quickly as halitosis (bad breath)? And the worst of it is that if you yourself have this insidious condition you may not even know it . . . or even realize that you are offending" (Listerine ad, *Red Star Mystery*, 10/40). "Halitosis" was popularized in the 1920s by advertising copywriters, who plucked it from medical literature, where it had been used since at least the 1870s. In Britain, the functional equivalent of "halitosis" is *oral offense.* See also BO.

handyman's special. In the real estate business, a building that has at least four walls. ". . . 'handyman's special' may walk you into the shell of a house, 'al afresco,' roofless" (*Brooklyn* [NY] *Phoenix*, 7/26/79). See also NEEDS SOME WORK and REALTOR.

hanky-panky. The general allusion to trickery may help cover up more serious matters. For example, in a discussion of what the FBI would call a SURREPTITIOUS ENTRY:

> "There's no hanky-panky about this, is there?"
> "Neither hanky nor panky. Nothing is to be abstracted from the house and nothing upset." (Josephine Tey, *The Singing Sands*, 1953)

Or, as President Richard M. Nixon said, when sorting out the reasons for getting the CIA to tell the FBI to call off its investigation of the Watergate CAPER:

> You open that scab, there's a hell of a lot of things and that we just feel that it would be very detrimental to have this thing go any further. This involves these Cubans, Hunt and a lot of hanky-panky that we have nothing to do with ourselves. (Tape of June 23, 1972, six days after the break-in)

Hannukah bush

"Hank-panky" also is useful for downplaying sexual high jinks, as in the following light verse by Balzac Schwenk about a great Transcendentalist:

> Thoreau, the misogynist Yankee
> Claimed that women and girls made him cranky;
> So both brunette and blonde
> He barred from his pond
> To make sure there was no hanky-panky.

The origin of "hanky-panky" is obscure. The "hanky" may come from the magician's handkerchief, with the "panky" being a repetition (or reduplication, as linguists say) of the first word's sounds. For another magical word, see JINGO.

Hannukah bush. A Jewish Christmas tree. "Hannukah bush" often is used facetiously and some Jews eschew the linguistic dodge and just say it like it is. By whichever name, and whether seriously or in fun, the object itself is devoid of Christian religious symbols. See also HEBREW.

happy hour. A time that is set aside for drugging the mind and loosening the inhibitions through consumption of alcoholic beverages. From a memo by the assistant chief of staff at Fort Benjamin Harrison, Indiana:

> The October Commander's call will be held at 1530, 20 October 1976. . . . The guest speaker will be Mr. Daniel J. Crowe, Indiana State Division of Addiction Services, who will discuss Industrial Alcoholism. . . . At the conclusion of the question and answer session, there will be a 'Happy Hour' in the Ballroom to afford everyone an opportunity to meet Mr. Crowe. (*Washington Monthly*, 12/76)

See also HIGH

Happy Hunting Grounds, gone to the. Dead. The pleasant circumlocution commonly is credited to the American Indians, but one wonders if the idea wasn't foisted off on them, considering that the earliest examples of the phrase's use in *A Dictionary of Americanism* come from such literary non-Indians as Washington Irving, who worked it into the *Adventures of Captain Bonneville* (1837), and James Fenimore Cooper (*The Pathfinder*, 1840). Meanwhile, during this same period, whites were referring to their heaven as "a happy land."

The Happy Hunting Grounds are only one of many possible places to which the DECEASED may be said to have traveled, depending on the persuasions of those left behind. These figures of speech were especially popular during the nineteenth century, when people stopped talking plainly about death. Among the others:

> *Abraham's bosom,* abode of the blessed dead, as in Luke XVI, 22: "the beggar died, and was carried by the angels into Abraham's bosom."
> *angels, joined the* or *with the.*
> *Arms of God, asleep in the.* Variants include *asleep in Jesus* and *safe in the arms of Jesus.*

better land/life/place/world, usually in the form of "He has gone to a better . . ."

beyond or *Great Beyond,* as in "He has been called to the beyond."

Confucius, seeing. An old Chinese saying, reportedly updated by Prime Minister Zhou Enlai who told visitors, when upon his own deathbed, "I shall soon be seeing Marx."

Davy Jones's locker. A sailor's grave. "Davy Jones," as the Devil or evil spirit of the sea, dates from at least the eighteenth century. "Davy" may come from the West Indian *duppy* (devil) and "Jones" may be a corruption of Jonah. Or Davy Jones may have been a pirate.

Eternal rest, heavenly rest, well-earned rest—all places, or states, to which one may be "called" or said "to have gone to."

Eternity, launched into. Not as an astronaut.

Fathers, gathered to one's.

glory, gone to.

Great majority, joined the. A more elaborate, more political variation is *slipped into the great democracy of the dead.*

Great Adventure, gone to the. Not an amusement park.

Green River, up. Among mountain men in the West in the nineteenth century, to send a man "up Green River" was to kill him. The phrase probably referred not so much to the Green River in Wyoming as to "Green River" knives, so stamped because they were made at the Green River works.

higher sphere, translated into. Note the elliptical verbs that are being used: *called, gone, joined, launched, slipped,* and now, *translated.* A variation: "He has been translated into another world."

home or *last home.* Informally: *gone home feet first.*

invisible choir, joined the.

Jordan's banks, went to. Or *to pass over the Jordan.*

kingdom come, gone to.

land of the heart's desire, gone to the.

mansions of rest, gone to the.

outer darkness. As a rule, bad people are said to be "cast into outer darkness," while good ones "slip into" it.

paradise, taken to.

reward, as in "He has gone to his final reward."

safe anchorage at last. A common epitaph for sailors.

Tap City. The place where high-rolling gamblers go; for a gambler, to be "tapped out" is to be broke.

undiscovered country, the. From a famous image in Shakespeare: ". . . death, The undiscovered country from whose bourn [border] No traveler returns . . ." (*Hamlet,* 1602).

valley, as in "He is asleep in the valley"; probably a discreet condensation of the twenty-third psalm, "Yea, though I walk through the valley of the shadow of death . . ." (King James Version, 1611).

wayside, fallen by the. While the rest of us go marching on?

west. The association between death and the West is old; see GO WEST.

And see also EXPIRE, PASS AWAY, REST, and SLEEP.

hard-of-hearing. Deaf; a *hard-of-hearing* person may also be said to be *auditory-impaired*. See also INCONVENIENCED and SIGHT-DEPRIVED.

harlot. A late-bloomer, comparable to PROSTITUTE for avoiding the older, harsher "whore." For example, where the first English translations of the Bible, the Wyclif versions of the fourteenth century, bluntly used *hoore*, translations of the sixteenth century frequently had "harlot," and when Noah Webster rewrote the Bible in 1833 (see PECULIAR MEMBERS for details), he cut out every single "whore," using "harlot" and other, still-blander expressions instead (e.g., *lewd woman*).

A "harlot" (from the medieval Latin *arlotus*, glutton) was originally a male, not a female—usually a boy or servant, in the sense of a buffoon, rascal, or fornicator, but also sometimes a regular fellow, a good guy. Geoffrey Chaucer employed it in the last sense when he wrote of the Sumonour in the *Prologue* to *The Canterbury Tales* (1387–1400):

> He was a gentil harlot and a kynde,
> A bettre felawe sholde men noght fynde.

"Harlot" was not applied to women until the fifteenth century, and then it encompassed such examples of feminine lowlife as jugglers, dancers, strumpets, and whores. As always seems to happen, the "worser" meanings became dominant: The term gradually was limited to women only, and to the worst kind of women at that.

"Harlot" also is distinguished for having one of the quaintest of all spurious etymologies, i.e., that it derived from the name of Arlette, or Herleve, daughter of Fulbert, a tanner of Falaise, and mother of William the Bastard, who became William the Conqueror. This etymology, favored for a long time by many students of language, was first proposed toward the end of the sixteenth century . . . which just goes to show that the whorish meaning of "harlot" had become dominant by that time.

harmonious. As applied to neighborhoods, "segregated." From a 1971 ruling in which a federal judge blamed segregation in Detroit schools on other institutions besides the school board: "For many years, Federal housing administrators and the Veterans Administration openly advised and advocated maintenance of 'harmonious' neighborhoods, i.e., racially and economically harmonious." See also MIDDLE CLASS, SEPARATE BUT EQUAL, and TURN.

harvest. The agricultural term becomes a euphemism for killing when it is applied to animals instead of vegetables.

While soft-spoken hunters of marine mammals tend to talk in terms of the annual *harvest* of seals or of gray whales, not the "catch" let alone the "killing" of them, it is the deer hunters who seem to be best at denying what they do. For example, an article on "Managing White-tailed Deer," in a New York State publication, *The Conservationist* (9–10/79), refers to the "harvesting of adult does," the "exploitation of the deer," the "annual buck take," and the issuance of "deer management permits," but not once to the "killing" of these animals. See also CULL, GAME MANAGEMENT, and SLUICE.

haystack (or **hayrick**). A haycock—and one of the many different kinds of "cocks" that Americans expunged from their language in the first decades of the nineteenth century; for details, see ROOSTER.

head. A toilet; originally a nautical expression, but now used generally on land as well as on sea, and not only by ex-military types, e.g., "'The head,' by which she meant the toilet, 'is just over there,' and she pointed to a little bucket behind a screen in the corner" (Maxwell Kenton, aka Terry Southern, *Candy*, 1965). In its original seagoing form, "head" was a topographical euphemism, alluding perhaps to a "bulkhead," next to which the "head" may be placed, but more likely to the front, or head, of a boat. On a sailing ship, this is the best place to PEE, with the sea in front and the wind behind. (And the direction of the wind is critical, as anyone who has ever tried to pee into it can testify.) See also TOILET.

health care. Medicine. Doctors who once practiced medicine now deliver *health care*, and "health" in this sense is a euphemism in the making. As Lewis Thomas says of "health" in *The Lives of a Cell* (1974):

> Sooner or later, we are bound to get into trouble with this word. It is too solid and unequivocal a term to be used as a euphemism and this seems to be what we are attempting. I am worried that we may be overdoing it, taxing its meaning, to conceal an unmentionable reality that we've somehow agreed not to talk about in public. It won't work. Illness and death still exist and cannot be hidden.

See also DELIVER.

health, reasons of. While people sometimes do have to leave jobs for *reasons of health*, this also is one of the standard face-saving explanations used to cover the exits of people who hadn't known their health was poor until they were LET GO. In the words of George Cassidy, telling why he was no longer race starter at Hialeah Park, then operated by Gene Mori: "I left for reasons of health. Mori got sick of me" (Red Smith, *New York Times*, 8/5/77). See also ILL/ILLNESS.

heavenly deception. A lie, as told by a member of the Unification Church (aka Moonie) to a nonmember. "He learned more about 'heavenly deception'—the Moonie euphemism for lying, for doing whatever is necessary to further the goals of the church" (review of Christopher Edwards's *Crazy for God*, in *The Sunday Record*, Bergen/Passaic/Hudson Counties, New Jersey, 4/1/79). The *heavenly deception* is OK because nonmembers of the church are, by definition, members of the world of Satan. "Heavenly deception" has a Fog or Pomposity Index of 7.7. See also WHITE LIE.

he-biddy. A nineteenth-century rooster or, more to the point, a cock. The euphemism was formed on the same principle as *he-cow* (for bull). See also ROOSTER.

Hebrew. Jew; once the standard euphemism, but now slightly archaic. "When the word ["Hebrew"] is used of a person in the United States today it is usually

heck

employed as a euphemism to avoid *Jew* . . ." (Bergen Evans and Cornelia Evans, *A Dictionary of Contemporary American Usage*, 1957). Theoretically, "Hebrew" should be reserved for discussions of the Jewish people of the distant past (i.e., the Hebrews of the Bible) or their language (Hebrew is the official language of the State of Israel). Its use as a euphemism for "Jew" probably is a function of Gresham's Law, as it applies to language (i.e., "bad" meanings drive out "good" ones), "Jew" having acquired many offensive associations through its misuse as a verb and adjective (to jew down, Jew boy, etc., ad nauseam). The result was that fastidious people, and nervous ones, began avoiding "Jew" even in proper contexts. Thus, as H. L. Mencken noted, "one often encounters" in newspapers "such forms as *Hebrew comedian, Hebrew holidays*, and even *Hebrew rabbi*" (*The American Language*, 1936). Use of the euphemism was by no means limited to non-Jews. A study of Jewish applicants to Yale in 1927 showed that 14 out of 91 (15 percent) answered "Hebrew" to the question "Church [*sic*] affiliation?" (Mencken, *The American Language, Supplement I*, 1945). This indecisiveness is perpetuated in institutional names, e.g., Hebrew Union College (founded 1875) and Jewish Theological Seminary of America (1876), and in the contrast between the many Young Men's (and Women's) Hebrew Associations and the various Jewish Councils and Jewish Community Centers. Nowadays, increasing pride in Jewishness has virtually overcome the word's older, negative associations, but the unusual amount of anxiety "Jew" used to cause is suggested by the number of other euphemisms for it. See also ANTI-SEMITIC, ARAB, JUICE HARP, and ZIONIST.

heck. Hell—as in "What the *heck*," "We had a *heck* of a time," "Just for the *heck* of it," "By *heck*," etc.

It wasn't so awfully long ago that American newspapers declined to print the proper name of the infernal regions, e.g., "Merlini, a magician, gets in a heck of a lot of trouble as he tries to solve a circus murder . . ." (*Columbus* [OH] *Citizen*, 9/22/40). Such reticence was by no means confined to the hinterlands. When H. L. Mencken said in a lecture on December 1, 1939, in Big Bad Gotham that "American grammar is fast going to hell" (a development that did not displease Mr. Mencken), the *Journal-American* reported on the morrow that Mr. M. had mentioned "h––l" (Mencken, "American Profanity," *American Speech*, 12/44). "Heck" seems to have come into the language about the middle of the last century, deriving perhaps from the dialectical *ecky* or *hecky*, or perhaps from "By Hector," referring to the Trojan hero. Today, it is the most common hellish euphemism, having superseded such dillies as BLAZES, HALIFAX, JESSE, SAM HILL, and THUNDER.

help. A euphemism both as a verb and a noun. As a verb, it means "to steal," in much the same sense as LIBERATE. "They helped themselves freely to the furniture of an uninhabited house" (E. Blackwell, *Booth*, 1883). As a noun, "help" quickly came to stand for "servant" in America, probably because *servant* stood for "slave." "I am Mr. ––––––'s *help*. I'd have you know . . . that I am no *sarvant*; none but *negers* are *sarvants*" (Charles W. Janson, *Stranger in America*, 1807). "Help" naturally led to *Help Wanted Ads*, frequently for such specialized positions as *Lady Help* (a servant who assisted the lady of the house; later called the MAID) or *Mother's Help*

134

(nowadays *helper*). Even *hired help* (or, more specifically, *hired man* or *hired girl*) was accepted by *the help* or *helps* themselves, where a mumbled "servant" would have caused them to walk off the job. See also SERVANT.

high. One of the older of the truly immense, not to say staggering, number of terms for describing a person who is staggering as a result of consuming too much alcohol. The oldest citation for "high" in the drunken sense in the *Oxford English Dictionary* is from 1627: "He's high with wine" (Thomas May, *Lucan's Pharsalia*). Other kinds of "high" in the seventeenth and eighteenth centuries included *altitudes* and *elevated*, as in "The man is in his altitudes, i.e., he is drunk" (Capt. Francis Grose, *A Classical Dictionary of the Vulgar Tongue*, 1796). In our own time, the meaning of "high" has been extended (along with other drinking terms, such as *buzzed, gassed, stoned,* and *zonked*) to cover the euphoria produced by non-alcoholic drugs—marijuana, for example: "The coarse seeds are made into cigarettes and the user smokes them in big puffs getting high—a state in which time seems to stand still, where the top of the head is filled with all heaven, and everything seems easy to do, better, stronger, and longer" (Stephen Longstreet, *The Real Jazz, Old and New*, 1956). The altitudinal metaphor may be reinforced by elaborating "high" into such phrases as *high as a kite* and *high spirits*, e.g.: "Once [in] a while a reporter writes that a Senator appeared in the Senate in 'high spirits.' Those on the in know the reporter means the Senator was drunk. The reader doesn't" (*New York Times*, 9/8/74).

Demonstrating the importance of alcohol in our culture, more synonyms are listed for "drunk" than for anything else in *The Dictionary of American Slang* (Harold Wentworth and Stuart Berg Flexner, 1975). The appendixes to this work include 356 terms for "drunk," and this listing is necessarily incomplete, since the set of drunken synonyms is continually changing, with old terms fading from use and new ones being created. Still, the Wentworth-Flexner listing suggests a considerable expansion in the drinker's working vocabulary from 1737, when Benjamin Franklin published a similar list of 228 terms. Franklin's listing, a continuation of a project that he had begun in 1722, at the tender age of 16, when he could find but 19 synonyms, included many words and phrases that are rarely, if ever, heard nowadays, e.g., *afflicted, been to Barbados* (where the rum came from), *cherry-merry, cherubimical, disguised, has his flag out, gold-headed, lordly, nimptopsical,* and *pigeon-eyed*. Other terms on his list are hardy perennials. Among them: *boozy, cockeyed, mellow, muddled, oiled, soaked, stewed, stiff, has a skin full,* and *half seas over* (*American Speech*, 2/40).

For other facets of what social scientists call "the drinking custom," see BEVERAGE HOST, INEBRIATED, LIBATION, SALOON, and TEMPERANCE.

highly confidential (or **sensitive) source.** A hidden microphone or wiretap, a bug; FBI-ese, from the long (1924–72) reign of J. Edgar Hoover as director of the bureau. Inanimate *highly confidential sources*, used in TECHNICAL SURVEILLANCE, should not be confused with the animate though usually cold-blooded CONFIDENTIAL SOURCE or SOURCE OF INFORMATION—FBI-ese for "informer," aka INFORMANT. See also SENSITIVE.

highly (or **usually) reliable source.** Journalese, in which "reliable" translates as "this source has supplied information before," while "highly" and "usually" mean "the information has not always been correct." Variations on the "source" theme include *highly-placed source, well-placed source,* and *responsible source.* (Can you imagine a reporter quoting an "irresponsible source"?) See also CONFIDENTIAL SOURCE, HIGHLY CONFIDENTIAL SOURCE, and SOURCE OF INFORMATION.

hit. To murder someone, or, the person who is murdered. The understated "hit" is a rare example of an evasion that is shorter than the word for which it stands. It has a negative FOP Index of -2.3. Of course, it comes from the underworld where, by definition, normal rules do not apply. "A murder is a contract. A hit is the sucker that gets killed. Remember those words, and use them. Then, even if the cops tap a phone, they won't know what you're talking about" (*The Enforcer,* film, 1950). An underworld *hit* (usually performed by a *hit man*) is the linguistic and functional equivalent of a governmental EXECUTIVE ACTION. As noted in one of the classic works of criminology:

> . . . persons with an extensive acquaintance with men of the lowest character know only too well what repugnance they feel in employing the correct expression. . . . Persons of a somewhat higher moral grade often shrink from using the word 'steal'; while the number of periphrastic expressions employed to avoid uttering the simple word 'kill' is extraordinary. (Hans Gross, *Criminal Investigation,* Norman Kendal, ed., 1934)

Among the circumlocutions: *bump off, cancel one's ticket (permanently), croak,* DISPATCH, *erase,* EXECUTE, FIX, *frag, give the business/heat/rap,* HOMICIDE, KILL (in very special circumstances), OFF, *put out,* REMOVE, RUB OUT, *score, silence, snuff out* (like a candle), *take for a ride,* TOUCH, WASTE, *wipe out,* and *zap.* For avoiding death generally, see PASS AWAY.

holy cow. New York Yankee announcer Phil Rizzuto's favorite oath (on the air, at least) and one of the most common of the many "holy" constructions available to those who wish to register shock, amazement, or whatever, without actually being profane. Others include *holy bilge water, holy cats, holy cripes, holy Egypt, holy gee, holy gosh, holy heck, holy hoptoads, holy Moses, holy smoke, Holy H. Smoke,* and *holy snakes.* Many of the combinatorial terms are euphemisms in their own right: see CRIPES, GEE, GOSH, and HECK.

home. When used to describe a private, detached dwelling, a genteelism for "house"; in all other instances, an out-and-out euphemism.

In the genteel sense, "home" was among the key words cited by Nancy Mitford as examples of the elegant and euphemistic speech by which non-Upperclass people betray their non-U-ness. Where non-U's say "they have a lovely *home,*" the U person has "a very nice *house*" (*Noblesse Oblige,* 1956). For more about U-ness and non, see DENTURES.

The tendency to drop the plainer "house" in favor of the fancier "home" shows up in many other ways. Contractors build *homes,* not *houses;* the people who buy the houses call themselves *homeowners,* not householders; the owners obtain the funds to enlarge their quarters with *home* (not house) *improvement loans,* and they fill their houses with *home furnishings* and *home appliances*. Still more euphemistically, "home" never really means "home" when used to describe an institution. Thus, a *boys' home* is a kind of jail; a *home for infants* or *children* is an orphanage; a *mental home* (see MENTAL) is a madhouse; a NURSING HOME is a combination hospital-dormitory-warehouse for old people; a *rest home* (also REST HOUSE) is the same, and a *memorial* or FUNERAL HOME is the living end. See also HOMEMADE, HOMEMAKER, and, for a notorious exception to the rule that the fancier houses are always homes, refer to HOUSE.

homemade. When pie—or anything else, for that matter—is described on a restaurant menu as "homemade," the most the diner can reasonably hope for is that it was made by human hands in the restaurant's own kitchen rather than by machines in a factory. The same principle applies in other fields. For example, the "homemade" signs displayed at political rallies usually are produced on an assembly-line basis. As one campaigner reported: "'Homemade' signs are another fraud. In a year of planning rallies, I doubt if I saw more than ten truly homemade signs, though I personally painted and distributed hundreds" (Timothy G. Smith, *New York Times*, 7/18/73). See also HOME.

homemaker. Housewife; the relevant committee of the National Organization for Women (NOW) is the National Homemakers Committee. (A divorced or widowed housewife is known technically as a *displaced homemaker*.) NOW is just following the example of other organizations. As early as 1939, the Long Island Federation of Women's Clubs "decreed that housewives should cease to be *housewives* and become *homemakers*" (H. L. Mencken, *The American Language, Supplement I*, 1945). The preference for "homemaker" reflects the general use of HOME in lieu of "house," possibly reinforced by the subconscious realization that "housewife" comes from the Old English *huswif*, which also has given us the modern "hussy."

homicide. The Latinate word for murder is preferred by police departments, as in *Homicide* Division, rather than Murder Division, although murder is their business. This usage has rubbed off on the people the police are trying to get. Thus, speaking of a Brooklyn street gang called the Crazy Homicides, Justice Sybil Hart Kooper said, "It's not a misnomer. The gang has been responsible for numerous murders" (*New York Times*, 3/28/78). Related Latinate murders include *fratricide, genocide, matricide,* and *suicide* (aka *felo de se*). See also HIT and MORALS DIVISION.

honorable, the. Mister or, with increasing frequency, Mrs. or Ms. (e.g., *The Honorable* Nancy Landon Kassebaum, Senator from Kansas).

"Honorable" is the standard honorific in a democratic society that supposedly abjures titles. It is routinely awarded to public servants from ratcatcher on up and, once given, is never given up. (A common practice: Military officers and university teachers also tend to carry their ranks with them into retirement.) To be perfectly "correct," one is led into such non sequiturs as *The Honorable* Richard M. Nixon. Perhaps this is what Elizabeth L. Post had in mind when she noted that "'The Honorable' is an expression that causes considerable confusion"

honorarium

(*The New Emily Post's Etiquette*, 1975). See also COLONEL, GENTLEMAN, and MADAM

honorarium. A payment. The Latin softens with "honor" the hard fact that the sum probably is smaller than it would be if it were called a "fee." See also EX GRATIA and REMUNERATION.

hook. To steal. An old English slang term (it goes back to the seventeenth century when hooks actually were used to steal merchandise out of store windows), the expression survives among modern youth, who dare one another to *book* small items from five-and-dime stores. The euphemistic value of "hook" ("stealing" is bad, but *booking* is OK) has been appreciated by the younger set for at least a century. For example, consider those conscience-stricken pirates, Joe Harper and Tom Sawyer: ". . . it seemed to them, in the end, that there was no getting around the stubborn fact that taking sweetmeats was only 'hooking,' while taking bacon and ham was plain simple *stealing*—and there was a command against that in the Bible" (Mark Twain, *The Adventures of Tom Sawyer*, 1876). See also APPROPRIATE and the etymology of HOOKER, below.

hooker. A whore; the slang term, paradoxically, is more acceptable in print and conversation than the honest Old English monosyllable, and so stands as a euphemism for it. "A doctor is dead—and a hooker is charged with murder! Jim Rockford is back . . ." (NBC ad, *New York Daily Metro*, 9/29/78). Even the whores themselves seem to prefer it, e.g., "'Well, I'm not a cocktail waitress, I'm a hooker, but I guess you sort of knew that'" (New York *Village Voice*, 1/2/78).

A rare, direct comparison of "hooker" and "whore," illustrating the greater palatability of the former, comes from an article in *MORE* (5/77) about the celebrities who hawk consumer products. There, the word "hooker" was always presented to readers without editorial qualification, i.e., "Nine years ago, says Jane Trahey . . . 'Nobody but hookers and Hadassah ladies wore dark fur'" or, again, referring to the many commercials for many different products by Joe Namath and Bill Cosby, "Too many hooks [meaning logical connections between celebrity and product] and one begins to smell a hooker." Whenever "whore" was used, however, the magazine carefully enclosed the stronger term in quote marks, i.e., ". . . he [meaning Cosby] threatens to replace Arthur Godfrey as the 'whore' of endorsers."

The origin of "hooker" is shrouded in mystery. The popularity of the term has been associated with Gen. Joseph ("Fighting Joe") Hooker, who commanded the Union armies for a time during the Civil War. In apparent tribute to the general's character, the women who inhabited Washington's brothels became known collectively as "Hooker's Division" or "Brigade." However, the earliest use of "hooker" to mean "whore" predates the Civil War. John Bartlett, in his *Dictionary of Americanisms* (4th ed., 1859), defined "hooker" as a "strumpet" or "sailor's trull" and opined that the term derived from the profusion of "houses of ill-fame" in Corlear's Hook, a notorious section of New York City (it also was home to a gang of river pirates called the Hookers). But Bartlett, a Bostonian, may have given sin city more than its due. The oldest citation for "hooker" in the 1976 supplement to the *Oxford English Dictionary* is from 1845 and a different part of the country: "If he comes by way of Norfolk he will find any number of pretty Hookers in the Brick row not far from French's hotel" (N. E. Eliason, *Tarheel Talk*, 1956). The use of "hooker" to mean "whore" might also stem from the usual *modus operandi*, in which the woman, like the angler-in-waiting, "hooks" her approaching customer-fish. Yet another possibility is that "hooker" acknowledges the thievery with which many whores supplement their basic earnings; a "hooker," in English slang of a couple centuries ago, was a petty thief (also called an *angler*), who used a stick with a hook on the end to steal goods out of shop windows. (See HOOK.) It may be purely a coincidence—an example of evolutionary convergence—but in Paris, the man who tries to steer pedestrians to the whorehouse for which he works is called an *accrocheur*, literally "hooker," from the verb *accrocher*, to hook. See also PROSTITUTE.

hoor (or **hooer**). Whore; the mispronunciation is an aural euphemism. See also BURLEYCUE and PROSTITUTE.

horsefeathers. Horse shit, aka horse MANURE. The term is thought to have been invented during the 1920s by William De Beck (d. 1942), a comic-strip artist, who also is credited with *heebie-jeebies, hot mama,* and *hotsy-totsy.* The euphemistic flavor of the expression is best conveyed by setting it in context. From John O'Hara's *Appointment in Samarra* (1934):

> "And my orders is to see that you keep your knees together, baby."
> "Horse feathers," she said.

hose. Describing "hose" as a "western" term in his *Dictionary of Americanisms* (1859), John Russell Bartlett explained: "Stockings is considered extremely indelicate, although long socks is pardonable." And even today, the entry for "Stockings-Women's" in the Manhattan, New York, *Yellow Pages* (1979–80) redirects one's fingers to the more genteel "Women's Hosiery" and "Hosiery-Retail." See also LIMB and LINGERIE.

Hospitable Sea. The *Euxine*—the ancient Greek name for the Black Sea, originally (and far more accurately) known as the *Axeinos* (inhospitable) sea. "Greeks were fond of describing the strange customs of the peoples of the Euxine, or 'Hospitable Sea', as they euphemistically called it . . ." (A. R. Burn, *A Traveler's History of Greece,* 1965). And what was life like in that part of the world? Burn continues: "The climate was described as 'four months cold and eight months winter', when (though really it was only true of some winters) the very sea froze, and metal wine amphoras had been known to crack, leaving the contents standing up. 'If you pour water on the ground, you will not make mud', says Herodotus, 'but if you light a fire, you will.'" Well over 2,000 years later, the Black Sea still retained its inhospitable reputation. As George Gordon Lord Byron noted in *Don Juan*:

> There's not a sea the passenger
> e'er pukes in,
> Turns up more dangerous breakers
> than the Euxine.

139

hot seat

For more about geographical euphemisms, see also GREENLAND.

hot seat. The electric chair; perhaps the most common of the many oblique references to this particular article of furniture. More picturesque is the rhyming variant "hot squat," as in "You couldn't ever rise from the hot squat" (A. Hynd, *Public Enemies*, 1949). In "American Euphemisms for Dying, Death, and Burial," (*American Speech*, 10/36), Louise Pound noted that the euphemisms for electrocution "are more terse and forbidding than the word itself, yet somehow suggestive of nonchalance in the face of punishment." In addition to the basic *burn*, *cook*, and *fry*, metaphors for the electric chair and the act of electrocution include *the chair*, *(take the) electric cure*, *electric stool*, *flame chair*, *(get a) permanent wave*, *hot plate*, *juice chair*, and *(ride) Old Smoky*. See also CAPITAL PUNISHMENT.

house. A brothel or whorehouse. *House of ill-repute* (or *ill fame*), *disorderly house*, and *sporting house* are among the printable euphemisms that came into vogue in American newspapers following the Civil War (H. L. Mencken, *The American Language*, 1936). Other *houses* of this kind include *accommodation house*, *assignation house*, *barrelhouse*, *bed house*, *boardinghouse*, *call house*, (see CALL GIRL), *case house*, CAT HOUSE, *crib house*, *doss house*, *fancy house* (see FANCY), *flophouse*, *joy house*, *occupying house* (see OCCUPY), *parlor house*, and *quean house* (see QUEEN). Then there is the French *maison close* (closed house) and the "little house" or BORDELLO. All the English houses probably derive from the STEW, or "hothouse," originally a public bathhouse. In William Shakespeare's *Measure for Measure* (ca. 1604), Mistress Overdone "professes a hothouse, which I think is a very ill house, too." See also MASSAGE PARLOR and PROSTITUTE.

hung. The generalization qualifies as a euphemism though it might also be described as a dangling past participle. Usually referring to male sexual equipment, the term appears in such combinations as *hung like a bull*, *hung like a chicken*, *hung like a horse*, and *hung like a rabbit* (the last is not a reference to size but to being continuously on the make). The basic expression is at least a couple hundred years old. The *Lexicon Balatronicum* (anon., "A Member of the Whip Club," 1811) translates the following sentence, "The blowen was nutts upon the kiddey because he is well-hung," as "the girl is pleased with the youth because his genitals are large." See also GENITALS.

ill/illness. Sick—or worse, even unto death. To those with sharp ears, who believe people define themselves by the words they use, "ill" is one of the key indicators for distinguishing non-Upperclass people from those Upperclass types who are "sick," have "false teeth," not DENTURES, and who live in "houses," rather than HOMES (Nancy Mitford, *Noblesse Oblige*, 1956). More seriously, there was the announcement on October 9, 1979, on Radio Kabul, Afghanistan, that former President Noor Mohammad Taraki had died "of a serious illness he had been suffering for some time." Later, it developed that Mr. Taraki had been either shot, or strangled, or perhaps, both. See also BRIEF ILLNESS; HEALTH, REASONS OF, and LONG ILLNESS.

illegal. Criminal. Some great minds are able to perceive a significant difference between "illegal" and "criminal," so they use the first as a euphemism for the second when they, their friends, or their friends' friends are caught in the act. Thus, Ronald Reagan, then governor of California, asserted that "criminal" was too harsh a word to apply to the burglars who pulled off the Watergate CAPER. "Illegal is a better word than 'criminal' because I think criminal has a different connotation," said Reagan, adding that it had been "sort of ignored" that those arrested were "well-meaning individuals" (UPI, 5/2/73). Subsequently, this usage was ratified by the head Watergater himself. Asked by David Frost about his approval of the Huston plan, entailing such criminal activities as burglary (SURREPTITIOUS ENTRY) and mail opening (MAIL COVER), Richard M. Nixon replied: "Well, when the President does it, that means it is not illegal" (Frost, *I Gave Them a Sword*, 1978). See also CRIMINAL (or ILLEGAL) OPERATION, IMPROPER, and, for more wit and wisdom from the Reagan family, CONSUMER COMMUNICATION CHANNEL.

imbibe. To drink alcohol, elegantly. "Imbibe" was once a general term for absorbing other things besides liquid—air, tobacco smoke, and knowledge among them. For example: "Young women are apt to imbibe another bad habit, namely the use of slang" (Josiah G. Holland, *Timothy Titcomb's Letters to the Young*, 1858). Today, however, the other meanings have been routed by the overuse of the affected "imbibe" for the act of consuming liquor, as in "What's wrong? Did you imbibe too much last night?" As a rule, those people who *imbibe* instead of "drink" become INEBRIATED instead of "drunk." One hopes their heads hurt just as much. See also HIGH and LIBATION.

impact attenuation device aka **impact attenuator.** A crash cushion, frequently a plastic barrel filled with sand or simply an old oil drum, placed between some unyielding highway obstruction and oncoming traffic. "Impact attenuation device" cushions "crash cushion" with a FOP Index of 2.5. See also MEDIAN DIVIDER and PERSONAL FLOTATION DEVICE.

improper. Wrong; not right. The prefix "im" comes from the Latin "in," meaning "not," but "im" doesn't sound nearly as bad as "not" in English. So, for those who wish to obscure a misdeed, the first step is to call it "improper." The psychology is the same as when ILLEGAL is substituted for "criminal."

Extremely artful use of "improper" was made by Patrick J. Buchanan, a speechwriter for President Nixon, when testifying to the Senate Watergate Committee in 1973 about the strategy he had advocated of interfering in the internal affairs of the Democratic party. The questioning went like this:

> SEN. DANIEL K. INNOUYE (D., Hawaii): Do you think it's ethical?
> BUCHANAN: I don't think it's unethical.

> SEN. JOSEPH M. MONTOYA (D., New Mexico): Do you think it's proper?
> BUCHANAN: I don't think it's improper.

As Hugh Rank pointed out in *Language and Public Policy* (1974), a landmark publication of the Committee on Public Doublespeak of the National Council of Teachers of English, Buchanan's testimonial technique was based on what George Orwell called the *not un*-formation. In Orwell's words: "It is easier—even quicker, once you have the habit—to say *In my opinion it is not an unjustifiable assumption that* than to say *I think*" (*Politics and the English Language,* 1946). Besides blurring the meaning, the *not un*-formation has the advantage of distancing the speaker from any ill consequences of his or her thought. (AFFIRMATIVE for "yes" has the same effect.) Orwell, in a rare moment of naïveté, suggested that it should be possible to laugh the *not un*-formation out of existence. He believed people might cure themselves of the habit by memorizing the sentence: "A not unblack dog was chasing a not unsmall rabbit across a not ungreen field." Unfortunately, this formula works only for those who actually want to kick the *not un*-habit—and not everyone does.

For more about the good work of the Committee on Public Doublespeak, begin with AIR SUPPORT.

incident. A generalized term for covering up crisis, catastrophe, death, disaster, etc. For example, the Japanese, foreshadowing American practice (cf., the Korean POLICE ACTION and the Vietnam CONFLICT), referred to the war that they started with China on July 7, 1937, as "the China incident." And some forty years later, when Japanese politicians were caught with wads of American money in their pockets, the scandal was called the *Rokkiedo Jiken,* or Lockheed incident. (See CONSULTANT.) On a more elementary level, an *incident* might be a fight, an automobile accident, or even a death. Thus, a psychiatrist, Dr. Milton C. Holar, told a Brooklyn, New York, court that some modest conditions might be attached to the release of a former New York City police officer from a mental institution (see MENTAL) because there had been an "incident"—meaning in this case the unprovoked killing of a youth by the officer (*New York Times,* 12/2/78). However, the potential of "incident" seems to have been realized most fully in the nuclear power business. (This is true also of the synonymous EVENT.) For example, practically everybody and his brother, from President Jimmy Carter on down, managed to refer to the 1979 crisis at the Three Mile Island nuclear plant in Pennsylvania as an *incident*. (Carter did so on April 1.) Even *Science*, which is relatively immune to this particular disease, and which did use the word "crisis," also allowed as how "The Three Mile Island incident has given a new credibility to antinuclear groups . . ." (4/13/79). Not all nuclear *incidents* are quite as scary as this one, but there are an awful lot of them. As the *New York Times* reported: "Atomic Plants had 2,835 Incidents in '78" (headline, 4/15/79). Going one step further down the blandness scale, the Nuclear Regulatory Commission files these *incidents* (malfunctions? mishaps? mistakes?) under the heading of *regrettable occurrences*. See also ACCIDENT, EPISODE, INVOLVEMENT, IRREGULARITY, PROBLEM, SITUATION, and THING.

inconvenienced. Crippled. The National Inconvenienced Sportsmen's League sponsors athletic competitions for people (i.e., women, too, despite the association name) who have lost—or lost the use of—their legs, arms, or eyes. See also HARD-OF-HEARING and SIGHT-DEPRIVED.

incursion. Invasion. The invasion that made the euphemism famous occurred in February 1971, when 16,000 South Vietnamese soldiers, supported by American artillery and airplanes, invaded Laos, hoping either to cut the Ho Chi Minh trail or to force the North Vietnamese to stand and fight a major battle in which they would surely be beaten. (Shades of Dienbienphu!) The operation was called an *incursion*, apparently in an effort to avoid the demonstrations (four students killed at Kent State University) that had been evoked by a similar invasion the previous year of Cambodia. As Edwin Newman reports: "Rarely had the importance the government attached to language been made so clear. An incursion, Washington called it, and there were official objections to our calling it an invasion, evidently in the belief that incursion implied something softer than invasion did, and that an incursion was permissible where perhaps an invasion was not" (*Strictly Speaking*, 1974).

A major battle was fought, as it turned out, but it was the invaders (incursers?) who were defeated, and forced to conduct a WITHDRAWAL, or hasty retreat. Administration apologists asserted that the return of the South Vietnamese proved the "invasion" to have been an "incursion" all along, but they obviously hadn't looked it up in their *Funk & Wagnalls*, which defines "incursion" as "A hostile, often sudden entrance into a territory; an invasion" (*Funk & Wagnalls Standard College Dictionary*, 1974). For other forms of incursion, see ACTIVE DEFENSE, OVERFLIGHT, and PROTECTIVE REACTION.

independent school. Private school. The exclusive connotations of "private school" do not sit well with liberal parents, many of whom attended public school themselves, so they prefer to bundle their kids off to *independent schools*, so named because they are "independent" of the public system. The private schools have even organized themselves into the National Association of Independent Schools.

in-depth treatment. An additional 30 seconds on a TV network news show, where ordinary stories are covered in one minute, 15 seconds, and more complicated, more important subjects, such as inflation or the energy crisis, may get the *in-depth treatment* of one minute, 45 seconds. For more TV talk, see ACTION and PROTECTIVE COVERAGE.

Indian. Nigger, as in the old counting rhyme, "Eenie, meenie, mine, mo/Catch an Indian by the toe." It is significant, too, that Agatha Christie's *Ten Little Indians* was originally published in England as *Ten Little Niggers* (1939). See also TIGER and TRAMP.

indicate. To say. The vague "indicate" (FOP Index of 3.3) makes a useful protective hedge for those who are speaking under oath. By testifying to what other people *indicated*, as opposed to what they actually "said," the witness gains a great deal of freedom in reconstructing events (invariably to the witness's own advantage) while minimizing the possibility of a perjury charge. So useful is the device that it tends to trip off the tongue even when there is no real need for it. Thus, during the Senate Watergate hearings in 1973, Jeb Stuart Magruder, deputy director of the Committee for the Reelection of the President, recalled an exchange with G. Gordon Liddy, counsel to CREP (pronounced "Creep") and its chief resident burglar: "Well, I simply put my hand on Mr. Liddy's shoulder, and he asked me to remove it, and indicated that if I did not, serious consequences would occur." Here, the "consequences" also were something of a euphemism. What Mr. Liddy *indicated* was that if the offending hand was not removed, he would kill Mr. Magruder.

See also AT THIS/THAT POINT IN TIME and NO RECALL (or MEMORY or RECOLLECTION) OF.

indigenous personnel. See also PERSONNEL.

indigent. Poor. "'Indigent circumstances'! sneered the other. 'Fine fancy words for saying he was hard up'" (John Dickson Carr, *The Bride of Newgate*, 1950). See also LOW-INCOME.

indisposed/indisposition. People who are *indisposed* are usually slightly and euphemistically sick. For example, when a woman is said to be *indisposed*, chances are she is suffering from an unmentionable *female complaint* (see MENSTRUATE), from an unspeakable diarrheal infection (see MONTEZUMA'S REVENGE), or from some entirely fictitious illness. The last was the case with Fanny Hill when Mr. H., her keeper of the moment, suddenly appeared and began making advances over terrain that a lusty servant boy had thoroughly conquered but a few minutes before. In Miss Hill's words: ". . . I pretended a violent disorder of my head, and a feverish heat, that indispos'd me too much to receive his embraces. He gave in to this, and good-naturedly desisted" (John Cleland, *Memoirs of a Woman of Pleasure*, 1749). Of course, men also may become *indisposed* or suffer *indisposition*. Male *indisposition* often comes out of a bottle, e.g., "There had been an officer 'staggering on parade' through 'indisposition' . . ." (Elizabeth Longford, *Wellington, The Years of the Sword*, 1969). See also DISPOSE.

industrial relations. Labor relations. The "industrial" avoids recognizing the existence of "labor" even while dealing with it. Some magnates, it seems, are physically unable to pronounce the word "labor"; whether the impediment is the result of a hereditary or occupational disease has yet to be determined. "Elizabeth Stanton Haight . . . was married yesterday afternoon to Matthew McGowan O'Connell . . . his father is vice president in charge of industrial relations for the Bethlehem Steel Corporation" (*New York Times*, 6/11/78). See also TECHNICIAN.

inebriated. Drunk; INTOXICATED. The long-winded "inebriated," with a FOP Index of 2.8, is something of a caste mark: As a rule, gentlemen are said to be *inebriated* (or *in their cups* or *under the weather* or *feeling no pain*, etc.) while the lower classes are "blotto," "stinko," "stewed," or "falling down drunk." The basic principle was expressed as early as 1839 in an essay by Henry Rogers: "To be 'drunk' is vulgar; but if a man be simply 'intoxicated' or 'inebriated', it is comparatively venial." See also HIGH and IMBIBE.

inexpressibles. Trousers, breeches; in extended usage, any form of underwear.
    "Inexpressibles" seems to be the oldest of a series of breathless euphemisms for the garments that cover—dare one say it?—the LIMBS. The series includes *indescribables, indispensables, ineffables, . . . unwhisperables*. For the full listing, see the reigning champ—UNMENTIONABLES.
    "Inexpressibles" comes out of the remarkable period of prudery that preceded Queen Victoria's long reign (from 1837). The oldest example of the euphemism in the *Oxford English Dictionary* is from *Rowland for Oliver* (1790), by Peter Pindar (John Wolcott):

> I've heard that breeches, petticoats, and smock
> Give to the modest mind a grievous shock,
> And that the brain (so lucky its device)
> Christ'neth them inexpressibles, so nice.

informant. Informer; a snitch or stoolie.
    Anthropologists routinely speak of their *informants* and so do the police. The more professional-sounding term, with its soft, French *ant* ending, has been popular in legal circles for some time, e.g., from Edmund Burke's *Report on the Affairs of India* (1783): "It was the last evidence of the kind. The informant was hanged." Today, *informants* are legion. A rule of thumb is that there are two for every regularly employed AGENT, which would mean that the Justice and Treasury departments alone account for some 30,000. The sheer number makes many people uneasy, including some *informants*, and they, accordingly, are casting around for a new name for their calling. Three government *informants* at a trial of antiwar veterans in Florida in 1973 described themselves variously as a *political monitor*, an *intelligence operative*, and a *source of information*. Other possibilities that have been suggested include *investigator* and *undercover operator*. See also CONFIDENTIAL SOURCE, FIELD ASSOCIATE, INVESTIGATOR, MONITOR, OPERATIVE/OPERATOR, and SOURCE OF INFORMATION.

inheritance tax. This puts the most beneficial construction on what is, in truth, a death duty. See also LIFE INSURANCE.

inmate. A convict or prisoner:

inoperative

"How does your institution function in regard to prisoners?"
"We call them inmates." (*The Jericho Mile*, WABC-TV, 3/18/79)

When *inmates* are feeling poorly they have what are known as *inmate health encounters*—in New York State, at least, where a memorandum of November 15, 1976, of the Department of Correctional Services not only specified that "Sick Call" henceforth would be called "Inmate Health Encounters," but decreed that medical treatment would be upgraded by changing the "Facility Hospital" in each of the state's prisons to an "Inpatient Component." See also CORRECTIONAL FACILITY.

inoperative. False; in the immortal word of Ronald L. Ziegler, press secretary to President Richard M. Nixon, on the afternoon of April 17, 1973: ". . . this is the operative statement. The others are inoperative." Those "others" were all the denials the White House had been making for months of any involvement in the Watergate COVER-UP. The occasion of Ziegler's great *mot* was a press conference, following an announcement by the president that there had been "major developments" and "real progress . . . in finding the truth" about Watergate. Prior to the announcement, Ziegler had consulted with the president about how to handle the questions he was bound to be asked. In particular, Ziegler was concerned about reconciling the new announcement with one by the president on August 29, 1972, in which he had said—citing a report by John W. Dean III, which Dean had never made—"I can state categorically that his investigation indicates that no one in the White House staff, no one in this Administration, presently employed, was involved in this very bizarre incident." Their conversation foreshadowed the famous reply:

> P: You could say that the August 29 statement—that . . . the facts will determine whether that statement is correct.
> Z: I will just say that this is the operative statement. (*The White House Transcripts*, 1974)

Which is what Ziegler tried to do at the press conference. A half-dozen times, he repeated, "This is the operative statement," until R. W. Apple, of the *New York Times*, asked if it would be fair to infer from this that the other statement "is now inoperative." Ziegler agreed and thus, in one glorious gulp, ate practically every word he'd said about Watergate for the previous 22 months. The overwhelming reaction of the press corps was summed up at a briefing the next day by Clark Mollenhoff, who shouted at Ziegler: "Do you feel free to stand up there and lie and put out misinformation and then come around later and say it's all 'inoperative'? That's what you're doing. You're not entitled to any credibility at all" (*New York Times*, 4/19/73).

See also CLARIFY, MISSPEAK, PLAUSIBLE DENIAL, and WHITE LIE.

insane. Crazy; a euphemistic stopover on the road from "mad" to *mentally ill.* See also MENTAL.

institute/institution. High-class names for such more-or-less grubby realities as industrial lobbies (the Manufactured Housing Institute represents the companies that make MOBILE HOMES); for schools of various sorts (from New York's Stenotype Institute and Speedwriting Institute to Princeton's Institute for Advanced Study); for jails, or penal *institutions,* for adults as well as for young people (Root-ee toot-toot/Root-ee toot-toot/We're the girls from the Institute); and for madhouses (mental *institutions*) and other places (*institutions* for the crippled, the deaf, or the blind) to which INCONVENIENCED people may be consigned or even *institutionalized.* When distinguished as "the institution" or, for emphasis,' "the peculiar institution," the reference is to the old-time American practice of keeping slaves. "If all earthly power were given me, I should not know what to do, as to the existing institution" (Abraham Lincoln, 10/16/1854, Peoria, Illinois). Lincoln, to his credit, did not, even at this early date, always speak in roundabouts. Later, in the same speech, he declared: "Slavery is founded in the selfishness of man's nature—opposition to it, in his love of justice." See also SERVANT.

instrument. A somewhat old-fashioned penis or vagina. *Instruments* have been employed at least since the time of Geoffrey Chaucer. For example, from *The Wife of Bath's Prologue* (ca. 1387–1400):

> In wyfhode wol I use myn instrument
> As frely as my Makere hath it sent.
> If I be daungerous [stingy], God yeve me sorwe!
> Myn housbonde shal it have bothe eve and morwe.

As for masculine *instruments,* we have it on the authority of Ms. Fanny Hill that bigger is not necessarily best: "Then I saw plainly what I had to trust to: it was one of those just true-siz'd instruments, of which the masters have a better command than the more unwieldy, inordinate siz'd ones are generally under" (John Cleland, *Memoirs of a Woman of Pleasure,* 1749). See also PENIS, VAGINA, and WEAPON.

intercourse. Short for "sexual intercourse," as in "One fifth of our eight million 13 and 14 year olds are believed to have had intercourse" (Planned Parenthood-World Population, fund-raising leaflet, rec'd 11/78). N.B.: The term may also apply to BISEXUAL doings, e.g., "Incredible as it may sound now, I still didn't accept that intercourse was possible between two men" (David Kopay and Perry Deane Young, *The David Kopay Story,* 1977).

"Intercourse" probably is the most common evasion today for what is usually known technically as COITION or COPULATION and informally as f—— or making love (see F—— and MAKE LOVE). The sexual connotations of "intercourse" are dominant today, but it was not always thus. The word's oldest meanings revolve around communication, as between countries or the inhabitants of different localities, especially with regard to commercial traffic. The oldest sexual "intercourse" in the *Oxford English Dictionary* comes from 1798, when the granddaddy of all population planners had occasion to refer to "An illicit intercourse between the sexes" (Thomas R. Malthus, *An Essay on the Principle of Population as It Affects the Future Improvement of Society, etc.*). Once the sexual meaning of "intercourse" was established, other meanings began to fall by the wayside. Exceptions to the trend include Intercourse, Pennsylvania, founded in 1813 (the original settlers are credited with having "commerce" or "trade" in mind) and the various nineteenth-century "intercourse laws," regulating trade between whites and Indians. Today, the sexual meaning is so dominant that it is asking for trouble to use the word in any other context—as evidenced by the brouhaha that was raised when the Swarthmore College catalog carried the announcement (ca. 1950) that "intercourse between male and female students will be under the direct supervision of the Dean of Women" (Mick Hill, M.D., personal communication, 1977).

As with other basic bodily functions, a great many euphemistic synonyms for "intercourse" exist. They can be divided into three somewhat overlapping categories: the Latinate, the slangy, and the bland metaphoric. Besides those already mentioned, they include:

The Latinate: CARNAL KNOWLEDGE, *conjugal rights* (see CONJUGAL), CUN-NILINGUS, FELLATIO, and FORNICATION.

The slangy (more commonly encountered in active form, as verbs): BANG, FRENCH, FRIG, GO (as in *go all the way, go the limit,* and *go on*), GREENS, IT, LAY, MAKE, ROGER, SCREW, SHACK UP (WITH), and SOIXANTE-NEUF.

The metaphoric: ACTION, BUSINESS, CONGRESS, CONNECTION, CONVERSATION, FAVORS, *fraternization* (military: see FRATERNIZE), GENERATION, INTIMACY, LIE/LIE WITH, OCCUPY, RELATIONS, SERVICE, and, finally, SLEEP WITH.

interesting condition or **situation** or **state.** Pregnant. Dating to the mid-eighteenth century, the euphemism was particularly popular in the nineteenth. See also EXPECTANT/EXPECTING.

interfere with. The British equivalent of the American MOLEST and, like it, both a generalization for sexual assaults other than rape and a euphemism for rape itself. The noun is "interference," as in "Before the War . . . the rape would have been mentioned delicately. 'Any sign of—interference?'" (Julian Symons, *Bloody Murder*, 1972). See also ASSAULT.

interment. A fancy burial, much favored by undertakers (FUNERAL DIRECTORS). The official organization in the field (so to speak) is the Interment Association of America. In general, *interment* involves the disposition of a CASKET in a CEMETERY or MEMORIAL PARK, while "burial" is of a "coffin" in a "graveyard." Technically, too, in *interment*, the grave, or SPACE, is neither "dug" nor "filled," but *opened* and *closed*. Variations on the "interment" theme include *entombment, inhumation,* INURNMENT, and, most beautifully, *sepulture*. See also PASS AWAY and PLANT.

intermission. Another term for yet another commercial break, usually qualified as a "brief intermission." See also MESSAGE.

intern. A prisoner or, as a verb, to hold prisoner, during time of war. Sometimes fancied up into "internee" (analogous to DETAINEE), the term is usually but not necessarily restricted to enemy nationals. Among the exceptions were Japanese-Americans in World War II, e.g., "Mr. [Frank] Tomori was interned at a Twin Falls, Idaho, detention camp because he was Japanese" (UPI, 4/29/76). See also DETENTION.

interpret the mood of. Stylish plagiarism in the fashion business, i.e., to knock off or rip off, as in, "Let's interpret the mood of Laurent's latest." And as more than one buyer has noted: There is no copyright on design. See also APPROPRIATE and REVERSE ENGINEERING.

interrogation. The general term for questioning often conceals the means by which the answers are elicited, i.e., torture. ". . . trained Brazilian torturers traveled to military academies in neighboring countries to conduct courses in what is euphemistically known as 'interrogation'" (Jean-Pierre Clavel, *New York Times*, 8/4/74).

Traditional forms of *interrogation* include beatings (aka the *third degree*), the application of electrical shocks (BELL TELEPHONE HOUR), and various forms of water torture (or WATER CURE). More subtle, and of more recent development, is *deep interrogation*, which borrows some of the techniques of brainwashing (e.g., sensory- and sleep-deprivation, starvation, and fatigue) to break victims psychologically. The British have used *deep interrogation* in Northern Ireland. In a letter reprinted in the *New York Times*, Graham Greene accused his countrymen of adopting a double standard, not hesitating to cry "torture" when *deep interrogation* was used by Communists or Fascists, but passing it off as "ill treatment" when they themselves were found doing it. He characterized the term, and the process, this way: "'Deep interrogation'—a bureaucratic phrase which takes the place of the simpler word 'torture' and is worthy of Orwell's '1984'—is on a different level [lower, for being better organized and more cold-blooded] of immorality than hysterical sadism or the indiscriminating bomb of urban guerrillas" (12/2/71). See also AVERSION THERAPY, BRAINWASH, and *the question* in AUTO-DA-FÉ.

intestinal fortitude. An elegant substitute for "guts," itself the mildest of the FOUR-LETTER WORDS. "Intestinal fortitude" is a rarity—a common euphemism whose invention can be attributed with some confidence to a particular person, in this case to Dr. John W. Wilce, who thought of the phrase two or three years after he joined the faculty of Ohio State University in 1913. At OSU, Dr. Wilce served as football coach as well as professor of clinical medicine and preventive medicine. One day, while traveling by streetcar between his football office and a class at the Medical College, the phrase popped into his head. No doubt the streetcar was near the midpoint of its journey and his mind was half on football and half on medicine. The invention was spurred by Dr. Wilce's dislike of the swearing that was rampant on football fields of the era. He used the phrase initially in a lecture to the football squad and the metaphor proved striking enough to be remembered and reused (Tom Burns Haber, *American Speech*, 10/55). For those who lack the *intestinal fortitude* to say "guts," other possibilities include PLUCK and the rather riskier COJONES.

intimacy/intimate. Euphemisms, as noun and adjective respectively, for sexual relations, usually illicit and usually heterosexual. In divorce court proceedings, *intimate relations* adds up to CRIMINAL CONVERSATION. People who enjoy *intimate relations* frequently are described as being *intimately acquainted*. Naturally, they get to know each other at *intimate meetings* (trysts). A very partial exception to the strictly sexual meaning of "intimate" occurs in the case of *intimate apparel*, or *intimates*, denoting the last feminine defenses to *intimacy*. See also INTERCOURSE and, for more about the euphemisms women wear next to their skin, continue with LINGERIE.

intoxicated. Drunk; one of the two (with INEBRIATED) most common highfalutin terms for describing a person whose system is overloaded with alcohol. "Intoxicated" derives from the Latin *toxicum* (poison), which in turn comes from the Greek *toxikon*, the poison that Homer's heroes put on arrowheads (the Greek word for "bow" was *toxon*). In the original sense, then, arrowheads were intoxicated, not people, and the word implied that the poison was smeared on, not IMBIBED. See also HIGH.

inurnment. The process of placing the ashes of a burnt body (the CREMAINS) into an urn and depositing it in a *cinerarium* or *columbarium* (CEMETERIES for pots); the act of *inurning*, or potting. "Inurnment" has flourished at least since the 1930s, especially in the hothouse atmosphere of Southern California, and not even Evelyn Waugh was able to kill it, though he gave it a good shot in *The Loved One* (1948): "Normal disposal is by inhumement, entombment, inurnment or immurement, but many people . . prefer insarcophagusment." See also INTERMENT and LOVED ONE, THE.

inventory leakage/shrinkage. Theft, as from a department store. See also APPROPRIATE.

investigative phase. Experimental. Asked how he got patients to agree to experimental operations, Dr. Denton Cooley, famed for his daring procedures, replied: "You don't tell patients it's experimental, you say it's in the investigative phase" ("Nova," WNET-TV, NYC, 2/23/78).

investigator. A detective. Sherlock Holmes, the greatest detective ever, was a private detective ("unofficial consulting detective," in his own words), but if he were detecting today, he would be listed in the *Yellow Pages* (Manhattan, New York, 1979–80) under "Investigators, Private." Even the police, who are public detectives, seem to be catching the disease, e.g.: "The detectives (now called 'investigators') resented the encroachment of younger patrol officers in the investigative work" (Joseph Wambaugh, *The Choirboys*, 1975). Scientists also like to dress up as "investigators," but the scientific "P.I." stands for "Principal Investigator," not "Private Investigator," as in the romantic James Rockford, P.I., of television's "Rockford Files." See also AGENT, CONSULTANT, and OPERATIVE/ OPERATOR.

invigorating. Cold. "Come on in; the water's invigorating" is the standard cry of shivering swimmers to warmer, smarter friends on the shore.

Invincible Armada, the. A gloriously exaggerated name for a most ingloriously fated fleet.
　　In Lisbon, in 1588, the Spanish collected a fleet of 130 ships for the invasion of England. Before sailing, the captain general of the armada, the duke of Medina

Sidonia, issued a report on the strength of his forces. It was a detailed report, the kind that would be stamped "top secret" today, but which the Spanish pridefully published, so that the whole of Europe, including the English if they cared to read it, would tremble at the armada's strength. Garrett Mattingly continues: "In the official publication . . . the fleet is called 'La felicissima armada'—the most fortunate fleet—but popular parlance at once substituted 'invincible' in tribute to its awesome strength. Thanks to the Spanish taste for irony, this armada has been known as 'La Invincible' ever since" (*The Armada*, 1959).

Of the 130 ships that left for England, barely half got back to Spain. Of course, the Spanish sense of irony is almost as exquisite as their tortures; see AUTO-DA-FÉ.

involved with/involvement. Whatever the context, the studiedly neutral "involve" ordinarily conceals more exciting action. Typically, the reference is to an AFFAIR. As Emily Post puts it: "A sensible executive who wishes to go far in his company does not become 'involved' with a woman in his office unless they are both free to do as they please" (Elizabeth L. Post, *The New Emily Post's Etiquette*, 1975). The meaning of "involvement" varies somewhat. A person who is *involved with* another person may be said to have an *involvement*, but when a nation has an *involvement*, it usually is fighting a war, e. g., the long American *involvement* in Southeast Asia. (See also ERA.) Then there is the nondescriptive "involvement," which can easily be a crime. For example: "Haldeman said that what he considered to be the real problem for the White House had nothing to do with the Watergate break-in itself, but concerned what he called 'other involvements'—things that an investigative fishing expedition into the break-in could uncover and exploit politically" (Richard M. Nixon, *RN: The Memoirs of Richard Nixon*, 1978). See also PROBLEM and THING.

irregularity. An omnibus term, useful for glossing over a wide range of theoretically abnormal conditions or actions. For example:

1. Constipation, as in the adman's discreet query, first posed in the 1930s, "Are you suffering from irregularity?"
2. Dishonesty, as when a spokesman for Canadian Prime Minister Pierre Elliott Trudeau's office said the PM would reimburse Air Canada for his wife, Margaret's, travel expenses if there were any "irregularities" in her use of her free pass for nonofficial trips (UPI, 4/2/77).
3. Pregnancy, as in the following advertisement by a nineteenth-century abortionist: "Madame Restell's experience and knowledge in the treatment of cases of female irregularity is such as to require but a few days to effect a perfect cure. Ladies desiring proper medical attendance will be accommodated during such time with private and respectable board" (*Boston Daily Times*, 1/2/1845).

See also ACCIDENT, INCIDENT, and REGULAR.

it. The neuter pronoun obviously can be made to stand for almost anything one prefers not to discuss in colorful detail and, over the years, "it" has. A century or so ago, when chamber pots were more common than they are today, "Fetch it," could mean "Get the CHAMBER." "It" also has served as a euphemism for the sexual organs, male and female, and for their mutual operation, e.g.: "The thing is, most of the time when you're coming pretty close to doing it with a girl—a girl that isn't a prostitute or anything, I mean—she keeps telling you to stop. The trouble with me is, I stop" (Holden Caulfield in J. D. Salinger's *The Catcher in the Rye*, 1951). Here, Holden is using "it" in precisely the same sense as Randle Cotgrave did more than 300 years previously, when defining *frétiller* as "to . lust to be at it," in his French-English dictionary of 1611. See also MAKE.

As a personal sobriquet, "it" is most closely associated with Clara Bow, who became the "It Girl" by starring in the movie *It*, based on Elinor M. Glyn's best-selling novel, *It*, of 1927. Clara's "It" was "sex appeal," sometimes coyly abbreviated to *SA*. So strong is the association with La Bow that it often is forgotten that Madame Glyn did not limit her definition of "it" in *It* to women, e.g., "He had that nameless charm, with a strong magnetism which can only be called 'It.'" It seems possible, too, that Glyn lifted "it" from Rudyard Kipling, who employed "it" this way in *Traffics & Discoveries* (1904): "'Tisn't beauty, so to speak, nor good talk necessarily. It's just It. Some women'll stay in a man's memory if they once walk down a street."

See also AFFAIR, BUSINESS and THING.

J

janitor. A caretaker; the person charged with cleaning and heating a building. Deriving from the Latin *janua*, door, which also gives us the god Janus and the month January, "janitor" originally meant a porter or doorkeeper, as in "The Keys for St. Peter, reputed the Janitor of heaven" (Robert Plot, *The Natural History of Staffordshire*, 1686). Caretakers began to assume the janitorial title about the beginning of the eighteenth century. The trend was especially noticeable in egalitarian America; the class-conscious English, by contrast, tended to retain "caretaker" and "porter," thus helping to keep those functionaries in their places. Of course, the upgraded *janitors* looked down upon those they had left behind, including feminine members of their—er—profession, e.g.: "The janitors object to allowing the janitresses to be so styled. 'Scrubwoman' is the term they insist on applying to their female rivals" (*New York Sun*, 11/29/1903). In time, the grimy connotations of the job wore off on "janitor," too. See also CUSTODIAN.

Jesse. Hell; a popular nineteenth-century euphemism, frequently used as a threat when about to scold or thrash a person, in such phrases as "If you don't watch out, you are going to catch Jesse," or "I'm going to give you most particular Jesse." The origin of the term is obscure. Since earlier examples exist, it definitely does not come, as some have thought, from the name of the wife of Gen. John C. Frémont, whose campaign for president in 1856 featured the slogan, "Give them Jessie!" The allusion may be to the biblical "rod out of the stem of Jesse" (Isaiah, XI, 1). "Give him Jesse" may or may not be entirely extinct; it *has* been a few years since it was last reported officially: "In February, 1946, I heard the expression used in a game of bridge by a player from Sidney, Nebraska, when her partner was ruffing an opponent's suit" (*American Speech*, 4/46). See also HECK.

Jiminy Cricket. The cute Walt Disney character notwithstanding, this is a euphemism for "Jesus Christ," on a par with *Judas Christopher, Judas Priest*, CRIPES, and JINGO. The "Jiminy" comes from "Gemini," which goes back to at least 1664, and which may derive from the Latin *Jesu domine*. "Jiminy" is sometimes used alone, as in "By Jiminy" or—perhaps a transitional form—"'Oh, geeminy, it's *him*,' exclaimed both boys in a breath" (Mark Twain, *The Adventures of Tom Sawyer*, 1876). "Jiminy" also may be finished off in other ways besides the cute "Cricket," e.g., *Jiminy Christmas, Jiminy crackers, Jiminy criminy, Jiminy cripes*, and *Jiminy whiz*. See also the basic GEE.

jingo, by. A euphemism for "By Jesus," the nonsense word having been substituted for the sacred name. ("Jingo" also has been used by conjurors for some hundreds of years; *hey jingo*, for making objects suddenly appear, is the opposite of *hey presto*, for making them vanish.) The euphemistic meaning is demonstrated clearly in the oldest of the citations for the word in the *Oxford English Dictionary*: Translating *Rabelais* in 1694, Peter Motteux began a sentence, "By jingo quoth Panurge   " where the French original started *"Par Dieu . . ."* Today, "jingo" more often refers to a bellicose patriot or warmonger. The modern meaning derives from the euphemism, as it was used in a British music hall ditty of 1878, written by G. W. Hunt, and popularized by "The Great MacDermott." The song was seized upon by home-front warriors who wanted England to fight Russia, then making one of her recurring expressions of interest in Turkey and the warm-water port of Constantinople. The chorus went:

> We don't want to fight yet by Jingo!
> if we do
> We've got the ships, we've got the men,
> and got the money too.
> We've fought the Bear before, and while we're
> Britons true,
> The Russians shall not have Constantinople.

To their great disappointment, no doubt, the original *jingoes* never got to fight. Great Britain sent its Mediterranean fleet into Turkish waters and Russia backed down. The euphemistic sense, however, is by no means obsolete. When Gen. Mohammad Zia ul-Haq, leader of the military government of Pakistan, was asked if he intended to yield power to civilians by holding elections, he replied: "By jingo, yes, unless the heavens fall, unless a new situation emerges that I have not foreseen and which I do not anticipate" (*New York Times*, 9/7/77). See also GEE and HANKY-PANKY.

job action. A strike or slowdown by public employees. Apparently created in response to laws forbidding public employees from going on strike, "job action" is a deliciously perverse phrase, a truly fine example of Reverse English, with its apparent, literal meaning being precisely the opposite of the actual meaning, i.e., job *in*action. A similar roundabout for "strike" in Britain is "industrial action." A wildcat strike in the United Kingdom is, by this token, an "unofficial industrial action." See also SICK OUT and WORKING TO RULE.

john. The most common American euphemism for (1) the toilet, and (2) a whore's customer or TRICK.
      The first kind of "john" is much the older. A Harvard College regulation of 1735 put it this way: "No freshman shall . . . go into the fellows' cuzjohn." This colonial "cousin john," to give it its full title, is apparently a close relative of *jakes*, *jacques*, and *jack's house* (or *place*), all of which were earlier forms of PRIVY. Naturally, this use of "john" elicited similar proper-name euphemisms. Thus, nineteenth-century Americans sometimes spoke of going to the *Joe* and even today a woman's toilet may be referred to as a *jane*. At Vassar, in the Roaring Twenties, the "john" was called "Fred." (Vassar girls have always been different.) Other proper names for the improper place include *Ruth*, MISS WHITE, and *Jones*, as in *Jones's place*, *Mrs. Jones*, and *Widow Jones*. See also TOILET.
      The "john" who patronizes a whore is a faceless person, in the sense of "John Doe," the fictional anyman and everyman created some centuries ago for use in court proceedings. Here "John," merely denotes "male," just as it does in such other expressions as *John Lack-Latin*, *John-of-all-trades*, *John Chinaman*, *Johnny-come-lately*, and JOHN THOMAS.

As a purchaser of sexual FAVORS, "john" once implied a steady, fairly durable RELATIONSHIP, in which the man paid for the woman's upkeep. "John" replaced "Daddy" (as in Cole Porter's "My Heart Belongs to Daddy," 1938) in this sense about 1945, according to the *Dictionary of American Slang* (Harold Wentworth and Stuart Berg Flexner, 1975). As time wore on, and the pace of modern life quickened, the term began to be applied to the male participants in relationships of ever shorter duration. Now, a couple of minutes suffices, e.g., "One night she brought in $1,000. Conventioneers make generous johns" (New York *Village Voice*, 1/2/78). See also PROSTITUTE.

John Thomas. The penis—and the most elegant of the various Christian names (e.g., *dick*, PETER, and ROGER) commonly bestowed upon it; perhaps from *John Thomson's man*, a Scottish expression, dating to the sixteenth century, for a man who was so devoted to (or browbeaten by) his wife as always to be guided by her. The penile sense was popularized by D. H. Lawrence: "'John Thomas! John Thomas!' and she quickly kissed the soft penis" (*Lady Chatterley's Lover*, 1928). Variations on the "John Thomas" theme, all with the same meaning, include *Jack*, *John*, *Johnnie*, and *Johnson*. See also ATHLETIC SUPPORTER, JOHN, and PENIS.

joint. The leg of a fowl in nineteenth-century America; the human PENIS in the twentieth. The earlier version of the euphemism amused and confused British travelers, who thought of a "joint" in terms of beef or VENISON. Thus, W. F. Goodmane wasn't sure what to do when asked "by a lady, at a public dinnertable, to furnish her with the first and second joint" (*Seven Years in America*, 1845). See also DRUMSTICK and WHITE MEAT.

journalist. Newspaper and magazine reporters can be forgiven for elevating themselves into "journalists," but there is no excuse for that oft-encountered contradiction-in-terms, the journalless "TV journalist." See also ENGINEER.

Jove. The name of the supreme Roman deity serves as a euphemism for "God" in such exclamations as "By Jove! here comes the Coroner" (Mary E. Braddon, *Wyllard's Weird*, 1885). "Jupiter," which means "father of the Gods" (from *Jovis* + *pater*), has been used in the same euphemistic way, e.g., "By Jupiter, I had it from her Arme" (William Shakespeare, *Cymbeline*, 1610?). Both forms remain current, at least in the comics. For example: "Jumpin' Jupiter, Buck. Barney and I need your help if we're gonna' claim all this uranium for earth before other planets find it. . . . [and later] By Jove, that will be the end of the evil Pounce!" (Robert C. Dille, *The World of Buck Rogers*, 1978). See also GOSH and GREAT SCOTT.

juice harp. Jew's harp. The name of the instrument has been associated with the Jews for some 400 years. It also used to be called a *Jew's trump* (or *trounk*). Whether or not the name was intended originally to be derogatory is not known, but it almost certainly was uneasiness over saying "Jew" that inspired the much later development of "juice harp," which was the standard euphemism in the 1940s and 1950s on radio and TV broadcasts. Other alternatives include *jaw harp* and, more discreetly and perhaps not even euphemistically (ignorance of the instrument's

true name may be the cause), *mouth harp*. For background on avoiding "Jew," see
HEBREW.

juvenile delinquency. Youthful crime, where the criminal is passed off as a
delinquent. "A high proportion of the world's famous gangsters—including most of
the gunmen of the Old West—were adolescents, and nobody paid much
attention to the fact. Today, offenses by high-school kids are 'juvenile
delinquency' rather than crime, which seems to put the matter in an entirely
different light" (Martin Mayer, *The Schools*, 1961).

K

Kamikaze. The Japanese word translates as *divine wind*, or *wind of the gods*, hardly suggesting to the uninitiated the terrible, suicidal airplane attacks to which it was applied. The Kamikaze Corps was organized in 1944. It was the Japanese response to the increasing skill of American pilots and the development of the proximity fuse, which caused antiaircraft shells to explode whenever they passed near their targets. The two factors had combined to make it virtually impossible for Japanese planes to get close enough to U.S. ships to damage them by conventional means. The World War II *Kamikaze* took the name from the *Kamikaze* of 1281, a real divine wind—a typhoon that wrecked an invading Mongol fleet. The explosive-laden *Kamikaze* planes often attacked in mass formation, inscrutably called *Kikusui*, or *floating chrysanthemum*. They exacted a fearful toll: In the Okinawa campaign alone, they sank 21 ships outright, damaged 43 others so badly they had to be scrapped, and put another 23 out of action for 30 days or more. See also DISPATCH.

keister; also **kiester, keyster, keester, kister.** An acceptable substitute for "ass," where the three-letter word might still be frowned upon. "A swift kick in the keester" (Garson Kanin, movie, *Born Yesterday*, 1951). ". . . if he moves his keister . . ." ("Kojak," CBS-TV, NYC, 9/2/77). "Keister" is a low slang term that has been generalized considerably; originally, it referred just to the anus or the VAGINA. This is because a "keister" also was a suitcase, satchel, trunk, or similar container—and people have often used their lower orifices as hiding places for jewels, heroin, skeleton keys, and what-have-you. The original sense of the word is retained in such underworld expressions as *keister buster* (a safecracker), *keister mark* (the victim of a luggage thief), and *keister plant* (narcotics concealed in the rectum). See also ARSE.

kept. Maintained or supported for sexual reasons or SERVICES. Traditionally, it was women, misses, mistresses, HARLOTS, and others of the feminine persuasion who were kept, as in "A kept mistress too! my bowels yearn to her already" (John Dryden, *The Kind Keeper; or Mr. Limberham, A Comedy*, 1678). Men, too, may be *kept*, but in that case they are usually called *gigolos*, which is the masculine counterpart of *gigole*, French for a tall, thin woman; a STREETWALKER, or dance-hall girl. See also PROSTITUTE.

kickback. A bribe. The distinction is fine, akin to that between ILLEGAL and "criminal," but nevertheless important to those in the business of disbursing them, since "kickback" puts the blame on the recipient, while "bribe" places the onus on the giver. For example, take Lockheed Aircraft Corp. and the $22 million in grease that it applied to palms abroad: "Daniel J. Haughton, Lockheed's chairman, in his testimony before the [Emergency Loan Guarantee] board refused to characterize the payments as bribes, explaining that one of his lawyers . . . preferred to call them 'kickbacks.'" In this instance, the translation was supplied immediately by Secretary of the Treasury William E. Simon, who, doubling as chairman of the loan guarantee board, took exception to Haughton's remarks and criticized Lockheed's "apparent long-standing practice of resorting to bribery to sell its products in foreign markets" (*New York Times*, 8/26/75). For more about Lockheed's *kickbacks*, see COMMISSION and CONSULTANT.

kill. Murder. As grim as it is, "kill," meaning "to deprive of life" (and in its very oldest recorded sense merely "to strike" or "to hit"), is a blander, less personal word than "murder," a legal term for an "unlawful, malicious, and intentional killing." Hence, in certain very special situations, "kill" can be used as a euphemism for taking the edge off "murder." Thus, commenting on the bombing that caused the death of Earl Mountbatten of Burma, a 79-year-old off on a family yachting outing, Tom Duffy, a spokesman for the Irish Republican Army in the United States, opined: "I think the killing—not the murder—was just part of the war that is going on" (*New York Times*, 8/29/79). See also EXECUTE (another favorite term of terrorists or, if you prefer, *freedom fighters*), HIT, SHOT, and YAH! YAH!

king-size. Doubletalk for longest, largest, biggest, in the case of products (except for cigarettes, which also come in the still-longer *super-king* size); a euphemism for fat, in the case of persons.

Bedding manufacturers turn out *king-size, queen-size,* and *regular* beds, with the royal nomenclature eliminating the necessity of ever having to refer to one of their items as "medium" or, worse yet, "small." *King-size* cigarettes work on the same principle. With people, though, the motive is different. As Bernard Levy, a clothier whose stores cater to "men of royal proportions" (sizes 44 to 60 regular), says: "Fat is one word we'd never, never dream of using. Nor are we fond of portly, oversized or heavyset. When referring to our customers, we much prefer to say king-sized" (*New York Times*, 5/5/78). See also LARGE, PORTLY, and REGULAR.

knock up. To render pregnant—the most common informal description of the DELICATE condition; usually encountered in the past tense. "Nicky is 14. She is one of Jolly Jim's main girls. She earns him $300 a night. And she's managed to get herself knocked up" (New York *Village Voice*, 1/2/78).

"Knock," minus the dangling preposition, is of some antiquity. Capt. Francis Grose began his definition of "knock" in *A Classical Dictionary of the Vulgar Tongue* (1796) with "To knock a woman; to have carnal knowledge of her." (See CARNAL KNOWLEDGE.) It is tempting to think that the sexual "knock" stems from "knock" in the sense of a sharp blow or rap, since this would tie in with the etymology of F——, but it is also possible that it comes from "nock," which was defined as "To perform the act of generation on a female," by John Ash, in *The New and Complete Dictionary of English*, of 1775. (See also GENERATE/GENERATION.) Still earlier, John Florio's Italian-to-English dictionary of 1598 translated the suspicious-looking *cunnata* as "a woman nocked." This kind of "nock," in turn, probably stems from "nock" in the sense of "notch" (e.g., the nock in the butt end of an arrow). The nock-that-is-a-notch is an old term both for the VAGINA and for the POSTERIORS, especially the cleft between them. In the asinine sense, "nock" is Standard

English, though not particularly polite. Witness the term's oldest example in the *Oxford English Dictionary*: "Yf hys tale be not lyckly Ye shall lycke my tayle in the nocke" (John Heywood, *The Play of the Wether*, 1533).

Coming forward in time, for a change, British derivatives of the sexual "knock" have included *knocking-shop* (or *-house* or *-joint*) for brothel; *knocking jacket* for nightgown; and *knocker* for the male thing that does the *knocking*. (This last is quite a difference from the American *knockers*, meaning breasts; see BOSOM.) Conspicuously absent from the British derivatives is "knocked up" in its pregnant sense. To the British, the phrase has entirely different meanings. For example, when Madame D'Arblay (Frances Burney) indited in her diary on February 7, 1770, "Here is a lady who is not at all tired . . . and here am I knocked up," she meant only that she herself was tired. For a time, this usage coexisted with the other in America. Thus, in 1864, Mary A. Dodge could mourn the language to which she, as a woman, was restricted by convention, complaining: "Men can talk slang. . . . But between women and these minor [slang] immoralities stands an invisible barrier of propriety—waves an abstract flaming sword in the hand of Mrs. Grundy. . . . I should like to call my luggage *traps*, and my curiosities *truck* and *dicker*, and my weariness being *knocked up* . . ." (*Country Living and Country Things*). Obviously, Ms. Dodge hadn't read *The Life of Col. David Crockett, Written by Himself*, and published four years before she herself wrote. In it, Colonel Davy noted: "Nigger women are knocked down by the auctioneer and up by the purchaser." (For a scholarly rewrite of Crockett's words, see NEGRO.) Within 20 years, however, the "bad" meaning of "knocked up" was well enough known that polite Americans were avoiding the phrase altogether. As Mark Twain explained to an Englishman: "When you are exhausted you say you are *knocked up*. We don't" ("Concerning the American Language," *The Stolen White Elephant*, 1882). Nor would an American host today ever say to a woman guest, as an Englishman might, "I'll knock you up at eight o'clock tomorrow," meaning only that he'll awaken her by knocking on her door at that hour. Numerous are the shoals of slang between England and the United States; for two of the most treacherous, see PECKER and SCREW.

know. The biblical verb for sexual INTERCOURSE, the reference being to knowledge in its fullest carnal sense. "And Adam knew Eve his wife; and she conceived, and bore Cain, and said, I have gotten a man from the Lord" (Genesis, IV, 1, King James Version, 1611). Though Eve assigned less than full responsibility to Adam, it is clear that from Adam's point of view, to know Eve was to love her. See also CARNAL KNOWLEDGE.

L

labor organizer. "This is the age of public relations. [He] is not a goon; he's a labor organizer" ("Rockford Files," WPIX-TV, NYC, 1/3/80). See also PUBLIC RELATIONS.

ladies/gentlemen. The politest of the various sex-related designations for public toilets; others include *ladies/gents; women/men; her/his; little girls'/boys' room,* and such local variants as *mermaids/mermen* (Gurney's Inn, Montauk, New York, 1979). Restaurants, meanwhile, tend to lapse into foreign languages on toilet doors even when their menus are in English, e.g., *damen/herren; femmes/hommes; señoritas/señores.*

While the simpler "women" and "men" probably are more common today, the upperclass "ladies" and "gentlemen" are routinely applied even in situations where there may be some doubt about the social standing of the users of the facilities. Thus, Green Point, a maximum security CORRECTIONAL FACILITY in New York State, boasts a *ladies room* for visiting wives and, uh, *lady friends* of the prisoners. For sheer subtlety, however, the United States is unable to hold a candle to the British (see RETIRING ROOM), let alone the South Africans. Consider the fine gradations on a row of 12(!) WC's at a railroad station outside Capetown (from *American Speech,* 10/49): First Class European Ladies; First Class European Gents; First Class non-European Ladies; First Class non-European Gents; Second Class European Ladies; Second Class European Gents; Second Class non-European Ladies; Second Class non-European Gents; Third Class European Ladies; Third Class European Gents; Third Class non-European Ladies, and, finally, Third Class non-European Gents.

A visiting American would, of course, be classified as "European" under this system (providing he or she were white). This system is known technically as SEPARATE DEVELOPMENT (or FREEDOMS). See also LATRINE, REST ROOM, and TOILET.

lady. Once a popular euphemism for WOMAN in the United States and Great Britain, "lady" has become virtually extinct in an age that prefers to pretend that class distinctions do not exist and that gracious behavior does not count. Occasionally, one does run across a "lady," e.g., the Ladies Professional Golf Association; The Ladies Clinic, of Omaha, Nebraska; in personal ads ("Looking for warm, healthy, home-oriented young lady, 22–34, for devoted relationship."); in public addresses ("Good evening, ladies and gentlemen"), and in public signs (see LADIES/GENTLEMEN). Then there are the poor, benighted males who are anxious not to offend liberated women by saying "girl friend" and so stumble onto "lady friend," thereby impaling themselves upon Eric Partridge's pointed opinion: "Only those men who are not gentlemen speak of their women friends as *lady friends,* and only those ladies who are not ladies speak of themselves as *charladies* and their men friends as *gentlemen friends*" (*Usage and Abusage,* 1973).

"Lady"—it comes from the Old English word, *blǽfdīge,* meaning "loaf-kneader"—originally denoted wives of lords and other women of comparatively elevated stations in life, but the word has been used loosely for a long, long time, e.g., *lady of the night*, *lady of pleasure*, and *lady of easy virtue*, all of which are euphemisms for PROSTITUTE. Thus, Samuel Pepys told his diary on May 30, 1668, that it "did make my heart ake" to hear the bawdy details of a friend's visit to "my Lady Bennet and her ladies; and there their dancing naked, and all the roguish things in the world" (*The Diary of Samuel Pepys*, Henry B. Wheatley, ed., 1893–99).

Not until the nineteenth century did "lady" take on airs of false refinement. In America, its heyday coincided with the Golden Age of euphemism—circa 1820–80, by H. L. Mencken's reckoning. A number of foreign visitors remarked on this usage. Mrs. Frances Trollope, mother of novelist Anthony, recalled with considerable irritation in *Domestic Manners of the Americans* (1832) that the residents of Cincinnati, Ohio, referred to every female in sight as a "lady," with the notable exception of herself. Speaking of themselves, the townfolk might say "the lady over that way takes in washing" or "that there lady, out on the Gulley, what is making dip-candles," but she herself was just "the English old woman." Several years later, Miss Harriett Martineau, another British tourist, was startled when a jailer in Nashville, Tennessee, replied to her request to see the "women's" cells by saying: "We have no ladies here at present, madam. We have never had but two ladies, who were convicted for stealing a steak . . ." And so it went. In 1838, James Fenimore Cooper inveighed against "lady" in *The American Democrat* (see SABBATH for details), but even he was unable to stem the tide. By 1845, New York City boasted such establishments as a Ladies Oyster Shop, a Ladies Reading Room, and a Ladies Bowling Alley.

Another development of this period was the rise of magazines for "ladies." *Ladies Magazine*, founded in 1828, merged nine years later with its leading rival, *Godey's Lady's Book*, whose publisher, Louis A. Godey, always spoke of his audience as "fair Ladies" or "fair readers." Declared Mr. Godey: "Nothing having the slightest appearance of indelicacy, shall ever be admitted to the *Lady's Book*" (John Tebbel, *Media in America*, 1974). *Ladies' Home Journal* came at the end of the Golden Age, growing out of a newspaper supplement started in 1879, but this was just about "lady's" last fling. Already, "woman" was being pushed to the fore by suffragists (not "suffragettes"; they were English). "Sales ladies" were being replaced by "saleswomen," and in 1897, when *Home* magazine took a new name, it became *Woman's Home Companion*. The English, by this time, had caught the "lady" disease themselves, but where the English used, and overused, *lady-doctor*, *lady-golfer*, *ladies' wear*, and even *lady dog*, Americans tended in the twentieth century toward woman doctor, woman golfer (except for the affected LPGA), and women's wear. A final, ladylike Anglo-American distinction is made in the case of LADYBIRD.

For more on the ups and downs of the general words for human beings of feminine gender, see FEMALE, MADAM, and WOMAN; for comparison's sake, see GENTLEMAN.

ladybird. An English or somewhat affected American ladybug. The English aversion to "bug" probably stems from the desire to avoid saying even one syllable of the dread word "buggery." (The English also have euphemized the common bedbug as a *B.*, *B. flat*, or *gentleman in brown*, while the innocent baby buggy is known to them as a "pram.") "Bug" itself has a curious origin, apparently stemming from the Middle English *bugge*, meaning an object of terror, such as a hobgoblin or scarecrow; this sense of the word survives in bogey, bogeyman, bugaboo, and bugbear. The "bugger" of buggery, meanwhile, comes from *Bulgarus* (Bulgarian), a term applied to a number of heretical sects, particularly the Albigensians of the twelfth and thirteenth centuries, who were accused of practicing this particular method of birth control. As for "ladybird," it is an old possessive form, equivalent to Our Lady's Bird (or Bug). As a term of endearment (e.g., Claudia Taylor "Ladybird" Johnson), it has been around for a while: "What, lamb! What, ladybird! God forbid!—Where's this girl?" (Shakespeare, *Romeo and Juliet*, ca. 1594). Of course, the Bard was, as almost always, playing with words: "Ladybird" in his time could mean a tart or lewd woman as well as a pretty little thing. Which is why the Nurse, suddenly aware of the double meaning, follows the endearment with "God forbid!"

landfill. Garbage; also a garbage dump. See also EFFLUENT and SANITATION MAN.

landscape architect. What the artful "gardener" blossoms into. See also ENGINEER.

lane. Alley. From the fourteenth through the mid-twentieth centuries, people bowled in "alleys," e.g., "An hundredth knightes, truly tolde/Shall playe with bowles in alayes colde" (*The Squyr of Lowe Degre*, pre-1400). Today, however, most "alleys" are called "lanes," thus dispensing with the grimy, back-alley connotations of the original term. At the same time, the "gutters" of the alleys have been converted to *channels*. It is probably no coincidence that these changes occurred as bowling was becoming a FAMILY recreation.

language arts. Educationese for what used to appear on report cards as "English"; variants include *language skills* and *communications arts*. "'Language Arts Dept.' is the English office" (Bel Kaufman, *Up the Down Staircase*, 1964).

large. All things are relative, but "large" is more relative than most, especially in stores and supermarkets. Olives, for example, are marketed in a host of exotic sizes, such as *behemoth, mammoth,* and *supercolossal,* all of which make *large* olives look pretty small. In another context, when gauging the sizes of women, the *large* or *larger* woman is fat. As with DELUXE and FIRST CLASS, the relativistic "large" causes displacements all along the scale. See also KING-SIZE, MEDIUM, PERSONAL, and REGULAR.

late. Dead—as in "the late lamented" or in the title of John P. Marquand's Pulitzer Prize winning novel, *The Late George Apley* (1937).

The main difficulty with "late" is knowing when to stop using it. It seems ridiculous to refer to "the late Mr. Jones," when Mr. Jones has not been on the premises for the last 15 or 20 years, or more. Yet this is done regularly. Consider the following invitation:

You are cordially invited to attend
the second
"COLONEL CHARLES LEWIS DAY"
in
Bath County, Virginia
honoring the 242nd Anniversary of
the birth of
COLONEL CHARLES LEWIS
late Commander of the Augusta County Regiment
who fell at
The Battle of Point Pleasant
October 10, 1774
opening engagement of the American Revolution

As if the confusion over time were not enough, "late" also creates redundancies, as in "Please accept my condolences upon the loss of your late husband," where "late" and "loss" (see LOSE/LOSS) refer to the same thing. About the best to be said for "late" is that it is by no means a late invention, e.g., from William Caxton's *The Book yf Eneydos* (1400): "Her swete and late amyable hosbonde." See also DECEASED.

latency period. This is how psychiatrists manage to drain the magic out of "youth." See also YOUNG.

late unpleasantness. A war, specifically the American Civil War, aka THE WAR BETWEEN THE STATES. Popularized by Petroleum Vesuvius Nasby (David Ross Locke, 1833–88), who meant it satirically, the phrase was taken seriously by Southerners who preferred not to discuss the lost war by name. Reports of the euphemism's death are probably premature: ". . . in many other Southern communities, the Civil War—that 'late unpleasantness' as it has been called in parlors from Charleston to Memphis—is finally losing its fascination" (*New York Times*, 7/26/75). See also TROUBLE and UNFORTUNATE INTERRUPTION.

latrine. A military toilet. The term comes immediately from the French, whose army seems to have had more influence linguistically than militarily (see MATERIEL, PERSONNEL, and TRIAGE), but it is rooted ultimately in the Latin *latrina*, a contraction of *lavatrina*, which, in turn, comes from *lavare*, to wash. See also LAVATORY and TOILET.

launder. A clean word for dirty business: For example, when dealers in used (or PREVIOUSLY OWNED) cars turn back odometers as, rumor has it, they do from time to time, it is correct to say that the mileage on the vehicles has been *laundered*. In politics, business, and organized crime, it is cash that is *laundered*, e.g., speaking of the funds used to finance the burglars who (almost) pulled off the Watergate CAPER: "They traced one check to a contributor named Ken Dahlberg. And apparently the money was laundered out of a Mexican bank and the F.B.I. has found the bank" (H. R. "Bob" Haldeman, quoting John W. Dean III

lavatory

in *The Ends of Power*, Haldeman with Joseph DiMona, 1978). See also CONTRIBUTION and SANITIZE.

lavatory. A Latinate WASHROOM, occasionally used for the principal fixture as well as for the place, e.g., "Albert closed the door and sat down on the lavatory" (J. T. Story, *Something for Nothing*, 1963). "Lavatory," sometimes abbreviated in Britain to *lav*, comes from the Latin *lavare*, to wash, as does LATRINE. Prior to the nineteenth century, a *lavatory* or *lavatorium* really was a place for cleaning up. Thus, the typical medieval monastery or convent had a *lavatorium*, which was for washing, and a *rere-dorter* (= behind the dormitory) or *necessarium*, which was not for washing. See also NECESSARY, REST ROOM, and TOILET.

law. The Lord, or *Lawd*; popular variations in the nineteenth century include *laws, lawsy, lawdy,* and *law sakes alive*, as well as such nonblasphemous exclamations as *Land alive!* and *Land's sake alive!* ". . . but laws-a-me! he's my own dead sister's boy . . ." (Aunt Polly, speaking of the hero of Mark Twain's *The Adventures of Tom Sawyer*, 1876). See also ADONAI and GOSH.

law and order. Doubletalk for social and political repression; a traditional rallying call for conservatives who wish to impose order without too fine a regard for law. The phrase is an old one, dating to at least the sixteenth century, and its true meaning is evident from the ways in which it has been used over the years in American politics. For example, in 1842, when Rhode Island presented the curious spectacle of having two sets of elected officials at the same time, one group having been elected "illegally" under a new constitution that gave the vote to all adult males, and the other having been elected "legally" under the state's seventeenth-century constitution, which restricted suffrage to property-owners (and which virtually disenfranchised Providence and other cities in the bargain), the party that opposed the more democratic system was, almost inevitably, "The Law and Order Party." In the next decade, another such party surfaced, this time in poor, bleeding Kansas. It, too, was highly antidemocratic: ". . . the pro-slavery party agreed . . . to change the name of the party from pro-slavery to the law and order party" (*Lawrence* [KS] *Republican*, 8/6/1857). In our own century, *law-and-order* signs sprouted on the floor of the 1920 Republican National Convention during a demonstration for Calvin Coolidge, whose only claim to fame was his declaration during the Boston police strike in 1919: "There is no right to strike against the public safety by anybody, anywhere, anytime." Most recently, in the tumultuous 1960s, "law and order" was repopularized by conservatives on the national and local levels, usually when attacking civil rights and antiwar demonstrators, Chief Justice Earl Warren and the Supreme Court, and "crime in the streets." As the Republican candidate for president in 1968, Richard M. Nixon denied that "law and order" is "a code for racism" (speech, Washington, D.C., 9/8/68), but those on the receiving end of "law and order," 1960s-style, saw things differently: "As black activist Floyd McKissick has remarked, 'Law and order really means "Let's keep the nigger in his place"'" (*New York Times Encyclopedic Almanac*, 1970). By the 1970s, the phrase had become so badly tainted by its conservative associations that when liberals decided to make *law and order* their issue, too, they had to scratch around for another name for it; see SAFETY IN THE STREETS.

lay. An informal but printable three-letter euphemism for the greatest of the FOUR-LETTER WORDS, as a verb and as a noun. Thus, *New York* magazine, which will only go so far as "f——k" (see F——), doesn't blink an eye at "lay," e.g., quoting TV producer Liz Bolen: "I want to show ballsy women who get laid—or who can say 'No I don't want to,' . . ." (5/29/78).

The most interesting thing, etymologically, about "lay" is its apparent newness, with the oldest example in the *Dictionary of American Slang* coming from as recently as 1930 (Harold Wentworth and Stuart Berg Flexner, 1975). The second most interesting thing, etymologically, about "lay" is that, in keeping with our increasingly liberated age, the term is no longer restricted to feminine objects. As one of the heroines of the British TV series, "Rock Follies" (aired in the United States on WNET-TV, NYC, in 1977), says to a once and future (male) bedmate: "As a human being you're a disaster area, but as a bundle of sexual energy, you're a great lay." See also INTERCOURSE, LIE/LIE WITH, and MAKE.

leak. Crude perhaps, but less so than "piss," and so marginally more acceptable. "Leak" has graced the writings of some of the greatest writers of all time, e.g., William Shakespeare: "Why, they will allow us ne'er a jordan [a chamber pot, or CHAMBER], and then we leek in your chimney . . ." (*Henry IV*, Part 1, 1597). Then there is Jonathan Swift, on the perils of consuming too much liquid on one's wedding night: "Twelve cups of tea (with grief I speak)/Had now constrain'd the nymph to leak" (*Strephon and Chloe*, 1731). It was also Shakespeare who provided one of the more elegant euphemisms for the euphemism in *The Winter's Tale* (1610–11) when the rogue, Autolycus, putting on the manner of a courtier, instructs Old Shepherd and his son: "Go.   I will but look upon the hedge and follow you." See also PEE.

learning situation. A classroom. See also SITUATION.

leave. Rank hath many strange and wonderful privileges: "An enlisted man goes on furlough; an officer goes on a leave" (Anatol Rapoport, *Semantics*, 1975). See also FURLOUGH, which itself becomes a euphemism in civilian life, and, for another of rank's privileges, OTHER THAN HONORABLE DISCHARGE.

lechery. Rape, Italian-style. "There are no reliable statistics on the number of rapes in Italy because most do not get reported. When they are, they are often listed as lechery" (*New York Times*, 12/5/76). See also MOLEST.

legend. A pack of lies, told by a spy. "'A legend is an operational plan for a cover,' according to one CIA official. 'A legend is a false biography,' according to a KGB counterpart" (*New York Review of Books*, 5/4/78). See also COVER STORY and WHITE LIE.

legislative advocacy leadership. Lobbying. "Learning the nuts and bolts of lobbying, students . . . attend classes in legislative advocacy leadership at Georgetown University" (picture caption, *Front Line*, 1/2/78).

le mot Cambronne. *Merde;* see SHORT FRENCH EXPLETIVE, A.

let go. To fire, as in "I'm sorry, but we will have to let you go." This is probably the most common of the many euphemisms for dismissal from a job. For sheer variety, this set of euphemisms rivals those for death itself (see PASS AWAY). The frequency says something about the necessity of employment in our society. See also AT LIBERTY, DISCHARGE, EXCESS, FURLOUGH, LOSE, OUTPLACEMENT, REDUNDANCY, RELEASE, RELIEVE, RETIRE, RIF, SELECT OUT, SEPARATE/SEPARATION, SURPLUS, and TERMINATE/TERMINATION.

liaison. Illicit sexual relations; lovemaking without marriage and, sometimes, without love, e.g.: "Of course it is manifest that my liaison with Mrs. Mayhew had little or nothing to do with love. It was demoniac youthful sex-urge in me and much the same hunger in her . . ." (Frank Harris, *My Life and Loves,* 1925). See also AFFAIR.

libation. An overly fancy drink, almost always alcoholic; a verbal pink lady for those who can't take their language straight. "—Have you time for a brief libation, Martin? says Ned" (James Joyce, *Ulysses,* 1922).

In ancient times, a "libation" was the wine or other drink poured out for the gods, but mere mortals have been taking sips for themselves for some centuries: "Libations to his health, or, in plain english, bumpers were poured forth to the Drapier" (John Boyle, fifth earl of Orrery and Cork, *Remarks on the Life and Writings of Dr. Jonathan Swift,* 1751). See also HIGH, IMBIBE, REFRESHMENT, SMILE, and WOOD UP.

liberate/liberation. To take what isn't yours, and the act thereof; ironically, to destroy something, usually a town.

The euphemistic noun seems to have come first, during World War II, when a patriotic editor of the *Richmond News-Leader* suggested that the Allies substitute "liberation" for "invasion." The idea was picked up by FDR. "At a press conference in May 1944, a month before D-day, President Roosevelt said that when our expected invasion of Europe began we would be using the word 'liberation—not invasion'" (Stuart Berg Flexner, *I Hear America Talking,* 1976). Thus, with the best of intentions, the word was *liberated* from its traditional moorings. Soon, soldiers in the armies of *liberation* began to speak of *liberating* chickens, bottles of wine, watches, and practically everything else that wasn't nailed permanently in place. In this way, "liberate" became World War II's counterpart of World War I's SALVAGE and the Civil War's APPROPRIATE. In the ironic sense, cities sometimes were *liberated* so thoroughly as to be hardly recognizable, e.g., "'This place sure has been liberated,' said an American M.P. . . . when eventually they reached the waste of brick and stone which had been Vire" (A. McKee, *Caen,* 1964).

The euphemism has withstood the test of time. Thus, in Israel, the territories that were taken from the Arabs during the Six-Day War of 1967 are never described by expansionists as "annexed," "occupied," or "administered," but as *liberated,* while in Cambodia, amid the confusion that attended the fall of Phnom Penh to Communist forces, Sydney H. Schanberg noted that "I even had time to 'liberate' a typewriter someone had abandoned, since the troops had 'liberated' mine earlier" (*New York Times,* 5/9/75). Mr. Schanberg also noted that the Communist troops called their military units "rumdos," which translates as "liberation forces." (When the Vietnamese invaded Cambodia in 1979, they also styled themselves as *liberation* forces.) In the United States, meanwhile, the crazies who murdered a black school superintendent and kidnapped Patty Hearst saw themselves as the Symbionese Liberation Army. And so it goes.

For more about invasions, see INCURSION.

liberty cabbage. Sauerkraut—perhaps the best-known of the super-patriotic attempts during World War I to prevent the American tongue from being sullied by Germanic words. Similar euphemisms included *liberty sandwich* for hamburger sandwich and *liberty measles* for that other kind of measles. During this period, too, German shepherd dogs were transmuted into *Alsatians*, frankfurters were sold more often as *hot dogs*, and German toast was dropped as an alternate name for *French toast*. People even went and changed their family names, most notably in Great Britain where the Battenbergs became the *Mountbattens* and the English division of the Saxe-Coburg-Gotha branch of the Wettin family metamorphosed into the House of *Windsor*.

There seems to have been less of this semantic tomfoolery in World War II. True, the collaborationist Vichy government in France gave VICHYSSOISE a bad name for a while, and some people had doubts about sending their children off to "kindergarten," but the proposal to change hamburger into *defense steak* was not approved by the National Association of Meat Merchants, and no one seems to have taken seriously the suggestion that Bismarck herring be relabeled *Eisenhower herring* (which would have been a dubious victory at best, one German name being substituted for another). See also SALISBURY STEAK.

lie/lie with. Because of the sexual connotations of LAY, squeamish souls tend to avoid it in any context, which results in such grammatical errors as "He has lain the newspaper down," where "laid down" is correct. The future, however, almost certainly belongs to the squeamish: "Lie" will become Standard English because the rules for using the ordinary, nonsexual "lay" are hardly ever taught anymore. As Sylvia Barrett was advised at the outset of her teaching career at Calvin Coolidge High: "Never turn your back to the class when writing on the board. . . . Never give a lesson on 'lie and lay'" (Bel Kaufman, *Up the Down Staircase*, 1964). As for "lie with," there should be no confusion: It has stood for sexual INTERCOURSE for more than 600 years. For example: ". . . if he had known me and how easy the trifle he aimed at was to be had, he would have . . . given me four or five guineas and have lain with me the next time he had come at me" (Daniel Defoe, *Moll Flanders*, 1722). Naturally, "lie with" also has been further euphemized. For instance, the Bowdlers had a colleague, the Reverend James Plumtre, who did for Shakespeare's songs what Dr. B. and his sister did for the plays. Thus, act II, scene 2 of *As You Like It* begins with Amiens entering, singing:

> Under the greenwood tree
> Who loves to lie with me

And Plumtre, thinking this too suggestive for FAMILY consumption, improved the verse thusly:

> Under the greenwood tree
> Who loves to work with me

life insurance. Death insurance; the policies are a provision against death, not continuing life. See also INHERITANCE TAX, MORTALITY RATE, and SUDDEN VICTORY.

limb. Leg. Considered more discreet for being more general, "limb" is widely acclaimed as one of the greatest euphemisms of the nineteenth century. Less often recognized is the fact that it has persisted well into the twentieth, e.g., describing Josephine Baker's memorable debut in Paris in 1925: "She made her entry entirely nude except for a pink flamingo feather between her limbs; she was being carried upside down and doing the split on the shoulder of a black giant" (Janet Flanner, *Paris Is Yesterday,* 1972).

Though associated mainly with the Victorian era, "limb" had a previous euphemistic incarnation: Men once had *privy limbs,* where the "privy" equaled the "private" in PRIVATE PARTS. Even in the leggy sense, "limb," like the related DRUMSTICK, came into fashion before Victoria became queen in 1837. It seems, too, that credit for popularizing "limb" must go to Her Majesty's former subjects, the Americans. This is evident from the confusion of such British visitors as Capt. Frederick Marryat, who reported in *A Diary in American* (1839) on the following incident at Niagara Falls:

> . . . I was escorting a young lady with whom I was on friendly terms. She had been standing on a piece of rock, the better to view the scene, when she slipped down, and was evidently hurt by the fall. . . . As she limped a little in walking home, I said, "Did you hurt your leg much?" She turned from me, evidently much shocked, or much offended . . . I begged to know what was the reason of her displeasure. After some hesitation, she said that as she knew me well, she would tell me that the word *leg* was never mentioned before ladies.

The captain apologized, attributing his "want of refinement" to his "having been accustomed only to *English* society" and asked how, if the occasion ever arose when he simply had to mention "such articles," he could do so without "shocking the company."

> Her reply was, that the word *limb* was used; "nay," continued she, "I am not so particular as some people are, for I know those who always say limb of a table, or limb of a piano-forte."

Some of Marryat's English readers probably thought he was pulling their—er—*limbs,* which he might have been, but only slightly, since this was also the age of the BENDER, the BOSOM, the JOINT, and such other quaint roundabouts as: "A bit of the wing, Roxy, or the—under limb?" (Oliver Wendell Holmes, *Elsie Venner: A Romance of Destiny,* 1860). See also EXTREMITY, HOSE, and UNMENTIONABLES.

limit, the. Sexual intercourse, the "limit" being the boundary that formerly (in stricter times than today) separated "nice" girls from those who weren't. "On the one hand, the all-American girl must not, as the poetry of our love-lore has it, 'go the limit.' On the other hand, she can't be prissy. She ends up a kind of perfumed puritan" (*Holiday,* 3/57). See also ALL THE WAY and, for the last stop before reaching the *limit,* DEMI-VIERGE.

limited war. Anything short of thermonuclear world holocaust. The comforting "limited" makes the prospect easier to live with, though it shouldn't, given recent history. (Both the Vietnam CONFLICT and the Korean POLICE ACTION were billed as *limited wars*.) Military planners also like to think that nuclear wars might in some way be *limited*. Technically speaking (in the sense that the number of grains of sand in the Sahara is limited), they may be right. The details are not very pretty to look at, however, e.g.: "A new Congressional study . . . says that even in a limited conflict as many as 20 million people would be killed in both the United States and the Soviet Union" (*New York Times*, 5/23/79). See also CLEAN BOMB, ESCALATION, MINI-NUKE, and SELECTIVE STRIKE.

lingerie. Women's underwear, French-style. In the original French, the primary meanings of "lingerie" have less to do with underclothing than with linen as a material, the true French equivalent of the English "linen" being *linge*. Our own "linen," of course, also is a euphemism for the various items worn next to the skin:

> MISS PRUE: I'm resolv'd I won't let Nurse put any more Lavender among my Smocks . . .
> FRAIL: Fie, Miss; amongst your Linnen you must say—You must never say Smock. (William Congreve, *Love for Love*, 1695)

The fancier "lingerie" is traced to 1835 in the *Oxford English Dictionary* as a collective term for all the linen items in a woman's wardrobe or trousseau. It took less than 20 years for the term to acquire its euphemistic meaning, circa 1852. Credit for popularizing "lingerie" in the modern sense is given to Sara Josepha Hale, longtime editor (1837–77) of *Godey's Lady's Book*, by Mary Brooks Picken, in *The Fashion Dictionary* (1973). Today, "lingerie" often classes as doubletalk as well as a euphemism, since the particular item in question may well be made of silk, nylon, rayon, or some other nonlinen material.

For another example of the influence of Mrs. Hale upon English, see FEMALE, and for more about women's wear, continue with BODY BRIEFER, BRASSIERE, CHEMISE, FOUNDATION GARMENT, HOSE, *intimates* (see INTIMACY/INTIMATE), PANTIES, UNDIES, and UNMENTIONABLES.

liquidate/liquidation. To kill or the act of killing, frequently on a mass basis. ". . . the Communists employ the euphemism 'liquidate' because they don't want to imagine the firing squad, the volley, the pool of blood . ." (John Moore, *You English Words*, 1962). "In Russia, after the revolution, massive killings of people accused of obstructing the regime were called 'liquidations,' a word previously meaning the disbanding of business enterprise" (Anatol Rapoport, *Semantics*, 1975).

The original Russian word was *likvidirovat* (to wind up) and it was converted into English at least by 1924, e.g., "In this way the 'Labor Opposition,' the 'Workers *Pravada*,' and a few other recalcitrant groups were all 'liquidated'" (*Yale Review*, XIII/24). Quickly, the euphemism entered the general vocabulary and was adopted in nonpolitical contexts. As the wonderful wizard said to Dorothy, upon being told how she had dissolved the Wicked Witch of the West with a bucketful of water: "You liquidated her; very resourceful" (*The Wiuzard of Oz*, film, 1939).

litter

See also ASSASSINATION; CULL; FINAL SOLUTION, THE; and NO RIGHT TO CORRESPONDENCE.

litter. Not necessarily candy wrappers and beer cans; see DOG DIRT/LITTER/ WASTE.

little (or small) people. Midgets. Like other minorities, they have banded together, and the name of their organization is the Little People of America. See also GOOD PEOPLE, THE.

long illness. Cancer; the unmentionable disease. "Cancer works slowly, insidiously: the standard euphemism in obituaries is that someone has died after a long illness" (Susan Sontag, *New York Review of Books*, 1/26/78). Variations include *prolonged illness* and *incurable illness*. Semantically as well as physically, cancer is the modern equivalent of TB, which was dreaded as much in its time as cancer is in ours, and which, accordingly, inspired a similar set of euphemisms. See also BRIEF ILLNESS; C, The Big; ILL/ILLNESS, and OBITUARY.

loo. A toilet; a British euphemism for yet another British euphemism, WC, occasionally encountered among jet-setters in the United States, too. A peculiarity of "loo" is that no one is quite sure where the word came from. High authorities have disputed learnedly over whether it is a corruption of the French *l'eau*, water; an abbreviation of *gardyloo*, an old warning that slops are descending (probably from *gardez l'eau*, or "Watch out for the water!"), or a misbegotten descendant of *lieux d'aisance*, or room of comfort—a French "water closet," in other words. It has even been argued that "loo" comes from "Waterloo," a word that has been imprinted indelibly on the British psyche. And perhaps the watery "loo" does pun on the battle, with an allusion to Napoleon going down the drain. Stranger things have happened in and to language. But not many. See also TOILET.

lose/loss. Discreet allusions to death. All connotations of casual negligence to the contrary, the report that "Mabel has lost her husband," doesn't mean that she has accidentally mislaid the poor man. Generals also have been known to *lose* people, and in large numbers, too, e.g., speaking of July 1, 1916, the first day of the Battle of the Somme: "In all the British had lost about sixty thousand . . ." (John Keegan, *The Face of Battle*, 1976). The basic construction is quite old: "We losten alle oure housbondes at that toun" (Geoffrey Chaucer, *The Knight's Tale*, ca. 1387–1400). See also CASUALTY and PASS AWAY.

love child. A bastard. "'You're taking it too hard. There's no disgrace in being a love child. How many of those kids in your class do you suppose were planned for?'" (Thomas W. Duncan, *Gus the Great*, 1947). Dating to at least the early nineteenth century, "love child" probably is shorthand for "love-begotten child," which was included along with the similar "merry-begotten" by Capt. Francis Grose in *A Classical Dictionary of the Vulgar Tongue* (1796). It remains the nicest of the many terms available to describe the issue of unmarried parents, e.g., *by-blow, by-child, by-scrape, by-slip, irregular child, natural child,* and *outside child*. See also

BASTARD; BLANKET, BORN ON THE WRONG SIDE OF; *sinfant* in ANTICIPATING; SOB; *trick baby* in TRICK, and WOOD COLT.

loved one, the. Dead person, the; frequently capitalized. "As for the Loved One, poor fellow, he wanders like a sad ghost through the funeral men's pronouncements. No provision seems to have been made for the burial of the Heartily Disliked One, although the necessity for such must arise in the course of human events" (Jessica Mitford, *The American Way of Death*, 1963). In spite of the valiant efforts of Mitford and, before her, Evelyn Waugh (i.e., *The Loved One*, 1948), "loved one" lives on: ". . . he never said 'your husband' but rather 'your loved one,' and 'when he dies' always became 'when he passes on.' No wonder there is so little reality about death. Even the people who make a living from it can't accept it" (Lynn Caine, *Widow*, 1974). See also DECEASED and PASS AWAY.

lovemaking. See also MAKE LOVE.

love that dare not speak its name, the. Late Victorian homosexuality. The phrase comes from a poem, "Two Loves" (1894), by Oscar Wilde's FRIEND, Alfred Lord Douglas (also known as Bosie), and it was made famous by its introduction on April 30, 1895, into Wilde's trial for violating a law, enacted 10 years previously, that made it a misdemeanor for any male to commit a "gross indecency" with another male, even in private. Seeking to establish what would be called today Wilde's SEXUAL ORIENTATION, the prosecutor quoted the following lines to the defendant:

> "Sweet youth
> Tell me why, sad and sighing, dost thou rove
> These pleasant realms? I pray tell me sooth,
> What is thy name?" He said, "My name is Love,"
> Then straight, the first did turn himself to me,
> And cried, "He lieth, for his name is Shame.
> But I am Love, and I was wont to be
> Alone in this fair garden, till he came
> Unasked by night; I am true Love, I fill
> The hearts of boy and girl with mutual flame."
> Then sighing said the other, "Have thy will,
> I am the love that dare not speak its name."

"Is it not clear," asked the prosecutor, "that the love described relates to natural love and unnatural love?"

"No," said Wilde.

The prosecutor pressed forward, "What is the 'Love that dare not speak its name'?"

And Wilde rose, most eloquently, to the challenge:

"The Love that dare not speak its name" in this century is such a great affection of an elder man for a younger man as there was between David and Jonathan, such as Plato made the very basis of his philosophy and such as you find in the sonnets of Michelangelo and

Shakespeare. It is that deep spiritual affection that is as pure as it is perfect. . . . There is nothing unnatural about it.

It was perhaps partly due to Wilde's eloquence that this trial ended in a hung jury. On retrial, however, Wilde was convicted and sentenced to two years of hard labor at Reading Gaol.

Aside from the general reluctance of Victorians to address sexual matters directly, the nameless love of Wilde and Bosie was nameless in the 1890s partly for lack of any "good" words for it. Even the word "homosexual" was still very new. The earliest example of the use of the word in the 1976 supplement of the *Oxford English Dictionary* is from a translation in 1892 of Baron Richard von Krafft-Ebing's *Psychopathia Sexualis* (1886). The term's newness in the 1890s also is evident from a note by H. Havelock Ellis in *Studies in the Psychology of Sex* (vol. 1, 1897): "'Homosexual' is a barbarously hybrid word and I claim no responsibility for it."

Of the words that proper Victorians could bring themselves to utter, *Uranian* love was perhaps the nicest appellation. (Urania was the muse of astronomy, and "Uranian love" was supposed to be especially heavenly or spiritual in nature.) BISEXUAL also dates to the nineteenth century. In addition, one could speak of FANCY gentlemen or, a vulgar rhyme, of a *Nancy* (a person might also be said to be "a bit nancy"). Otherwise, such discussions as took place tended to be couched in terms of *inverts* and *inversions; perverts* and *perversions; unspeakable* or *nameless acts* or *crimes; gross indecency* and *indecent assault; abominable offenses; crimes against nature* and UNNATURAL acts. Everything is different nowadays: The "bad," inverted words have been shoved back into the closet, and GAY has emerged, sweeping all before it.

low-income. Poor; a classic bureaucratic dodge. "The Census Bureau has decided to say 'low-income' instead of 'poverty' in its official releases" (*New Republic*, 8/7&14/71). The bureau seized upon "low-income" because of all the publicity given to a Census report three months previously that showed an embarrassing increase (the first in a decade) of, as the *New Republic* put it, "the number of people below the poverty level, if you'll pardon the expression." See also BLACK, DISADVANTAGED, and INDIGENT.

madam. A brothel-keeper; the honorific goes with the managerial position. "In a few moments the 'madam,' as the current word characterized this type of woman, appeared" (Theodore Dreiser, *The Financier*, 1912).

"Madam," or "my lady," corresponds etymologically to "madonna" and may originally have been the child's form of address to its mother (*ma dame*, with "dame" meaning "mother"), but the recipient of the title in the earliest written examples is a queen or other high-ranking woman. Subsequently, in Chaucer's time (ca. 1343–1400), the wife of an alderman qualified for it; nuns also were addressed as "madam" until the Reformation. By 1700, "madam" had acquired such pejorative meanings as "a kept mistress" or "whore." The "madam" as manageress probably dates from this time, and it has gradually superseded the other titles for women who ran brothels, including *abbess, lady abbess* (whose husband or other male companion was called the *abbott*), and *aunt*, the last being "a title of eminence for the senior dells who serve for instructoresses, midwives, &c." (Capt. Francis Grose, *A Classical Dictionary of the Vulgar Tongue*, 1796). The gradual reduction in the status of "madam" parallels the devolution of LADY. See also HONORABLE and PROSTITUTE.

Madame. The guillotine. Gallows humor is not limited to the gallows itself and the point of such jokes, regardless of the means of execution, generally is euphemistic, with a lighthearted term or phrase substituting for a dreaded one. "Madame Guillotine," the name to the contrary, was not created solely by Dr. Joseph Ignace Guillotine. Similar though cruder devices had been used since at least the sixteenth century, and Dr. Guillotine almost certainly knew something about them when he proposed to the French National Assembly, in 1789, that this means of execution be adopted. Guillotine's objectives were not only humanitarian (the machine eliminated grisly human error) but in keeping with revolutionary ideals of social equality (previously, commoners had been hanged, while beheading was a privilege of nobility). The first "Madame" went into operation in 1792 and by the time she was retired had lopped off some 8,000 heads but not, as legend has it, Dr. Guillotine's. He died in bed in 1814, after which his children escaped the cloud that had become attached to his name by officially changing theirs.

The use of "Madame" for the guillotine is the leading example of the tendency to attribute feminine qualities to deadly instruments. The immediate ancestress of "Madame" was the *maiden*, a crude guillotine used in Edinburgh and other places (it was also known as the *Halifax gibbet*). There was also the infamous *iron maiden*, used by torturers; *the duke of Exeter's daughter*, which was the name of the rack in the Tower of London (apparently so-called in tribute to the duke who introduced this method of questioning during the reign of Henry VI); and *the scavenger's daughter* (also used during the Tudor period, it nicely complemented the rack, squeezing a person into a ball instead of pulling him apart). See also CAPITAL PUNISHMENT and PRIEST.

made a trumpet of his ass. Farted. A poetic euphemism by a great poet, Dante

Alighieri. From Canto XXI of *The Inferno* (ca. 1315), as translated by John Ciardi (1954):

> They [the demons] turned along
>   the left bank in a line;
> but before they started, all of them
>   together
> had stuck their pointed tongues
>   out as a sign
> to their Captain that they wished
>   permission to pass,
> and he made a trumpet of his
>   ass.

Ciardi adds in a note that "mention of bodily function is more likely to be more shocking in a Protestant than a Catholic culture. . . . the offensive language of Protestantism is obscenity; the offensive language of Catholicism is profanity or blasphemy. . . . Dante places the Blasphemous in Hell as the worst of the Violent against God and His Works, but he has no category for punishing those who use four-letter words. . . . Chaucer, as a man of Catholic England, took exactly Dante's view of what was and what was not shocking." See also FOUR-LETTER WORD.

It should not diminish our appreciation of Dante's metaphor to know that it may not have been entirely a figment of his poetic imagination. People called "posterior trumpeters," who could play tunes, or airs, with their airs, are reliably reported to have existed. In the seventeenth century, a pamphlet on the subject was issued under the pseudonym Don Fartando, and a few people still living may remember performances by Joseph Pujol (1857–1943), who wowed audiences at the Moulin Rouge and other *boîtes* with recitals on his peculiar instrument. Cynics contended that Pujol, who performed under the name Le Petomane, was a fraud but, if so, he was a good one, for he hoodwinked the physicians who examined him. He could mimic cannon, imitate the calls of animals, and blow out candles from several feet away, but his crowning achievement is generally conceded to have been his rendition of *Clair de Lune*. See also BREAK WIND.

maid. A woman servant, DOMESTIC, or HELP. "There were   . three females . . . and Miriam Brackett, a 'maid'—so called because the preacher had hired her for the 'in door work'" (John Neal, *Brother Jonathan*, 1825). See also SERVANT.

mail cover. Postal spying. "Covering," or recording, the names and addresses on envelopes is legal in certain circumstances, but the term becomes a euphemism when it leads (as it always seems to) to illegal mail opening. Thus, as the Senate Intelligence Committee learned in 1975, the CIA ran a *mail cover* operation in New York City for 20 years, starting in 1952, during which the agency screened 28 million letters—secretly, and illegally, opening and photographing nearly 250,000 of them. FBI agents also opened other people's mail; agents referred to this illegal investigative technique as the *mail run*. See also AGENT and ILLEGAL.

major. An honorary rank bestowed on such functionaries as railroad conductors. It is one step below COLONEL.

make. To seduce, to engage in INTERCOURSE, or, as a noun, the person who is seduced, "an easy make" being essentially the same as "an easy lay" (see LAY). "A considerable degree of manipulativeness was condoned in the behavior of a young man who was in the process of trying to 'make' a young woman. He was almost expected to be false and seductive . . . in the interest of getting her to 'come across' and go to bed with him" (Barry McCarthy, *What You Still Don't Know About Male Sexuality*, 1977). Of course, it takes only a small change in emphasis to depersonalize the seduction: "The old phrase, 'Did you make her?' has been changed because 'making her' is personal, intimate, warm. The cool cats say, 'Man, don't think I didn't make it with her.' The insertion of the word 'it' cools it, depersonalizes it—and coolness is all" (*Playboy*, 2/58). See also IT.

Like "lay," "make" seems to have picked up its sexual connotations comparatively recently. Eric Partridge says the term has been used in the sense of "to cöit (with a girl)" since about 1918 by the Canadians, who picked it up from the Americans (*A Dictionary of Slang and Unconventional English*, 1970). The widespread currency of the term south of the border about this time is suggested by the pun contained in "Let's eat, drink, and make merry, for tomorrow Mary may reform," a remark that Americans still considered quite witty in the 1920s. (A New York City joke of the same vintage is about the man and woman who were canoodling on the train. The conductor came into the car, announced "Jamaica," and the man got up and punched him in the eye.) Muddying the etymological waters are such related expressions as *make good, make time with, on the make,* and MAKE OUT, all of which have sexual aspects, as well as the now-archaic use of "make" for simply making a good impression on a person of the opposite sex, e.g., "Look at that big stiff tryin' to make that dame!" (*American Magazine*, 6/1918).

make love. With SLEEP WITH, the most common euphemism for the great FOUR-LETTER WORD that is itself euphemized as F——. The interchangeability of the terms is evident from the following communication to *Playboy* (7/78), from F. H., of San Mateo, California:

> We made love in the top of an 80-foot tree on a platform tree house in the spring. We fucked in rainstorms until we steamed. We made love on the frozen surface of a river. We made love in the closet of a Unitarian church.

The relevant noun is "lovemaking," as in "Several times we were right in the middle of lovemaking when our families dropped in unexpectedly" ("Dear Abby," *Boston Herald American*, 7/14/77).

"Make love" once had a more general meaning and, in fact, seems to have evolved from a euphuism into a euphemism. As a euphuism, it was the flowery equivalent of "to pay court" or "to woo," and the oldest example of the phrase in the *Oxford English Dictionary* comes from the progenitor of all euphuisms, John Lyly, who created the character that gave the flowery style its name: "A Phrase now there is which belongeth to your Shoppe boorde, that is, to make loue" (*Euphues and His England*, 1580). The *OED* did not recognize "make love" in its euphemistic, copulative sense until publication of the 1976 supplement and then the earliest example given is from 1950. Older citations, however, are to be found by those who search for them. Thus, from the great Victorian underground autobiography, *My Secret Life*:

> . . . I began those exquisite preliminaries with this well-made, pretty woman . . . but . . . was impatient . . . Smiling she [asked] "Shall we make love?"

This particular "make love" may date from as early as 1851, when the incident took place, though the anonymous autobiography, extensively rewritten, did not go to press until about 1890. See also INTERCOURSE.

make out. In Standard English, the phrase may mean, among other things, "to make shift" or "to get along," and these general senses are mirrored in slang, where "make out" covers a wide range of sexual activity. Thus, on the authority of Ann Landers: "Among high school and college kids, making out can mean anything from holding hands to going the whole route" (*Washington, D.C., Daily News*, 3/4/63). The evidence suggests that the heavier, more euphemistic sense is the older. For example: "When I was young, if one 'made out,' his accomplishment was a good deal more total than was implied by either *to neck* or *to pet*, or both" (*American Speech*, 2/62). A person who is noted for *making out* may be known as a *make-out* or even a *make-out artist*. See also NECK and PET.

make (or **pass**) **water.** To piss. The "water" is the euphemism, of course, although "make" occasionally is used in other ways, e.g., *make wee wee* or, simply, *make* (the latter usually meaning to DEFECATE). "Water" has stood for "urine" for the past 600 years or so. A famous example comes from the first of the articles of impeachment against Quinbus Flestrin, aka the Man-Mountain: "Whereas, by a statute made in the reign of his Imperial Majesty Calin Deffar Plune, it is enacted, that whoever shall make water within the precincts of the royal palace, shall be liable to the pains and penalties of high treason . . ." (Jonathan Swift, *Gulliver's Travels*, 1726). See also PEE, PUMP SHIP, and URINATE/URINATION.

male. Homosexual, as in "Male movies," a marquee ad for films in which the female roles are played by males in drag. See also FEMALE and GAY.

mammary glands. Breasts; the reference to function almost invariably conceals a prurient interest in form. See also BOSOM and GLANDS.

man. Servant; a euphemistic shortening of "manservant" or "hired man." Also, in some constructions, such as *bellman* and *houseman*, a euphemism for "boy." See also GARÇON, GENTLEMAN, SERVANT, and SCOUTING/USA.

manure. The word originally meant "to work with the hands"; it stems from the Latin *manus*, hand, and is closely related to "maneuver," which is something to remember next time you read about the army going out on them. Today, of course, "manure" is one of the more common euphemisms for "shit," as in "What I liked about her, she didn't give you a lot of horse manure about what a great guy her father was" (J. D. Salinger, *The Catcher in the Rye*, 1951). See also HORSE-FEATHERS.

People first began spreading manure in the sixteenth century; before that, going back to the thirteenth, they spread MUCK. See also DEFECATE/DEFECATION, FERTILIZER, and NIGHT SOIL.

marital aid (or **device**). A vibrator or other gadget used in sexual activity. "Sex toys are known by many names: marital aids, dildos, adult novelties, etc. None of the 'trade names' are very descriptive" (ad for *The Spirit of Seventy Sex, Penthouse,* 1/77). See also CORDLESS MASSAGER and MASTURBATION.

marketing. Sales. "Marketing is a fashionable term. The sales manager becomes a marketing vice-president. But a gravedigger is still a gravedigger even when he is called a mortician—only the price of burial goes up" (Peter Drucker, quoted in John J. Tarrant, *Drucker: The Man Who Invented the Corporate Society,* 1976). See also ENGINEER and MORTICIAN.

marry. An archaic exclamation of surprise, which started off as a euphemistic oath, this being short for the "Virgin Mary." See also GEE and GOSH.

massage parlor. A brothel or HOUSE. The phenomena of "massage parlors" that specialize in providing sexual SERVICES dates to before World War I: "Along with them go the announcements of 'massage parlors' (an all-too-obvious euphemism), free whiskies, and other agencies of public injury" (*Colliers,* 1/25/13). And Ernest Weekley, defining "stew" in 1921, had this to say: "The public hot-air baths acquired a reputation like that of our massage establishments some time ago" (*Etymological Dictionary of Modern English*).

All reports to the contrary, there are still some massage parlors that provide nothing but massages. A few of these have even traded on the existence of the fake *massage parlors* to boost their own business. For example, consider this strange situation in Las Vegas, Nevada, possibly the only American city in which a massage parlor could be closed for *not* offering sex to customers: "After trying unsuccessfully with other legal tactics to close the two large massage parlors, the city got two linguistic experts to testify that the . . . parlors' graphic advertisements in tourist newspapers were explicitly promising sexual liaisons [see LIAISON] when, in fact, they were offering only massages" (*New York Times,* 10/4/76).

Just as there are many different kinds of HOUSES, so the *massage parlor* has evolved into different forms. There are *nude encounter centers; rap clubs,* RAP PARLORS, and *rap studios; relaxation clubs* and *parlors; sensitivity meeting centers;* and *sex therapy clinics.* New York City used to have a well-stacked *library,* complete with "librarians to better serve you," and Las Vegas has boasted *co-ed wrestling studios.* The euphemisms are so diverse that legislators are reduced to vague generalizations when drafting laws to restrict them, e.g., a 1975 New York City zoning proposal to limit the proliferation of "physical culture and health establishments." See also ADULT, CLUB, PARLOR, and STUDIO.

master. An older athlete. The Amateur Athletic Union has a *masters* program. Swimmers, divers, and water polo players who are older than 25 are *masters.* Track-and-field athletes, aged thirty-five or more, are *masters,* except for distance runners, who become *masters* at forty. Professional tennis players go the AAU one better: When they turn 40, they blossom into *grandmasters*. See also MATURE.

masturbation. The currently dominant Latinate euphemism for what was politely described during most of the last three centuries as *onanism, self-abuse,* or *self-pollution.* "Don't knock masturbation. It's sex with someone I love" (Woody Allen in *Annie Hall,* film, 1977).

The origin of "masturbation" is mysterious, etymologically. Some people believe it to be constructed out of the Latin *manus,* hand, and *stuprare,* to defile; others, including Eric Partridge, have argued for *mas,* semen, and *tubare,* to agitate. As early as 1621, Robert Burton referred to "rapes, incests, adulteries, mastuprations," etc. in *The Anatomy of Melancholy.* The modern "masturbation" did not appear until considerably later, with the oldest example in the *Oxford English Dictionary* coming from the title of a work that was published in 1766: *Onanism: or a Treatise upon the Disorders produced by Masturbation.*

The "polite" terms, such as *self-abuse* and *self-pollution,* that "masturbation" gradually superseded are simultaneously pejorative and circumlocutory—that is, they reveal society's official attitude toward this "vice" without actually describing the action at hand. For example, the *OED* (vol. M. prepared 1904–08) defined "masturbation" as "The action or practice of self-abuse." In the United States, the first dictionary to carry a nonopaque definition was *Webster's Unabridged,* of 1957, i.e.: "Production of an orgasm by excitation of the sexual organs as by manipulation or friction." Previously, *Webster's* definition had been "Onanism; self-pollution" (from Noel Perrin, *Dr. Bowdler's Legacy,* 1969). See also COME and FRIG.

The older terms are still encountered every once in a while. For example, in the 1970 film *M.A.S.H.,* Hawkeye says to Major Burns: "A bunch of the boys asked me to ask you about Major Houlihan. Is she better than self-abuse?" This is definitely an exception, however. In truly liberated circles, even "masturbation" seems to be on the way out; see SELF- (or MUTUAL) PLEASURING.

materiel. Military material, i.e., equipment and supplies. A French import, *materiel* crossed the Channel to England at about the same time as its counterpart, PERSONNEL, and in the same way, appearing first in Anglicized form, e.g.: "Their [the French] baggage, equipage, tumbrils, artillery, the whole of what is called *material,* were taken" (*Quarterly Review,* XIII, 1815). See also LATRINE, SORTIE, and TRIAGE.

matinee. Sex in the afternoon. "The most sensible of all New York [City governmental] traditions was the setting aside of Monday and Thursday as Official Mistress Nights. . . . With the advent of Lindsay [Mayor John V., elected 1965] and the Reformers, the institution fell into disrepute, do-gooders preferring things like 'matinees' . . ." (*New York Times,* 2/6/74). A variant is "funch," which is sex during the lunch hour, and which is a portmanteau word. See also AFFAIR and ASSIGNATION.

mature. An exceedingly generalized term that blankets all ages from semiadult through old; an exception occurs in the case of advertisements for women's clothes, where a *mature* woman may be a "fat" woman. Usually, it is people who are characterized as *mature*, but there are exceptions, e.g., businesses and economies. In general, a *mature* economy—such as that of several of the nation's northeastern cities—is an economy that is old and ailing. As for people: On the lower end of the age range, a movie for *mature* audiences is one that parents are supposed to treat as "discretionary viewing" because it includes partially unclad human bodies. And on the upper end of the people scale, there is "the woman in the home for 'mature' people discovering that the years after retirement are not always 'golden'" (*New York Times*, 3/24/76). It was the latter kind of "mature" that also was meant at the 1964–65 New York World's Fair, where the Dynamic Maturity Pavilion had a garden and benches on which *mature* people (and others) could rest. See also ADULT; AGE, OF A CERTAIN; GOLDEN AGE/YEARS, and YOUNG.

meaningful dialogue. Conversation; occasionally the preliminary to a MEANINGFUL RELATIONSHIP. "The American vice is explanation. This is because there is so little conversation (known as 'meaningful dialogue' to the explainers) in the greatest country in the history of the greatest world in the Milky Way" (Gore Vidal, *New York Review of Books*, 2/9/78).

meaningful relationship. An illicit sexual relationship, longer than a one-night stand, but frequently shorter than an AFFAIR. "I never could have a meaningful relationship with anyone who wore a polyester suit" ("Rockford Files," WNBC-TV, 1/5/79). "Meaningful" has to be one of the most overworked, least meaningful words of our time; here, it functions only as a signpost, calling attention to the sexual significance of RELATIONSHIP.

means. Wealth, riches, as in "Mr. Johnson is a man of means." See also MODEST and, for one of the many advantages of *means*, refer to MENTAL HOSPITAL.

median divider. Highway department doubletalk for the center strip of a highway, as in "Do not cross the median divider." The fancy "median divider" has a FOP Index of 1.5. See also IMPACT ATTENUATION DEVICE.

medication. Medicine. "Bayer Aspirin has relieved more pains, aches, and flu than any other medication in history" (TV commercial, 2/10/78). ". . . our society, like our language, is in serious trouble when . . . nobody takes medicine but rather medication. Indian tribes soon will have medication men" (Edwin Newman, *Strictly Speaking*, 1974). "Medication" sins for pompously pretending to be something more than it really is. It has a FOP Index of 1.4.

medium. One of the many labels that manufacturers use in preference to the hateful "small." "*Small* is disguised as . . . *medium* (the dental liquid *Cue* divides itself into *medium*, *large*, and *giant*) [sizes] . . ." (*American Speech*, 4/42). See also LARGE.

meeting. A duel or affair; also, somewhat more specifically but still euphemistically, a "private meeting." "A meeting took place . . . between Mr. O. Joynt and Mr. P. Mckim . . . when on the first fire, the latter was struck in the forehead" (*Annual Register*, 1812). The English euphemism imitates French practice, *rencontre* (meeting) also being used for duels across the Channel. See also AFFAIR.

megadeath. One million dead people. "'Fifty-five megadeaths' does not sound as bad as 55 million Americans dead" (Ralph E. Lapp, *Kill & Overkill*, 1962). "Megadeath" also has the advantage of being less gruesome than "megacorpse," a synonym attributed to Herman Kahn, who specializes in thinking the UNTHINK-ABLE. Both are spin-offs of "megaton" as in "India is reported to have exploded a five-megaton device." See also DEVICE.

member. The penis; a generalization (technically, any separable, nonthoracic part of the body qualifies as a "member"), whose meaning is usually clear enough from the context, as in the following description of Nell Gwynne's ministrations to His Majesty Charles II, attributed to the decidedly irreverent John Wilmot, second earl of Rochester (1647–80):

> This you'd believe, had I but time to tell you
> The pain it costs to poor laborious Nelly,
> While she employs Hands, Fingers, Lips, and Thighs
> E'er she can raise the Member she enjoys.

"Member" in this sense is by no means obsolete, e.g., "Regard how I have willed my member: no base or material desire is connected with it, yet it resembles the so-called sexual erection" (Maxwell Kenton, aka Terry Southern, *Candy*, 1965). Somewhat confusingly, in the distant past, "member" also referred to the external sexual organs of women. Thus, Geoffrey Chaucer had both sexes in mind when he wrote, "Telle me also, to what conclusion/Were membres maad of generacion/ . . . Trusteth right wel, they were nat maad for noght" (*The Wife of Bath's Prologue*, ca. 1387–1400). Other archaic variants include *carnal member, male member, privy member, virile member*, and, in the poetic words of Robert Burns (1756–1796), *dearest member*. For those who prefer to cloak their thoughts in Latin, there is always *membrum virile*. Of course, care must be taken not to mistake the penile *member* for Noah Webster's PECULIAR MEMBERS (the testicles) or the *unruly member* (the tongue, so-called after the biblical passage: ". . . the tongue is a little member . . . the tongue can no man tame; *it is* an unruly evil . . ." (James III, 5–8, King James Version, 1611). Finally, a chamber pot, or CHAMBER, used to be called a *member mug* (or *thunder mug*, from its resonance). See also PENIS.

memorial park. A burying place; a graveyard, cemetery, or mausoleum. The type specimen is in Glendale, California, where, in 1917, an old, run-down cemetery was reborn as Forest Lawn Memorial-Park. Other parts of the country have also been blessed with *memorial parks* and the closely related *memorial gardens*, e.g., two East Coast mausoleums, Rose Hills Memorial Park in Putnam County, New York, and "Italy's Pompeii inspired" Woodbridge Memorial Gardens, in Woodbridge, New Jersey. "Memorial" also takes some of the sting out of death in such allied constructions as *memorial association* (funeral society), *memorial bronze* (grave marker), *memorial chapel* (an undertaker; see CHAPEL), *memorial counselor* (cemetery plot salesman), and *memorial estate* (grave site). See also CEMETERY, ESTATE, and GARDEN OF HONOR.

menstruate. "The habit of creating euphemisms dates back at least to the Norman Conquest of England in 1066. At that time the community began to make a distinction between a genteel and an obscene vocabulary, between the Latinate words of the upper class and the lusty Anglo-Saxon of the lower. That is why a duchess *perspired* and *expectorated* and *menstruated*—while a kitchen maid *sweated* and *spat* and *bled*" (Peter Farb, *Word Play*, 1974). The Latin root of "menstruate" is *mensis*, meaning "month" (see MONTHLIES). The strength of the taboo against female bleeding is reflected by the number of euphemisms and circumlocutions for it. A compilation by Natalie F. Joffe (*Word*, vol. 4, 1948) contained nearly 100 such expressions, and more were included in an article by Lalia Phipps Boone (*American Speech*, 12/54). Most of them can be grouped into six somewhat overlapping categories:

> The idea of illness or inconvenience: *come sick, cramps, curse, curse of Eve, feeling that way, fall off the roof, female complaint* or *disorder, illness,* INDISPOSED, *poorliness, problem days, stub one's toe* (see ANKLE, SPRAIN AN), *tummy ache, unwell, watertight.*
> The color red: *bloody Mary, flagging, red devil, red light, the Red Sea's in, show.*
> Periodicity: *bad time, calendar time, courses, full moon, monthly blues, Old Faithful,* PERIOD, *that time, that time of month, wrong time, wrong time of month.*
> The idea of a visit ("visit" itself being an old code word for menstruation): *Aunt Flo has come, entertaining the general, grandma's here from Red Creek, little sister's here.*
> Sanitary measures: *covering the waterfront, having the rag on, in the saddle, in the sling, riding the white* (or *cotton*) *horse, wearing the rag, wearing the manhole cover.*
> Sexual unavailability: *beno* (a contraction of "There'll be no fun"), *ice-boxed, out of this world, today I'm a lady, wallflower week.*

mental. Mad, insane (itself a euphemism for "mad"); a discreet condensation of "mentally deranged," or "mentally ill," as in, "I gather she was a little queer towards the end—a bit mental, I think you people call it" (Dorothy L. Sayers, *Unnatural Death*, 1927). "Mental" is merely one of the latest in a long string of euphemisms for "mad." As Eric Partridge points out: "Frequently, euphemism causes successive synonyms to be suspect, displeasing, indelicate, immoral, even blasphemous. . . . An excellent example is afforded by *mad*, which became *crazy*, which became *insane*, which became *lunatic*, which became *mentally deranged*, which became *deranged* and, a little later and in slang, *mental*" (*Usage & Abusage*, 1973).

"Mental" also appears in various euphemistic combinations, such as *mental depression* or *mental fatigue* (which is another way of saying "depression"; see FATIGUE); *mental job*, which is slang for someone who is, or is suspected of being, mentally unwell; and *to go mental*, for becoming mentally disordered. A *nonmental*, by the laws of reverse psychology, is a sane person, as in, "The Secret Service continued today to press its investigation of what was described as a 'very serious, very large' conspiracy by 'nonmentals' to assassinate President Nixon during his visit to New Orleans yesterday" (*New York Times*, 8/22/73)

mental hospital. A present-day madhouse or insane asylum; variants include *mental health center, mental home,* and *mental institution.* "They pushed him in a Mental Home, And that is like the grave" (Rudyard Kipling, *Limits & Renewals,* 1932). "Modern madhouses are called 'mental hospitals.' If they cater to people of means (another euphemism for 'rich people') they are called 'sanatoria,' 'rehabilitation centers,' or 'Esalen'" (Anatol Rapoport, *Semantics,* 1975). See also ASYLUM, INSTITUTION, REST HOUSE, SANATORIUM/SANITARIUM, and STATE HOSPITAL.

merde. Shit—in elegant, bilingual society.
    E. E. Cumming's *The Enormous Room,* as originally published in 1922, contained the lament, "My father is dead! Shit. Oh, well. The war is over." However, the "shit" so offended John S. Summer, secretary of the New York Society for Suppression of Vice, that the publisher agreed to ink it out in every copy of the first printing. Five years later, in 1927, a second edition was released, in which Cummings converted the entire passage into French: *"Mon père est mort! Merde! Eh bien! La guerre est finie."* And this time, Mr. Summer did not object, thereby demonstrating once again the enormous euphemistic power of French. See also SHORT FRENCH EXPLETIVE, A.

mess. Excrement, usually that of a pet, e.g., from an inside-the-kennel account of a presidential dog-keeper: "The dogs constantly 'make messes.' And when they are not making messes, they 'water the tulips,' 'decorate the rug,' and 'leave a present'" (*New York Times Book Review,* 8/3/75 quoting from Traphes Bryant and Frances Spatz Leighton, *Dog Days at the White House*). See also DOG DIRT/LITTER/WASTE.

message. Euphemistic shorthand for the clearer but crasser "commercial message," or advertisement, typically encountered in the form of: "We'll have more baseball and more interviews after these messages from your local station" (WNBC-TV, NYC, 7/29/78). More complex is the *message* that corrects previous *messages,* such as: "Do you recall some of our past messages saying that Domino sugar gives you strength, energy and stamina? Actually, Domino is not a special or unique source of strength, energy and stamina" (from an advertisement that Domino was required to run by the Federal Trade Commission in 1973). A variant is the *message unit.* As Paul V. Higgins, senior vice-president of the Lieberman-Harrison advertising agency, has said: "I don't like to use the word 'commercial.' I prefer to call our spots 'message units'" (from *Saturday Review/Education,* 12/2/72). See also INTERMISSION and WORD FROM OUR SPONSOR, AND NOW A.

micturate/micturition. The commendably complete index of the underground classic, *My Secret Life* (anon., ca. 1890), translates the Latin succinctly: "Micturating frolics (See pissing)." The noun continues to be printable, even in FAMILY newspapers. As Russell Baker pointed out in connection with the Supreme Court's 1978 ruling on FOUR-LETTER WORDS: ". . in the case of 'micturition,' 'defecation,' and 'incestuous male issue,' the use of Latin is commonly adopted to take people's minds off what is being said" (*New York Times,* 7/11/78). See also PEE and WATER SPORTS.

middle class. White. "'The underlying assumption has been all along that the [urban brownstone] renovation movement is a white thing—when you say middle-class, you mean white'" (*Brooklyn* [NY] *Phoenix*, 7/15/76). See also ETHNIC and HARMONIOUS.

Middle Eastern dancing. Belly dancing. See also ABDOMEN.

military intelligence. To paraphrase someone or other: Military intelligence is to intelligence as military music is to music.

mini-nuke. A smallish nuclear bomb, with a throwaway name. "One risk of developing tactical nuclear weapons, especially those now euphemistically called 'mini-nukes,' is that they may create the illusion that a limited war can be fought" (*The Defense Monitor*, 2/75). See also LIMITED WAR and TACTICAL NUCLEAR WEAPON.

minority. Black and/or Hispanic; as contrasted with ETHNIC, which stands for "white."
   "How far have minority journalists come since the sixties? White editors emphasize gains, but blacks and Hispanics complain of shell games and gestures" (subhead, *Columbia Journalism Review*, 3–4/79). "Minority" is a traditional euphemism that may be on its way out. At their 1979 convention, the National Association of Black Social Workers vowed to stop using the term. The trouble with it, according to Cenie J. Williams, the organization's executive director, was that other groups—white women, veterans, homosexuals, Asians, and American Indians, among them—were also being classified as "minorities," enabling them to compete for governmental and corporate funds in programs that were originally designed for blacks. "The term minority has been bastardized to the extent that it has caused black people to receive less than an equitable share of available resources," he said in his annual report (*New York Times*, 4/22/79). See also BLACK.

miscarriage. A spontaneous abortion. "Miscarriage" is preferred because "abortion," though perfectly correct, has overtones of a formerly illegal operation. Society's divided feelings on the issue of abortion are evidenced by the number of euphemisms that cluster around the topic. See also CRIMINAL (or ILLEGAL) OPERATION, PROCEDURE, PRO-CHOICE, and THERAPEUTIC INTERRUPTION OF PREGNANCY.

misspeak. To make a blooper; especially useful for taking back impolitic statements by American presidents. "'The President,' [Ron] Ziegler said, 'misspoke himself.' He explained that the President . . . had another case in mind when assuming personal responsibility for Fitzgerald's being 'fired, or discharged, or asked to resign'" (*Harper's Magazine*, 6/73). Ernest Fitzgerald, an air force cost analyst, was LET GO in a "routine reorganization" after letting Congress know about a $2 billion cost overrun by Lockheed on the C-5A supercargo plane. The president, Richard M. Nixon, "misspoke" at a press conference, declaring, "No, this was not a case of someone down the line deciding he should go. It was a decision submitted to me. I made it, and I stick by it."

Miss White

Presidents come and presidents go, but the terminology remains the same: ". . . Mr. Carter seemed to go a bit further than he intended in his response to a question about the possible prosecution of Richard Helms, a former Director of Central Intelligence. . . . That, in White House jargon, was Presidential misspeaking" (*New York Times*, 9/30/77). See also CLARIFY and INOPERATIVE.

Miss White. The toilet. Speaking of Cissy Caffrey: ". . . or when she wanted to go where you know she said she wanted to run and pay a visit to Miss White" (James Joyce, *Ulysses*, 1922). See also TOILET and, for more about Cissy's way with words, BOTTOM.

mixed breed. A pedigreed euphemism for "mongrel." In the words of a representative of the Society for Prevention of Cruelty to Animals: "At the ASPCA, the dogs we love most are the mixed breed dogs" ("Romper Room," WOR-TV, NYC, 2/2/78). See also SOB.

mobile home. A trailer. "Mobile homes have of course an unhappy history to live down, and the industry would like to bury its past in new nomenclature. Hence, the euphemism 'mobile home' itself, instead of the old 'trailer'" (*New York Times*, 7/4/76). See also HOME.

model. Alas for the reputation of legitimate models, this is also a euphemism for "whore." In England, some shopwindows are crowded with notes from *models*, advising the public of their availability, while in the United States, more or less amateur *models* may advertise themselves in such publications as *Ace* (undated, ca. 1976):

> ATLANTA NUDE MODEL DISCREET UNINHIBITED . . . looking for sgl swinging studs that know how to turn me on and make me do my thing. 38-22-34.

See also PROSTITUTE and SWINGING.

moderate. More or less liberal. In 1976, four years before Rep. John Anderson made his bid for the presidency, Elizabeth Drew noted that the Illinois Republican, along with other "moderates" in both political parties, was not using the word "liberal" anymore (*The New Yorker*, 10/25/76). Anderson ran on his own ticket, of course, after trying, but failing, to win the Republican presidential nomination from Ronald Reagan. Thus, history repeated itself. In 1964, Nelson A. Rockefeller and other "liberal" Republicans became "moderates" in an effort to stop another conservative, Barry Goldwater, from getting their party's presidential nomination, and they had no more luck than the *moderate* Mr. Anderson.

modest. Poor; typically encountered in such phrases as *modest means, modest accomplishments,* and *modest record,* e.g., "He has a modest record for having served so long in the House." See also MEANS.

molest. The American term for sexual assaults in general and rape in particular is comparable to the basic British INTERFERE WITH.

Since World War II, FAMILY newspapers have started to print "rape," with the result that "molest" is used more accurately, as well as less often, than formerly. Even the best of newspapers, however, still fall back on it occasionally. Thus, in the case of a girl who had been killed by numerous stab wounds and whose body had been partly burned, it was reported: "The state police and the medical examiner declined to say whether the victim had been molested" (*New York Times*, 7/30/79). Probably, "molest" should be confined to historical fiction, where cardboard characters do not bleed:

> Shanna's eyes narrowed as she gritted, "You vulgar beggar, they should hang you for a molester of women!"
> His eyes gleamed like hard brittle amber, and his quip jarred her. "Madam, I believe that's what they intend." (Kathleen E. Woodiwiss, *Shanna*, 1977)

See also ASSAULT, CANOLA, and LECHERY.

monitor. To eavesdrop, or one who engages in this practice; a spy. As an example of *monitoring* on a grand scale, there is friendly old Ma Bell, otherwise known as the American Telephone and Telegraph Co. At a House subcommittee hearing in 1975, company officials admitted that Ma, besides regularly *monitoring* the phone conversations of her one million employees, also conducted a special program during 1965–70, in which some 30 million calls were *monitored*, with tape recordings being made of all or portions of some 1.5 million to 1.8 million of these. See also INFORMANT and TECHNICAL SURVEILLANCE.

monosyllable. For most of the eighteenth and nineteenth centuries, this was the most common slang euphemism for one of the most dreaded of the FOUR-LETTER WORDS, i.e., "cunt." The earliest example in *Slang and Its Analogues* (J. S. Farmer and W. E. Henley, 1890–1904) is from 1714: "perhaps a bawdy monosyllable, such as boys write upon walls" (Theophilus Lucas, *The Memoirs of Gamesters and Sharpers*). The first person to include "monosyllable" in a dictionary, according to Eric Partridge (*A Dictionary of Slang and Unconventional English*, 1970) was Capt. Francis Grose, who defined the term as "A woman's commodity," in the 1788 edition of *A Classical Dictionary of the Vulgar Tongue*. When speaking, "monosyllable" ordinarily was prefaced by the article "the," which resulted in a second-order euphemism. Thus, Jon Bee noted that "of all the thousand monosyllables in our language, this *one* only is designated by the definite article; therefore do some men call it 'the article,' 'my article,' and 'her article,' as the case may be" (*Slang: A Dictionary of the Turf*, etc., 1823). Bee, by the way, was a pseudonym; his real name was John Badcock—making him a formidable rival to Grose for the honor of being The Most Aptly Named Authority on Slang.

Though now obsolete in its classical, anatomical sense, "monosyllable" still crops up every once in awhile as a synonym for "four-letter word." Thus, Bernard De Voto noted in a discussion of some of Mark Twain's uncensored language that "the taboo of these monosyllables remained almost though not quite absolute until 1930, when it began to relax" (*Harper's Magazine*, 12/48). See also VAGINA.

Montezuma's revenge. Diarrhea and/or dysentery; the chief Mexican version of worldwide illnesses, which almost always are called by some other, more picturesque name. "The North American in Mexico has coined a number of names for the inevitable dysentery and diarrhea: 'Mexican two-step,' 'Mexican fox-trot,' 'Mexican toothache,' and less directly if more colorfully, 'Montezuma's revenge,' 'the Curse of Montezuma,' and the 'Aztec hop'" (*Western Folklore*, XXI, 1962). In other parts of the world, the same gastrointestinal complaints appear as the *Cairo Crud* (see CRUD), *Delhi Belly*, *Gyppy* (i.e., "Egypt") *Tummy*, *Hong Kong Dog*, *Rangoon Runs*, and *turista* (or *turistas*). Soldiers everywhere have suffered from the *GI's*.

N.B.: *Montezuma's revenge* and friends are not restricted to the poorer, "dirtier" parts of the world. In most cases, the illness probably is just the result of new microbes, or species and strains thereof, being introduced into the traveler's intestines. For this reason, visitors to the "clean" old U.S.A. have been afflicted by the *Bronxville* (New York) *Bomb*, the *L.A.* (California) *Belly*, and similar, not-so-exotic complaints. See also INDISPOSED/INDISPOSITION and STOMACHACHE.

monthlies. An oblique reference to the cycle (or PERIOD) of menstruation. "That squinty one is delicate. Near her monthlies, I expect, makes them ticklish" (James Joyce, *Ulysses*, 1922). See also MENSTRUATE.

monument. A tombstone or other grave marker. Thus, the uninitiated person who looks up "tombstones" in the *Yellow Pages* (Manhattan, New York, 1979–80) is told to "See 'Monuments.'" See also SPACE.

Morals Division. "Immorals Division" would be more accurate, this being the modern police department name for what used to be called the "Vice Squad." See also HOMICIDE.

mortality rate. Death rate; the "mortal" derives ultimately from the Latin *mors* (death) but does not sound nearly as harsh to Anglo-Saxon ears. See also LIFE INSURANCE and PASS AWAY.

mortician. Undertaker. Modeled along the lines of "physician," this represents one of the bolder attempts of the people in the funeral business to increase their prestige by trading on that of the medical profession. "Mortician" was formally proposed in the February 1895 issue of *Embalmer's Monthly*, and was received enthusiastically by those sensitive souls who did not think "funeral director," the reigning alternative to "undertaker," to be sufficiently high-toned. Thus, a mere six months later, the *Columbus* (OH) *Dispatch* carried a notice (8/14/95): "We, Mank & Webb, are the only Morticians in the city who do not belong to the Funeral Director's Protective Association." Columbus also was the founding place of the National Selected Morticians (9/17/17), an exclusive trade group that is still alive and kicking. On the whole, though, "mortician" is showing a lack of staying power. This may be partly because the prefix "mort," from the Latin *mors*, death, is a shade too explicit. (MORTUARY also has faded, probably for the same reason.) "Mortician" also lost a lot of professional sheen on account of all the imitations it inspired. Of these, BEAUTICIAN and COSMETICIAN have lasted the longest, and probably hurt the most; others, dating from the 1920s and 1930s, included *bootblackitician*, *fizzician* (soda jerk), *locktician* (locksmith), *shoetrician* (cobbler), and *whooptician* (cheerleader). Whatever the exact cause, the effect is beyond dispute. The supreme authority is the *Yellow Pages*, and the 1979–80 Manhattan, New York, edition includes "mortician" only as a cross-reference to that old standby, FUNERAL DIRECTOR.

mortuary. A deadhouse—and a relatively newfangled one at that, with the oldest example in the *Oxford English Dictionary*, in the sense of a temporary abode for the dead, coming from 1865. Previously, a "mortuary" had been a payment or gift from the estate of the dead person to the parish priest, a funeral, and an OBITUARY.

   Mortuaries come in various sizes. Thus, there are *mortuary chapels* and there are *mortuary coolers;* Bally Case & Cooler, Inc., makes a "2-3-Mini-Walk-In" *mortuary cooler* and a "5-7-Junior-Walk-In with Add-on Capability" (ad, *Casket & Sunnyside*, 1/80). Not that there isn't good precedent for such fancy terminology. The ancient Egyptians, whose accomplishments in this particular field have rarely been equaled, let alone surpassed, called the workshop in which their embalming was done *the beautiful house*. See also CASKET, CHAPEL, and FUNERAL HOME/ PARLOR.

motel. It sounds a lot posher than "auto camp," which is what "motels" started out as. It took awhile for auto camp entrepreneurs to find a suitably elegant name for themselves, but they persisted, developing ever fancier ones, e.g., *auto court, tourist court, cottage court, motor court, motor lodge,* and *motor hotel,* until 1930, when a West Coast operator, Oscar T. Tomerlin, compressed "motor hotel" into "motel" (*Saturday Evening Post*, 7/5/47). Other West Coast condensations that never quite made it included *autotel* and *autel.* Meanwhile, an anchorage for boats may be known as a *boatel*.

mother. Euphemistic shorthand for "motherfucker," which has not only taken over the position once held by "fuck" as the most obscene of the standard obscenities, but has replaced The Great American Epithet, "son of a bitch," in most of its many applications. See also F—— and SOB.

   "Motherfucker" is black slang, introduced to the rest of society during World War II and the immediate postwar years, thanks largely to the leveling influence of the United States Army. As the power of "fuck" was diminished through overuse, "motherfucker" naturally came to the fore—and along with it came the requisite set of euphemisms. Thus, Gen. Alexander Haig, Jr., told White House aide John Scali in December 1972: "This man [Pres. Richard M. Nixon] is going to stand tall and resume the bombing and put those B-52 mothers in there and show'em we mean business" (from Bob Woodward and Carl Bernstein, *The Final Days*, 1976). Euphemistic synonyms of "mother" include *mother-flunker, mother-grabber, mother-jumper, mother-lover, mother-raper,* and *mother-rucker,* as well as the black-slurred *mo'-fo'* and *muh-fuh,* and the fancy permutation, *triple-clutcher,* popularized during the Korean POLICE ACTION by black truck drivers in construction battalions.

motion discomfort. Motion sickness. "I was sitting at the edge of my seat . . . pondering airline euphemisms—the bag labeled 'for motion discomfort,' the card telling me what to do in the event of 'a water landing,' the instructions for using

187

oxygen masks 'should the occasion arise'" (*Saturday Review*, 3/4/72). Another term for that "container," sometimes known as a *comfort container*, is "barf bag." See also STOMACHACHE, UPCHUCK, and WATER LANDING.

motorized transportation module. A school bus, in educationese. See also VERTICAL TRANSPORTATION CORPS.

muck. Most commonly encountered today in the compound "muckraking," "muck" is just an old form of MANURE, itself a euphemism for "shit." As Francis Bacon put it, when explaining why it was not good policy to allow "the Treasure and Moneyes" of a nation to be gathered into a few hands: "For otherwise, a State may haue a great Stock, and yet starue. And Money is like Muck, not good except it be spread" ("Seditions and Troubles," *Essays*, 1625). The journalistic "muckraking" was popularized in 1906 by President Theodore Roosevelt, who drew the metaphor from John Bunyan's *The Pilgrim's Progress* (1684). Bunyan's figure of a man working so busily with a muckrake that he never looked up to see the celestial crown being offered to him stood for the man of the world whose heart had been carried away from God by absorption with earthly things. In TR's version, "the men with the muckrakes" were the antibusiness crusaders who were "often indispensable to the well being of society; but only if they know when to stop raking the muck, and to look upward to the celestial crown above them, to the . . . beautiful things above and round about them" (speech, 4/14/06). Even though it hadn't been intended entirely as a compliment, Lincoln Steffans and other muckrakers were glad to accept the label. For another TR-ism, see VOLUNTARY.

MUF. A wonderfully euphemistic acronym, given the connotations of its sound-alike, "muff," this by-product of the atomic energy business stands for "Materials Unaccounted For." The "materials" in question are SPECIAL NUCLEAR MATERIALS, i.e., uranium and plutonium that have been enriched sufficiently for the making of a bomb (aka DEVICE). Processing operations inevitably result in some *MUF*, but it is possible that thieves also have been at work. In 1977, the federal government said that some 8,000 pounds of highly enriched uranium and plutonium seem to have been lost in some way over the years. To make a bomb, perhaps a thousandth of this amount would be required; see SIGNIFICANT QUANTITY.

mutilated. Castrated; the general term for being deprived of a limb or other organ may serve as a code word for the loss of a very particular organ. ". . . the lively, supple Greek/And Swarthy Nubia's mutilated son" (George Gordon Lord Byron, *Childe Harold's Pilgrimage*, 1812). See also BILATERAL ORCHIDECTOMY.

native. Nonwhite, usually but not necessarily "black." To the white inhabitants of the Union of South Africa, for example, no white person is ever a "native," since that term is reserved exclusively for the original inhabitants of the continent. Not only South Africans speak this way, e.g.: "The [Memphis, Tennessee] *Commercial Appeal*'s history of excesses reads like journalistic folklore. Under former editor Frank Ahlgren, no citizen could ever be referred to as a native of Arkansas. Natives were Africans" (*[MORE]*, 5/74). The nonwhite meaning of "native" also is dominant in such expressions as *the natives are restless, to go native,* and even *Native American,* which seems to be replacing "American Indian." However, not all nonwhites class as *natives.* For example:

> The Japanese were at one time *natives,* but are now foreigners. . . . This metamorphosis is to be attributed to the progress of Japan within a few generations from a harmless and insular existence to her present power and pretensions, as the rival of European countries in the Western arts of bullying, murdering, looting, swaggering, lying, moralising, faking and cheating, and in all the industrial crafts that are necessary to support such activities, especially the manufacture of lethal weapons. As it is unthinkable that a *native* should own anything so civilised as a battleship, a bomber or a mechanised army, the Japanese are manifestly no longer *natives* . . . (Reginald Reynolds, *Cleanliness and Godliness,* 1946)

See also DARKY, SEPARATE DEVELOPMENT (or FREEDOMS), and UNDERDEVELOPED.

necessary. A privy—occasionally a rather elaborate affair, judging from *The Connoisseur* (no. 120, 1756): "The Connoisseurs in Architecture, who build . . . necessaries according to Palladio." Before the advent of indoor plumbing, there were also *necessary houses,* as well as *necessary places, stools,* and *vaults,* e.g., from 1780: "In my Botanical Garden, next the Necessary House, was sown 3 rows of Grass-seeds" (George Washington, *Diaries . . . 1748–1799,* 1925). See also PRIVY.

neck. To engage in amorous play. Roughly equivalent to PET, "neck" is more or less euphemistic depending on the degree to which the participants focus their attentions on the anatomical part named. "In general . . . petting that is confined to lip kissing and mild embracing is referred to as necking" (Robert A. Harper, "Petting," *Aspects of Sexuality,* Albert Ellis and Albert Abarbanel, eds., 1967).

"Neck," "necker," and "necking" were still relatively new terms in 1927 when Damon Runyon noted in his report on the celebrated separation suit between Edward W. "Daddy" Browning, New York real estate operator who admitted to age 51, and his wife, Peaches (*née* Frances Belle Heenan), age 15: "It seems that she made record [in her diary] of the little episodes of her girlhood such as casual 'neckings' with the flaming youth of her acquaintance. When your correspondent was a 'necker' of no mean standing back in the dim and misty past, they called it 'lally-gagging.' Times have changed" (*American Speech*, 2/62).

The origin of the expression "to neck" is shrouded in appropriate darkness. Most authorities date it to about 1910 and say that it became common around 1920, all of which fits well enough with Runyon's testimony. True, the 1976 supplement to the *Oxford English Dictionary* gives citations going back to 1825 for "neck" in the sense of "To clasp (a member of the opposite sex) round the neck; to fondle," but when forced to choose, one leans toward Runyon, who probably was more expert on this particular subject than any dictionary editor. See also MAKE OUT.

necktie party or **sociable.** A hanging, usually but not necessarily a lynching. "Mr. Jim Clemenston, equine abductor, was . . . made the victim of a necktie sociable" (*Harper's Magazine*, 11/1871). This is only one of a great many euphemisms for hanging that flourished in nineteenth-century America. Dating mostly from the 1860s and 1870s, they indicate the way justice was dispensed in the Wild West. Among them: *cause to die of hempen fever, dance, dance on a rope, die in a horse's nightcap, exalt, go up a tree, hoist, jerk to Jesus, give a necking, kicked the clouds (air or wind), legally lasso, neck, put on the hempen collar (cravat, necktie, necklace, etc.), put in a state of suspense, run up, string up,* and *swing* (*American Speech*, 10/36 and *The American Thesaurus of Slang*, 1953). See also CAPITAL PUNISHMENT.

needs some work or **some work needed.** In the realm of real estate, a light reference to a major renovation. See also HANDYMAN'S SPECIAL.

negative. No, with a FOP Index of 5.0. In the military, the use of "negative" has been developed into a form of high art. For example, from J. Irving's *Royal Navalese* (1946): "Orders for a Church Parade 'Dress for Officers No. 3 negative swords'." See also AFFIRMATIVE.

negative reinforcement. Among behavioral psychologists, the opposite of a reward; a punishment. See also AVERSION THERAPY.

Negro. A word that has had wildly different connotations over the past several centuries, depending on time, place, and circumstance, and which, even today, may serve both as a euphemism for "nigger" and a dysphemism for "black." As a euphemism: In *A Dictionary of Americanisms* (Mitford M. Mathews, ed., 1951), a quote from *The Life of Col. David Crockett, Written by Himself* (1860) is rendered as "Negro women are knocked down by the auctioneer and up by the purchaser," where the redoubtable Davy originally wrote "Nigger women," etc. As for "Negro" as a dysphemism: Discussing the ways the *Saint Louis Globe Democrat* lards news stories with its editorial opinions, including its general hostility "to anyone unfortunate enough to be poor, black, or, in some instances, even young," [MORE] reported (5/74): "Long after black Americans had indicated their preference for being called 'blacks,' for example, the *Globe* insisted on calling them 'Negroes,' and Muhammed Ali was Cassius Clay in the *Globe* probably longer than any place else."

"Negro" has an unusual history, having twice swung in and out of fashion. In the eighteenth century, "Negro" was a common euphemism for "slave," a word that inspired so much guilt that even slave-owners were reluctant to pronounce it. Thus, "Negro quarter" is first recorded in 1734, more than a century before the initial appearance of "slave quarter" in 1837. The euphemistic aspect also is clear from Capt. Francis Grose's definition: "NEGRO. A black-a-moor: figuratively used for slave. I'll be no man's negro; I will be no man's slave" (*A Classical Dictionary of the Vulgar Tongue*, 1796).

As the abolitionist movement slowly made headway in the early decades of the nineteenth century, "Negro" came to be avoided because of its slavish associations—particularly by those blacks who were not slaves. By the 1840s, free blacks were appending to their signatures *f.m.c.* or *f.w.c.* for *free man* (or *woman*) *of color*. Other terms were floated in this period, e.g., *Africo-American* (1835), *ebony* (ca. 1850), and *Afro-American* (1880), but "colored" remained dominant for about a century. The Census Bureau, on the advice of Booker T. Washington, adopted "Negro" in 1891. However, the National Association for the Advancement of Colored People was founded in 1909, and as late as 1937, Dr. Kelly Miller, a black man, could worry over the question, *"Negroes or Colored People?"*—the title of an article by him in *Opportunity*, published by the National Urban League. While conceding that "such terms as *colored lady*, *colored gentleman*, and *colored society*" still sounded "more polite than the corresponding *Negro* equivalents," Miller plumped generally for "Negro," which had in fact reestablished itself among blacks as well as whites of the better sort. (The *New York Times* began capitalizing the "N" in "Negro" in 1930; the Government Printing Office did the same thing in 1933.) "Negro" remained ascendant until the mid-1960s, when it was again cast off by a new generation in need of new terms to symbolize its revolt against the status quo, e.g., the Black Panthers (1965), "black power" (1966), and "black is beautiful" (1967).

See also BLACK, COLORED, DARKY, MINORITY, NIGRA, RACE, SERVANT, and TIGER.

nether parts. The unspeakable area below the waist. The expression sounds so archaic as to be obsolete, but it isn't: "The attachments became very strong, the monkeys becoming greatly agitated if separated from their dog. The latter undertook its parental role, grooming and licking the nether parts of the baby" (*New York Times*, 3/25/74).

"Nether" has long been used as an oblique reference to the lower anatomical parts: "Lest he . . . make hym lame of his neder limmes" (John Skelton, *Why Come Ye Not to Court?*, 1522). Later generations managed even to dispense with mention of "limmes" and "legs" in this connection, referring instead to *nethers, nether man*, or *nether person*. The *nether parts* were covered by, naturally, *nether garments*, known generally today as "trousers," e.g., "Long before the old porter could pull his legs through his nether garments" (Capt. Frederick Marryat, *Japhet in Search of a Father*, 1835). See also PRIVATE PARTS and UNMENTIONABLES.

neutralize/neutralization. To take out of action, to render harmless, to kill; the acts thereof. The methods of *neutralizing* people run the gamut from character assassination through assassination. For example, on the least violent end of the spectrum: "Neutralization of [Daniel] Ellsberg . . . I am proposing a skeletal operations plan aimed at building a file on Ellsberg that will contain all available overt, covert and derogatory information. This basic tool is essential in determining how to destroy his public image and credibility" (memo from E. Howard Hunt, Jr., PLUMBER, to Charles W. Colson, special COUNSEL to the president of the United States, 7/28/71, as quoted by Leon Jaworski, special prosecutor, in *The Right and the Power*, 1976). In other contexts, such as the United States-financed Phoenix counterinsurgency program in Vietnam, the sense is more violent: "Despite the fact that the law provided only for the arrest and detention of the suspects, one-third of the 'neutralized agents' were reported dead" (Frances FitzGerald, *Fire in the Lake*, 1972). Even in death, there are different kinds of *neutralization*. Thus, speaking of one of the army officers accused of covering up the My Lai massacre: "His lawyer discussed 'precise neutralization' (the killing of a villager determined to be a Communist) and 'imprecise neutralization' (the killing of a villager not quite determined to be a Communist)" (John J. O'Connor, *New York Times*, 4/7/71). See also ASSASSINATION, COVERT OPERATION, PACIFY/PACIFICATION, and RECONNAISSANCE IN FORCE.

night soil. Human excrement. Nowadays, *night soil* usually is collected from cesspools and other depositories in the mornings, but back in the eighteenth century, when the euphemism appears to have originated, the job actually was performed under cover of night, as awkward as that might seem. As a result, the poor fellow who was saddled with it was sometimes called the *night man*. Other titles for this position have included *gold finder, honey-dipper, jakes farmer,* and *lavender man.* See also MANURE and PRIVY.

nigra; also **nigrah** and **niggra.** An aural euphemism for "nigger." People who say "nigra" sometimes contend that it is a legitimate southern pronunciation of "Negro" and, in defense of alternate pronunciations, they can always point to the father of American dictionary-makers, Noah Webster (1757–1843), who used "neger" all his life. (He also spelled "zebra" as "zeber" until his revision of 1828.) But times have changed, and the people who say "nigra" today usually are self-conscious enough to lower their voices when they say it—particularly if any *nigras* are about—and they never talk about being bit by a "chiggra" except when making a bad joke. See also NEGRO.

no Mayday. In hospital parlance, this translates as "Do not resuscitate this patient." It derives from "Mayday," the international radio-telephone distress call (in turn, from the French *m'aider*, help me). Another way of telling hospital workers not to make extraordinary efforts to keep terminally ill patients alive is to specify that "Routine nursing care [only] to be provided." Both are less drastic than "pull the plug," i.e., to disconnect life-sustaining apparatus. See also NOT DOING WELL and TRIAGE.

nondiscernible microbionoculator. A poison dart gun developed by the CIA. Electronically operated and almost silent, it could shoot a tiny dart about 100 meters. See also ASSASSINATION.

No Outlet. On traffic signs, the upbeat version of "Dead End," euphemistically comparable to the sports announcer's SUDDEN VICTORY.

no recall or **memory** or **recollection of.** "No recall of" and its friends are legalistic hedges for protecting witnesses from committing perjury and their appearance ordinarily should be interpreted as a sign that whoever is asking the questions is getting too warm for the witness's comfort. The underlying principle was explained in a meeting on March 21, 1973, of President Richard M. Nixon and Messrs. H. R. "Bob" Haldeman and John W. Dean III. The conversation (as recorded in Leon Jaworski's *The Right and the Power*, 1976) went this way:

> DEAN: You just can't have a lawyer before a grand jury.
> HALDEMAN: Okay, but you do have rules of evidence. You can refuse to talk.
> DEAN: You can take the Fifth Amendment.
> PRESIDENT: That's right. That's right.
> HALDEMAN: You can say you forgot, too, can't you?
> PRESIDENT: That's right.
> DEAN: But you can't . . . you're in a very high risk perjury situation.
> PRESIDENT: That's right. Just be damned sure you say I don't remember. I can't recall. I can't give any honest . . . an answer that I can recall. But that's it.

Similar hedges include *no personal knowledge* and *to the best of my knowledge*. See also INDICATE and PLAUSIBLE DENIAL.

no right to correspondence. Executed; the official euphemism in Stalin's Russia. Variants included *deprived of the right to correspond* and *sentenced without right to correspondence*. "Or else the answer is tossed out: . . . 'No right to correspondence'—and that almost for certain means: 'Has been shot'" (Aleksandr I. Solzhenitsyn, *The Gulag Archipelago 1918–1956: An Experiment in Literary Investigation*, 1974). See also LIQUIDATE/LIQUIDATION and SHOT.

not doing well. Dying; a circumlocution used by nurses in hospitals when breaking the bad news to the patient's doctor. See also EXPIRE.

nude. Naked. There is more to nudity than meets the eye. A woman may pose for an artist in the "nude," but if she is seen minus her clothes by a Peeping Tom, then she is "naked." And if, as happened once in an art class I attended, the unauthorized viewing is done during the posing, then the model is simultaneously "nude" and "naked." In this instance, the model immediately grasped the semantic point as well as her robe, and would not resume her pose until the cops had been called and the peeper chased away.

Typically, the harsher, starker "naked" is an Anglo-Saxon word. The softer, more-refined "nude" comes from the Latin *nudus*, with some help from the obsolete French *nud*, and is a much later, eighteenth-century addition to English. See also ALTOGETHER, AU NATUREL, BIRTHDAY SUIT, BUFF, and OPTIONAL SWIMSUIT AREA.

nuisance. A general-purpose euphemism, usually proceeded by the word "commit," as in, "Dammit—Fido's committed a nuisance on the Oriental." See also DOG DIRT/LITTER/WASTE.

number one and/or **two.** Potty talk for "piss" and "shit," dating from at least the nineteenth century and still current on the nation's airwaves, in public prints, and among consenting adults, e.g., referring to water conservation measures during a California drought: "I understand that you can now flush the toilet after going number one in Marin County" (Johnny Carson, WNBC-TV, 1/19/78). And on the grimmer side, reporting on the miseries of being a prisoner on a prison train in Russia: "Sometimes the orders came before you even started: 'All right, number one only!'" (Aleksandr I. Solzhenitsyn, *The Gulag Archipelago 1918–1956: An Experiment in Literary Investigation*, 1974). The euphemism here is the translator's adaptation, the equivalent Russian terms being "little" and "big" (Thomas P. Whitney, trans., and Frances Lindley, ed.). See also DEFECATE/DEFECATION and PEE.

nurse. Suck. Embarrassment over the animalistic—ugh!—act of sucking dates to the great period of pre-Victorian prudery. For example, Noah Webster substituted "to nurse" or "to nourish" for "to give suck" when he bowdlerized the Bible in 1833. But Webster's hang-ups (see PECULIAR MEMBERS for more details) were by no means peculiar to him. Consider the lengths to which proper English LADIES went just two decades later: ". . . there was the unpleasant association with a ceremony frequently gone through by little babies; and so, after dessert, in orange season, Miss Jenkyns and Miss Matty used to rise up, possess themselves each of an orange in silence, and withdraw to the privacy of their own rooms, to indulge in sucking oranges" (Elizabeth C. Gaskell, *Cranford*, 1853). And a proper young man of the time, when given an orange, is said to have announced, "If you will excuse me, I think I will nurse mine."

nursing home. An old-age home, and a rare double-euphemism, the "nursing" implying a degree of loving tenderness that is seldom encountered, while the "home" conceals an institution that at best has all the hominess of a good hospital and at worst is a chamber of horrors. "'If I put a man in a room, beat him, starved him, didn't give him any water, the state would put me in jail,' Dr. [Isa] Goldman said. 'If I own a nursing home and do it, the state pays me'"(*New York Times*, 1/3/75).

"Nursing home" is a fairly new import from Britain. As recently as 1945, H. L. Mencken noted: "It would be hard to imagine any American male of the plain people using such [British] terms as *rotter, braces* (for *suspenders*), *boot-shop, . . . nursing home* or *master's bedroom*" (*The American Language, Supplement I*). In that era, the standard American euphemism for "old-age home" was *private hospital*. See also ADULT, CONVALESCENT HOSPITAL, RESIDENT, and the basic HOME.

nuts. Euphemistic slang for the balls or TESTICLES. "Oh nuts!" is the functional equivalent of "Oh balls!" while "Nuts to you!" is an emphatic "No!" (People also *go nuts* when they go crazy and sometimes they even wind up in the *nut house*, but these usages derive from "nut," singular, as slang for "head.") Because of its lower anatomical meaning, "nuts" has been euphemized as *nerts* or *nertz*, and it has also—getting to the main point of the present entry—served as a euphemism for still stronger language.

By far the most famous euphemistic "nuts" is that attributed to Brig. Gen.

Anthony McAuliffe, who, as acting commander of the 101st Airborne Division, is said to have given this one-word reply to the Germans on December 22, 1944, at the height of the Battle of the Bulge. McAuliffe had been asked to surrender Bastogne, a key road junction. His troops were outnumbered four to one and completely surrounded. According to the Authorized Version of history, McAuliffe said "Nuts!" as he dropped the German surrender note on the floor. One of his regimental commanders then translated the reply for the enemy officers who had brought the demand: "If you don't know what 'Nuts!' means, it is the same as 'Go to hell!'" (Frank James Price, *Troy H. Middleton, A Biography*, 1974).

McAuliffe always will be remembered for this brave answer, but it seems most unlikely that he ever said it. Ordinarily, the general used stronger language and people familiar with his speech patterns believe that he ran true to form on this occasion, saying something just as brave but not as printable. In the words of a well-informed infantry scout, Kurt Vonnegut, Jr. (he was captured during the Battle of the Bulge): "Can you imagine the commanding general of the 101st Airborn saying anything but 'shit' . . ." (personal communication, via Walter James Miller, 1979). In this connection, it seems highly significant that McAuliffe was known fondly to his troops as "Old Crock." Vonnegut adds that the general's remark may have been "a plagiarism"; for the source from which McAuliffe (perhaps unconsciously) stole, see SHORT FRENCH EXPLETIVE, A.

O

obituary. A death notice; from the Latin word for death, *obitus*, which is something of a euphemism, too, with the literal meaning of "a going down" (from *obire*: *ob-*, down + *ire*, to go). As a record or announcement of a person's death, the short "obit" preceded "obituary" into English by a couple hundred years, "obit" dating to the mid-fifteenth century, while the long form isn't recorded until the beginning of the eighteenth (*Oxford English Dictionary*). See also PASS AWAY and PREPARED BIOGRAPHY.

obscene, derogatory, and scatological. On October 4, 1976, Earl L. Butz was forced to RESIGN as secretary of agriculture for having said something that only two newspapers in the land dared print—the *Capital Times*, of Madison, Wisconsin, and the *Blade*, of Toledo, Ohio, according to a poll by the Associated Press. For the rest, euphemism and circumlocution reigned, as the nation's editors ganged up to run Butz out of town but without letting their readers know exactly why. Leading the pack was that great FAMILY newspaper, the *New York Times*, which initially informed the masses that President Gerald R. Ford was reprimanding Mr. Butz because the secretary had told an anecdote "in which black people were referred to as 'coloreds' and described as wanting only three things. The things were listed, in order, in obscene, derogatory, and scatological terms" (10/2/76). The *Times* stuck to this prissy description on the following day and, on October 5, after Butz had resigned, became only slightly more explicit, telling readers that Butz's anecdote had revolved around "'coloreds'" wanting "satisfying sex, loose shoes and a warm place for bodily functions—wishes that were listed by Mr. Butz in obscene and scatological terms." With this, the *Times* surpassed its best previous euphemistic effort (BARNYARD EPITHET). Other versions of Butz's anecdote, arranged in order of increasing clarity, included:

> The Associated Press: "'blacks' alleged preferences in sex, 'shoes,' and bathrooms."
> United Press International: "good sex, easy shoes and a warm place to go to the bathroom."
> The *Washington Post*: "Coloreds only want . . . first, a tight (woman's sexual organs); second, loose shoes; and third, a warm place to (defecate)."
> The *San Francisco Sunday Examiner*: "First, a tight p————, second, loose shoes, and third, a warm place to s———."

The dashes are an old euphemistic convention (see F———), and here they stand, of course, for the extra letters of "pussy" and "shit" (the former being a euphemism in its own right; see PUSSY). The inflammatory language had been elicited from Mr. Butz by a serious question from Pat Boone, the singer, who had wanted to know why the Republican party couldn't attract more black voters. To which Butz had replied, jokingly, that "coloreds" were interested in only three things, etc., etc., etc. The remark was delivered shortly after the Republican

National Convention, in an airplane en route from Kansas City to Los Angeles, and in the presence of John W. Dean III, who at this time was no longer White House COUNSEL but—equally dangerous—acting as a reporter for *Rolling Stone.* Mr. Dean kindly attributed the remark only to a "shirt-sleeved cabinet member" in his account (10/7/76), but *New Times,* by checking the traveling schedules of all 11 cabinet secretaries, quickly fingered the guilty party. Boone told *New Times:* "He [Butz] knew he was talking to a reporter, and he may have thought what he said was unprintable. It occurred to me right then that it might be printed. I cringed for him" (10/15/76).

As unedifying as Butz's remark was, the spectacle of his being forced out of office for unstated reasons was still more curious. In resorting to euphemisms, most of the newspaper editors were being not only high-minded but high-handed, taking it upon themselves to make a decision about Butz that should have been left to their voter-readers. Robert Malone, managing editor of the *Capital Times,* put the case for printing all the news this way: "We think readers have the right to know exactly what Mr. Butz said and judge for themselves whether his remarks were obscene and racist in character; the paraphrasing we've seen doesn't carry off the same meaning as the actual words" (*Columbia Journalism Review,* 11–12/76). Of course, this wasn't the first time Butz's sense of humor had gotten him in trouble; see GAME for the second-most-famous Butz joke.

occupy. In the seventeenth and eighteenth centuries, this was the principal euphemism for cohabitation in general and sexual INTERCOURSE in particular. Consider the following ditty, from Capt. Francis Grose's *A Classical Dictionary of the Vulgar Tongue* (1796):

> All you that in your beds do lie
> Turn to your wives, and occupy:
> And when that you have done your best,
> Turn a-se to a-se, and take your rest.

So tarred was "occupy" by its secondary, euphemistic meanings that it was virtually banned from polite English in any sense at all for almost 200 years. As early as 1597, William Shakespeare noted *what* was happening in *Henry IV,* Part 2: "A captain! God's light, these villains will make the word as odious as the word 'occupy,' which was an excellent good word before it was ill-sorted . . ." Some years later, his contemporary, Ben Jonson, explained *why* it happened: "Many, out of their own obscene apprehensions, refuse proper and fit words—as *occupy, nature,* and the like; so the curious industry of some, of having all alike good, hath come nearer a vice than a virtue" (*Timber: Or Discoveries Made Upon Men and Matter,* "De Stilo," ca. 1640). The shunning of "occupy" was so total that the *Oxford English Dictionary* included a special note on the phenomenon: "The disuse of this verb in the 17th and most of the 18th c. is notable. Against 194 quots. for 16th c., we have for 17th only 8, outside the Bible of 1611 (where it occurs 10 times), and for 18 c. only 10, all of its last 33 years. . . . This avoidance appears to have been due to its vulgar employment . . ." See also F——.

odds bodkins. God's Little Body. The euphemistic nonoath derives from *ods bodikins,* where "od" is a shortening of "God" that first appeared around 1600.

"'Oddsbodikins!' said the sergeant of police, taking off his helmet and wiping his forehead" (Kenneth Grahame, *The Wind in the Willows*, 1908). The basic "od" also produced such other euphemistic exclamations as *od rabbit it, od rat it* (which may have led to the common *drat*), *odsoons* (wounds), and *odzooks* (hooks). See also GADZOOKS and ZOUNDS.

off. To kill or to SCREW, the commingling of death and sex in a single word being fairly standard practice (see DIE). "The Organization had ordered him to mess up a couple of guys, but instead he offed them" (John Godey, *The Taking of Pelham One Two Three*, 1973). "You may not believe this . . . when I off a nigger bitch, I close my eyes and concentrate real hard and pretty soon I get to believing that I'm riding one of them bucking blondes" (Eldridge Cleaver, *Soul on Ice*, 1968).

Among British soldiers in World War I, "off" also was slang for "die," and before that (ca. seventeenth to twentieth centuries) "off" and "go off" already stood for going off to sleep or—to sleep's look-alike—death, e.g., "The doctors told me that he might go off any day" (Sir H. Rider Haggard, *Colonel Quaritch, V.C.*, 1888). At home in the 1960s, meanwhile, the same demonstrators who favored nonviolence in Southeast Asia frequently shouted "Off the pigs," when the police moved in on them. See also HIT and INTERCOURSE.

officer. A common title for elevating the status of various trades, e.g., *animal welfare officer* (dogcatcher), *correctional officer* (prison guard), *information officer* (press agent), *pest control officer* (a British ratcatcher), *truant officer*, and, of course, the simple police *officer* (if those on patrol are *officers*, then what are the lieutenants and captains back at the station house—*officer officers?*). See also ENGINEER.

old man's friend, the. Pneumonia; a friendly name for an illness that was dreaded, and rightfully so, especially by the aged, prior to the discovery of penicillin. See also C, THE BIG and TB.

open marriage. Open adultery; the smart new term not only dispenses with the sinful connotations of the traditional one but puts monogamists on the defensive. The psychology of the terminology is the same as with PRO-CHOICE. See also AFFAIR and EXTRAMARITAL.

open shop. Nonunion shop; another victory for management, which tends to win semantic battles more often than contractual wars. See also RIGHT-TO-WORK.

opera house. The grandiose appellation for the auditorium that once played such a vital part in small-town American life, and in which operas were seldom, if ever, performed. Discussing the typical *opera house* offerings in the 1890s: "These were the great days when *Uncle Tom's Cabin*, with 'fifty men, women, and children, a pack of genuine bloodhounds, grandest street parade ever given, and two bands,' packed the Opera House to capacity" (Robert S. and Helen Merrell Lynd, *Middletown* [Muncie, Indiana], 1929). The Muncie Opera House eventually gave way to a movie house. For a note on its offerings, see also PET.

operative/operator. A classy detective, INVESTIGATOR, or spy; a secret AGENT.

Domestically, the high-toned term was popularized about the turn of the century by the most famous of detective agencies, i.e.: "The word 'detective' became so offensive . . . that it was dropped by some agencies. The word chosen by the Pinkertons to take its place was 'operative'" (*New York Press*, 10/23/05). Then there is John D. Ehrlichman, who began his political service for Richard M. Nixon in 1960 by spying on Governor Nelson Rockefeller and on the Democratic National Convention. He didn't use the word "spy," of course. "Because of his anonymity, Ehrlichman said, he was assigned to 'operative work' stalking Rockefeller" (Evans and Novak, *New York Post*, 6/2/73). Fittingly, having begun his political career as an *operative*, Ehrlichman ended it with a COVERT OPERATION.

option. Choice. The harder sound of the two-syllable word makes the choices themselves sound harder and suggests, by association, that the people making them have harder noses, too. The vogue for "option" began in the early 1960s as the Kennedy Administration built up conventional military forces so that the nation could wage small wars instead of having to rely exclusively on the threat of massive retaliation, e.g., "The new approach . . . was recommended by Secretary [of Defense Robert S.] McNamara as part of his build-up of options" (Theodore C. Sorensen, *Kennedy*, 1965). Subsequent administrations retained the terminology. Thus, discussing Watergate burglar E. Howard Hunt, Jr.'s threat to tell all to the prosecutors unless he received $120,000, President Richard M. Nixon told John W. Dean III:

> Just looking at the immediate problem, don't you think you have to handle Hunt's financial situation damn soon? . . . It seems to me we have to keep the cap on the bottle that much, or we don't have any options. (3/21/73, *The White House Transcripts*, 1974)

For more about *options* in the Pentagon, see SCENARIO; for the *option* the president elected in Hunt's case, continue with EXPLETIVE DELETED.

optional swimsuit area. The tongue-tied city fathers' way of saying "nude bathing permitted." Speaking of La Jolla, California: "The city ordinance passed this spring proclaiming that a 900-foot-long strip of Black's Beach was an 'optional swimsuit area' was made possible by a 1972 California Supreme Court ruling that nude sunbathing was not illegal if it took place on beaches secluded from the public view" (*New York Times*, 6/24/74). See also NUDE.

ordnance. The generic term, classically taken to mean cannon and their supplies, conceals such modern uglies as bombs and napalm. Thus, speaking of the intentionally bland reports given by American military briefers in Vietnam:

> Their language, which has no connection with everyday English, has been designed to sanitize the war. Planes do not drop bombs, they 'deliver ordnance.' Napalm is a forbidden word and when an American information officer is forced under direct questioning to discuss it, he calls it 'soft ordnance.' In the press releases and the answers to

newsmen's questions, there is never any sense, not even implicit, of people being killed, homes being destroyed, thousands of refugees fleeing." (Sydney H. Schanberg, "The Saigon Follies, or Trying to Head Them Off at the Credibility Gap," *New York Times Magazine,* 11/12/72)

Another kind of "ordnance" is *incontinent ordnance,* which are bombs that fall where they're not supposed to (e.g., on friends instead of foes). Such miss-hits also may be disguised as *accidental delivery of ordnance equipment,* perhaps due to a *navigational misdirection.* See also CASUALTY, DELIVER, FRIENDLY FIRE, and SELECTIVE ORDNANCE.

organ. Women have internal organs but as a rule only men have external, euphemistic *organs,* i.e., the penis (aka the *male generative organ* or the *reproductive organ*), the testicles (or *male organs*), and the collective *organs of generation* (see GENERATE/GENERATION). However, the single word usually is enough to get the message across. As a letter writer to *Playboy* (9/76) put it: "Some just like the visual turn-on; others say a big organ feels better in their hand."

Modern usage is even blander than that of the Victorians, who actually referred to "sex organs," sometimes even in the feminine sense. As past masters of the art of double-think, however, the Victorians could pretend when the occasion demanded that their women had no "reproductive organs." Thus, Dr. William Acton, a sexologist before that term was invented, published a great work in 1857, entitled *The Functions and Disorders of the Reproductive Organs, in Childhood, Youth, Adult Age, and Advanced Life, Considered in Their Physiological, Social and Moral Relations.* The only trouble with this title, as Steven Marcus pointed out, is that "it is altogether misleading and inaccurate. The book is entirely about men and male sexuality" (*The Other Victorians,* 1964). See also PENIS and TESTICLES.

osculate. The high point of first-year Latin for many students is learning that "osculate" means "to kiss," the English word deriving from the Latin *osculum,* "little mouth." Such are the unexpected advantages of a classical education. "Osculate" also has acquired other esoteric meanings. Thus, biologists say that two species, or genera, "osculate" when they are connected by common characteristics, while mathematicians use the word to describe the bringing of two curves or surfaces into close contact so that they have three or more points in common—a definition that covers all but the shyest of ninth-grade *osculators.* See also EXPECTORATE.

other than honorable discharge. The military services maintain the discriminations of rank to the bitter end; thus, an officer will get an *other than honorable discharge* where an enlisted person will receive an undesirable discharge. See also LEAVE.

outhouse. An outdoor PRIVY; the generalization originally concealed the errand. Technically, an "outhouse" could be any "outbuilding." In fact, the *Oxford English Dictionary* defined "outhouse" in the following, careful manner: "A house or building, belonging to and adjoining a dwelling-house, and used for some subsidiary purpose, e.g., a stable, barn, washhouse, toolhouse, or the like" (vol. O, prepared 1902–04). In this instance, "or the like" must be regarded as a euphemism. See also TOILET.

outplacement. Finding a job for someone who is being LET GO (as contrasted with "placement," which is jargon for finding a job for someone who wants in). "Alan Sweetser is president of Compass Incorporated, a local executive outplacement counselling firm" (*Minneapolis Tribune*, 7/23/78). Synonyms for "outplacement" include *recruitment, dehiring,* and *constructive termination.* See also TERMINATE/ TERMINATION.

Oval Office. The president of the United States; topographical doubletalk, whereby a person is described indirectly in terms of the physical location of the body. This kind of talk may be used to elevate the stature of job-holders (as in BENCH, THE); it also introduces an element of imprecision that can be useful in establishing a PLAUSIBLE DENIAL. For example: "In fact, Krogh had told me it [approval of the Fielding break-in] came from the Oval Office, but I was still keeping the President out of things" (John W. Dean III, *Blind Ambition,* 1976). For more about the Fielding break-in, see also COVERT OPERATION.

overapplied for. Talking about doubletalk: "'It gets worse and worse,' said Henry Steele Commager in an interview. 'Did you hear Caspar Weinberger, the Secretary of HEW, explain that we have enough medical schools—they are just over-applied for?'" (Israel Shenker, "Zieglerrata," *New Republic,* 4/13/74). The Ziegler of Zieglerrata is, of course, Ron; see INOPERATIVE.

overflight. An illegal flight over an international boundary.
The most famous American "overflight" occurred in 1960 when a U-2 spy plane (the "U" is for "Utility") piloted by Francis Gary Powers was shot down near Sverdlovsk, nearly 1,300 miles inside Russia, but it was by no means the first such mission. As early as September 5, 1949, two CIA-trained Ukrainian nationalists were flown home from a base in the American zone in Germany. Referring to plans for this and other "overflights" to infiltrate AGENTS into the Soviet Union: ". . . the A-2 [Air Force chief of intelligence] also pointed out that the Soviet ground reaction to our overflights would provide him with the first hard intelligence on the state of Soviet ground defenses against air attack" (Harry Rositzke, *The CIA's Secret Operations,* 1977). See also COVER STORY and INCURSION.

overqualified for. Doubletalk; used when rejecting job applicants, this usually translates as "I'm afraid that you'll quickly become bored and unhappy with the miserable, low-paying job for which you've applied." Occasionally, it may also mean "You are too old" (the point being that it took many years to get all those qualifications) or "I'm afraid to hire you because you're smarter than I am." "Overqualified" women frequently end up as ADMINISTRATIVE ASSISTANTS.

P

p——. The euphemistic dash lives on in the nation's FAMILY newspapers. "Whether or not Sally Quinn . . . made up another quote . . . what we want to know is if [Hamilton Jordan, assistant to the president] is the kind of person who'd tell this same assemblage, 'This administration has to take a p———.' We already know the *Washington Post* is too icky poo to print the *iss* . . ." (*MORE*, 2/78). See also F—— and PEE.

pacify/pacification. Gentle terms for not-so-friendly forms of persuasion: to repress, destroy, lay waste, and the acts thereof. "In czarist Russia, detachments sent to punish striking workers were called 'pacifying detachments' . . ." (Anatol Rapoport, *Semantics*, 1975). As George Orwell explained: ". . . political language has to consist largely of euphemism, question-begging and sheer cloudy vagueness. Defenceless villages are bombarded from the air, the inhabitants are driven out into the countryside, the cattle machine-gunned, the huts set on fire with incendiary bullets: this is called *pacification*" ("Politics and the English Language," 1946). A quarter-century later, the phraseology and the technique remained essentially the same, i.e.: "Under the so-called Accelerated Pacification Campaign the U.S. Ninth Division almost literally 'cleaned out' the Front-held regions of the northern Mekong Delta, bombing villages, defoliating crops, and forcing the peasants to leave their land" (Frances FitzGerald, *Fire in the Lake*, 1972). However, *pacification* by means of fire and sword is not just another example of newspeak; thus: "To send fourtie . . . men of weir to the West Bardour for helping to pacifie the cuntre" (*The Register of the Privy Council of Scotland*, 1565). See also NEUTRALIZE/NEUTRALIZATION.

palpitators. Nineteenth-century American falsies, also known as *palpitating bosoms* or *patent heavers*. In the fractured English of Petroleum Vesuvius Nasby (David Ross Locke): "I am a bridegroom, wich cometh from his bride on the mornin feelin releeved ub the knowledge that she wore not palpitators, nor calves, nor nothing false, afore she was hizn" (*Swinging Round the Cirkle*, 1867). See also BOSOM, BRASSIERE, and GAY DECEIVERS.

panties. Women's underpants; the diminutive minimizes the sexual associations by casting the adult wearers in the roles of children or little girls.

When "panties" first appeared on the scene, back in the 1840s, they were men's underpants—*small trousers*, as they were also called. The men's "panties" derived from "pants," naturally, with the latter being a new and still somewhat disreputable abbreviation of "pantaloons." Liberated women in the nineteenth century also wore "pants," but when that word was used in a feminine context, the reference was to "pantalets" or "bloomers." True *panties* for women do not seem to have come into style until after the turn of the century. Eric Partridge dates this sense of the word to 1905 (*A Dictionary of Slang and Unconventional English*, 1970), while Mario Pei says its real use did not begin until the 1920s (*Words in*

Sheep's Clothing, 1969). Probably, the great change in women's fashions that took place around the time of World War I (see BRASSIERE) had much to do with the adoption of "panties," actually as well as linguistically. In addition, women wear a number of other similar euphemisms, including:

Briefs: A product of the early 1930s, whose appearance was soon protested, but to no effect: "I'm bored to tears with 'scanties'/I'm sick to death of 'briefs' . . ." ("Too Much of Too Little," *Books of To-day*, 11/10/34). "Briefs" also was adopted in France, to the despair of middle-aged French writers, who tried to have the term banned from the dictionaries because it was not the one (i.e., *pantalon de femme*) they had learned as youths (Cecil Saint-Laurent, *A History of Ladies Underwear*, 1968). Indicative of the current feminization of men's fashions is the fact that since about 1950, men also have been wearing *briefs* (along with the older, longer "shorts" or "undershorts"). As yet, men have not taken to wearing *brevities*, but this, too, may well come to pass.

Drawers: An old and now somewhat antiquated term, the first reference to "drawers" in the *Oxford English Dictionary* is from 1567. In the beginning, the word seems to have been applied to "stockings" as well as to undergarments of varying length (sometimes to the ankle), depending upon the fashion of the time. The word actually describes the way the garment is drawn on, not the garment itself, giving it the same euphemistic quality as the later *pull-ons* and *step-ins*.

Knickers (or *knicks*): Loose, short (originally knee-length) underpants, worn by British women (and children) since the late nineteenth century. The term is an abbreviation of "knickerbockers," which are men's knee-length pants (also called "plus fours" when cut in an exceptionally baggy manner, four inches too long). The acronym *NORWICH*, composed by some unknown but lonely British serviceman in World War II, stands for "Nickers Off Ready When I Come Home."

Scanties: "Scanty trousers" appears in the *Oxford English Dictionary* from 1874, but the pantielike "scanties" of today come from the same era as *briefs* above.

Step-ins: A common euphemism of the 1930s and 1940s, e.g., "She came out [of the water], pulling her soaking step-ins about so as to get a maximum of modesty" (John O'Hara, *Appointment in Samarra*, 1934). N.B.: "A step-in" is an anagram of "panties."

See also LINGERIE, UNDIES, and UNMENTIONABLES.

paramour. An illicit lover of either sex. In French, *par* plus *amour* equals "by or through love," and the early connotations were not necessarily impure. In medieval times, for instance, a knight might refer to his lady love as his "paramour," and have only high-minded thoughts. The allusion might even be religious, as in a poem from 1492, in which the Virgin Mary addresses Christ as "Myne owne dere sonne and paramoure." Nevertheless, the more sensual connotations developed quickly: "My fourthe housbonde was a revelour; This to seyn he hadde a paramour" (Geoffrey Chaucer, *Prologue to the Wife of Bath's Tale*, ca. 1387–1400). "Paramour" sounds archaic, but it is not, to wit: ". . . the state's Welfare Inspector General, Richard V. Horan, has singled out the case of a 31-year-old Queens woman who together with her five children and 'paramour,' has managed to collect $88,268.17 in benefits over the last five and one-half years . . ." (*New York Times*, 10/13/76). See also AMOUR and FRIEND.

parlor. A euphemism for a business establishment. While the domestic parlor has been largely superseded by the living room, the business *parlor* lives on in a variety of forms, among them: *beauty parlor, betting* (or *horse*) *parlor, billiard parlor* (also called an *academy*), FUNERAL PARLOR, *ice-cream parlor*, MASSAGE PARLOR, RAP PARLOR, and *shoeshine parlor*. Barbershops used to be known as *tonsorial parlors*; the first movie houses were *movie parlors* (later they became *theaters, palaces,* and even *cathedrals*); and some of the more expensive whorehouses were called *parlor houses*. In railroad lingo, meanwhile, a *parlor car* was either a Pullman (the Pullman firm was proudly incorporated in 1867 as the Pullman Palace Car Company) or, less romantically, a caboose. A *parlor cattle car*, by contrast, is a superior car for taking cattle to market.

Before the term was adopted in the business world, a *parlor* was purely a place for conversation; the French *parler* or, in its Latin form, *parlatorium*, was a room in a monastery or nunnery in which inmates could talk to visitors. See also EMPORIUM, SALON, SHOPPE, and STUDIO.

parson-in-the-pulpit. The common name of the wild arum lily, formerly known as the "cukoo pintile" (or "pint") and "priest's pintle"—"pintle" being an old (ca. 1100) word for "penis." See also CANOLA and PENIS.

partner. A person who is living with another person in an unsanctified relationship. The relationship is usually but not necessarily a RELATIONSHIP, i.e., sexual, and the *partners* themselves may be of either, and not necessarily the opposite, sex. The term was adopted officially by the Census Bureau for the 1980 census, with "partner, roommate" being one of the four categories to which all persons "not related to person in column 1" (the de facto head of the household) could assign themselves. See also FRIEND and ROOMMATE.

party. Whether as a verb or noun, the festive term covers an exceedingly wide range of behavior, from the traditional tea or cocktail *party*, to the teen-age *petting party* (see PET), to even heavier get-togethers, featuring nonalcoholic drugs and/ or group sex. ". . . the straight call girls . . . are nothing at all compared to their society's stars, the women who run the ritzier houses, where prices start at $50 for a half-hour and can go as high as $1,000 for a 'bachelor party' or orgy" (*New York Times*, 8/9/71). See also CALL GIRL and HOUSE.

pass away. To die; an old euphemism, dating at least to the fourteenth century, which flowered in the fertile soil of pre-Victorian prudery, being well watered with tears of artificial sentimentality. The basic "pass" comes from the French *passer*, which the French themselves use euphemistically in place of *mourir*, to die. Variants include *pass beyond, pass on, pass out,* and *pass over*, frequently elaborated, usually in the past tense, into such poetic figures as *passed over the river* and *passed over the Great Divide*.

The prettying up of death in the decades just before Victoria ascended the throne in 1837 was recorded for posterity in the changing styles of tombstones. As one graveyard (or CEMETERY) visitor reports:

During the eighteenth century, according to my churchyard observations, people were allowed, quite simply to die. Towards the end of that period they begin to "depart this life." That is a fuller term, but there is no evasion about it. . . . But about the year 1830 everything goes. . . . Simplicity vanishes as well as the stately and sonorous rhythm. People no longer die, like Adam: they pass over, they go home, they are carried to rest, they fall asleep, they are removed to the divine bosom, or whisked to other celestial and possibly embarrassing niches. Anything but the plain fact of death. (Ivor Brown, *A Word in Your Ear* and *Just Another Word*, 1945)

Though we are now, supposedly, well out of the Victorian era, "pass away" and its principal variants are still commonly encountered on OBITUARY pages as well as in funeral establishments (see LOVED ONE for an example). Of course, the ways of not talking about death are legion, as every good FUNERAL DIRECTOR knows. Many of the euphemisms and circumlocutions are phrased in terms of REST and SLEEP (e. g., *laid to rest* and *fell asleep*); others refer to the places to which living people like to think dead people go (see HAPPY HUNTING GROUNDS, GONE TO THE), and still others refer with varying degrees of vagueness to the act of dying (see CROSS OVER, DEMISE, EXPIRE, and GO). Special vocabularies also have been developed for different kinds of untimely death; see ASSASSINATION, BITE THE DUST, BRIEF (or SHORT) ILLNESS, CAPITAL PUNISHMENT, CULL, and PUT AWAY/DOWN/OUT/TO SLEEP. And these only scratch the surface: There are hundreds of other euphemistic metaphors for the untoward event. Herewith, a sampling:

> *answer the last muster* (or *roll call*). An old soldier's death.
>
> BALL GAME, END OF THE. One of many game-playing analogies; see the entry.
>
> *call to one's reward*. Other "calls" include *called home, called to God,* and *called beyond*.
>
> *close one's eyes*. Not just a blink.
>
> *decease*. A legal term that becomes a euphemism in nonlegal contexts; see DECEASED.
>
> *depart*. Somewhat more precise than most similar circumlocutions, even in such a flowery setting as "John has now departed this vale of tears," but clearly a euphemism when referring to John himself as *the departed*; see DEPARTED.
>
> *fade*. A pleasant regionalism, from the hills of Tennessee, as in "Aunt Hattie faded last night."
>
> *give* (or *grant*) *the quietus*. An accounting term; see QUIETUS.
>
> *in the grand secret*. "He or she is in the grand secret; i.e., dead" (Capt. Francis Grose, *A Classical Dictionary of the Vulgar Tongue*, 1796).
>
> *kick the bucket*. In use since the eighteenth century, probably referring to the bucket on which the suicidal farmer stood in order to hang himself.
>
> *lay down one's knife and fork* (or, depending on one's station in life, *one's pen, shovel and hoe,* etc.).
>
> *make one's final exit*. Usually reserved for actors and others with large roles upon the stage of life; informally: "It's curtains for you."

pay the debt of (or *to*) *nature.*

shuffle off (or *step off*) *this mortal coil.* From the Shakespearean phrase, "For in that sleep of death what dreams may come, when we have shuffled off this mortal coil" (*Hamlet,* 1601). "Coil" is here used in the sense of the bustle or turmoil of life. The word's origin is unknown; it may have arisen into literary use from slang, as did "rumpus," "hubbub," and other words of similar meaning.

slip one's cable. A sailor's death.

step off. As in "He has stepped off to eternity" or, less formally, "He has stepped off the deep end."

take the last count. For ex-boxers.

turn up one's toes to the daisies. Informally: *pushing up daisies.* The French have a similar expression, *manger les pissenlits par la racine,* which means "eating dandelions by the root." (It would be the French, of course, who would think of death in edible terms.)

went to one's last roundup. For cowboys.

went to the races. For sporting types.

wink out. What candles do.

yield up the ghost (or *breath* or *soul* or *spirit*). Basically the same as *give up the ghost.* From the Bible (1611): "And when Jacob had made an end of commanding his sons, he gathered up his feet into the bed, and yielded up the ghost, and was gathered unto his people" (Genesis, XLIX, 33).

patellar reflex. A fancy "knee jerk"; doctor talk. See also BILATERAL ORCHIDECTOMY.

patron. A customer. "Patron," from the Latin *pater,* father, flatters by implying that the customer is the protector of the establishment—a patron saint practically. This sense of the word is preserved in French and Spanish, where the *batron* or *padron* of an inn is the innkeeper, not the customer. In English, however, the *patron* is no longer even a regular customer, but anyone who darkens the door momentarily, as in "Notice to our patrons: The Management is not responsible for articles left in the checkroom." See also CLIENT

pecker. The penis, in American English, but something quite different in British English, where the expression, "Keep your pecker up," translates innocently as "Keep your courage up," or, more freely, as "Never say die." Both the American and British "pecker" probably derive from that barnyard pecker, the cock, aka ROOSTER.

The anatomical meaning of "pecker" has produced other, complex semantic ripples in some parts of the United States. For example, one of the reasons fastidious Tennesseans in the 1920s preferred to call the "woodchuck" a "groundhog" was that "woodchuck" also was the local name for a kind of woodpecker, and "pecker" was a word that could never be uttered before women "without the offender being guilty of a serious and practically unpardonable social blunder" (*American Speech,* 5/52). There is a kind of logic here, though it takes some thinking about. See also PENIS and TIMBERDOODLE.

peculiar members. The balls or TESTICLES—and by all odds, the most peculiar of the many euphemisms produced by Noah Webster, when that great lexicographer turned his attention to the Bible, publishing in 1833 a new version "with Amendments of the language." Thus, Leviticus, XXI, 19–20, "Or a man that . . . hath his stones broken" (King James Version, 1611) became, in Webster's version, "Or a man that . . . have his peculiar members broken." (See MEMBER and ROCKS.) The egregiousness of Webster's euphemism is mitigated only slightly by knowing that he was using "peculiar" not in the sense of that which is odd, strange, or queer, but in its original primary sense, relating to personal property, possessions, or privileges.

In rewriting Holy Writ, Webster was following closely in the mincing footsteps of Henrietta and Thomas Bowdler, who had already cleaned up the greatest secular works in the language, with *The Family Shakespeare* (1807, rev. ed. 1818). Webster even defined his objective in virtually the same terms as the Bowdlers (see FAMILY), explaining in a letter of 1836 that his aim had been to remove those words and phrases that "cannot be uttered in families without disturbing devotion." The extraordinary expurgatory efforts of Webster and the Bowdlers are landmarks in the period of prudery beginning in the mid-eighteenth century, that led up to full-fledged Victorianism. Webster's "peculiar members," along with his other "amendments" to the Bible, practically constitute a map of the proto-Victorian psyche, indicating the acts, ideas, and bodily parts whose names were subject to the greatest taboos. Among his other euphemisms, as recorded by Allen Walker Read in "Noah Webster as a Euphemist" (*Dialect Notes*, vol. VI, Part VIII, 1934):

> *Breast*, a generalization for "teat," which he consistently deleted. ("Pap" was occasionally allowed to stand.) See also BOSOM.
>
> *Harlot, lewd*, or *lewd woman* for "whore." Webster completely de-whored the Bible. "To play the whore" became "to be guilty of lewdness." In Revelation, XVII, 1, "the great whore that sitteth upon many waters" became "the great harlot." For "whoredom," Webster substituted such expressions as *carnal connection, idolatries, impurities, lewd deeds, lewdness,* and *prostitution*. See also HARLOT and PROSTITUTE.
>
> *Ill smell, ill savor, odious scent,* and *putrid* were among Webster's euphemisms for "stink," another word that he invariably excised. Thus, in Exodus, VII, 18, "the river shall stink" was rendered as "shall be offensive in smell." (For the ultimate in "stink," see FRAGRANCE.) Curiously, while avoiding "stink," Webster did not worry much about "dung," which he changed only a few times. Nor was "dunghill" ever touched. "Piss," however, was verboten; he took it out every time. See also PEE for an example.
>
> *Lewd deeds, lewdness,* or *impurity* for FORNICATION.
>
> *Male organs*, used as a synonym for those peculiar *peculiar members*. See also ORGAN.
>
> *Nurse* for the more vivid "suck." Thus, "woe unto them . . . that give suck in those days!" became "that nurse infants in those days!" (Matthew, XXIV, 19).
>
> *Secrets*, for the *peculiar members* and PENIS, considered collectively, with "He

that is wounded in the stones, or hath his privy member cut off, shall not enter into the congregation of the Lord" (Deuteronomy, XXIII, 1) being watered down to "He that is wounded or mutilated in his secrets." See also MUTILATED and PRIVATE PARTS.

Of Webster's many circumlocutions, perhaps the most inspired (i.e., most opaque) is his rendering of the famous passage about Onan's seed (Genesis, XXXVIII, 9), wherein it is reported that when Onan "went in unto his brother's wife, that he spilled *it* on the ground . . ." In Webster's version, this became "in to his brother's wife, that he frustrated the purpose." This passage gave rise to the terms "Onanism" or the "Sin of Onan," which the Victorians associated with MASTURBATION, though it is clearly *coitus interruptus* (see COITION) that is described. One suspects the Victorians fixed upon *Onanism* as the name because the biblical penalty was so dreadful: The Lord, after all, slew poor Onan for having practiced birth control.

pee, also **P, pea,** and **pee pee.** Potty talk for "piss," the "pee" and its variants all serving to soften the sibilant sound of a word that itself is probably of onomat-opoetic origin.

> Knock knock?
> Who's there?
> Santa.
> Santa who?
> Centipede on the Christmas tree.
> (Grade-school humor, ca. 1954)

"Piss" was not always regarded so badly as today. It came into English about the thirteenth century, its immediate ancestor being the Old French *pissier.* It also passed into other Teutonic languages—e.g., German, Swedish, and Icelandic—as, of all things, a euphemism.

In times that were franker than our own, Chaucer, Shakespeare, Dryden, and Swift were among the many writers who committed "piss" to paper. The term even appears in the King James or Authorized Version of the Bible (1611), e.g., "the men which sit on the wall . . . may eat their own dung, and drink their own piss . . ." (2 Kings, XVIII, 27). In this instance the divines who translated the Bible were more explicit than the original author, their "piss" appearing in place of a euphemistic Hebrew expression, "the water of their feet."

The increasing prejudice against "piss" toward the end of the eighteenth century coincides with the general increase in pre-Victorian linguistic delicacy. Thus, when Noah Webster bowdlerized the Bible in 1833, he deleted every single "piss," with the previously mentioned passage in 2 Kings being changed to "the men which sit on the wall . . . may feed on their vilest excretions." (For more about the Webster Version of the Bible, see PECULIAR MEMBERS.) For other alternatives to "piss," see CALLS (or NEEDS) OF NATURE, CAUGHT (or TAKEN) SHORT, DUTY, ELIMINATE/ELIMINATION, GO, LEAK, MAKE (or PASS) WATER, MICTURATE/MICTURITION, NUMBER ONE AND/OR NUMBER TWO, P——, PIDDLE, POWDER MY NOSE, PUMP SHIP, RELIEVE, RETIRE, URINATE/URINATION, WATER SPORTS, and WEE WEE.

penguin. A creature raised semisurreptitiously on kibbutzim in Israel, under the auspices of the Institute of Animal Research. The Israeli *penguin* is a breed apart: It has four legs, a curly tail, and says "oink, oink." Up to 3,000 of these *penguins* (also sometimes called "ducks") are slaughtered each year, and their flesh is served in restaurants as *white meat* or *white steak*. In a state that is at once religious and secular, the doubletalk helps disguise a flourishing industry in, and growing appetite for, pork—despite the traditional dietary laws that proscribe this meat for Jews. See also FILET MIGNON, FRAGRANT MEAT, and WHITE MEAT.

penis. "Children in English-speaking communities learn early that their communities regard certain words as 'dirty' and instead offer euphemisms that usually are of Latin or French derivation. Instead of *prick*, the child is supposed to say *penis*, and he is expected to substitute *vagina* for *cunt* . . ." (Peter Farb, *Word Play: What Happens When People Talk*, 1974).

"Penis," like other Latin terms for sanitizing sexy objects, is a relative newcomer to English. The oldest "penis" in the *Oxford English Dictionary* comes from a medical dictionary that was translated in 1684 and published in 1693. There, the word was defined in terms of an older euphemism, the YARD. In the original Latin, "penis" meant "tail," and "tail" in English is an old (circa fourteenth century) term for the "penis" as well as for its female opposite; see TAIL.

Like other key components of human anatomy (e.g., ARSE and BOSOM), the *penis* has (and has had) a wide variety of other names and sobriquets. Following is a partial listing, divided into six broad categories:

1. Personal names: *Dick/Dicky* (see DONKEY), JOHN THOMAS, PETER, and ROGER.
2. Weaponry: The analogy of the *penis* to a pointed weapon is old. The Romans referred to it casually as a *gladius* (sword). Naturally, the *gladius* fitted into a VAGINA (Latin for "sheath"). The English "prick," though not a weapon per se, but something with a point that pierces, continues the thought. Then there is TOOL (in the sense of "sword"), the more-complicated *engine* (meaning a battering ram, an engine of war), *machine, truncheon,* and the highly generalized WEAPON. Finally, the age of gunpowder has brought forth the GUN, the *pistol,* and the SHORT ARM.
3. Anatomical allusions: JOINT, MEMBER, ORGAN, *pizzle* (from an old Germanic word for "sinew"), PRIVATE PARTS, SEX.
4. Miscellaneous metaphors: *bat* (and *balls*), *bishop, bone* (see ENOB), *cock* (see ROOSTER), *goober* (i.e., a peanut), *horn, ladies delight, manhood, manroot,* PECKER, *pego* (probably from the Greek word for "spring" or "fountain"), *rod,* YARD.
5. Generalizations: AFFAIR, *apparatus,* BUSINESS, *equipment,* GADGET, INSTRUMENT, *movement,* THING, THINGUMBOB, *whang* (probably from the "whang" that is a resounding blow or BANG), *works.*
6. Nonsense and baby talk: DING-A-LING, *peenie, pintle* (see PARSON-IN-THE-PULPIT), *weenie,* WEE WEE.

people's republic. Government of the masses by a dictator or oligarchy, with the trappings of communism or socialism; sometimes, more elaborately, a *people's democratic republic*. Since, by definition, sovereignty in a republic resides with people, "people's republic" is a redundancy, and the unnecessary duplication reminds one of the person who doth protest too loudly. Consider, for example, such bastions of people's republicanism as the People's Republic of Albania, People's Republic of Angola, People's Republic of China, Democratic People's Republic of Korea, People's Republic of Mongolia, etc. See also DEMOCRACY.

period. The allusion is to the "menstrual period"; probably the most common of the host of ways of referring to this natural phenomenon. See also MENSTRUATE.

perpetual care. An obligation that is manifestly impossible to fulfill, but which CEMETERIES and *mausoleums* gladly undertake anyway—in return for a surcharge of 10 to 25 percent of the price of graves or crypts. The beauty part of *perpetual care* is that all the funds collected need not be spent right away, giving the cemetery operator a bankroll for other investments. "Perpetual care? . . . in the cemetery business, it means they mow the lawn" ("Lou Grant," WCBS-TV, 10/25/78). See also PRENEED.

person. Once a human being of either sex (from the Latin *persona*, a mask worn by an actor when impersonating someone else) but now usually a woman rather than a man, especially in such pseudo-neuter compounds as *chairperson*, CLEANING PERSON, *committeeperson, congressperson, copyperson, councilperson,* and *selectperson*. For example: "Lee Sternlight, a Park Slope resident, is chairperson of the Central Brooklyn Branch, New York City League of Women Voters" (Brooklyn [NY] *Phoenix*, 9/9/76). Admittedly, appearances can be deceiving. Thus, a sharp-eyed editorial writer for the *Saint Petersburg* (FL) *Times* noticed that Sen. Edward M. Kennedy (D., Massachusetts) had revised a line from Thomas Wolfe's *You Can't Go Home Again* when announcing his candidacy for the 1980 Democratic presidential nomination: Where Wolfe had written, "So, then, to every man his chance . . . to work, to be himself," Kennedy, mindful of women voters, orated: "So, then, to all persons their chance . . . ."
The increasing sexualization of "person" also is apparent in other ways. For example, the plural "persons" often is seen nowadays where, only a few years ago, "people" would have been used. Consider the following report on a new design for *The Nation:* "The new look was designed by Walter Bernard and Milton Glaser 'in consultation with all the persons who help produce our magazine'" (*Columbia Journalism Review,* 11–12/78). Another indicator of the extent to which "person" has become identified with "woman" is the frequency with which high-status women object when the womanly (i.e., low-status) "person" is applied to them. For instance, under the dateline, Amherst, Massachusetts: "Town meeting members have voted, 140 to 70, last night against changing the job title of selectman to selectperson. Among the defenders of the established designation were Nancy Eddy and Diana Romer, the two women members of Amherst's five-member Board of Selectmen" (AP, 5/1/76). "Person" suffered a similar setback in Berkeley, California, where the city council made an exception to its policy of desexing job titles and other terminology when a *councilperson* objected to the preparation of bids for *personhole covers* instead of manhole covers. "'The cover on a

sewer,' she said, 'is not an acceptable desexed word'" (*Playboy*, 9/76). But Amherst and Berkeley are exceptional cases. "Person" definitely seems to be riding the wave of the future. Some *persons* are even changing their names to it, e.g., Donna Ellen Cooperman (*née* Donna Ellen Bloom), who won a year-long legal battle in New York in December 1977 when a State Supreme Court judge granted her request to become Donna Ellen *Cooperperson*. In *Words and Women* (1976), Casey Miller and Kate Swift point out: "*Salesperson* is a word that doesn't seem to throw anyone into a tizzy. . . . As more women serve in posts once exclusively held by males, -person compounds will come to seem more natural." They are probably right—except for *personhole* covers, of course.

For more about the great and continuing effort to neuteralize the language, see, for example, AGENT, ADMINISTRATIVE ASSISTANT, FIRE FIGHTER, FLIGHT ATTENDANT, HOMEMAKER, RACE RIDER, REPRESENTATIVE, and SUPERVISOR.

Personal Assistant to the Secretary (Special Activities). A cook—and a classic demonstration of the general bureaucratic rule that the longer the title, the more menial the position. "Personal Assistant to the . . ." has one of the highest FOP Indexes in captivity: 17.8.

The *Personal Assistant to the* . . . was Willy Barnes, a retired marine, who was hired at $12,763 per annum, to cook for Joseph A. Califano, secretary of Health, Education and Welfare. The official description of Mr. Barnes's job, as approved by Mr. Califano, contained 402 words, not one of which was "cook." It began: "This position is to provide a confidential assistant to the Secretary to assist in providing a broad range of personal services for special activities." For his mastery of bureaucratese, Mr. Califano received one of the 1977 Doublespeak Awards from the Committee on Public Doublespeak of the National Council of Teachers of English. For another 1977 winner, see VERTICAL TRANSPORTATION CORPS.

personal flotation device. A life jacket or vest, courtesy of the United States Coast Guard. See also CUSHION FOR FLOTATION and IMPACT ATTENUATION DEVICE.

personnel. Human beings, people—considered collectively and impersonally. The effect of "personnel" is to permit whoever wields the term to treat individuals as though they were inanimate objects. As army orders so often begin: "All personnel will report bag and baggage at 0600 hrs."

"Personnel" weaseled its way into English toward the beginning of the last century, coming from the French, where *le personnel* distinguished an army's human assets from its nonhuman ones, i.e., *le matériel*. (See MATERIEL.) Attempts were made at first to Anglicize "personnel," e.g., "The personal of the army or navy" (*Westminster Review*, 4/1833), but by mid-century, the French spelling was not only winning out but spreading to nonmilitary areas. Today, private as well as governmental endeavors are replete with *personnel, personnel administrators, personnel managers, personnel offices, vice-presidents for personnel,* and—another military variant—*indigenous personnel,* who are native employees, usually KP's. See also ANTIPERSONNEL WEAPON and TRIAGE.

perspire. To sweat; the manly form of GLOW. People have been perspiring instead of sweating since the eighteenth century: "It is well known that for some time past, neither man, woman nor child . . . has been subject to that gross kind of exudation which was formerly known by the name of *sweat,* . . . now every mortal except carters, coal-heavers and Irish Chairmen . . . merely *perspires"* (*Gentleman's Magazine,* LXI, 1791).

"Perspire" is preferred by the fastidious because it is Latinate (the root *spirare* means "to breathe"), while "sweat" positively reeks of Old English. The earliest example in the *Oxford English Dictionary* of "perspire" in the sweaty sense comes from 1725. The present meaning of "sweat," by contrast, dates to at least 1375, and before that, the word referred not to the moisture exuded through the body's pores but to the very blood of life. See also ANTIPERSPIRANT, BO, GLOW, and UNDERARM WETNESS.

pet. To kiss, hug, fondle; an exceedingly vague term, roughly equivalent to NECK. ". . . petting is necking with territorial concessions" (Frederic Morton, *The Art of Courtship,* 1957). "The techniques used in petting include almost every type of physical contact imaginable" (Robert A. Harper, "Petting," *Aspects of Sexuality,* Albert Ellis and Albert Abarbanel, eds., 1967). For the sake of clarity, sexologists and others sometimes divide the activity into *light petting* (hands above the waist) and *heavy petting,* with the latter frequently serving as a euphemism for what Alfred Kinsey called *petting to climax.*

Before they began to *pet* (ca. 1910, about when "neck" also came in), Americans had been known to *bundle, canoodle, court, lallygag, spark,* and *spoon.* "Pet" naturally gave rise to "petting parties" and even, in centers of higher learning, the study of "petology." In the Flapper era, particularly, *petting* was all the rage, as evidenced by the flaming ad copy for *Alimony,* when that film played at the old OPERA HOUSE in Muncie, Indiana, circa 1925: ". . . brilliant men, beautiful jazz babies, midnight revels, petting parties in the purple dawn, all ending in one terrific smashing climax that makes you gasp" (from Robert A. and Helen Merrell Lynd, *Middletown,* 1929). See also DEMI-VIERGE and MAKE OUT.

peter. The penis. The term is in widespread use but of obscure origin; it may simply be a euphemistic deformation of "penis." Another possibility, in keeping with the common metaphor of the penis as a weapon (e.g., GUN), is that "peter" is a corruption of "petard," an old-fashioned explosive device for blowing holes through fortress gates and walls. (The petard, whose name derives from the French *péter,* to break wind, in the sense of "to fart," frequently misfired; hence, the expression "to be hoist with one's own petard.") Whatever the derivation, the use of "peter" for "penis" has naturally caused some people to have second thoughts about the Christian name. Thus, talking about folkways in the Ozarks: "Very straight-laced old-timers seldom name a boy Peter. I recall an evangelist from the North who shouted something about the church being founded upon Peter, and he was puzzled by the flushed cheeks of the young women and the ill-suppressed amusement of the ungodly" (Vance Randolph and George P. Wilson, *Down in the Holler: A Gallery of Ozark Folk Speech,* 1953). See also BREAK WIND and PENIS.

pharmacy. Drugstore. The *Yellow Pages* of Ma Bell's phone book are a practically infallible guide to pretentious diction. Thus, the entry for "drugstore" in the Manhattan, New York, *Yellow Pages* (1980–81) reads "See 'Pharmacies.'" Of course, the *pharmacies* themselves sometimes adopt even more esoteric guises. Thus, Manhattan is home to Downing Chemists Ltd., while, across the river, Brooklynites may get their drugs from the Clinton Apothecary.

physical. In sports: rough, tough, often dirty. A *physical* team leaves its opponents with bruises at the least—and, possibly, assorted sprains, strains, breaks, and bites.

physique. Body in general, but when referring to a woman, almost invariably a circumlocution for "large breasts." In the still circumlocutory vernacular, the fancy "physique" translates as "build." For example: "Tanya has a great [pick one] physique or build." See also BOSOM and DERRIÈRE.

piddle. To piss; potty talk, dating to at least the eighteenth century. As is generally true of potty talk, the older the user, the more euphemistic the expression, e.g., "The young lady's room was opposite to mine, and . . . I could not restrain myself from listening to hear when she piddled . . ." (anon., *My Secret Life*, ca. 1890). See also PEE and WEE WEE.

pish/pshaw. Two effete exclamations of contempt or disgust, formerly used by well-brought-up ladies and gentlemen, e.g.: "She writh'd with impatience more than pain, And utter'd 'pshaws!' and 'pishes!'" (Thomas Hood, *Miss Kilmansegg and Her Precious Leg*, 1840). Samuel Johnson, defining "pish" in his great *Dictionary of the English Language* (1755), noted: "This is sometimes spoken and written pshaw. I know not their etymology and imagine them formed by chance." Which may be so. Nevertheless, the resemblance between "pish/pshaw" and "piss/shit" is suspicious. See also SHUCKS.

plant. To bury; an Americanism, dating to the middle of the nineteenth century. "I don't want any absurd 'literary remains' and 'unpublished letters of Mark Twain' published after I am planted" (Samuel L. Clemens, letter to his brother, Orion, undated but obviously post-1863, when he adopted his pen name). See also INTERMENT and REMAINS.

plausible denial. Official ignorance, official lying. "Whether he [Secretary of State Henry A. Kissinger] was telling the truth about the CIA's noninvolvement in Chile or was simply indulging in a bit of official lying (called 'plausible denial'), he along with the President would have made the crucial decisions on the Chilean situation" (Victor Marchetti and John D. Marks, *The CIA and the Cult of Intelligence*, 1974). The official doubletalk seems to have been developed for overseas operations and only later applied domestically. Speaking of CIA practice: ". . . the theory of 'plausible denial' . . . requires that no covert operation can be traced back to the U.S. government. . . . It means that an operation, even if it is blown, can be denied as an officially sponsored act without the government's being caught in a barefaced lie" (Harry Rositzke, *The CIA's Secret Operations*, 1977).

On the domestic side, considerable efforts were made in the Nixon White

pledged

House to ensure that the president was never without *plausible denials*. Thus, John W. Dean III reports how he had traced an anonymous instruction back to its source: ". . . the President, I was told . . . had scrawled my orders in the margin of his daily news summary. No one had to explain why the President's name was not used. He was always to be kept one step removed, insulated, to preserve his 'deniability'" (*Blind Ambition*, 1976). The president, for his part, was properly grateful for this. As he said to John D. Ehrlichman in the course of a conversation on the morning of April 14, 1973:

> E: There were 8 or 10 people around here who knew about this, knew it was going on. Bob knew, I knew, all kinds of people knew.
> P: Well, I knew it. I knew it.
> E: And it was not a question of whether—
> P: I must say, though, I didn't know it but I must have assumed it though but you know, fortunately—I thank you both for arranging it that way and it does show the isolation of the President, and here it's not so bad. (*The White House Transcripts*, 1974)

See also ASSASSINATION and NO RECALL (or MEMORY or RECOLLECTION) OF.

pledged. Pawned, hocked.

pluck. Guts. "He wants pluck; he is a coward" (Capt. Francis Grose, *A Classical Dictionary of the Vulgar Tongue*, 1796). As a byword for courage, "pluck" seems to have appeared before "guts," but it arose the same way and remains as a euphemism for what is now considered to be the stronger term. In truth, "pluck" really is just another word for "viscera" (i.e., g—ts). For example: "I saw . . . five unpleasant-looking objects stuck on sticks. They were the livers and lungs, and in fact the plucks, of witch-doctors" (Mary Kingsley, *Travels in West Africa*, 1897). See also BOTTOM, FRY, and INTESTINAL FORTITUDE.

plumber. An agent of the Nixon White House, a burglar. The *plumbers* were supposed to fix leaks, particularly the gusher represented by Dr. Daniel Ellsberg's disclosure of "The Pentagon Papers" in 1971. The name comes from the sign, "The Plumbers," on the door of Room 16 in the basement of the Executive Office Building where the group, formally known as the Special Investigations Unit, was headquartered. The sign was the work of David R. Young, co-chairman of the unit, according to William Safire (*Safire's Political Dictionary*, 1978).

The operations of the *plumbers* involved some of the choicest euphemisms, circumlocutions, and doubletalk of the Watergate era. The *plumbers* were organized following a meeting of John D. Ehrlichman and Egil "Bud" Krogh, Jr., with President Richard M. Nixon on July 24, 1971, in the OVAL OFFICE. Four days later, E. Howard Hunt, Jr., who had been working for the White House as a CONSULTANT, wrote a memo proposing the NEUTRALIZATION (public smearing) of Ellsberg. One of Hunt's ideas was to get the files of Ellsberg's psychiatrist. On August 11, Krogh and Young recommended to Ehrlichman that this be done by means of a COVERT OPERATION (burglary). Over the Labor Day weekend, a team of burglars under Hunt and G. Gordon Liddy broke into the psychiatrist's offices but could not find the files on Ellsberg. The failed operation (also called "Hunt-Liddy Special Project #1") became a key element in the Watergate THING after Liddy and Hunt were implicated in yet another break-in—the Watergate CAPER of June 17, 1972. Hunt's threat to spill the beans to prosecutors about his earlier jobs, unless he was given some $120,000 and the assurance of clemency (see EXPLETIVE DELETED), then became a powerful force in drawing the president himself ever deeper into the COVER-UP.

plump. Overweight; the feminine counterpart of PORTLY.

police action. A war; specifically, the Korean War, aka CONFLICT or *emergency*. "In this war, long called a 'police action,' the United Nations suffered casualties totaling about 74,000 killed, 250,000 wounded, and 83,000 missing and captured" (*Encyclopedia Americana*, 1965).

The war could not officially be called a war because it was never legally declared by Congress to be one. The phrase, "police action," was popularized by President Harry S Truman, but as often turns out with such utterances, the words were put into the famous man's mouth by a lowly reporter. It happened this way:

On June 27, 1950, at his first press conference after the start of the war two days before, Truman said the United States was repelling a raid by "a bunch of bandits." A reporter then asked if "it would be correct . . . to call this a police action under the United Nations?" The president replied, "Yes, that is exactly what it amounts to." This was all the newspapers needed to justify such headlines as "Truman Calls Intervention 'Police Action.'" In *Thunder of the Captains* (1977), David Detzer suggests that the anonymous reporter, in turn, got the phrase from a Senate speech made earlier that day by William F. Knowland (R., California), who compared the role of the air force to that of the police, chasing a burglar away from the scene of a crime. Asserted Knowland: "The action this government is taking is a police action against a violator of the law of nations and the Charter of the United Nations."

Technically, the Korean *police action* was classed as a LIMITED WAR. See also the Vietnam ERA.

polygraph interview. A lie detector test.

pooper-scooper. A small shovel for picking up DOG DIRT. Potty talk. See also WEE WEE.

poor. Black; the honest word for the lack of money becomes a dishonest word for something else when the subject under discussion is something else.

"But when white professionals busy themselves with birth control for the poor (meaning blacks) it strikes many blacks as a racist plot" (*New Republic*, 8/7&14/71). See also BLACK and DISADVANTAGED.

poppycock. Shit. The word's aboveboard interpretation is "rubbish" or "nonsense," but it actually means "soft dung," from the Dutch *pappekak*. See also BS.

portly. Fat. "Don's a little portly now," observed New York Yankee announcer

position

Phil Rizutto, as Don Zimmer, roundish manager of the Boston Red Sox, ambled toward the pitcher's mound to gain some time for a relief hurler to warm up (WPIX-TV, NYC, 6/14/77).

"Portly" people tend to move in a slow, dignified manner, much like ocean liners docking, and the word itself once meant "stately," "dignified," "majestic," "handsome." Thus, Christopher Marlowe did not mean "fatty" when he referred to "my queen and portly empress." The Elizabethans, however, did use "portly" both ways, with that famous fat man, Sir John Falstaff, no doubt getting a laugh when he described himself as "A goodly portly man, i'faith, and a corpulent . . ." (William Shakespeare, *Henry IV*, Part 1, 1597). See also BROAD-BEAMED, BUXOM, KING-SIZE, and STOUT.

position. A "job" in managerial guise. Where an executive is ASSOCIATED WITH a company in a particular *position* or CAPACITY, his [*sic*] secretary has a job, unless she [*sic*] is an ADMINISTRATIVE ASSISTANT, in which case she may be said to have a *position*, too. "Position" has a FOP Index of 3.3.

posterior(s). The ass; an elegant Latinized euphemism, comparable in a topographical sense to the more mundane BACKSIDE or REAR. Thus, Fanny Hill described one of her co-workers: "Her posteriors, plump, smooth, and prominent, form'd luxuriant tracts of animated snow, that splendidly filled the eye . . ." (John Cleland, *Memoirs of a Woman of Pleasure*, 1749). People have been sitting upon their *posteriors* at least since the seventeenth century. No doubt, it is merely a strange—not to say unnatural—coincidence that the oldest examples in the *Oxford English Dictionary* of "posteriors" and the related DERRIÈRE both have to do with spanking. In the case of the former, the illustration is of "A poor pedantick schoolmaster sweeping his living from the posteriors of little children" (William Drummond, of Hawthornden, *Notes of B. Jonson's Conversations with D.,* 1619). See also ARSE.

posttraumatic neurosis. A psychiatric casualty; the latest (ca. Vietnam) version of a military affliction known as *battle* (or *combat*) *fatigue* during the Korean POLICE ACTION and World War II, and as *shell shock* during World War I. By whatever name, the condition is relatively new. Typically, it results from the length of exposure to combat; prior to the twentieth century, however, battles rarely lasted more than two or three days—not long enough to break men down this way. See also CASUALTY and FATIGUE.

powder my nose, I have to. Use the toilet, i.e., *powder room*—a common public excuse for a private errand involving neither powder nor nose.

> HONEY: I want to . . . put some powder on my nose.
> GEORGE: Martha, won't you show her where we keep the .
> euphemism? (Edward Albee, *Who's Afraid of Virginia Woolf,* 1962)

"Powder my nose" is used mainly, but not exclusively, by women. Fast women, as well as fast-talking ones, may also adopt the jocular variant, "I have to powder my puff." Men, meanwhile, have their own separate euphemisms for the same mission: Perhaps the most common is "I have to see a man about a dog." A man who wants to demonstrate his *savoir faire* may vary this, announcing that he has to "see a dog about a man." This is guaranteed to impress. (In one way or another.)

Other examples of the ingenuity of mankind (and womankind) in explaining away the CALLS or NEEDS OF NATURE include:

cash (or *write*) *a check*
consult Mrs. Jones
feed a dog
freshen up
give a Chinaman a music lesson
go feed the goldfish (see also GO)
go see the baby
go to Cannes or *Deauville* (two famous watering spots) or *Egypt* or *Lulu's* (see LOO)
go to the bank
go water the lawn (or *the petunias* or *the stock*)
mail a letter
pay a visit (to the old soldiers' home)
PUMP SHIP
see Johnny (see JOHN)
shake hands with an old friend
sharpen the skates
shoot a dog (American) or *a lion* (English)
spend a penny (English)
visit the chamber of commerce
wash my hands

See also DEFECATE/DEFECATION, PEE, TOILET, and WASHROOM.

prairie oysters. The testicles of a bull calf when presented as a delicacy for eating. Of course, flatlanders are not the only people to enjoy such fare. Gourmets in the hills eat those of boar and sheep as well as those of bulls, but to the uplanders, these dishes are known as *mountain oysters*. See also FILET MIGNON, FRY, and TESTICLES.

prat. The ass. An old word, "prat" is related to "pretty"; both are of obscure origin. The Old English *praett* meant a trick, or prank, while the Old English "pretty," *praettig*, meant cunning or sly. Examples of *praett* in the *Oxford English Dictionary* go back to about the year 1000, while the oldest citation for a "prat" as "A buttocke" comes from 1567. In modern times, theater people, especially, are prone to fall on their *prats* or to take *pratfalls*, usually by intent in comedy routines. (Note the retention of the "trick" element in the word's meaning after nearly a thousand years.) See also ARSE.

precipitation. Water from the sky. The generalized "precipitation" is favored by meteorologists and TV weather PERSONS, partly because the Latin term sounds altogether more professional, more scientific, and partly as a way of hedging their bets, since general forecasts have a greater chance of being correct than such specific ones as "rain," "snow," or "hail." See also SHOWER ACTIVITY.

precision bombing. The deceptively precise name that helped Americans rationalize air bombardment of civilian populations—a distinguishing feature of World War II, as opposed to World War I, which at least had the virtue of limiting battle deaths almost exclusively to the battlefield.

   Precision bombing, according to the chief of the army air force, Gen. Henry H. "Hap" Arnold, "aimed at knocking out not an entire industrial area, nor even a whole factory, but the most vital parts of Germany's war machine, such as the power plants and machine shops of particular factories" ("Air Strategy for Victory," *Flying*, 10/43). On paper, this looked fine, but in practice dropping bombs on smallish targets from high altitudes under combat conditions wasn't as easy as the general implied. In 1943, only 15 percent of the bombs dropped by the Eighth Air Force hit within 1,000 feet of their aiming points; in 1945, after two years' practice, accuracy improved to 60 percent. "American precision bombing had proven [this was by the spring of 1944] to be not so precise as had been hoped. . . . Even the relatively precise bombing of industrial targets inevitably killed and maimed large numbers of civilians hitherto exempt from the most direct horrors of war" (Russell F. Weigley, *The American Way of War*, 1973). *Precision bombing*, as carried out in daylight raids by B-17 FLYING FORTRESSES, contrasted with nighttime AREA BOMBING, popularized by the British Royal Air Force. For other ways of improving bombing accuracy through the power of words, see SPECIFIED STRIKE ZONE, *strategic bombing* in STRATEGIC, and SURGICAL STRIKE.

precleared fire zone. One of the substitutes for "free fire zone" in Vietnam, after "free fire zone" became verboten. See also SPECIFIED STRIKE ZONE for more details.

preemptive strike. A surprise (i.e., sneak) attack, also called a *preemptive first strike*.

   The uncanny resemblance between the dispassionate war-gamer's "preemptive strike" and what Japan did to the United States on December 7, 1941, was noted by Attorney General Robert F. Kennedy, when such an attack was proposed as a quick solution to the Cuban missile crisis of October 1962. Partly paraphrasing Kennedy's words, Theodore C. Sorensen reports: "A sudden airstrike at dawn Sunday without warning, said the Attorney General, would be 'a Pearl Harbor in reverse, and it would blacken the name of the United States in the pages of history' . . . the Cuban people would not forgive us for decades; and the Soviets would entertain the very dangerous notion that the United States, as they had feared all these years, was indeed capable of launching a pre-emptive first strike" (*Kennedy*, 1965). See also ACTIVE DEFENSE, PREVENTIVE ACTION/ DETENTION/WAR, and SURGICAL STRIKE.

preliterate. The modern anthropologist's tactful, oh-so-scientific replacement for "savage" and "primitive." See also UNDERDEVELOPED.

preneed. Predeath; the usual way of characterizing cemetery sales that are made while the prospective users of the SPACE are alive and kicking, as opposed to *at need* or *postneed*, when they aren't. The aggressive cemetery promoter focuses on *preneed* selling because the market is much larger and because it enables him to close deals long before the MORTICIAN, with whom he increasingly competes, can get *his* foot in the door. *Preneed* selling also brings in cash for MONUMENTS and PERPETUAL CARE that doesn't have to be spent right away; such monies are put into trust funds whose size has been known to tempt some operators from the strict paths of righteousness. The advantages of *preneed* selling, or something very similar, have been recognized for some time. Hubert Eaton, The Dreamer, who made Forest Lawn what it is today, began work for that cemetery in 1912 as agent for "before-need" sales. See also CEMETERY and MEMORIAL PARK.

pre-orgasmic. Taking the optimistic view, the Sex Advisory and Counseling Unit of the University of California Medical School in San Francisco classifies women who have never had an orgasm as "pre-orgasmic" (*Time*, 4/1/74). Meanwhile, in New York City, the 1978–79 catalog for the Institute for Rational Living and the Institute for Rational Emotive Therapy included a "Pre-Orgasmic Women's Group" for those "who have not experienced orgasm or who have rarely reached orgasm." See also COME.

prepared biography. A notice of a death that has not yet occurred; an OBITUARY. "Richard Nixon's political obits—the Associated Press prefers the euphemism 'prepared biography'—are set in type and are on tape and film at a dozen major news organizations, where they are freshly updated" (*New York* magazine, 12/17/73). See also PROTECTIVE COVERAGE.

preplan. Plan; the addition of the unnecessary "pre" produces a FOP Index of 2.0. Used mainly in bureaucratic contexts, "preplan" appears to reflect the delight that bureaucrats take in attending meetings. In order to prepare themselves for "planning" meetings, these cagey types gather in advance sessions that are called—naturally—"preplanning" meetings. Of course, "preplan" is gobble-degook, as demonstrated by the fact that the plain "plan" invariably can be substituted for it with no loss in meaning. For example, consider the following sinister malarkey: "Once the inhabitants of a pre-planned target area have been adequately warned that the area has been selected as a target and given sufficient time to evacuate, the area may then be struck without further warning" (MACV Dir525–13, 5/1/71). For more about this directive, see SPECIFIED STRIKE ZONE.

prevaricate. A long-winded, soft-sounding, Latinized "lie." "Prevaricate" and its related nouns, *prevarication* and *prevaricator*, derive from the Latin *praevaricari*, meaning "to walk a crooked course" and, hence, to deviate from the straight path of truth. See also FABRICATION and WHITE LIE.

preventive action/detention/war. "Preventive" whitewashes dirty business in much the same way as "protective" (e.g., PROTECTIVE CUSTODY). Thus, *preventive action*, as practiced in the FBI's Counterintelligence Program (Cointelpro to the pros), included a wide range of criminal acts, such as burglaries (BLACK BAG JOBS), mail openings, forgery, and entrapment. Meanwhile, the motive behind *preventive detention* is to rationalize the confinement of people who haven't committed crimes and might never do so, thus perverting the traditional presumption of innocence into a presumption of guilt. See also DETENTION.

Of course, the most dangerous of the "preventives" is "war." The true nature of "preventive war" has been recognized even by generals. Thus, Henry Cabot Lodge reported that Dwight D. Eisenhower "did not believe there was such a thing as preventive war . . . [and] would not even listen seriously to anyone who talked about it" (Lodge, *As It Was*, 1976). In Ike's words: "Many thousands of persons would be dead and injured and mangled, the transportation systems destroyed, and sanitation systems all gone. That is not preventive war—that is war" (press conference, 8/16/54). Not all men in all generations have had such keen perception, e.g.: "A preventive war, grounded on a just fear of invasion, is lawful" (Thomas Fuller, *The Historie of the Holy Warre*, 1639). See also DEFENSE, DEPARTMENT OF and PREEMPTIVE STRIKE.

previously owned. Used; "preowned," for short. Honor for popularizing the fancy phrase goes to the Cadillac people. New York's Potamkin Cadillac, among others, regularly offers "preowned vehicles" (ads, WINS, radio, NYC, 1977). Other more-or-less euphemistic terms for cars that have had multiple owners include *rebuilt, reconditioned,* and *repossessed.* Used automobile tires, meanwhile, are known generally as *recaps* or *retreads.* As long ago as 1945, H. L. Mencken reported in his first supplement to *The American Language* that Los Angelinos were buying *experienced* tires, and the term has since been applied in other parts of the country to the cars themselves. For more about the *previously owned* car business, see LAUNDER.

priest. The mallet or other weapon used to administer the last rites to a fish that has been caught. The principle is the same as with the medieval *misericord* (literally: compassion, mercy), which was the dagger used by one knight when delivering the coup de grâce (literally: stroke of grace) to another. At one time "priest" also was a euphemism for the person who did the killing, e.g.: "Seeing the deed is meritorious/And to preserve my sovereign from his foe/Say but the word, and I will be his priest" (William Shakespeare, *Henry VI*, Part 2, 1590–91). See also MADAME.

private parts aka **privates, lower parts,** and **sensitive parts.** The external sexual organs, whether male or female; the GENITALS. "He went to a doctor with a rash on his private parts and the doctor diagnosed syphilis. The sailor became depressed and hanged himself. Then it was discovered that he did not have syphilis after all" (Norman Moss, *The Pleasures of Deception*, 1977).

The "private" construction is old, with the earliest "private parts" in the *Oxford English Dictionary* coming from 1634. Before that, going back to the thirteenth century, people had *privy limbs* (see LIMB), *privy members* (see MEMBER), and *privy parts* (see PRIVY).

privy. The general term for that which is private, intimate, concealed, and done by stealth has been used to designate an outdoor toilet (a *privehouse* or *privy house,* in full) since at least the fourteenth century. A "privy stool" was the same as a "close stool" (see STOOL). People also used to have *privy parts*, an early form of PRIVATE PARTS, while to be *privy* with another person could imply a sexual RELATIONSHIP.

"Privy" usually denotes a structure of some sort (an OUTHOUSE, in effect). In the past, unenclosed *privies* were a frequent menace. To wit: "A very pretty Boy of 4 years old . . . fell into a scurvy open Privy before night; of which loathsom Entertainment he died in a day or two" (*The Diary of Samuel Sewall*, 9/28/1708). See also NECESSARY and TOILET.

problem. The most common of the common denominators for converting all life's difficulties, from the most trivial to the most horrible, into a uniformly bland and boneless mush. No one has explained the psychology of the term better than the former COUNSEL to the president of the United States, John W. Dean III, who said of "problem": "That was the word of common currency in the Administration; a 'problem' could be anything from a typographical error to a forty-year jail sentence. The word drained the emotional content from tense discussions. It helped us maintain the even, robotlike composure we considered vital to effectiveness" (*Blind Ambition*, 1976). Or, as the former president himself explained: "South Vietnam would not have gone down the drain if I hadn't had my problem" (Richard M. Nixon, as quoted by Harry Dent, a former aide, Reuters, 8/4/75).

There is absolutely no end to the world's *problems*. When New York City had a *liquidity problem* (i. e., near-bankruptcy), municipal bond dealers sagely attributed their difficulties in selling their wares to a *market psychology problem* (investors were scared out of their wits). The state of Florida, meanwhile, has *problem alligators* (so many of them that some Floridians are scared out of their wits). And there is Amtrak, which had to lower the speed limit for its 150 GM diesel locomotives because, in the words of a Federal Railroad Administration official (*New York Times*, 2/1/77): "There is a problem with that locomotive on curved tracks" (meaning it tends to jump off them). Finally, there is the *problem* that is an unmitigated disaster. Thus, after Rep. Wayne L. Hays (D., Ohio) admitted in a speech to the House to having had a RELATIONSHIP with Ms. Elizabeth Ray, one of his colleagues, Rep. Philip Burton (D., California) told him, "Wayne, you've got a problem" (*New Times*, 10/15/76). But perhaps the greatest understatement of all was the message from *Apollo 13* on April 13, 1970, when, 56 hours after launch, an oxygen tank blew up, cutting off electrical power and oxygen for the command module: "Houston, we've got a problem." See also SITUATION, THING, and TROUBLE/TROUBLESOME.

procedure. An operation. In the words of a doctor who didn't know his voice was being recorded but who was so eager to perform abortions that he didn't always check to be sure his patients were really pregnant: "I'm just about to give you a procedure" (WCBS-TV, 2/23/79). See also MISCARRIAGE.

pro-choice. Pro-abortion. "Almost no one mentions the word abortion; one is pro-life or pro-choice" (*New York Review of Books*, 7/20/78). Thus, depending on whose terminology is being used, opponents are left with the unenviable task of seeming to argue against either "life" or "choice." See also MISCARRIAGE and, for

product

more about loading arguments in advance, OPEN MARRIAGE, OPEN SHOP, and RIGHT-TO-WORK.

product. A bland, impersonal, opaque word, straight off the assembly line, now being applied regularly to items that once were thought to have the distinction, character, and quality associated with handmade manufacture.

One expects the huge corporations that turn out autos, toiletries, cereals, and other mass-produced, homogenized items to speak of their *products* and it is, somehow, not terribly surprising to find that the CIA regards information as a *product,* e.g.: "In various ways, the Central Intelligence Agency is going public, partly to improve its image and partly to improve its 'product,' high-ranking agency officers said in interviews last week" (*New York Times,* 5/9/78). The august Metropolitan Museum of Art in New York City is heavily into *product* (but this will not shock anyone who knows about that institution's record of *deaccessioning* —a euphemism for "selling off"—its treasures): ". . . the Metropolitan is 'developing an extensive product line,' as Mr. [Thomas P. F.] Hoving put it, of replicas and mementos of ancient Egyptian works of art" (*New York Times,* 7/15/76). Even the good, gray *New York Times* has been infected. As publisher Arthur Ochs Sulzberger said, when announcing the newspaper's change to a six-column format: "These changes will not affect content or the quality of our product" (*New York Times,* 6/15/76). Saddest of all are the book publishers who have capitulated. For example, an executive of Harcourt Brace Jovanovich reported: "From our mass market line, you'll now be seeing a well-planned product with first rate solicitation and promotion . . ." (*Bestsellers,* 9/77). Confirming this view was the art director at Harper & Row who opined: "A book is really a product—it must look like a unified package" (*Art Direction/The Magazine of Visual Communication,* 4/78). And over at Doubleday and Co., a research analyst who hoped to become a "product manager," said of book publishing: "It isn't that different from consumer goods. Instead of marketing Brillo pads, for instance, membership in a book club is the product" (*New York Times,* 5/25/75). Book-lovers also will be interested to know that, technically speaking, books are "crossover products" because, "Like women's stockings, books are sold in both grocery and retail drugstores" (Association of American Publishers, Book Distribution Task Force, Information Bulletin No. Seven, 4/78).

professional car. A hearse; part of the sickly sweet terminology of the death business. "For over one hundred years funeral directors have chosen the uncompromised excellence and value of the Hess & Eisenhardt professional car" (ad, *Casket & Sunnyside,* 1/80). Other bywords for the deathly "hearse" include *coach, casket coach, funeral car, limousine,* and *service car.* See also FUNERAL DIRECTOR.

projection. The scientific version of what, if uttered by a Nostradamus or a Jeane Dixon, would be called a "prediction."

"Predictions—or projections, a distinction made by some academics who define them as mere extrapolations of today's situation into the future; really a psychological distinction rather than a real one—invariably turn out to be wrong" (Norman Metzger, *Energy: The Continuing Crisis,* 1977). See also SCENARIO.

prosthesis aka **prosthetic device.** A piece of artificial anatomy, such as a leg, arm, breast, or tooth. For example, a false tooth is, technically, and fastidiously, a *dental prosthesis*. To refer to a "prosthesis" instead of an "artificial leg," say, is the verbal equivalent of averting one's gaze from the area of the amputated LIMB. See also DENTURES.

prostitute. Whore. "Prostitute" comes from the Latin *pro* (forward) plus *statuere* (to set up or to place) and so translates as "to expose publicly" or "to offer for sale." (Note the parallel to the modern slang expression, "to put out," said of a woman who too freely bestows her sexual FAVORS.) The Latinate word came into English as a euphemism for the blunt English one, itself apparently a euphemism for a word so old it has been forgotten: The Old English *hōre* is cognate with the Latin *cara*, wich simply means "dear" or "darling."

"Prostitute" appears first in the *Oxford English Dictionary* as a verb in a work of 1530 that would have been of some assistance to English visitors in France: "I prostytute, as a comen woman dothe her self in a bordell house, *je prostitue*" (Jehan Palsgrave, *Lesclarcissement de la Langue Francoyse*). In the nineteenth century, Noah Webster changed "whore" to "prostitute" (or "lewd woman") when he bowdlerized the Bible (see PECULIAR MEMBERS for details), and as late as the 1930s, some New York City newspapers wouldn't print "whore." For example, one of the members of the cast of *Within the Gates*, which opened in 1934, was listed simply as "The Young Whore," but the *Sun* changed this to "The Young Prostitute," the *World-Telegram* to "The Young Harlot," and the *American* to "A Young Girl Who Has Gone Astray" (Robert Benchley, *The New Yorker*, 11/3/34). Even today, most people tend to steer clear of the harsher-sounding term. This includes those people who are whores: They are more likely to refer to themselves as HOOKERS or WORKING GIRLS.

There are (and have been) a tremendous number of ways of implying "whore" without actually coming out and saying the word. Among them:

> *abandoned woman* (a profligate Victorian male might be called "an abandoned man"); *anonyma; Aspasia* (a learned allusion to the learned woman who was mistress to Pericles in Athens in the fifth century B.C.);
> *bad girl* (a euphemism by way of understatement); B-GIRL; *brothel* (the word referred to a person—a scoundrel or good-for-nothing, if a man, and a whore, if a woman—before it came to mean a bawdy house); *buttock* (in many combinations, such as *buttock-broker*, a procuress or brothel manager, and *buttock and file*, a whore who was also a pickpocket);
> CALL GIRL, *cat* (see CAT HOUSE); COMMODE; CONVENIENCE; COURTESAN; *crack; Cyprian* (referring to Venus, goddess of love);
> *demimondaine* (from *demimonde*, coined by Alexandre Dumas *fils*, 1824–1895, for the class of woman whose loose behavior had caused them to lose social position); *Dutch widow* (as contrasted with a life-size, mechanical *Dutch wife* or *Dutch husband*—machines for masturbating with);
> *erring sister;*
> FALLEN WOMAN; *fancy woman* (see FANCY); FILLE DE JOIE; *fire ship* (also, a woman infected with venereal disease);

game (a collective term, late seventeenth to early nineteenth centuries, when a young whore or a girl who was well on her way to becoming one might also be called a *game pullet*—and see GAME); *girl of ease; girl of the* (or *about*) *town;*

HARLOT; *houri* (from the Arabic word—meaning "black-eyed" or "to be gazellelike in the eyes"—for the beautiful virgin given to every deserving male Moslem upon obtaining Paradise); HOOR (an aural euphemism);

incognita; industrial debutante (one who works business conventions);

joy sister;

Kate (an especially attractive whore);

lady of easy virtue/of the evening/of the night/of pleasure (see LADY);

MADAM; *miss* (a mistress in the seventeenth century and later a strumpet or whore); MODEL; *moll* (the type specimen being Moll Flanders, heroine of Daniel Defoe's picaresque novel of 1722); *moose* (American military usage in the Far East, from the Japanese *mus*, short for *musume*, a young girl or inamorata); *mort* (any woman or any girl but also, from the sixteenth through early twentieth centuries, a loose woman or whore—see the *muff* in VAGINA);

nymph du pave;

one of the Burlap sisters (i.e., a bag); *one of the frail sisterhood* (Victoriana);

painted (or *scarlet*) *woman; Paphian* (alluding to the "Paphian goddess," worshiped orgiastically at ancient Crete and identified by the Greeks with their own Aphrodite); *patriotute* (one who specializes in servicemen, for "patriotic" reasons; *pavement princess; piece of trade, puella* (Latin for "girl"); *punk* (today, sexually speaking, usually a catamite, but a conventional feminine whore from Elizabethan to Victorian times, e.g.: "At London I at first took fancy again for women in the suburbs, punks who would let me have them for half a crown . . ." (anon., *My Secret Life*, ca. 1890); *pure* (an ordinary mistress or whore, late seventeenth to early eighteenth centuries); *purest pure* (a classy mistress or whore of the same period);

quean (see QUEEN);

red-light sister;

SPORTING GAL (or WOMAN); STEW (a woman as well as a brothel); STREETWALKER;

TAIL; *tart* (once a term of honest endearment, comparable to "sweetheart"); *town* (short for *woman of the town*); *trading girl;* TRAMP; TRICK; *trumpery* (an old whore or valueless goods, eighteenth century);

UNFORTUNATE;

Vestal (referring to the virgins who attended the sacred fire in the Temple of Vesta, Roman goddess of the hearth and protectress of the state); VICTORY GIRL;

woman of easy virtue/of the town (see WOMAN); WORKING GIRL.

protective coverage. From the TV news business: "Sending a correspondent and camera crew to church with the president is part of what the networks euphemistically call 'protective coverage.' That means they don't want to miss the pictures if someone takes a shot at the president" (Ron Nessen, *It Sure Looks*

Different from the Inside, 1978). See also IN-DEPTH TREATMENT and PREPARED BIOGRAPHY.

protective custody. The self-serving "protective" operates in the same manner as "preventive" (e.g., PREVENTIVE ACTION) and should be treated accordingly, i.e., ignored. "Protective custody" just means "custody." The essential slipperiness of "protective" is most evident when examined from the point of view of those who are about to be *protected:* "De Geer in his broadcast declared The Netherlands would resist with arms any attempt by a foreign power to extend protective help to her" (*Topeka* [KS] *Journal,* 4/19/40). And the sham is fully revealed for what it is in the case of Nazi Germany, where "protective custody" was the official euphemism for imprisonment in a CONCENTRATION CAMP: "A cloak of legality was given to arbitrary arrests and imprisonment of victims in concentration camps. The legal-sounding term was *Schutzhaft,* or 'protective custody,' based on the law of February 28, 1933, which suspended the clauses of the constitution guaranteeing civil liberties" (Nora Levin, *The Holocaust,* 1968). *Protective custody* was one of the first steps in Germany toward achieving the FINAL SOLUTION. See also the American *custodial detention* in DETENTION.

protective reaction. Bombing; specifically, an air attack on enemy territory— and one of the more contorted circumlocutions of the Vietnam ERA. "Protective reaction" was the Nixon Administration's pretext in 1969 for resuming air raids on North Vietnam. Supposedly, the attacks were just on antiaircraft positions. However, ". . . it developed that the Seventh Air Force under General John D. Lavelle adopted a very broad interpretation of 'protective reaction,' including raids on such targets as oil and truck dumps" (Russell F. Weigley, *The American Way of War,* 1973). The men who actually flew the missions were even more outspoken. As one pilot told the *New York Times* (6/15/72): ". . . protective reaction was just a euphemism for the F-4's to stage raids over Laos and North Vietnam and bomb the hell out of them." See also ARMED RECONNAISSANCE, ERRONEOUS REPORT, INCURSION, and RECONNAISSANCE IN FORCE.

public relations or **PR.** The general euphemism for projecting a sympathetic image for a corporation, institution, or PRODUCT, by means of news management, propaganda, outright lies, and, when push comes to shove, silence. ". . . President [Nixon] seemed to be willing to give the aggressive and ambitious [Kenneth W.] Clawson the inclusive sway that he wanted over every aspect of White House 'public relations,' the official euphemism for overt propaganda as distinct from what passes for information" (John Osborn, *New Republic,* 5/4/74). See also SCENARIO.

Practitioners of *public relations* (see PUBLICITOR) generally insinuate the views they wish the public to hold into the news without paying for space or air-time; in this sense *public relations* is the dark side of advertising (see MESSAGE). Somewhat unfairly, news people, while relying heavily upon PR people for stories, tend to look down upon them. As one newsman is said to have told a co-worker, when his pal announced that he was quitting the paper for a job that paid three times as much in *public relations:* "Frankly, I'd rather see you handing out towels in a Hackensack [New Jersey] whorehouse."

publicitor. One who engages in PUBLIC RELATIONS; a grandiloquent press agent. "We were startled . . . yesterday by a dispatch fresh from American League offices stating that news of the Athletics' move to Kansas City was given in an announcement by the League's 'publicitor.' We take this to mean press agent" (*Birmingham* [AL] *News*, 10/14/54).

"Publicitor," formed on the same principle as REALTOR, is a particularly classy version of the basic "publicist"; other variations include *public relations counsel* (a borrowing from the legal COUNSEL, made in 1919 by Edward L. Bernays and Doris E. Fleischman); *public relations officer* (see OFFICER); *publicity engineer* (see ENGINEER); *publicity director*, and *publicity representative* (see REPRESENTATIVE). These are titles that *publicitors* (the even wilder "publicator" also has been reported) give to themselves; to those on the receiving end of the never-ending barrage of publicity releases, they are generally known as "flacks," from *flak*, the World War II abbreviation of *fliegerabwehrkanone*, the German antiaircraft cannon.

Sometimes, one or the other of the fancy publicity titles may also serve as a cover for an entirely different occupation—selling, say, or procuring. In the first, marketing sense: "We were book [encyclopedia, door-to-door] salesmen! They didn't call us that, not at first, and they didn't tell us our pay would come by commission, either. My title in the company was Publicity Representative" (*Atlantic*, 6/74). And in the second: "The girls were found by the publicist, and there is, as a matter of fact, a touch of humor to the designation 'publicist,' because one of his main functions is to keep his client's name out of the papers. The other is, of course, to provide company" (*New York* magazine, 5/26/75).

pudendum. The external sexual organs, converted into Latin for decency's sake. The literal meaning of the term is "that of which one ought to be ashamed," and it says a great deal for the consistency of attitudes toward sex in our society that the first example of "pudendum" in the *Oxford English Dictionary* comes from 1398. The term often is used in the plural, *pudenda*, and is sometimes fancied up into *pudendum muliebre* (from *mulier*, woman). Although correctly applied to males as well as females, it is much more often encountered in the feminine sense, as in the old (ca. nineteenth-century) limerick:

> That naughty old Sappho of Greece
> Said: "What I prefer to a piece
> Is to have my pudenda
> Rubbed hard by the enda
> The little pink nose of my niece."

See also GENITALS, PENIS, and VAGINA.

pump ship. British: usually translated as to MAKE WATER or, a secondary meaning, to vomit. Though obviously of nautical origin, the expression has been generally adopted by landlubbers. Thus, a very famous soldier, the duke of Wellington, when asked if he could produce some motto that had served him in all his campaigns, is said to have replied: "Certainly, sir; never lose an opportunity to pump-ship." See also PEE.

pupil station. A school desk.

pussy. For the many people who do not feel comfortable with the technical VAGINA (the equally technical PENIS is much more widely accepted), this is probably the most common substitute for the FOUR-LETTER WORD "cunt."

"Pussy" may be a translation of the French *chat*, cat, or *minette*, kitten or pussy, both of which carry the same slang meanings in French as in English. Or it may simply be a case of parallel evolution. "Puss," "pussy," and "pussycat" all seem to have been used to refer to women generally (usually in a contemptuous manner), and to the female PUDENDUM in particular, since at least the seventeenth century. "Cat," meanwhile, is an even older word for "whore," going back at least to the beginning of the fifteenth century (see CAT HOUSE), and it has also been used in the same way as "pussy" since the nineteenth century. As common as it is in private talk, "pussy" is bothersome enough to be euphemized by most newspapers; see OBSCENE, DEROGATORY, AND SCATOLOGICAL.

put away/down/out/to sleep. To kill; four different ways of not mentioning death—usually used in connection with animals whose lives have become burdensome to themselves, their owners, or, as in the following example, their owner's owners: "You have that bleed'n mongrel put down" (Mrs. Louisa Trotter, proprietor of the Bentinck Hotel, to Starr, the doorman, on the subject of his beloved Fred; "Duchess of Duke Street," WNET-TV, NYC, 1/5/79).

People as well as animals may be *put away* and *put down*, though not always with lethal results. Thus, it used to be said that a husband *put away* his wife when all he did was to divorce her. Or a person may be *put away* in a MENTAL HOSPITAL. To *put down* another person, meanwhile, may mean only that one has publicly humiliated the other, which is the functional equivalent of death but, still, preferable to the real thing. In the past, people occasionally *put down* themselves, and with more lasting effect. For example: "Word came that Eppy Telefer had 'put down' herself over night, and was found hanging dead in her own little cottage at daybreak" (Blackwood's *Edinburgh Magazine*, XXI, 1827).

Finally, there is the Macbethian use of "put out" by seventy-one-year-old Maria Petra Ramsay, who was convicted of trying to kidnap her former husband, an eighty-two-year-old multimillionaire. As recorded in a taped conversation with an undercover cop:

MRS. R.: I have no regrets. I do wish to have my husband and the people who are controlling him should be put out, because otherwise, they'd put me out.

COP: By "out," you telling me to kill them?

MRS. R.: Absolutely, if it could be done, yes. (*New York Times*, 1/24/79)

See also ASSASSINATION, HIT, and SLEEP.

quaint. Small, especially in real estate listings. ". . . being a naive real estate shopper, I was in for a seminar in semantics: . . . 'Quaint' and/or 'cute' mean essentially the same thing: one could never lose sight of one another within the house . . ." (Aldo Bianchi, *Brooklyn* [NY] *Phoenix*, 7/26/79). See also HANDY-MAN'S SPECIAL.

quarantine. Blockade. During the Cuban missile crisis of 1962, when the United States and Russia teetered on the brink of nuclear war, President John F. Kennedy and his advisers talked of a "blockade" as being one of their OPTIONS, but when the president told the nation in a televised address on October 22 what was happening, he used the euphemistic "quarantine" instead. "The President . . . adopted the term 'quarantine' as less belligerent and more applicable to an act of peaceful self-preservation than 'blockade'" (Theodore C. Sorensen, *Kennedy*, 1965). For other *options* that were considered, see PREEMPTIVE STRIKE and SURGICAL STRIKE; for their likely consequences, see also ESCALATE.

queen. Nowadays, a male homosexual who plays the female part, but before that, as quean, a bold or ill-behaved woman, specifically, a whore: "Here's to the flaunting extravagant quean. And here's to the housewife that's thrifty" (Richard Brinsley Sheridan, *School for Scandal*, 1777). Back in Sheridan's era, "quean-house" was another term for "brothel" and "queanery" equaled "harlotry" (see HARLOT). "Quean" is related to, among other words, the royal queen; the Dutch *kween* (a barren cow); the Chaucerian *queynte* (cunt); the Gothic *qino* (woman); and the Greek *gyne* (also "woman," and from which descend both "gynecology" and "misogynist"). Homosexual "queens," meantime, have been flourishing under that title for the past century or so, but "straights" have not always understood the meaning of the term. For example, during a trial in 1890, Sir Charles Russell, the Queen's *[sic]* Counsel, cross-examined John Saul, a male prostitute, to this effect:

> "Did you live with a woman known as Queen Anne in Church Street, Soho?"
> "No, it is a man. Perhaps you will see him later on." (From H. Montgomery Hyde, *The Cleveland Street Scandal*, 1976)

See also GAY, a word first recorded as being used in its modern sense by the same John Saul.

questionable. Wrong—usually in a criminal as well as a moral sense.
From the euphemistic axiom that the real meaning of a word or phrase always is worse than the apparent meaning, it follows remorselessly that the explicit acknowledgment of doubt in "questionable" is tantamount to an admission of guilt. "Questionable" pops up in many contexts, e.g., *questionable act, questionable practice,* and *questionable reputation,* but the most common kind of "questionable" in recent years is the *questionable payment,* used to grease the ways of

international business. Of the 300 or so American firms that have confessed to the practice, the leading dispenser of *questionable* payments seems to have been the Lockheed Aircraft Corp., which shelled out $38 million in this manner between 1970 and 1975, and whose former president, A. Carl Kotchian, put the question this way: "Some call it gratuities, some call them questionable payments. Some call it extortion, some call it grease. Some call it bribery. I look at these payments as necessary to sell a product" (*New York Times*, 2/16/79). See also COMMISSION and CONSULTANT.

quietus. Death; originally a receipt or acquittance showing that a debt had been paid or accounts cleared, the meaning of "quietus" was extended to include the discharge of a person from the obligations of office, as well as from life itself, and finally, the method—a blow, say—by which the discharge may be accomplished, e.g., "When he himself might his quietus make/With a bare bodkin [i.e., dagger]" (William Shakespeare, *Hamlet*, 1602). See also PASS AWAY and TERMI-NATE/TERMINATION.

R

rabbit. Various meats have been billed euphemistically as "rabbit" from time to time. For example, speaking of the 135-day Siege of Paris in 1870–71, "'Rabbit' became a common euphemism for cat or kitten, often smothered in onions or served as a stew" (*Natural History*, 10/77). During this siege, Parisians also consumed some 70,000 horses as well as uncounted numbers of rats. Curiously, "lamb" continued to be sold even as the city's dog population dropped precipitously. (For more about eating meat, see FILET MIGNON.)

On a much profounder level, psychologically as well as semantically, "rabbit" also is a euphemism for "cony," a word that conjured up extremely bad thoughts in the minds of our early nineteenth-century ancestors. To begin at the beginning:

"Rabbit" originally referred only to the young of the long-eared *Lepus cunicula*, an adult of the species was a "cony" (also spelled *coney, coniq, conynq, cunning, cunny*). The distinction was maintained at least until the early seventeenth century, but was lost by the middle of the eighteenth, with Dr. Johnson using the two words interchangeably in his *Dictionary of the English Language* (1755). Thereafter, though still used by those people who were most familiar with the animal (e.g., gamekeepers, poachers, furriers, cooks), "cony" faded from general use, with "rabbit" taking over in its place. The *Oxford English Dictionary* (vol. C, 1888–93) refers guardedly to the "obsolescence" of "cony" without attempting to explain what happened. Yet the reason is clear enough to anyone who knows how the bad meanings of words tend to drive out the good ones (Gresham's Law again) and who also knows that from the sixteenth century, if not before, "cony" was both a term of endearment for a woman and a nickname for her most PRIVATE PARTS. Thus, as an endearment: "He calleth me his whytyng, His nobbes and his conny" (John Skelton, *The Tunnyng of Elynor Rummyng*, ca. 1528). Meantime, the use of "cony" in the other, strictly anatomical sense was reinforced not only by the physical resemblance (as with PUSSY) but by the semantic relationship, since "cony" probably is cognate to the heavily tabooed "cunt" (or VAGINA). In fact, "cony" originally was pronounced to rhyme with "honey" or "money," e.g., "A pox on your Christian cockatrices! They cry, like poulterers' wives, 'No money, no coney'" (Philip Massinger and Thomas Decker, *The Virgin Martir, A Tragedie*, 1622). Moreover, "cony" had other pejorative meanings: *cony* or *Tom cony* once stood for "simpleton"; to engage in *cony catching* was to live by tricking or swindling (see STREETWALKER for the book title that made the term a popular one for some sixty years); a *cony* (or *cunny*) *warren* was a brothel; and to make a fist with the thumb inside, as girls often do, was to be *cunny thumbed*. (At the same time, "bun," as in "bunny," also stood for "cunt." For a sailor, "to touch bun for luck" before going on a voyage was something like—but not too much like—rubbing a rabbit's foot.)

With all these circumstances combining against "cony," it is not hard to see why "rabbit" became the term of choice among polite people, who were not so polite that they didn't know what cony-pronounced–cunny sounded like. There was still an annoying difficulty, however: "Cony" appeared in the Bible. What to do when reading sacred Scripture? And with women in the congregation! Not until the start of the nineteenth century did incipient Victorians arrive at the proper solution, i.e., *change* the pronunciation of "cony." As the *Oxford English Dictionary* notes, John Walker, whose pronouncing dictionary was published in 1791, knew only the "cunny" pronunciation, but Benjamin H. Smart, who revised Walker's opus in 1836, knew both. While admitting that the word "is familiarly pronounced *cunny*," Smart ordained that *cony* is "proper for a solemn reading." And so it is, even unto our own day, that milady may wear a "cony" coat, but only with a long "o," and that we do not say "cunny" when we speak of visiting Coney Island (New York) or Coney Creek (Colorado).

For other animals that have had difficulties with their names, see ROOSTER.

race. Black; a general substitute for the more explicit word, once resorted to by blacks as well as whites. "In 1923, pianist Clarence Williams was helping Frank Walker initiate Columbia's 'Race Record' series, a new venture for the company. . . . The series was inspired by the success of such labels as Okey and Paramount in capturing the vast black blues market" (Chris Albertson, "Empress of the Blues," notes for the reissue of Bessie Smith's surviving recordings, *Bessie Smith—The World's Greatest Blues Singer*). For more on the exceedingly tricky color question, see NEGRO.

race rider. A woman jockey—"jockey" having been associated for so long with masculine riders that some people felt an entirely new term was needed when feminine ones started mounting up at thoroughbred racetracks. See also PERSON.

rap parlor. In theory, "to rap" is "to talk," as in "rap session," but conversation is not of the essence in a "rap parlor" (or "club" or "studio"), which is merely another kind of MASSAGE PARLOR, or brothel. "In the face of a crackdown on street prostitution many of the girls . . . are taking refuge in 'rap clubs'—which have replaced [??] massage parlors in the sex-for-sale world" (*New York Post*, 6/22/73).

There is more to this euphemism than meets the uninitiated eye: Since freedom of speech is protected by the Constitution, it may be more difficult to devise legislation against *rap parlors* than *massage parlors*. As Columbia Law School Professor Curtis J. Berger has pointed out: "I suppose there are some people who just like to talk on the lap of a naked lady for a half hour. If that is all that happens, I think you have First Amendment problems with this [proposed New York City] ordinance. When you talk about 'rapping,' you are moving somewhat closer to the range of constitutionally protected activity" (*New York Times*, 11/3/75). See also ADULT.

Realtor. A real estate agent/broker/man/person. Employing one word in place of three is almost always commendable but "Realtor" is an exception to the rule. (PUBLICITOR is another.) It is an exception because of the motive: self-aggrandizement. In the words of George Follansbee Babbitt: "We ought to insist that folks call us 'realtors' and not 'real-estate men.' Sounds more like a reg'lar profession" (Sinclair Lewis, *Babbitt*, 1922).

"Realtor" was still a new term when Babbitt spoke, having been coined in

1915 by Charles N. Chadbourn, of Minneapolis, Minnesota, who wanted to distinguish himself and fellow members of the local Real Estate Board from those dealers in land who weren't certified board members. The new handle was enthusiastically adopted by the locals and, in 1916, by the National Association of Real Estate Boards, which subsequently won a number of court battles to prevent nonboarders from using it, too. (Hence, the capital "R" awarded "Realtor" in dictionaries.) Cynics suggested that "Realtor" was compounded of two Spanish words, *real* (royal) and *toro* (bull), but the originator, Mr. Chadbourn, produced another explanation for H. L. Mencken: *"Real estate* originally meant royal grant. It is so connected with land in the public mind that *realtor* is easily understood, even at first hearing. *Or* is a suffix meaning a doer, one who performs an act, as a *grantor, executor, sponsor, administrator. Realtor:* a doer in real estate" (*The American Language: Supplement I*, 1945). As Mencken also points out, the *or* ending itself has especially classy connotations, probably because it stands for the Latin *ator* or the French *eur*, whereas *er* to indicate "doer" is strictly English. Thus, *advisor* and *insuror* have better vibes than ADVISER and "insurer"; an AUTHOR is esteemed more than a "writer," and both *educator* and *professor* outrank "teacher." At various times, furniture dealers have tried to turn themselves into *furnitors*, merchants into *merchantors*, and welders into *weldors*. It is a small wonder that the world does not also have *preachors* and wild animal *trainors*.

For more about building professional images, see also ENGINEER, and for more about the work of *Realtors*, continue with ADORABLE, DEVELOP/DEVELOPER/ DEVELOPMENT, EAT-IN KITCHEN, HANDYMAN'S SPECIAL, HARMONIOUS, MIDDLE CLASS, NEEDS SOME WORK, and QUAINT.

rear. The ass; another of the many discreet allusions to the piece of anatomy with which everyone is blessed but whose name is deemed too vulgar to mention. "Do you think I'm too fat? Does my rear look too big in these pants?" (Consuelo Saah Baehr, *Report from the Heart*, 1976). See also ARSE.

recession. Hard times; a small depression; an economic THING. "In the 1920's, Wesley Clair Mitchell, the great business cycle analyst who was the founder of business cycle theory, offered 'recession' as a description of a relatively mild transition from 'prosperity' to 'depression.' The word it was designed to replace was 'crisis'. . . ." (*New York Times*, 12/24/78). The new term became popular among politicians, for whom "depression" was unutterable (if their party happened to be in office when one occurred), e.g., ". . . the nation's economy . . . suffered, from 1957 through 1958, the third and deepest recession since World War II. . . . By June, unemployment had climbed to 5,437,000—an unwanted pinnacle, unmatched since the days before World War II" (Emmet John Hughes, *The Ordeal of Power*, 1963). With "recessions" of this ilk coming along so regularly, the euphemism soon began wearing thin. This led to labeling all *recessions* as "temporary," and to characterizing them, when possible, as *growth recessions* (meaning that the economy is expanding but so slowly that the unemployment rate is nevertheless increasing) Innovative minds also developed completely new euphemisms, such as *downturn* (and the more eloquent *mild but necessary downturn*), *high-level stagnation, rolling readjustment, slowdown* (frequently qualified as a *healthy slowdown*), and *slump* (or *mini-slump*).

Attempting to distinguish "recession" from "depression," economists have produced complex definitions of the former, the simplest of which is Arthur M. Okun's definition—an empirical description, really—of a "recession" as a decline in the real gross national product for two consecutive quarters. For the average person, an even more elemental definition, also empirical, is contained in the adage, "A recession is when you lose your job; a depression is when I lose mine."

For more about the dismal science of economics, see ADJUSTMENT DOWN-WARD, GROWTH STOCK, STABLE GROWTH, and TECHNICAL ADJUSTMENT

reconnaissance in force. Search and destroy. Other, still-softer variants include *search and clear, search and sweep, sweeping operation,* and *reconnaissance forces sweeping operation.*

The basic "search and destroy" dates from 1966, when the United States went on the offensive in Vietnam, with Gen. William C. Westmoreland launching six major search-and-destroy attacks. As military phrases go, this one was unusually vivid. (See CASUALTY for more on the blandness of military talk.) It took awhile, however, for the general to appreciate the semantic error. In his own words:

> . . . many Americans apparently failed to comprehend "search and destroy," possibly because detractors of the war chose to distort it. . . . many people, to my surprise, came to associate it with aimless searches in the jungle and the random destroying of villages and other property. . . . I was long unaware of how twisted the meaning of the term had become. . . . Not until early in 1968 did . . . John Charles Daly call my attention to it. "General," John Daly told me during a visit to my office, "you are your own worst enemy to perpetuate a term that has become so distorted." Although those who saw the war as a political issue could no doubt have twisted any term, I changed it without fanfare to "sweeping operation" or "reconnaissance in force." Yet the term still stuck in the minds of many. . . . (*A Soldier Reports,* 1976)

One reason the term "stuck" was that on March 16, 1968, around the time Westmoreland and Daly were chatting, C Company of the First Battalion, 20th Infantry Brigade, Americal Division, entered the village of My Lai and massacred (or WASTED, as Lt. William L. Calley, Jr., put it) some 300 to 500 women, children, and old men. Charlie Company was on a routine search-and-destroy mission at the time, and it was hard to pass off the event as a *sweeping operation, reconnaissance in force,* or what-have-you. See also NEUTRALIZE/NEUTRALIZATION, PROTECTIVE REACTION, and SPECIFIED STRIKE ZONE.

recycler. A junkman; an operator of a junkyard. The trade association of the junkmen is the National Association of Recycling Industries. This is only their newest, recycled name; previously, this organization was known as National Association of Secondary Material Industries and, before that, as the National Association of Waste Material Dealers.

The *recycling* business, like most other businesses, has its specialists. Thus, in the state of Pennsylvania, the operators of automobile junkyards are officially—

redundancy

by act of the state legislature—known as *automotive dismantlers and recyclers*. See also LANDFILL and RESALE SHOP.

redundancy. In Britain, the usual excuse for reducing work forces by dismissing employees who can't be fired for cause; comparable to the American EXCESS. "Penguin Books Ltd. . . . has announced cuts in its publishing program of 22%, staff redundancies of nearly 100 and economies in overhead . . ." (*Publishers Weekly*, 2/8/80). See also LET GO.

refreshment. An alcoholic drink, a LIBATION. "We then visited another public place, and after a few refreshments Mrs. Battistella became ill, and I enlisted the help of others in our group to assist me in seeing her safely home" (Rep. Wilbur D. Mills, D., Arkansas, statement to the press, 10/10/74).

Nostalgia Department: Mrs. Battistella, better known professionally as Fannie Fox, the Argentinian Firecracker, was an ECDYSIAST. After the car in which she and Mr. Mills were traveling was stopped for reckless driving in the wee morning hours of October 7, near the Jefferson Memorial in Washington, D.C., she made waves—literally and figuratively—by leaping out of the car and into the chilly waters of the nearby Tidal Basin. For Mr. Mills, chairman of the House Ways and Means Committee, and commonly described as one of the most powerful men in Washington, this was the beginning of the end of his congressional career. See also HIGH.

regular. Another of the ways for manufacturers to avoid tagging their merchandise with the supposedly unsalable word "small." A "regular" cigarette, for example, is a small one, compared to a KING-SIZE or *super-king* cigarette. And in quite another product category: "*Small* is disguised as *regular* ('Giant, family or regular size package of White King'—handbill distributed in Los Angeles, 8 Aug. 1940) . . ." (*American Speech*, 4/42). For other kinds of "small," see MEDIUM and LARGE, and for another kind of "regular," see IRREGULARITY.

relations. Uncles? Aunts? Cousins? Uh-uh. As with INTERCOURSE, it is the prefatory "sexual" that has been delicately omitted, e.g., "They smoked some grass and then they had relations." See also SEX.

relationship. In the absence of compelling evidence to the contrary, it is always safe to assume that the bland, impersonal "relationship" is sexual. Moreover, though married and homosexual couples occasionally are said to have "relationships," the term usually implies illicit, hetero goings-on—what previous generations would have called an AFFAIR, AMOUR, or CONNECTION. Frequently, signposts are put up, just to be sure that everyone gets the message. This results in such combinations as *close personal relationship, long and deep personal relationship,* MEANINGFUL RELATIONSHIP, and *special relationship*. Short and long forms often appear cheek by jowl, proving their essential synonymity. Thus, on May 25, 1976, Rep. Wayne L. Hays (D., Ohio) admitted to the House of Representatives that "for an extended period of time I did have a relationship with Elizabeth Ray," and then, a minute or so later, referred to "my personal relationship with Miss

Ray." And "sex," of course, was at issue, though not explicitly mentioned; see also FAVORS.

On the whole, "relationship" seems well-suited for the modern world. It is a denatured, pseudo-scientific word that might better be reserved for inanimate objects than animate, sexual ones. It suggests that feelings are functional and more the result of physical positional relationships than anything else, e.g.: "I firmly believe that if you find something you really enjoy, do *it*—often! I give everything I have to my job, and my relationships (especially with Sean) . . . I guess you could say I'm that COSMOPOLITAN Girl" (ad for THAT magazine, *New York Times*, 10/17/77). Or as a Cosmo girl might also say, abusing "relationship" in a different way: "The bubble burst when a relationship in which I had invested four years of role-playing rode off into the sunset without a trace" (Paula Becker, et al., *The Strategic Woman*, 1977).

release. To fire from a job; frequently said of professional athletes, even the best of whom commonly are *released* at about age thirty-five, which is when the legs start to go. See also LET GO.

relieve. (1) To fire from a job, i.e., to come to someone's assistance (or *relief*) by freeing (or "relieving") that person of the onerous obligations of showing up at the office; to LET GO an employee. (2) To reduce (or *relieve*) internal bodily pressures by expelling waste matter; to EASE oneself. "James Gordon Bennett, publisher of the Paris *Herald* . . . exiled himself to France in 1877—ostracized by society for relieving himself while drunk in the fireplace [or, some say, the grand piano] of his fiancée's home" (Henry Serrano Villard, *Contact: The Story of the Early Birds*, 1968). See also PEE.

remains. A dead body. The oldest "remains" in the *Oxford English Dictionary* come from John Dryden's translation of Ovid's *Metamorphoses* (1700): "Of all the mighty man the small remains/A little urn and scarcely fill'd contains."

The term is still used commonly by FUNERAL DIRECTORS and others, e.g.: "REMAINS SHIPPED WORLDWIDE" (ad, Manhattan, New York, *Yellow Pages*, 1979–80). From a strictly euphemistic point of view, however, "remains" is of interest today primarily for its metamorphosis into one of the ickier neologisms of our time—CREMAINS (aka ashes). See also DECEASED.

remove. To kill, as in "The spy had been 'removed from circulation'" (William Stevenson, *A Man Called Intrepid*, 1976). This particular spy, or AGENT, was *removed* while crossing Broadway at Times Square: A taxi knocked him down and a follow-up car completed the *removal* by running over him. See also RUB OUT and the general HIT.

remuneration. Pay, wages, salary; linguistically comparable to the HONORA-RIUM given to someone who is not on the regular payroll.

repose. Originally, only a temporary rest, especially one gained from sleep, by the nineteenth century "repose" had become a euphemism for the rest from which there is no waking. Churches celebrated the Festival of the Repose of the Virgin and some of them had Altars of Repose. FUNERAL HOMES, meanwhile, converted their laying-out rooms into *reposing rooms* or *slumber rooms*. The euphemism sounds quaint but is by no means obsolete, as evidenced by the sweetly solemn advertisement, cited by Edwin Newman in *Strictly Speaking* (1974), of Unity Funeral Chapels (see CHAPEL) of New York:

> But even Roses with all their splendor and heart
> Will one day their beautiful petals fall apart.
> Man too, has his season like the Rose.
> And then, one day, he also must repose.

See also REST and SLEEP.

representative. Formerly a euphemism for "man," as in *manufacturer's representative, publicity representative,* and *sales representative,* but now that so many women are in business, too, a euphemism for "person." See also PERSON and TRAIL REPRESENTATIVE.

resale shop. A junk shop that has metamorphosed halfway into an antique store. All the goods in a *resale shop* are PREVIOUSLY OWNED. See also RECYCLER.

resident. (1) A patient in an institution for old people, aka NURSING HOME; (2) a prisoner in an institution for bad people, aka CORRECTIONAL FACILITY.

resign. To be fired or LET GO. One of the many privileges that rank hath is that of being allowed to resign: "A cabinet minister is asked to resign; a factory worker is fired" (Anatol Rapoport, *Semantics*, 1975).

respect. Fear.
  A baseball thrown at 85 or 90 miles an hour is a projectile that can—and has—killed. Despite this, hitters never admit to "fear." The correct term, as Roger Angell has pointed out, is "respect" (*The New Yorker*, 10/4/76). If a hitter really digs in, or otherwise fails to show sufficient *respect* (by hitting a homerun, say), the next pitch he sees may be up around the eyeballs—just as a reminder. The euphemism and the implied threat appear off the playing field, too. Thus, when an angry father announces to his heir apparent, "I'm going to teach you some respect," junior correctly understands this to mean, "The old man is about to give me a licking," and when The Godfather raises his voice, everyone scampers for safety, for he is a man of *respect,* and feared accordingly.

response form. Complaint form. Tell Amtrak that you want to make a complaint and you will be handed a *passenger response form* (personal communication from Janet Baker, who was given one, 2/26/80).

rest. The relaxation that is obtained through death, as in *eternal rest, called to heavenly rest, go to rest,* and *laid to rest.* A *place of rest* is a grave, or SPACE, while "RIP," for *rest in peace,* is a common epitaph on MONUMENTS. (The jocular *rest in pieces* is reserved for those who have had accidents with dynamite.) See also HAPPY HUNTING GROUNDS, GONE TO THE and PASS AWAY.

rest house. Madhouse. "'I knew this would end up in the nut house.'' . . . I say rest house.'" (Joseph Kesselring, *Arsenic and Old Lace*, film, 1944). See also MENTAL HOSPITAL.

rest room. A public toilet. "While the carnivorous rodent was being chased about the darkened theater, it fled into the rest room" (*Lubbock* [TX] *Morning Avalanche*, 2/23/49). "Rest room" seems to be a genuine Americanism, with the oldest example of such a FACILITY in *A Dictionary of Americanisms* (Mitford M. Mathews, ed., 1951) coming from 1900. "Rest room" is one of the most common, as well as most discreetly generalized, of the many euphemisms for this kind of public CONVENIENCE. See also CLOAK ROOM, COMFORT STATION, LADIES/GENTLEMEN, LAVATORY, RETIRING ROOM, TOILET, VESPASIENNE WALK, WASH ROOM, and WC.

retire. An omnibus term that coyly covers a variety of unseemly actions. For example, to say that "she has retired," may mean—depending on context—either that "she has gone to bed," or that "she has gone to the toilet" (also known in some circles as the RETIRING ROOM). On the other hand, when soldiers *retire*, they are retreating—a movement that may also be described as a RETROGRADE MANEUVER.

retiring room. A toilet.
      Demonstrating once again the remarkable flair of the British for pageantry: "It has been announced that the retiring rooms specially erected at Westminster Abbey for Coronation Day will be severally marked as follows: 'Peers,' 'Gentlemen,' 'Men,' and 'Peeresses,' 'Ladies,' 'Women'" (*New York Herald Tribune*, 5/7/37). See also REST ROOM, TOILET, and, for the other side of the social coin, the South African examples in LADIES/GENTLEMEN.

retrograde maneuver. A military retreat—an orderly one, supposedly. Referring to the decision of South Vietnamese President Thieu in the spring of 1975 to shorten his lines of defense by abandoning several central and northern provinces: "A 'retrograde' maneuver—as the experts euphemistically term such a withdrawal—requires extensive planning and a coordinated command structure" (*Time*, 4/14/75). Euphemisms for "retreat" probably began coming into existence shortly after the first army made the first one; see STRATEGIC MOVEMENT TO THE REAR.

reverse engineering. Copying; specifically, in electronics, taking apart a chip, or miniature integrated circuit, in order to determine how it was made. The Japanese (according to Americans) are notorious for copying; Americans only engage in *reverse engineering*. See also INTERPRET THE MOOD OF.

RIF. The acronym for Reduction in Force, most commonly encountered in governmental bureaucracies, civilian as well as military, where it is used generally as a verb meaning "to dismiss" or LET GO, e.g., "Poor Capt. Jinks has been riffed because he was three years overage in grade." See also SELECT OUT.

right, not. In the art world, a common circumlocution that enables experts to deliver general opinions without descending into specifics on which they might later be shown to be wrong. From an interview with Alan Shestack, director of the Yale Art Gallery: "'Right' . . . keeps one from having to say whether it's a forgery or a fraud or an imitation. You say, 'It doesn't look *right* to me,' and that can mean anything: that it *was* executed by the artist but on a day when he wasn't feeling well, or that it's by one of his followers or students, or even that it's a fraudulent imitation intended to deceive" (*Yale Alumni Magazine*, 2/76). See also AUTHENTIC REPRODUCTION.

right-to-work. Management's fair-sounding term for what labor calls "union-busting." The *right-to-work* movement is rooted in section 14-b of the Taft-Hartley Act of 1947. This section permits states to pass laws banning "union" (or "closed," in management's lexicon) shops that employees must join, or pay dues to, if they are to work for unionized firms. See also FAIR TRADE, FREE ENTERPRISE, OPEN SHOP, and PRO-CHOICE.

rock lobster. Crayfish, commonly served up on restaurant menus as *South African Rock Lobster Tail*, which certainly has a more appetizing ring than "South African Crayfish Tail." Another kind of undersea "rock" is the *rock salmon*, aka dogfish. See also CAPE COD TURKEY and FILET MIGNON.

rocks. The testicles; probably inspired by the much older (from the twelfth century) *stones* and perhaps reinforced by the modern slang meaning of "rocks" as diamonds, i.e., precious stones, or FAMILY JEWELS. Thus, commenting on the surprisingly effete language of the American West: "The wives and daughters of the senators and representatives of the young states, occasionally it is true, . . . gave different names to various animate and inanimate objects; such as 'little rocks' for stones, 'rooster' for game-cock" (Hugo Playfair, *The Hugo Playfair Papers; or, Brother Jonathan, the Smartest Nation in All Creation*, 1841). See also PECULIAR MEMBERS and ROOSTER.

rodent operator. An English ratcatcher.

roger. The penis; another of the many personal names that have been bestowed upon this part of the male anatomy, e.g., *dick*, JOHN THOMAS, and PETER. "Roger" may come from the habit of farmers in the seventeenth and eighteenth centuries of giving this name to their bulls. Sometimes spelled "rodger," it also became a byword for the sexual act, e.g., "I rogered her lustily" (L. B. Wright and M. Tinling, eds., *The Secret Diary of William Byrd of Westover, 1709–1712*, 1941). As commonly happens, the euphemism was tarred by association with that for which it stood, so that a half-century later, another journalist, James Boswell, resorted to euphemistic dashes, i.e., "r-g-r," in his entry for the riotous evening of June 4, 1763. It seems probable, too, that the euphemistic connotations of "roger" were known to the unknown composer of the following old limerick:

> There was an old maid from Cape Cod
> Who thought children were made by God,
>   But it was not the Almighty
>   Who lifted her nightie,
> It was Roger, the lodger, by God!

Roman candle. A parachutist whose chute doesn't open. "Then that rare and tragic nightmare of all paratroopers occurred: the chute came out of the bag and streamed unopened behind him. The man catapulted to earth. He had become what paratroopers call 'a Roman candle'" (Stewart Alsop and Thomas Braden, *Sub Rosa—The O.S.S. and American Espionage*, 1946). The OSS, or Office of Strategic Services (described by its critics as Oh So Social, Oh So Secret, and Oh So Silly), was the predecessor of the CIA; see CASUALTY, COMPANY, and STRATEGIC.

romance. Love without marriage (at least not to the lover in question) or, more specifically, sex (with or without marriage). In the more general sense: ". . . she was not difficult to love. Though I knew the guilt of a longtime family man with a loyal wife and five children, I did nothing to discourage our romance once it began" (Bobby Baker, *Wheeling and Dealing*, 1978). And more specifically: "Romance does not take as much energy as an equal amount of time spent throwing a Frisbee. True or false?" ("Hollywood Squares," WABC-TV, 9/11/78). From the undercover meanings of "romance" comes "romansion," a portmanteau term for a highfalutin whorehouse. See also LOVE and SEX.

    P.S. The answer to the game-show question is "True." Throwing a Frisbee is a better way of losing weight, if that is what interests you.

Roman culture. Orgies, group sex, the swinging party scene; personal-ad code, often shortened to *Roman*: "ITALIAN LADY SEEKS men women cpls for fr and roman cult. Have a well endowed male friend" (*Ace*, undated, ca. 1976). See also ENDOW/ENDOWMENT, FRENCH, and SWINGING.

roommate. When the collegiate term is applied to old grads, the emphasis is on the "mate" part, as the dormitory is usually co-ed and the relationship sexual but unsanctified. A variant for those with more spacious accommodations is *housemate*. See also PARTNER.

rooster. Cock. On account of its remarkable versatility, "rooster" ranks as the greatest of all barnyard euphemisms. It is also one of the hallmarks of the period, dating from about 1750, of pre-Victorian prudery.

    Deriving from the Old English *hrost*—the spars or rafters of a house, a perch—"rooster" has always been more popular among Americans than the English themselves. The oldest example of the term in *A Dictionary of American English* (1944) is from 1772. A half-century later, "rooster" was still strange enough to British readers that James Flint felt he had to explain to them that the

"Rooster, or he-bird [is the] Cock, the male of the hen" (*Letters from America*, 1822). The reason for making the change didn't have to be explained, at least not to Americans. Even the bumpkin Jonathan, the best comic creation of Royall Tyler, the first successful American playwright, was sensitive enough to language to know that he didn't like the sound of "cock" (he didn't like SERVANT either), telling how "One sailor-looking man . . . clapt me on the shoulder and said, 'You are a d——d hearty cock, smite my timbers!' I told him so I was, but I thought he need not swear so, and make use of such naughty words" (*The Contrast*, 1787).

The "naughty word" is, of course, one of the traditional ones for what is now known politely as the PENIS. The origin of "cock" in this sense is itself decently lost in the mists of lexicography. The earliest example in the *Oxford English Dictionary* (1972 supplement) is from 1618, but William Shakespeare punned upon this meaning two decades before, when he had Pistol yell at Nym: "Pistol's cock is up . . ." (*Henry V*, 1599). The original metaphor may have derived from the proud, procreative "cock" or from the "cock" that is a spout or faucet, but it probably did not come to the fore until the fifteenth or sixteenth centuries, since in the fourteenth century and earlier, "cock" (or "gock") was a euphemism for "God" ("cokkes bones" was a good Chaucerian oath), and it seems unlikely that the word could have borne two such disparate meanings simultaneously.

"Rooster" was not the only word to supplant "cock." CROWER, HE-BIDDY, and even *barn-door he-biddy* also have been reported. "Crower," for example, was especially popular in the Ozarks, where, Vance Randolph relates, "I myself have seen grown men, when women were present, blush and stammer at the mere mention of such commonplace bits of hardware as *stop-cocks* or *pet-cocks*, and avoid describing a gun as *cocked* by some clumsy circumlocution, such as *she's ready t'go* or *th' hammer's back*" (*Dialect Notes*, vol. VI, Part I, 1928). The southern nervousness about "cock" may also reflect the word's use as a euphemism of sorts for the corresponding female part. It can be mildly disconcerting (to a northerner) to hear a good ole boy tell how "She kept pushing my hand away but finally I was able to get it on her cock" (personal communication; Fort Sam Houston, Texas, 1957). Still, the squeamishness is by no means limited to any one part of the country and it is nevertheless real for sometimes being half-masked by jocularity. Consider the following:

Apricots were once apricocks or apricox.
The "cockchafer" ("chafer" does mean "teaser," but this is a kind of beetle, believe it or not) had its name shortened to *chafer*.
The "turkey cock" was converted into the *gentleman turkey*.
"Haycocks" are now *haystacks*.
The original emblem of the Democratic party was "the cock," but it became a *rooster* before the nineteenth century was out.
Roostercade has been reported for "cockade."
"Cockroaches" in the nineteenth century turned into *rooster roaches* or, as today, *roaches*.
Rooster fighting gained in popularity during the second half of the nineteenth century at the expense of "cockfighting."
The old "cock and bull tale" became, in the Ozarks at least, a *rooster and ox*

story. This is a rare, triple euphemism, since "tale," a homophone of TAIL, is being replaced as well as the sexually charged "bull."

The "cocktail" occasionally metamorphosed into the *roostertail,* and some wags suggested (to avoid "tail" again) that it be called a *rooster's shirt.*

T. C. Haliburton may have been exaggerating in *Sam Slick* (1843–44) when he had a young man tell a maiden that her brother had become a *roosterswain* in the navy, instead of a "coxswain," but the thought is true to the time.

The American "woodcock" became the TIMBERDOODLE.

"Weathercocks" today are usually known as *weathervanes,* even when shaped like *he-biddies.*

The author of *Little Women, Little Men, Under the Lilacs,* etc., is Louisa May Alcott because her father, Amos Bronson, changed his last name from "Alcox." (Previously, it had been "Alcock" and, before that, probably "Allcock," which seems to reflect well on one of Louisa May's ancestors.)

For more on the richly euphemistic subject of animal names, see COW BRUTE, DONKEY, GENTLEMAN, RABBIT, SIRE, SLUT, and the *groundhog* in PECKER.

rubber. A general reference to an embarrassing article, i.e., a condom, also known as a *disposable sanitary device* (in the United States) and as a *specialty* or *circular protector* (in the United Kingdom). Condoms have been euphemized visually as well as verbally. Thus, in a Bill Mauldin cartoon ("Wisht I could stand up an' git some sleep"), one of two GI's in a foxhole at Anzio has stuck a tin can over the business end of his rifle to keep the rain out. As Mauldin pointed out on the Dick Cavett show (WNET-TV, NYC, 12/28/78), GI's usually improvised with "other objects for which there was no use at the time," but the tin can was "pictorially more acceptable." See also the *French letter* in FRENCH and SAFETY.

rub out. To kill; the expression comes not, as one might expect, from the city streets of the twentieth century, but from the American West of the nineteenth, e.g.: "If you are fortunate you will discover the Black Feet before they see you. . . . If they discover you first, they will rub you all out" (J. P. Beckwourth, *Life and Adventures,* T. D. Bonner, ed., 1856). "Rub out" almost certainly derives from "erase," but "erase" itself, as a byword for "murder," seems to be more popular among literary men than HIT men. See, however, the analogous REMOVE, which is used by certain high-toned practitioners of the trade.

ruddy. Bloody. "All I've got to say, is to say you've got a ruddy good billet" (Lord Charles Beresford, *Memoirs I,* 1914).

An old and perfectly legitimate word in its own right, "ruddy" was drawn into service as a euphemism toward the end of the last century. The British aversion to "bloody" is itself a relatively recent phenomenon, arising around 1750, at the outset of the euphemistically important pre-Victorian period. The taboo against "bloody," which probably derives from plain, ordinary "blood," rather than "By Our Lady," "God's Blood," or any of the other exotic sources that have been proposed, remained strong until the 1920s, despite the liberating influence of the bloody-Great-War. In 1914, its use in George Bernard Shaw's *Pygmalion* ("Walk!" said Eliza. "Not bloody likely. I am going in a taxi.") caused such a great sensation that newspapers, which had previously been rendering the term as "b——y," started referring to *the Shavian adjective* (see also ADJECTIVE/ ADJECTIVAL) and to the adverb, *pygmalionly*. Besides "ruddy," the taboo spawned such other euphemisms as *bally, bleeding* (see BLEEDER), *blooming, rose-colored,* and (jocularly) *sanguinary*. A highlight of the ban on "bloody" was the deletion of "ruddy" from *Ruddigore,* the Gilbert and Sullivan operetta of 1887. It had opened as *Ruddygore,* but some people thought this was too risqué; hence the substitution of the "i" for the "y" after the fourth performance.

Sabbath. For those Christians who wish to revel in religiosity, the first day of the week; Sunday.

James Fenimore Cooper, in a remarkable anticipation of Nancy Mitford's disquisition on U and non-U (see DENTURES), had this to say about "Sabbath": "One of the most certain evidences of a man of high breeding is his simplicity of speech . . . . He does not say, in speaking of a dance, that 'the attire of the *ladies* was exceedingly elegant and peculiarly becoming at the late assembly,' but that 'the *women* were well dressed at the last ball'; nor is he apt to remark 'that the Rev. Mr. G. —————— gave us an elegant and searching discourse the past *Sabbath*,' but that 'the parson preached a good sermon last Sunday'" (*The American Democrat*, 1838). See also LADY.

sacrifice. To kill an animal in the name of science. The euphemism is the term of choice among those who can only examine the insides of test animals by performing autopsies on them, e.g.: "Sacrificing these newly hatched wild chicks, he found that they had larger brains and adrenal glands than do domesticated or hybrid turkeys" (*Science*, 3/7/80). See also CULL and, for more lab talk, STRESS-PRODUCING STIMULUS.

saddleblock anesthesia. So-named in preference to mentioning that portion of the anatomy that would be in contact with a saddle if only the patient (usually a woman in labor) were riding a horse instead of an operating table.

safety. A condom; sometimes shortened to "safe." See also RUBBER and, for a short history of "condom," refer to the *French letter* in FRENCH.

safety in the streets. Law and order; doubletalk by liberals who objected so strongly to conservative calls for law and order that they felt unable to use the same phrase when they also decided to exploit crime as a political issue. An alternative slogan is *domestic tranquillity*.

> Representative Mario Biaggi was talking about crime. Only a few years ago, he was saying, "law and order" were dirty words among liberals, coded language for antiblack attitudes. "Now my opponents in the Democratic primary for Mayor have discovered the issue but they call it 'safety in the streets.' They've just discovered that the poor and the black are the most victimized by crime. That makes it O.K. to talk about." (*New York Times*, 3/18/73)

Biaggi, a much-decorated policeman prior to his entry into politics, didn't get the nomination, but the issue—and the code phrase—has remained very much alive.

Salisbury steak

Salisbury steak. Hamburger. When a restaurant lists *Salisbury steak* on the menu instead of "hamburger," the diner should expect to pay more for it. The expensive term comes from Dr. J. H. Salisbury, a turn-of-the-century food faddist, who urged people to eat hamburger at least three times a day. It took World War I, however, with the attendant, patriotic attempt to cleanse the language of Germanic words, to convert "Salisbury" into a full-fledged euphemism. A quarter-century later, as meat-packers prepared to fight World War II, some thought was given to changing "hamburger" to *defense steak,* but nothing came of it, "hamburger" having been thoroughly Americanized in the meantime. "Hamburger" also has been disguised as *Bifteck à la Cuisinart, chopped steak, entrecôte haché grillé, fried steak, Golden Kazoo Burger, O.K. Corral Manhandler, onion steak, Swiss steak, trailmaster steak, Wisconsin cutlet* (cheeseburger), and *Zapata Burger.* In England, meanwhile, "Wimpyburger" is regarded as a euphemism for a real-meat hamburger by those who have sunk their teeth into the real American McCoy.

For more about the great effort to de-Germanize the language, see LIBERTY CABBAGE, and for more about the meats we eat, continue with FILET MIGNON.

salon. A Frenchified shop, as in the Chatter Box Beauty Salon (Brooklyn, New York, *Yellow Pages,* 1979–80). A "salon," back when the word came into English in the early eighteenth century, was the drawing room or reception room of a palace or great house. Thus the modern beauty *salon* is the true euphemistic equivalent of the beauty PARLOR. (Acceptable alternatives in the beauty biz include *lounge,* SHOPPE, and STUDIO.) See also BEAUTICIAN.

saloon. A bar or tavern; a nineteenth-century euphemism that fell from grace as a result of the campaign of the Anti-Saloon League. "After going into the saloon (grog-shop) to 'freshen the nip'— . . . they led me into the upper tier of boxes" (*The Southern Literary Messenger,* VII, 1841).

A *saloon* originally was a drawing room or parlor, i.e., a SALON, and the term was applied to business establishments of many kinds—*beauty saloons, bowling saloons,* and *ice-cream saloons,* among them. The smell of whiskey was so strong, however, that it was generally recognized that *saloonkeepers, saloon-men, saloonists,* and, most poetic, *saloonatics,* were not curling hair, setting up bowling pins, or selling ice cream. Although the Noble Experiment of Prohibition (see TEMPERANCE) failed, the euphemism was so tainted in the process that when the old *saloons* reopened, they did so as *bars, cocktail lounges, taprooms, taverns,* and so forth. In some backward localities, laws against using "saloon" were left on the books, and it is for this reason that actor Patrick O'Neal's restaurant in New York City is called O'Neals' Baloon, not Saloon. For more about drinking alcohol, a custom that has inspired far more than its share of euphemisms, see HIGH.

salvage. To take without asking, to steal, as in "Let's salvage that case of wine." "Salvage" is the First World War's equivalent of the Second World War's LIBERATE and the Civil War's APPROPRIATE.

Sam Hill. Hell. The euphemism seems to be a product of the early Victorian period, with the first example in *A Dictionary of Americanisms* (Mitford M.

Mathews, ed., 1951) dating to 1839: "What in sam hill is that feller ballin' about?" (*Havanna* [NY] *Republican*, 8/21). See also HECK.

sanatorium/sanitarium. A cleaned-up tuberculosis clinic or a madhouse. "The fancies associated with tuberculosis and insanity have many parallels. In both diseases, there is confinement. Sufferers are put into a 'sanatorium' (the common word for a clinic for tuberculars and the most common euphemism for an insane asylum)" (Susan Sontag, *New York Review of Books*, 1/26/78).

N.B.: It used to be that the people in the businesses of treating tuberculars and mad people tried to make a distinction between *sanatorium* and *sanitarium*, maintaining that the former had more of the characteristics of a spa, while the latter was more like a hospital. However, the distinction was too fine for ordinary people—as well as for dictionary-makers—to comprehend, and so the two words are treated correctly as synonyms. See also MENTAL HOSPITAL and TB.

sanitation man. Garbage man. By all odds, the cleanest thing about garbage is the language associated with it. In New York City, "garbage man" was changed officially to *sanitation man* as long ago as 1939. Today, the city's 8,000-odd *sanitation men* generally refer to themselves as *Sanmen*. They work for the *Sanitation Department*, formerly known as the Bureau of Street Cleaning, and they belong to one of the most powerful municipal unions in the country, the Uniformed Sanitationmen's Association.

New York is by no means alone in this regard. The countryside is dotted with *sanitary landfills* (dumps) and many other cities have *sanitation departments*. At least one, Pasadena, California, even boasted a *Table Waste Disposal Department* (H. L. Mencken, *The American Language, Supplement I*, 1945). Garbage men in other cities also have been known as *sanitary engineers* or *sanitary officers*. (See ENGINEER and OFFICER.) Meanwhile, back in the Big Apple, the city Health Department has *sanitarians*, whose duties include enforcement of the local canine WASTE law. It is unlikely that the ultimate in this category is the Portable Sanitation Association, of Washington, D.C., but it will do until a better example comes along: The PSA, among other functions, offers rewards for the apprehension of people who damage or deface public toilets. See also LANDFILL, RECYCLER, and TOILET.

sanitize. To destroy evidence; specifically, to remove or change portions of a memorandum, record, or similar written DOCUMENT (paper) in order to protect the writer from embarrassment and/or criminal prosecution. Papers to be *sanitized* usually are characterized as being SENSITIVE; the act of *sanitizing* them may be a crime (destruction of evidence).

"Sanitize" seems to have originated in the intelligence COMMUNITY. The final report of the Senate Intelligence Committee in 1976 included a glossary of terms, among which was: "Sanitize—to delete or revise a report or document so as to prevent identification of the intelligence sources and methods that provided the information." And the CIA is a very efficient cleaner-upper. As noted in the House ("Pike Committee") report on the agency: "We were given heavily 'sanitized' pieces of paper. 'Sanitized' was merely a euphemism for blank sheets of paper . . ." (New York *Village Voice*, 2/11/78). See also DEEP SIX and LAUNDER.

scenario. A plan, a possible sequence of actions; specifically, during the Watergate affair, a plot or scheme; a charade. "As we kicked 'scenarios' around the room, a public-relations strategy emerged around two central themes: hide the facts and discredit the opposition" (John W. Dean III, *Blind Ambition*, 1976). "I would like also a scenario with regard to the President's role . . ." (President Richard M. Nixon, 4/15/73, *The White House Transcripts*, 1974). See also PUBLIC RELATIONS.

"Scenario" had been a popular word among military planners since at least the early 1960s. Thus, discussing the Cuban missile crisis of October 1962: "The air-strike advocates in our group prepared an elaborate scenario, which provided for a Presidential announcement of the missiles' presence Saturday, calling Congress back into emergency session, and then knocking the missiles out early Sunday morning, simultaneously notifying Khrushchev of our action and recommending a summit" (Theodore C. Sorensen, *Kennedy*, 1965). *Scenarios* can be a lot more complicated than this, of course. For example, William P. Bundy (brother to McGeorge CAPABILITY Bundy) directed the preparation of a 30-day-long *scenario* of political and military moves leading up to full-scale bombing of North Vietnam. This *scenario* was dated May 23, 1964, more than four months before North Vietnam handed the United States the excuse it needed for conducting the first air raids by attacking two destroyers in the Gulf of Tonkin. A truly sophisticated *scenario* encompasses many different possibilities, e.g., "OPTION C. Progressive squeeze-and-talk. . . . The scenario would be designed to give the U.S. the option at any point to proceed or not, to escalate or not, and to quicken the pace or not" ("Action for South Vietnam," second draft, Assistant Secretary of Defense John T. McNaughton, 11/6/64, *The Pentagon Papers*, 1971).

One would have thought the combined influence of the Pentagon and White House to be so baleful as to deter other people from adopting "scenario," but this is not the case. For example: "As long as there have been fossils to study, investigators have devised scenarios to describe the history of the human lineage" (*Science*, 7/15/77). See also ESCALATE, OPTION, and PROJECTION.

scientific and literary investigation. Theft and vandalism.

After the army of Gen. William Tecumseh Sherman captured the capital of Georgia, in November 1864, the troops went on the rampage, stealing and destroying. Then, in the tactful words of *New York Herald* correspondent David Conyngham: "Colonel [William] Hawley, of the 3d Wisconsin, was appointed commandant of the post, and established his headquarters in the State House, after which all scientific and literary investigation were put a stop to" (Conyngham, *Sherman's March Through the South*, 1865). For more about theft—and about Sherman's men, too—see APPROPRIATE.

Scouting/USA. The nonboyish name for what is still, legally, the Boy Scouts of America. A memo to editors about the name change explained: "The word 'boy' is objectionable to minorities, our young adult (male and female) leaders and naturally to the young women enrolled in our coed Exploring program." While continuing to enroll boys, ages eight to 18, the new "communicative" name is to be used on billboards, letterheads, etc. Not to be outdone, the old Campfire Girls later degirled themselves, becoming Campfire, Inc. See also MAN and PERSON.

screw. Whether in the literal sense as a verb, "to screw," or as a noun, "a screw," or in such figurative senses as "screw off" and "screw up," this is essentially a softer, euphemistic, five-letter version of the FOUR-LETTER WORD, "fuck." Its usage has been sanctioned by our most conspicuously religious president: "Christ says, Don't consider yourself better than someone else because one guy screws a whole bunch of women while the other guy is loyal to his wife" (Jimmy Carter, *Playboy* interview, 11/76). Illustrating the difference in attitudes toward the literal and figurative, the *New York Times* declined to print Carter's remark in toto, substituting "sexual intercourse" in place of the operative verb (9/21/76), though it later ran the complete transcript of David Frost's TV interview (5/4/77) with Richard M. Nixon, in which the former president said of Watergate: "I screwed up terribly in what was a little thing and became a big thing."

The sexual sense of "screw" seems to have arisen in the eighteenth century, possibly to fill the vacuum created by the banning of "fuck." For example, while forced to resort to dashes when defining "F——K" in *A Classical Dictionary of the Vulgar Tongue* (1796), Capt. Francis Grose felt no inhibitions when he reached "TO SCREW." In Grose's time and later, the word also has had other nonsexual, metaphorical meanings. Among them: A *screw* may be either a skeleton key or a prison guard (perhaps from "turnkey," perhaps from the "screw" in "thumbscrew"); *to be screwed* may just mean that one is drunk (see HIGH); and, in England, a *screw* may be a person's wages or salary, as in "I get a good weekly screw." That "screw" retains these other meanings makes it one of the few exceptions to Gresham's Law as it applies to language, i.e., that "bad" meanings drive out "good" ones. See also F—— and FORNICATE/FORNICATION.

sea squab. The blowfish; also called the *globefish, porcupine fish, puffer, swellfish,* or— getting back to real euphemisms—the *chicken of the sea*. The latter may even be served up as *chicken sea legs*, which do, as it happens, bear a passing resemblance to DRUMSTICKS. In fish markets, customers may also have a difficult time deciding between *sea squab* and *sea trout*, the latter being the more edible name that is given to any of several fishes, especially the weakfishes. Variations on the "sea trout" theme include *gray trout, saltwater trout, shad trout,* and *sun trout*. See also CAPE COD TURKEY.

seat. The ass, or ARSE; by transference, the word for the thing upon which one sits became a euphemism for the anatomical part that does the sitting. Examples in the *Oxford English Dictionary* date to 1607. The term was sometimes elaborated into *seat of honor, seat of dishonor, seat of shame,* and *seat of vengeance,* e.g.: "A well-ventilated [bicycle-] saddle is the best preventative for those blisters which favour the seat of honour" (*Athletic World,* 5/10/1878).

seat belt. Safety belt. A subtle distinction drawn originally by airlines and seconded strongly by automobile manufacturers, the point being that the mere mention of "safety" might cause people to begin thinking about the danger of accident. It is for this reason, too, that when a FLIGHT ATTENDANT offers a small round candy with a hole in the center to a passenger, she says "Mint?" not "Life Saver?" See also WATER LANDING.

seclusion. Solitary confinement. The euphemism is used both in prisons (see ADJUSTMENT CENTER) as well as in institutions for the retarded and mentally unwell. See also MENTAL HOSPITAL.

secure facility. A jail from which escape is supposed to be difficult. "Only those considered 'seriously assaultive,' . . . are housed in the one remaining 'secure facility'" (Jessica Mitford, *Kind and Usual Punishment: The Prison Business*, 1974). *Secure facilities* contrast with *residential facilities*, from which escape is no problem. See also CORRECTIONAL FACILITY.

select out. To fire, to dismiss. "The Senate [Foreign Relations] panel's action stems largely from concern following the suicide last April of Charles W. Thomas, a 48-year-old Foreign Service officer who was 'selected out'—dismissed—without pension in 1969 after 18 years of service" (*New York Times*, 4/24/72). See also CULL and LET GO.

selection room. The sales room for coffins in a FUNERAL HOME. "Leave it to [National Selected Morticians] to come out with new names for old things. We've passed through the period of the 'backroom,' the 'show room,' the 'sales room,' the 'casket display room,' the 'casket room.' Now N.S.M. offers you the 'selection room'" (*Mortuary Management*, 1951, from Jessica Mitford, *The American Way of Death*, 1963). See also CASKET and MORTICIAN.

selective ordnance. Napalm, with a FOP Index of 3.5. "Have you heard of *napalm* lately? No, but you may have heard of *selective ordnance*—though how napalm is 'selective' I do not know" (Peter Klappert, "Let Them Eat Wonderbread," *Saturday Review*, 10/7/72). Other ways of *not* saying "napalm" include the pleasant-sounding *napthagel* and the new and improved *incendijel* (Napalm-B), also called (in a semantic corruption that more accurately describes the results) *incinderjell.*

Napalm is perhaps the world's most awful Valentine's Day present, i.e.: "On Feb. 14 [1942] we reported . . . development of two lines of gels . . . . To one . . . I gave the name Napalm" (L. F. Fieser, *Scientific Method*, 1964). Napalm is similar in composition and effect to the Byzantine Greek Fire, also called "wildfire," whose raging action inspired Geoffrey Chaucer to write in the prologue to *The Wife of Bath's Tale* (ca. 1387–1400): "Thou liknest wommenes loue . . . to wilde fyr/The moore it brenneth the moore it hath desir." See also ORDNANCE and SOFT.

selective strike. Something less than total obliteration. "The Defense Department has significantly increased its estimates of civilian casualties that would result from a 'selective' Soviet nuclear strike against military bases on the United States" (*New York Times*, 9/17/75). The estimates were raised from a range of .8–3 million to 3.5–22 million casualties. See also CASUALTY; DEFENSE, DEPARTMENT OF; LIMITED WAR, and SURGICAL STRIKE.

self- (or **mutual**) **pleasuring.** Masturbation, alone or cooperatively.

The "pleasuring" is another step in the long campaign by the enlightened to convince people that they should not feel guilty about indulging in the near-universal practice of what used to be called "self-abuse" or "self-pollution," e.g.: "'Self-pleasuring' or 'solitary sex' are less pejorative terms, and one physician calls it 'the thinking man's television.' . . . Masturbation is important in learning to give and receive pleasure . . . Petting is a further step, with mutual pleasuring short of intercourse—a meaningful transition to full sexual partnership" (E. James Lieberman, "Teenage Sex and Birth Control," *Journal of the American Medical Association*, 7/21/78).

Another modern variation is "self-love," as in the title of Betty Dodson's manual on the subject, *Liberating Masturbation: A Meditation on Self-Love*. Ms. Dodson, who seems to think men are superfluous, runs workshops on *self-love*, complete with lectures, slide shows, group discussions, and demonstrations. See also MASTURBATION.

senior citizen. Old person; sometimes telegraphed to *senior*. "And what's wrong with 'older man'? Why has he got to be a 'senior citizen'? There is an unwillingness to face life and like it" (Jacques Barzun, age sixty-seven, in the *New York Times*, 6/17/75, upon the occasion of his retirement from the faculty of Columbia University).

As happens to all euphemisms in time, and as Professor Barzun's opinion suggests, the gold plating on "senior citizen" is beginning to wear thin and efforts are under way to replace it with something more awful. For instance: "According to [Mario] Cuomo, who is 46, we wouldn't even use the euphemism, senior citizens. We would call old people the Longer Living" (Anthony Burton, [New York] *City News*, 9/26/78). Cuomo, the New York State secretary of state, then running for lieutenant governor, also suggested that the Department of the Aging be renamed "Department of the Longer Living." See also GOLDEN AGE/YEARS.

sensitive. Secret; frequently morally wrong and/or criminal as well. Thus, *sensitive source* was an FBI euphemism of the Hoover era for an illegal wiretap or bug; a *sensitive gift* is the same as a QUESTIONABLE payment, and a *sensitive matter* almost surely involves HANKY-PANKY. ". . . Bob Mardian . . . had to speak directly with the President about a matter so sensitive he couldn't tell me a thing. . . . I was impressed and bested, since I could say only that I had to speak directly with [John D.] Ehrlichman on a matter so sensitive I couldn't tell Mardian a thing" (John W. Dean III, *Blind Ambition*, 1976). In this case, Mardian's *sensitive matter* was his fear that J. Edgar Hoover might be able to blackmail the administration because he knew about its illegal wiretaps against 13 government employees and four newsmen. Dean's *sensitive matter* was his fear that Charles Colson was going to order the firebombing of the Brookings Institution in Washington, D.C. See also HIGHLY CONFIDENTIAL (or SENSITIVE) SOURCE, ILLEGAL, and TOP SECRET.

separate/separation. To dismiss or fire; the act of so doing. "Separate" and "separation" seem to be as American as apple pie in this sense, with the oldest example of an involuntary separation in *A Dictionary of Americanisms* (Mitford M. Mathews, ed., 1951) coming from 1779 and the writings of Thomas Jefferson. The terms usually but not necessarily refer to the severing of people from jobs Herewith, another kind of dismissal: "He would feel [sorrow] at what the official college gracefully terms the 'separation' of Billy from the University" (Charles M. Flandrau, *Harvard Episodes*, 1897). See also LET GO.

separate but equal. The official euphemism in the United States for three generations for keeping blacks in what whites construed to be "their place." The phrase obtained the force of law in 1896 when the Supreme Court used it in *Plessy* v. *Ferguson* to rationalize the constitutionality of a Louisiana law requiring segregated railroad facilities; "separate but equal accommodations," according to the Court majority, did not necessarily imply that the "colored race" (see COLORED) was inferior. Reinforcing the concept of "separate but equal" were the pre-Darwinian arguments of those who believed the different races were created separately. "Was Adam the progenitor of all people or only of white people? Are blacks and Indians our brothers or merely our look-alikes? In logic, separate needn't mean unequal . . . . In fact, I know of no American 'polygenist'—as advocates of separate species called themselves—who did not assume that whites were separate *and* superior" (Stephen Jay Gould, *Natural History*, 6–7/78).

On May 17, 1954, the Supreme Court finally reversed itself in *Brown* v. *Board of Education of Topeka*, concluding after a study of the effects of segregation that "in the field of public education the doctrine of 'separate but equal' has no place. Separate educational facilities are inherently unequal." Though qualified in application (it affected public schools in just 21 of the states and the District of Columbia), this decision demolished the fiction of separate equality so thoroughly that segregationists had to retreat to other euphemisms; see also HARMONIOUS.

separate development or **freedoms.** In the Republic of South Africa, euphemistic replacements for *apartheid*, itself an opaque term that translates simply as "apartness" or "separateness."

"The frank language of white supremacy in South Africa has been officially replaced by such terms as 'apartheid' (separateness) and more recently the blander 'separate development' and 'separate freedoms'" (Anthony Lewis, *New York Times*, 8/30/76). Still another euphemism of the same ilk is "plural democracy." By whatever the names, however, the underlying idea is that some 4.3 million whites should control 87 percent of the nation's territory, while some 18.6 million blacks enjoy the remaining 13 percent for their "homelands." See also NATIVE, SINGLE MEN'S QUARTERS, and, for the application of *separate freedoms*, etc., on an extremely elemental level, refer to LADIES/GENTLEMEN.

serious and candid. A diplomatic way of characterizing a meeting (usually between diplomats) at which there has been serious disagreement. See also FRANK.

servant. Slave; a euphemism in colonial America that went decidedly out of fashion in the early nineteenth century because white servants who weren't slaves refused to accept the same label as black *servants* who were. The euphemism was used by slave-owners as well as by the slaves themselves. Thus, speaking of William Penn (1644–1718): "He was a slaveholder but he used the less pejorative term 'servant' instead of 'slave.'" (*History Book Club News*, 4/75). And referring to a slave of Penn's period: "He said he was a free Negro, . . . but upon being sent to Prison, he owned he was a servant" (*Boston News-Letter*, 7/17/1704). So well recognized was the servant-slave equation that in the statutes of the state of Connecticut, "servant" was used in place of "slave"—"a violation of terms for which it would not perhaps be difficult to assign the motive" (E. A. Kendall, *Travels Through the Northern Part of the United States*, 1809). And by Kendall's time, of course, the euphemism was so thoroughly tainted that nonslaves would no longer accept it. As James Fenimore Cooper explained: "In consequence of the *domestic servants* of America having once been Negro slaves, a prejudice has arisen among the laboring class of the whites, who not only dislike the term *servant*, but have also rejected that of *master*" (*The American Democrat*, 1838). And Cooper was, if anything, understating the prejudice. Nearly half a century before, Jonathan, the comic hero of Royall Tyler's *The Contrast* (1787), bridled at the "servant" label, snapping back at Jessamy, who had called him one: "Servant! Sir, do you take me for a neger,—I'm Colonel Manley's waiter." For more about slavery, see INSTITUTION, and for the "servant" problem, continue with BOSS, CLEANING PERSON, DOMESTIC, HELP, MAID, and MAN.

service. A sexual act or, as a verb, the performance of one. "Service" seems to have come full circle. As far back as the fourteenth century, sexual INTERCOURSE was sometimes described as "the flesh's service" or "the service of Venus," but the term later was limited mainly to barnyard doings, except in the language of slang, e.g., Capt. Francis Grose's definition of "stallion" as "A man kept by an old lady for secret services" (*A Classical Dictionary of the Vulgar Tongue*, 1796). Subsequently, the Victorians who put together the *Oxford English Dictionary* decided the sexual "service" was obsolete except in an animalistic sense, restricting their definition to "The action of covering a female animal." (See COVER.) Today, however, people have taken back the word and started applying it in ways that would shock most right-thinking horses. For example: ". . . I sincerely hope that some day soon Tom will recuperate from his sexual depression. After all, what are the four of you doing to help *him*. . . . Doesn't he want to service his own wife? . . . I can't imagine that their marriage will improve all that much if he remains just an impotent spectator" (Xaviera Hollander, *Penthouse*, 1/77). Note, too, that the modern, "with-it" whore may combine new and old meanings by describing her business as a *social service*; see also WORKING GIRL.

Service, Internal Revenue. A "service" that most taxpayers feel they could do without. Formerly known as the Bureau of Internal Revenue, it used to be headed by a "collector," a title that fairly reflected the function. Now, the top dog is the *"director."* See also DEFENSE, DEPARTMENT OF.

service station. A filling station, aka gas station. Obsolete? The quality of the euphemism is (was?) best appreciated when seen through a dirty windshield, darkly.

serviette. An affected table napkin. Much used by Victorians, the term has been regarded since the turn of the century as a symptom of vulgar, lower-class non-U speech. Some English, now that they have turned against "serviette," like to think it is an Americanism. They are wrong. *Serviettes* appeared on English tables as long ago as the fifteenth century. The term fell into disuse, only to be revived in the opening decades of the nineteenth century as a French import. For more about U and non-U, see DENTURES.

sex or **s-e-x (when children are present).** Usually, "sex" is encountered in the phrase "to have sex," which is something that everyone has all the time, if the words are to be taken at face value—which, of course, is never the euphemizer's intention. Careful analysis of the context in which the phrase appears generally reveals its true meaning. For example: "When *Screw* publisher Al Goldstein ran an ad parody . . . showing Poppin' Fresh and his friend Poppie Fresh having sex in a skillet, and appropriating the company's slogan, 'Nothing says lovin' like something from the oven . . . and Pillsbury says it best,' the folks at Pillsbury . . . slapped Goldstein with a $1.5 million suit for trademark and copyright infringement" (*MORE*, 6/78). On a more elevated plane, Bertrand Russell used the same euphemism when he wrote in *Marriage and Morals* ("Prostitution," 1929): "Marriage is for women the commonest mode of livelihood, and the total amount of undesired sex endured by women is probably greater in marriage than in prostitution."
   "Sex" also may be used in place of the real names of the sexual organs, whether male or female. Thus, Frank Harris fondly recalled one of his youthful conquests: ". . . the end of it was that right there on the porch I drew her to me and put my sex against hers and began the rubbing of her tickler and front part of her sex that I knew would excite her" (*My Life and Loves*, 1925). See also FOXY, INTERCOURSE, PENIS, and VAGINA.

sexually explicit or **oriented.** Pornographic; two positive alternatives to the pejorative term.
   "Using the 'I know it when I see it' test for hard-core pornography, nearly all of *The Illustrated Report* is the real stuff. Or, if you prefer, 'sexually explicit material'" (Mary Ellen Gale, [*MORE*], 2/76). See also EROTICA.

sexually otherwise. A catchall for a variety of sexual practices that used to be categorized as "perverted." As Chip Durgom, the director of an Off-Off Broadway show, *Another Way to Love*, told *Penthouse* (1/77): "We don't like to use the term S. and M. That's offensive. That's like using the word *nigger*. Instead, we'd like it to be called 'sexually otherwise' or 'kinky sex' or 'sexual variants.' And those who are into it should be called 'sex fantasists.'" See also S/M.

sexual orientation. Homosexual orientation; the phrase has been popularized by GAY activists seeking to escape the stigma attached to the other word. Thus, speaking of a proposed bill of homosexual rights in New York City: "The bill, which prohibits discrimination in jobs, housing, and public accommodations on the basis of sexual orientation, had been defeated in committee four times in the past three years" (*New York Post*, 4/19/74). This particular bill defined "sexual orientation" as "the choice of sexual partner according to gender," which would mean nothing to anyone who didn't already know the intent of the legislation. Several years later, because they did know what she had in mind, gays in the crowd cheered when Bella Abzug carefully thanked everyone "of whatever sex or sexual orientation" who had worked in her losing campaign in the New York City mayoralty primary (9/8/77). See also LOVE THAT DARE NOT SPEAK ITS NAME, THE.

sexual variety. Promiscuity. Reviewing the Kinsey Institute study, *Homosexualities*, Martin Duberman pointed out that "many now affirm that 'sexual variety' (the term 'promiscuity' is itself rapidly going out of favor) contributes positively to the well-being of the individual *and* to the partner relationship in which he or she may be involved" (*New York Times Book Review*, 11/26/78). See also AFFAIR and SWINGING.

shack up with. To spend one or more nights with a person to whom one is not married. "Christ said, 'I tell you that anyone who looks on a woman with lust has in his heart already committed adultery.' I've looked on a lot of women with lust. I've committed adultery in my heart many times. . . . God forgives me for it. But that doesn't mean that I condemn someone who not only looks on a woman with lust but who leaves his wife and shacks up with somebody out of wedlock" (future president Jimmy Carter, *Playboy* interview, 11/76).

"Shack up" may predate World War II slightly. Truck drivers and traveling salesmen are reported to have used the phrase circa 1940, back when most auto camps (see MOTEL) were mere collections of ricky-ticky shacks. (Hobos of the period would *jungle up* in hobo camps, or "jungles.") The phrase was popularized during the war when many servicemen set up light housekeeping with women who lived in rented quarters just off-post. (The woman in such a case might be referred to as a "shack job" and the fellow as a "shack man" or "shack rat.") It didn't hurt the phrase's popularity that in postwar Japan, where houses were exceptionally flimsy by American standards, even a poorly paid private could afford to *shack up* with his *moose* (see PROSTITUTE).

The etymology of "shack" itself is unusual: In the housing sense, it might come from the "shackle" of "ramshackle," but this explanation is not nearly as appealing as the possibility that it derives from an Aztec word, *xacalli*, or wooden hut, via the Mexican-Spanish *jacal*, formerly written *xacal* and pronounced as though spelled *shacal*. The congruence of "shack" and "shag" in many senses also is noteworthy. Thus, outfielders are sometimes said to "shack" fly balls, and sometimes to "shag" them. "Shack" and "shag" also may be used interchangeably to mean "fallen" or "refuse grain," an "idle" or "rascally fellow," and a "shaking, tossing motion," as of a horse. Finally, "shag," as a verb, has meant "to copulate" since at least the eighteenth century. See also COPULATE, FORNICATE, and INTERCOURSE.

shmo. A shmuck (or schmuck), i.e., a PENIS or, more colloquially, a "prick."
   "Never utter *schmuck* lightly, or in the presence of women and children. Indeed, it was the uneasiness about *shmuck* that led to the truncated euphemism *shmo*—and any *shmo* knows what *shmo* comes from" (Leo Rosten, *The Joys of Yiddish*, 1968). The Yiddish *shmuck* comes from the German *schmuck,* an ornament, jewelry. (The analogy is reminiscent of the English FAMILY JEWELS.) Of course, in casual use, in a conversation that is being conducted mainly in English (e.g., "Oh, what a *shmuck* Jerry is"), the term does not always carry the powerful meaning of the Yiddish original. In translation, Jerry may be simply a fool or a jerk. See also TUSHIE.

shoot. In the expletive form, "Oh shoot," it is a euphemistic mispronunciation of "shit"; see BS and SHUCKS.

shoppe. Shop; an Old Englishification, with a FOP Index of 1.5. See also SALON.

short arm. The penis, especially in the military, where the troops are checked for signs of VD in a ceremony known variously as *short-arm drill* or *short-arm inspection.* This is another example of the penis being compared to a weapon, with the "short-arm" metaphor deriving from the frequent inspections of the soldier's "long arm," or rifle. See also GUN and PENIS.

short French expletive, a. On June 18, 1815, as Napoleon's once-Grand Armée dissolved in panic on the field of Waterloo, General Pierre-Jacques-Étienne Cambronne, commander of the Old Guard (from which conservative "Old Guard" Republicans in the United States obtained their name), supposedly disdained an invitation to surrender, replying (according to polite historians and the monument erected to his memory in Nantes), *"La Garde meurt mais ne se rend pas!"* ("The Guard dies but never surrenders"). Discussing this "phony quotation" in the *New York Times* (4/5/76), William Safire could come no closer to the real reply than the parenthetical explanation: "(What Cambronne did say was a short French expletive later used frequently by Hemingway in his novels and to this day referred to as *le mot Cambronne.*)" And what, non-Hemingway fans may ask, does this mean? Is Safire referring to *Zut,* which is short, French, and an expletive—and which is often used with *alors* to convey anger, scorn, or flat refusal? *Mais non!* Safire, remember, is writing for a FAMILY newspaper, and this means that he cannot always express himself with his usual precision. Actually, Cambronne, who was captured anyway, was understood at the time to have said *"Merde!"* (shit), and this is what Safire meant by "a short French expletive."
   The lofty sentiment that flowered from the *merde* of Waterloo should be

compared with NUTS, supposedly uttered by an American general some 78 miles to the southeast and 129 years later. See also MERDE.

shot. Executed. In the real world, the one word could not be a euphemism for the other, but in Russia, in early 1918, when all was topsy-turvy, some strange distinctions were made. Thus, the sentencing of Admiral Aleksei Shchastny "To be shot within twenty-four hours" caused something of a stir among courtroom spectators, who knew that the Soviet government had abolished the death penalty just a few months previously. "Prosecutor Krylenko explained: 'What are you worrying about? Executions have been abolished. But Shchastny is not being executed; he is being shot'" (Aleksandr I. Solzhenitsyn, *The Gulag Archipelago 1919–1956: An Experiment in Literary Investigation,* 1974). The nonexecution of Shchastny was carried out, and 20 years later, in another, far greater purge, Peoples Commissar Nikolai Vasilyevich Krylenko himself met the same fate. See also CAPITAL PUNISHMENT, EXECUTE, and NO RIGHT TO CORRESPONDENCE.

shower activity. Rain, with a FOP Index of 4.75. See also PRECIPITATION.

shucks. The interjection has been used since at least the middle of the last century as an expression of disgust, regret, or impatience, making it a euphemism for "shit" in all senses. Dictionary-makers tend to derive "shucks" from the worthless "shuck," or husk, of corn, but a hint that the word arose strictly as a euphemism is contained in the oldest example of its use in *A Dictionary of Americanisms* (Mitford M. Mathews, ed., 1951). It comes from Edward M. Field's *The Drama of Pokerville* (1847): "And Mr. Bagley was there . . . [to shoot] any gentleman who might say 'shucks!'" Which does seem to be excessive punishment if the word stood merely for disgust, regret, impatience. See also BUSHWA, PISH/PSHAW, and SUGAR.

shy-poke. The euphemistic version of "shite-poke," the vulgar but popular name of the green heron, so-called because of the bird's tendency to DEFECATE when flushed and taking to wing. See also ROOSTER and TIMBERDOODLE.

Sicilian Vespers. The Sicilians have a mordant wit akin to that of the Spanish (see INVINCIBLE ARMADA, THE). The "Sicilian Vespers" is the name of a massacre of the ruling French in 1282; its ferocity is indicated by the simple fact that it is still remembered. The uprising began in Palermo and was repeated in other cities. The bell for the evening service—Vespers—was the signal to begin, whence the name.

sick out. A strike by public employees who are legally forbidden to go on strike; if the antiwork bug bites the police, it may be called the *blue flu.* See also JOB ACTION.

sight-deprived. Blind, with a FOP Index of 3.4. "The blind are now 'sight-deprived,' as if to refute any suspicion that they got that way voluntarily" (Gary Jennings, *Personalities of Language,* 1965). The related "partially sighted," translates as "nearly blind," the distinction being that one can retain a modicum of vision while still qualifying for such dubious benefits of legal blindness as an income tax exemption. Finally, those who are merely color-blind are said to be *color deficient*. See also INCONVENIENCED.

significant quantity. The amount of enriched uranium-235 required to make an atomic bomb (aka DEVICE). "The United States Atomic Energy Commission has set five kilograms [11 pounds] as the amount at and above which the material is 'significant.' . . . The Atomic Energy Commission, now much occupied with the growth and development of the peaceful nuclear-power industry, wants the atom to make a good impression on the general public. In the frankly bellicose days of the somewhat forgotten past, the term used was not 'significant' but 'strategic.' Unofficially—around the halls and over the water cooler—five kilos is known as 'the trigger quantity'" (John McPhee, *The Curve of Binding Energy*, 1974).

Five kilos is a rather arbitrary figure. Much depends on the skill of the bomb-maker and the type of facilities that he or she has available. For a crudely engineered bomb, as much as 10 kilos might be needed, but a more sophisticated bomb might be made with less than the officially designated *significant quantity*. Most worrisome, the *significant quantity* is just a drop in the bucket compared to the amount of uranium and plutonium that has been "lost" in recent years; see MUF as well as SPECIAL NUCLEAR MATERIALS.

sign off. To approve, to agree to; the circumlocution minimizes personal responsibility in much the same way as AFFIRMATIVE waters down "yes." Thus, H. R. "Bob" Haldeman reported to President Richard M. Nixon on how it came to pass that John N. Mitchell approved a quarter-million-dollar budget for an intelligence-gathering operation that was to include the great Watergate CAPER: ". . . [Jeb Stuart] Magruder told Mitchell . . . that [Gordon C.] Strachan had told him to get it going on Haldeman's orders on the President's orders and Mitchell signed off on it. He said, 'OK, if they say do it, go ahead'" (3/27/73, *The White House Transcripts*, 1974).

Despite the notoriety that "sign off" received as a result of Watergate, the expression continues in use. Thus, referring to a period when she hadn't yet admitted to herself the extent of her addictions, Betty Ford noted that when "my son Steve, caught by a reporter outside the hospital, said I was fighting the effects not only of pills but alcohol, I wasn't enchanted. I wasn't yet prepared to sign off on that" (*The Times of My Life*, with Chris Chase, 1978).

silly. Feebleminded, from at least the sixteenth century. Among the examples in the *Oxford English Dictionary*: "The King's uncle, being rather weak in intellect, was called Silly Billy" (Goldwin Smith, *Lectures and Essays*, 1881). See also SPECIAL.

single-men's quarters. The migrant NATIVE (i.e., black) workers at South African diamond mines are housed in *single-men's quarters*, formerly known as *hostels*, and before that, as "compounds" (personal communication, David E. Koskoff, 1979). See also SEPARATE DEVELOPMENT.

sire. One of the euphemistic alternatives available to those who believe "stud," "studhorse," or even "stallion" are too sexy. Other possibilities include *he-horse, male horse, seed horse, stable horse, stock horse, stone horse,* and *top horse.* Of these, "stone horse" is slightly on the risky (or *risqué*) side, for reasons that will become apparent after consulting ROCKS. See also COVER, SERVICE, and the analogous COW BRUTE.

sit-me-down-upon. The ass or ARSE. "He left the impression of his sit-me-down-upon on the cushion" (Dorothy L. Sayers, *Clouds of Witness,* 1926). Obviously, the "sit-me-down" and the slightly more ornate "sit-me-down-upon" are connected closely with *sit-down-upons, sit-upons,* and *sit-in-'ems,* all of which denote breeches or trousers, aka UNMENTIONABLES.

situation. An omnibus term, equally suitable for filling verbal vacuums when the mind itself has gone blank or, more seriously, for scaling down the dimensions of catastrophe and crisis. For example, consider the studiously bland opening of the minutes of the emergency meeting of the Nuclear Regulatory Commission after a nuclear power plant outside Harrisburg, Pennsylvania, released "puffs" of radiation in the spring of 1979: "As the Three Mile Island situation developed beginning Wednesday, March 28, the commissioners met to discuss the nature of the event." (See also EVENT and INCIDENT.)

Situations come in all shapes and sizes. In the strictly mindless category, there are the *punting situations, first-down situations,* and *jump ball situations,* encountered so often in football and basketball, e.g., "He's going to call a jump ball situation" (WABC-TV, 10/2/78). Then there is the military, where, partly through mindless reflex and partly to minimize disaster, ships that go bump in the night are said to get into *collision situations.* Teachers, meanwhile, do their stuff in a *learning situation,* i.e., classroom (note the flattering assumption that learning is taking place), while child psychologists examine the *play situation* (which certainly seems to be a good way of taking the fun out of play). A recent (ca. 1978–79) program of New York's fancy Lincoln Center even told of a singer "in an operatic situation," i.e., onstage. On the more serious, more euphemistic side there was the "Eagleton situation" (letter to the *New York Times,* 7/12/76), a discreet allusion to the dropping of Sen. Thomas F. Eagleton (D., Missouri) from the Democratic national ticket in 1972 because of his history of *mental fatigue* (see FATIGUE). And the president of the United States occasionally receives briefings (*situation reports*) in the White House Situation Room.

Besides Three Mile Island, the nation has suffered through a number of other *crisis situations,* in which the semantically unnecessary "situation" takes the edge off the "crisis." In particular, there was the "Vietnam situation," so-called by a CIA witness during the Senate Intelligence Committee hearings (9/25/75), the oft-mentioned "Watergate situation," and—an earlier and less-serious scandal— "the 1919 Chicago White Sox situation" (Ralph Kiner, WOR-TV, NYC, 4/20/80).

"Situation" may be used more or less interchangeably with another of the great omnibus terms, PROBLEM. Attempts have been made to distinguish the two, but not with notable success. Thus, when Boston Celtics center Dave Cowens decided to take a vacation from basketball, leaving the team in something of a lurch, he explained that, "the problem—no, not the problem; it's not a problem, it's a situation—has been weighing heavily on my mind for a long time"(*New York Times*, 11/13/76). Final confirmation of "situation's" great utility comes from knowing that it is also used in other languages in the same mind-numbing way. Thus, the siege mentality in Israel is known to those enduring it as *hamatzau*—the situation.

See also INVOLVEMENT, IT, and THING.

slack fill. The positive way of saying a container is partly empty and that the customer is receiving less than meets the eye. "A good deal of creative effort goes into making packages seem bigger than they are, or seem to hold more than they do. We have no basis for accusing cereal-makers of intentional deception. But, on average, one-fifth of their boxes contained air rather than cereal. That's called 'slack fill'" (*Consumer Reports*, 2/75). For more about the wonders of packaging, see LARGE.

sleep. Death—and the most common way of denying death's permanence.

This euphemistic "sleep" is encountered in many forms, perhaps most often today in the phrase, PUT TO SLEEP, which is how many domestic animals meet their deaths. And in CEMETERIES, their masters are still described on MONUMENTS as *Fallen Asleep, Not Dead but Sleeping, Asleep in Jesus* (a common child's epitaph in the nineteenth century). The basic idea is at least a couple thousand years old. Callimachus, the Alexandrian librarian and poet (ca. 310–240 B.C.), expressed it this way in one of his epigrams: "Here sleeps Saon, of Acanthus, son of Dicon, a holy sleep; say not that the good die" (J. Banks, trans., *The Works of Hesiod, Callimachus, and Theognis*, 1856). And in the harder-boiled prose of Raymond Chandler (1888–1959): "What did it matter where you lay once you were dead? In a dirty sump or in a marble tower on top of a high hill. You were dead, you were sleeping the big sleep, you were not bothered by things like that" (*The Big Sleep*, 1939).

It can be argued that "sleep" is a harmless euphemism—a poetic metaphor that doesn't really fool anyone—and it would be relatively easy to accept this proposition if it were not for the recent example of the Reverend Jim Jones, who leaned heavily on the idea of death-as-sleep when persuading some 900 followers to commit suicide at the Peoples Temple commune of Jonestown, Guyana, in 1978. From the tape recording of his final exhortation:

> Adults, adults. . . . I call on you to quit exciting your children when all they're doing is going to a quiet rest. Quit telling them they're dying. All they're doing is taking a drink they take to go to sleep. That's what death is: sleep. (*New York Times*, 3/15/79)

See also PASS AWAY, REST, and the different SLUMBER constructions.

sleep with. Along with MAKE LOVE, one of the two Standard English (as opposed to the Latinate COPULATE and FORNICATE) euphemisms for "fuck," the need for "sleep" being the last thing that is on the minds of the parties involved and, usually, the last thing that happens, e.g.: "I slept with her, and never had a more voluptuous night" (anon., *My Secret Life*, ca. 1890).

People who *sleep with* other people more or less indiscriminately are said to *sleep about* or *sleep around*. Some keep running counts of their partners. "Sexually promiscuous Lisa Menzies . . . slept with over 425 men in the last two years of high school" (picture caption, *Book Review Digest*, 8/77). Even those who *sleep with* others for pay use the phrase. Quoting a PROSTITUTE named Michelle: "You need someone to come home to—you sleep with 10 men in a night, you're a little bit whacky" (*New York Times*, 4/9/71).

Because of its euphemistic vagueness, "sleep with" has caused scholarly disputes. What, for example, did Walt Whitman mean in the following entry from his diary for 1862–63:

> Horace Ostrander Oct. 22 '62 24 4th av. from Otsego co. 60 miles west of Albany was in the hospital to see Chas. Green about 28 y'rs of age—about 1855 went on voyage to Liverpool—his experiences as a green hand (Nov. 22 4th av.) slept with him Dec. 4 '62. . . .

Whitman's diary tells of meetings with many young men and this entry is one of four that includes "slept with." Whitman denied that there was a homosexual element in his poetry, and he also claimed (probably falsely) that he had fathered six illegitimate children. The diary entries do make one wonder, however. While it is impossible to tell if Whitman had the euphemistic meaning in mind, it is quite possible that he was aware of it, since "sleep" has been used to imply sexual intimacy or cohabitation since at least the ninth century A.D. Poets who have employed the term include Chaucer and, much closer to Whitman's time, Percy Bysshe Shelley. From *The Cenci* (1819):

> Cristofano
> Was stabbed in error by a jealous man,
> While she he loved was sleeping with his rival

See also F——, INTERCOURSE, and SHACK UP.

slow. Retarded, disturbed—a catchall euphemism for children who, for one reason or another, are not performing as well as their peers in school; somewhat archaic now that EXCEPTIONAL and SPECIAL have appeared on the scene.

sluice. In the American West, to shoot a sitting duck; also, the correct euphemism for shooting eagles from a helicopter. "Testifying before a Senate subcommittee, James Vogan, a balding, heavyset helicopter pilot from Murray, Utah, told how he had ferried sharpshooters and so-called 'sportsmen' over ranches in Colorado and Wyoming to 'sluice' the eagles" (*Time*, 8/16/71). The airborne marksmen were reported to have killed 770 golden and bald eagles. See also CULL and SPORTSMAN.

slumber cot/robe/room. The "slumber" is very deep, for this is the sleep of the dead. A *slumber cot* is a coffin; a *slumber robe* is (or was—they're not so common anymore) a shroud, and a *slumber room* is a laying-out room in a FUNERAL HOME. See also REPOSE and SLEEP.

slut. A (canine) bitch. Female dogs became "sluts" or "slut-pups" in the nineteenth century, since no polite person wanted to say the other word, especially when ladies were present. See also SOB.

S/M. Sadomasochism. It sounds less painful when abbreviated. Variants include *SM, S-M, S and M, S&M,* and *sm.*

Sadomasochism is the practice of obtaining sexual pleasure through pain: The sadist gives, the masochist receives. The term honors Count (usually called "Marquis") Donatien Alphonse François de Sade (1740–1814) and Leopold von Sacher-Masoch (1836–1895), whose names became associated with sexual cruelty through their writings and the peculiarities of their personal lives. De Sade, who liked to torture people, is best remembered for *Justine, or Good Conduct Well Chastised* (1791), while Sacher-Masoch, who liked to be whipped, revealed his proclivities in such novels as *The Legacy of Cain* (1870–77) and *False Ermine* (1873). Both men died in insane asylums.

The flavor of *S/M* today is conveyed in the following classified:

> DOMINATRIX, YOUNG beautiful seeking slaves for sm, bondage, humiliation and spanking. If you are not interested, dont write. (*Ace*, undated, ca. 1976)

See also BD, ENGLISH GUIDANCE, SEXUALLY OTHERWISE, and TV.

smile. A shot of alcohol. "Want to join me in a little smile?" asked Frank Skeffington, as he walked over to the liquor cabinet (Edwin O'Connor, *The Last Hurrah*, TV movie version, 1977). See also LIBATION.

snafu. The euphemistic acronym for what is euphemistically translated as "Situation Normal: All Fouled Up."

"Snafu" seems to have been invented by some unsung genius in the British army about 1940, and it was picked up by the Americans soon after they entered the war. Since confusion is the normal state of human affairs, the expression has found wide application in nonmilitary contexts. Its use is by no means limited to lower rankers. Thus, in 1951, the tremendously urbane American secretary of state, Dean Acheson, apologized for the United States not having let Britain know in advance of its plan to bomb North Korean power plants along the Yalu River by saying: "It is only as a result of what is known as a snafu that you were not consulted about it" (*American Speech*, 5/55).

So successful was "snafu" that it spawned a host of imitations, some of which were wildly popular for a time but none of which have demonstrated the staying power of the original. Among the imitations:

fubar. Fucked Up Beyond All Recognition.
fubio. A linguistic memento of VJ day: Fuck You, Bub. It's Over.
fubiso. A variant of the above: Fuck You, Buddy, I'm Shipping Out.

gfu. General Fuck Up; usually said of an individual who continually made mistakes.

janfu. Joint Army-Navy Fuck Up.

mfu. British: Military Fuck Up, dated by Eric Partridge to 1939 and so, possibly, the progenitor of "snafu" rather than an imitation of it (*A Dictionary of Slang and Unconventional English*, 1970).

samfu. Also British: Self-Adjusting Military Fuck Up. (A cousin to the British *sabu*: Self-Adjusting Balls Up.)

sapfu. Surpassing All Previous Fuck Ups.

snefu. A British variation of the basic "snafu": Situation Normal: Everything Fucked Up.

susfu. Situation Unchanged: Still Fucked Up.

tarfu. Things Are Really Fucked Up.

tuifu. The Ultimate in Fuck Ups.

In view of the plenitude of *FU*'s, it is surprising the Allies won the war. For some typical euphemistic abbreviations, as opposed to acronyms, continue with BS and SOB.

snowing down south, it's. Back in the premini, prepants-suit days, when women were ladies (see LADY), and most of them wore a full complement of undergarments most of the time, "It's snowing down south" was the delicate way of telling a PERSON that her slip was showing. Still more anciently, the phrases were "shimmy showing" (a "shimmy" being a CHEMISE) or "petticoat peeping." These could be further disguised with initials. Thus, one *s.y.t.* (sweet young thing) might whisper to another at a mixer, "Psst S.S." (or "P.P.")—as the case might be. Of course, the slip that shows is only one of several common disarrangements of clothing. Others include:

Your booby trap is sprung. Your brassiere has slipped. (See BRASSIERE.)
Jack White is out of jail. Your shirttail is out.
It's one o'clock at the waterworks. Your fly is open.
Johnny's out of jail. Again: Your fly is open. (See also JOHN THOMAS.)

so-and-so. A euphemism for a stronger but unexpressed thought, usually "bastard" or "son of a bitch." "I think I'll sue the so-and-so" (Heywood Broun, *New Republic*, 8/17/38). Thirty years later, though most of the rest of the world had changed in the interim, the *New Republic* still held fast to its principles. In 1967, it fastidiously translated *Illegitimi non Carborundum* (Don't let the bastards grind you down) as "Don't let the so-and-so's shut you up" (from William Safire, *Safire's Political Dictionary*, 1978). See also SOB and, for the many terms for real as opposed to figurative bastards, LOVE CHILD.

SOB. This classes as The Great American Euphemism, assuming "son of a bitch" is The Great American Epithet, and a strong case can be made for the latter. For example, those impartial observers, the French, heard Americans use the expression so often during World War I that they called the Yanks *les sommobiches*,

social disease

just as their fifteenth-century ancestors referred to the English as the GODDAMS.

The basic "son of a bitch" has been traced back to 1712 by Eric Partridge (*A Dictionary of Slang and Unconventional English*, 1970). In effect, it is merely a long way around of saying BASTARD and is equivalent to the older "son of a whore" or "whoreson." The use of initials seems to have been an American invention, made in the decade or so prior to the Civil War. Other euphemisms for "son of a bitch" include *son of a bachelor, son of a bee, son of a Beechnut Gum* (among grade-schoolers), *son of a biscuit eater, son of a bum, son of a Dutchman, son of a female canine, son of a horse thief, son of a sea cook,* and *son of a gun,* the last of which dates to the early eighteenth century and whose etymology is perhaps too good to be true: Coming from an era when wives and other women sometimes went to sea, and occasionally gave birth while afloat, the phrase supposedly alludes to the place where such deliveries were accomplished, behind a canvas screen set up on the gun deck. Thus, any child born at sea might be called "a son of a gun" and, in cases of doubtful parentage, the child might be officially designated as a "Son of a gun" in the ship's log (from *Brewer's Dictionary of Phrase and Fable,* rev. by Ivor H. Evans, 1970).

Another standard way of sanitizing "son of a bitch" for public consumption is to dash out all or part of the expression. The classic example of this sort comes from Owen Wister's *The Virginian* (1902), where the dashed-out expression elicited one of literature's most celebrated replies:

> Trampas spoke: "Your bet, you son-of-a-————."
> The Virginian's pistol came out, and his hand lay on the table, holding it unaimed. And with a voice as gentle as ever . . . he issued his orders to the man Trampas:—
> "When you call me that, *smile.*"

See also SLUT and, for more about euphemistic dashes, F————.

social disease. Venereal disease; specifically, syphilis or gonorrhea. Until the 1930s, only a few newspapers were bold enough to print the names of the venereal diseases; many even shied clear of the very word "venereal." And for good reason: The Post Office, in the person of Special Agent Anthony Comstock, secretary of the New York Society for the Suppression of Vice, might threaten to lift their mailing permits. For example, after *The Call,* a New York socialist publication, ran an article on gonorrhea, as part of a series by Margaret Sanger, entitled "What Every Girl Should Know," Comstock told the paper its mailing permit would be revoked if Sanger's installment on syphilis were printed. Thus, the left-hand column of the women's page of *The Call* on February 9, 1913, was blank except for the message: "What Every Girl Should Know. NOTHING. By order of the Post Office Department" (from Lawrence Lader, *The Margaret Sanger Story,* 1955).

Despite the best efforts of Comstock, the existence of venereal disease could not be ignored completely, and so a host of euphemisms and circumlocutions was begat. Along with "social disease," they included *blood disease, blood poison* and *specific blood poison, a certain disease, communicable disease, preventable disease, secret disease,* and *vice disease.* Even doctors were not immune from this sort of linguistic contamination. According to Dr. Morris Fishbein, longtime editor of the *Journal of the American Medical Association,* when one doctor told another that patient Jones had a "specific stomach" or "specific ulcer," that meant the diagnosis was "syphilis" (H. L. Mencken, *The American Language,* 1936). Most of the euphemisms were forgotten during World War II, when it became necessary to discuss venereal disease in the plainest of terms in order to be sure that servicemen got the message. The exception is "social disease" which, having outlived the need for which it was created, is still commonly encountered, e.g., "Hey, I've got a social disease" (Stephen Sondheim, "Gee, Officer Krupke!" *West Side Story,* 1957). See also the *French disease* in FRENCH and VENUSIAN.

soft. Military targets are of two kinds: hard and soft. *Hard* targets are made of brick, concrete, steel, etc. *Soft* targets are made of flesh and bone. "The conventional bombs also will still have a role in attacking dispersed 'soft' targets, such as troops in a battlefield" (*New York Times,* 3/18/74). Especially suitable for attacking *soft* targets is *soft ordnance,* i.e., napalm. See also ORDNANCE in general and SELECTIVE ORDNANCE in particular.

soixante-neuf. Mutual oral-genitalism; a borrowing from the French, who are popularly believed to be especially attached to this form of sexual exercise. The numbers—*sixty-nine* or *69,* in translation—apparently refer to the positions assumed. The practice is not necessarily heterosexual. For example, one of the earliest examples of *soixante-neuf* on record involves two women: Flossie, the heroine of the late (undated and anonymous) Victorian novel, *Flossie, a Venus of Sixteen,* and Eva Letchford, her—ah—guardian. As Flossie tells Captain Archer: " . . occasionally, too we perform the *'soixant neuf.'"*

It is perhaps significant that "soixante-neuf" merely replaced an earlier French term, "gamahuche" (from *gamahucher* and, possibly, some Arabic original). In the parlor games that Flossie played with Captain Archer, she cast herself in the role of "The White Queen of the Gama Huchi Islands." (Guess what the queen's scepter was?) And in the greatest work of underground nonfiction of this period, *My Secret Life* (ca. 1890), the anonymous author devotes much space to "gamahuching" in all possible combinations, while only occasionally adopting modern terminology. (An exception occurs in volume eight: "Then again came my sudden impulse of lust . . . 'Lay over, make me sixty-nine.'") Another popular term of this period was *minette* (French for "pussy"); the participle, as taken into English, was *minetting.* (See PUSSY.) Frank Harris probably came close to the original construction when he told of a Parisian woman who asked him, "Why not *faire minette?"* (*My Life and Loves,* 1925). See also CUNNILINGUS, FELLATIO, and FRENCH.

soldier's disease. Opium addiction (*dependence,* in modern jargon). Toward the end of the nineteenth century, *soldier's disease* was an all-too-common complaint of Civil War veterans who had been given too much pain-killer for too long (courtesy of Walter James Miller, poet and professor, whose great-grandfather suffered from it).

solitary sex. Masturbation; see SELF-PLEASURING.

sortie. The term conjures up the image of knights charging over a drawbridge to engage in a melee, but in the modern world it means one mission by one airplane, French being the language of war (e. g., MATERIEL and PERSONNEL) as well as diplomacy. "The air campaign against heavily defended areas costs us one pilot in every 40 sorties" ("first rough draft" of a memo from Secretary of Defense Robert S. McNamara's office to President Lyndon B. Johnson, 5/19/67, *The Pentagon Papers*, 1971). See also the *strategic bombing* in STRATEGIC.

source of information. A spy or informer. ". . . the CIA considered using Mr. [Thomas] Riha as a 'source of information' while he was an exchange student in 1958–59 at the University of Moscow" (*New York Times*, 9/28/76). See also AGENT and HIGHLY (or USUALLY) RELIABLE SOURCE.

space. A grave site. "The 'space and bronze deal,' as it is called by the door-to-door sales specialists, is exciting, heady work, full of the romance of a new Gold Rush and the conquest of new frontiers" (Jessica Mitford, *The American Way of Death*, 1963). "Bronze" here is short for "memorial bronze," or MONUMENT. Indicative of the heady, Gold Rush atmosphere is the record of Mililani ("Gates of Heaven") Memorial Park, near Honolulu, where, Ms. Mitford reports, $1,090,408 in installment sales were racked up in a four-week period. Innovative cemetery operators also extract the maximum return from their land by selling *companion spaces*, which are double-decker graves, one deeper than the other, for husbands and wives, and by reserving some plots for *babyland* (three graves in the place normally occupied by one). Other, less-formal bywords for "grave" include *deep six, dust bin, earth bath, the Great Divide, last home, long home, narrow house,* and *place of rest*. See also BUY THE FARM, CEMETERY, PASS AWAY, and REST.

special. Retarded, mentally crippled, or handicapped; formerly *dull*, SILLY, or SLOW. For example, *The Special Child*, by Robin White, is "a comprehensive guide for the parents of children who suffer some form of brain handicap (retardation, epilepsy, cerebral palsy, autism, learning disabilities)" (Little Brown and Co., summer/fall catalog, 1978). And the "Special Olympics" is an athletic competition for mentally retarded people. A qualitative description of "special" comes from Michael Harrington: "But perhaps the saddest group of all were the students in the special class. They had IQ's so low that any attempt to bring them a standard education would inevitably fail" (*The Other America*, 1962). See also EXCEPTIONAL.

special nuclear materials. Uranium or plutonium that is rich enough for making a DEVICE (bomb), i.e., weapons-grade materials. A loss of as little as 11 pounds of *special nuclear materials* is of concern, as that is the SIGNIFICANT QUANTITY.

special treatment. Mass murder. Discussing the destruction of European Jewry in the Holocaust: "Strict secrecy governed the death camps, with severe isolation from the outside world, garden landscaping as camouflage, and euphemisms as further concealment: Killing was 'special treatment,' gas chambers were 'bath houses'" (*New York Times*, 4/18/78). See also FINAL SOLUTION, THE.

specified strike zone. A free fire zone in South Vietnam after May 1, 1971; also called a PRECLEARED FIRE ZONE. A new set of rules for use of firepower in the Republic of Vietnam that was issued on that date by the U.S. Military Assistance Command substituted "specified strike zone" for "free fire zone," specifying that henceforth "the term 'free fire zone' will not be used under any circumstances." See also PREPLAN, RECONNAISSANCE IN FORCE, and, for a historical parallel, CONCENTRATION CAMP.

speculate. Gamble. No one likes to think that our great free enterprise system depends on anything as chancy as gambling. Therefore, Wall Streeters are said to *speculate*. Though the literal meanings, or denotations, of the two words are the same, the connotations are so different that even the better gamblers avoid the dicier term. Thus, after an afternoon during which he had won about $200 at the Resorts International casino in Atlantic City, New Jersey, Howard Grossman, an expert blackjack player, declared "I don't gamble. I invest with a risk" ([New York] *City News*, 10/8/78). See also SPORTSMAN and TURF ACCOUNTANT.

sporting gal or **woman.** A whore. "'Of course, we called them sporting gals,' Lewis Gibson, the assistant police chief [of Fairbanks, Alaska], said. 'They weren't called prostitutes'" (*New Republic*, 11/1/75). See also PROSTITUTE.

sportsman. (1) A gambler, especially one who plunges heavily; (2) a hunter, especially one who takes no chances. The first sense was included by John Russell Bartlett in his *Dictionary of Americanisms* (1848) and *sportsmen* of this stripe are still sighted occasionally, as in a "Talk of the Town" piece on Jack Dempsey's restaurant in *The New Yorker* (10/21/74). As for the second kind of "sportsman," see SLUICE.

stable growth. Slow growth. On the authority of Hamilton B. Mitchell, chairman of the board of Dun & Bradstreet Companies, Inc., at a meeting of The Investment Analysts Society of Chicago, 11/1/73:

> Q: What percentage of your revenues are in the slow growth and what are in the fast growth areas?
> A: Well, it used to be that 75% were in the slow growth or we might say the stable growth, if you permit me to use that word instead of slow growth.

"Stable" has a FOP Index of 1.75 compared to "slow." See also ADJUSTMENT DOWNWARD.

state farm/hospital/training school. The "state" is a signpost word, indicating that a euphemism follows. For "state farm," read "prison," as in the Cummins State Farm, in Arkansas, where, it was rumored, some 200 prisoners had been murdered, and where, on January 29, 1968, three decapitated skeletons were found in shallow graves in the mule pasture. (For taking the pains to search out the *state farm's* unsavory past, the SUPERINTENDENT, Thomas O. Murton, was dismissed by Governor Winthrop Rockefeller, while a local grand jury considered indicting him for "grave robbing.") As for "state hospital," read "mental hospital," and for "state training school," read "reformatory" or "children's prison." Both the latter euphemisms are wearing thin, and new terms are coming to the fore as replacements. Thus, in New York State, the name of Matteawan State Hospital (for the criminally insane) was changed to the even blander "Correction Center for Medical Services," while the *training school* at Goshen, which features barbed wire on top of the fence around the playground, steel mesh screen over the windows, and heavy, locked doors, goes by the name of the Goshen Center for Boys. See also CORRECTIONAL FACILITY and MENTAL HOSPITAL.

State Research Bureau. In Idi Amin's Uganda, the secret police. "The State Research Bureau—the secret police—was set up as a military intelligence agency to replace [former President Milton] Obote's bodyguards, and its successor fulfills the same function for Amin. The people—about 2,000 at any one time . . . are Amin's keys to power" (Henry Kyemba, *A State of Blood: The Inside Story of Idi Amin,* 1977). The euphemism has inspired at least one imitation—in Oman, which boasts a similar *Research Department* ("60 Minutes," WCBS-TV, 3/9/80). "State Research Bureau" was one of the runners-up to CONSUMER COMMUNICATIONS CHANNEL for the 1976 Doublespeak Award of the Committee on Public Doublespeak of the National Council of Teachers of English. See also the CIA's semantically similar *Health Alteration Committee* in EXECUTIVE ACTION.

statutory offense. Sodomy in the newspapers. See also ASSAULT.

stew. A brothel, circa thirteenth to nineteenth centuries; also, a woman who worked in one. "Stew," as brothel, derives from "stew," meaning a "heated room," or "bath," in which people "stewed" themselves in hot air or steam. The extension of the word's meaning to include "brothel" was the natural result of the frequent misuse of the public bathhouses of medieval London and other cities for immoral purposes. Public baths, it seems, have always had a bad reputation. Other forms of "brothel" in the seventeenth and eighteenth centuries included the *bagnio* (from the Italian *bagno,* bath) and the *hummums* (from the Arabic *hammam,* a hot bath). From an early date, there were also *stews* for homosexuals. In 1530, William Tyndale noted the existence in Rome of "a stues not of women onely, but of the male kynde also agaynst nature" (*An Answer Vnto Sir Thomas Mores Dialoge*). See also HOUSE and PROSTITUTE.

stomachache. Bellyache. People suffered "bellyaches" for some two centuries before the first "stomachache" was recorded, with examples of the two terms in the *Oxford English Dictionary* going back to 1552 and 1763, respectively. Thus, "stomachache" classes as another pre-Victorianism. Not surprisingly, the more refined "stomach" comes from the Old French (and ultimately from the Greek *stomachos,* gullet), while "belly" is Old English (from *belg, belig,* bag).

Today, "stomach" continues as the preferred prefix when referring to internal disturbances, e.g., *stomach awareness* and *stomach distress*, for the queasy realization that one is about to lose one's cookies, and *stomach disorder*, for the actual event. For example, reporting on one of the *Skylab* missions: "In the voluminous interior of the space station . . . . Carr, and particularly Pogue, were having more serious symptoms of what the flight surgeons referred to as 'stomach awareness.' Looking at Pogue, Gibson remarked, 'Ole sweaty-palm time there.' Pogue threw up" (Henry S. F. Cooper, Jr., *A House in Space*, 1976). See also ABDOMEN, MOTION DISCOMFORT, and UPCHUCK.

stonewall. To obstruct (justice), to say little or nothing, to COVER UP.

As President Nixon told his men on March 22, 1973, in a segment of the conversation that was *not* included when the White House transcripts were made public on April 30, 1974, but which was preserved for posterity by the House Judiciary Committee: "I don't give a shit what happens. I want you all to stonewall it, let them plead the Fifth Amendment, cover up, or anything else, if it'll save it—save the whole plan. That's the whole point. . . . We're going to protect our people if we can."

This use of "stonewall" probably is a tribute to Confederate Gen. Thomas Jonathan Jackson, who became "Stonewall" Jackson after conducting a resolute defense at the first Battle of Bull Run in 1861. "Stonewall" also has an obstructionist meaning in politics in Australia and New Zealand, where it is a parliamentary stalling tactic involving long speeches (akin to a filibuster) and other delaying actions. This usage apparently derives from cricket, where a batsman who plays purely defensively is said "to stonewall."

A recent innovation is *semistonewalling*. Thus, an industry official said the Bituminous Coal Operators Association had adopted a "semi-stonewalling position" when it agreed to resume negotiations with the United Mine Workers union, which had been on strike for more than two months (*New York Times*, 2/22/78).

stool. Either the seat or the fecal matter expelled while sitting upon it; originally a *close stool, privy stool*, or *stool of ease*, and later the action ("to be at stool") as well as the result. The basic stool-that-is-a-seat is of some venerability, dating to at least the fifteenth century. The *Oxford English Dictionary* includes such classic examples as "I send them by his advice to sit upon the stool and strain" (Milton, *Colasterion*, 1645). See also EASE, PRIVY, and TOILET.

story. A lie, from at least the seventeenth century. The liar, meanwhile, is the "storyteller" or, especially among English children, simply "a story," as in "You story, you!" Slangy variations include *bedtime story, cock-and-bull story, fairy story, ghost story*, and *tall story*, as well as such specific *stories* (or "yarns") as the *barroom story, bunkroom story*, and *fish story* (aka *piscatorial prevarication*). See also COVER STORY and WHITE LIE.

stout. Fat; sometimes, *stylishly stout*. See also KING-SIZE and PORTLY.

strategic. An overarching word for justifying whatever means are necessary to obtain a particular end; frequently ·sed when contemplating the UNTHINKABLE. John Kenneth Galbraith described the mentality this way: ". . . recent experience shows that presidents cannot survive the strategic mind. If life on this planet dissolves one day in an intense sheet of flame with great over-pressure, the guidance of our demise will have been given by a relentless strategic mind, a particularly tough exponent of global balance" (*New York Review of Books,* 10/12/78).

The combinations in which "strategic" appears are awesome to behold. For example, there is *strategic bombing,* which in World War II meant the bombing of cities, and which has since been developed into the idea of *strategic nuclear war,* also called an *all-out strategic exchange* (see EXCHANGE). A war of this sort would be waged by .he Strategic Air Force (whose motto is "Peace Is Our Profession"); by *strategic submarines,* such as the Poseidon; and by *strategic nuclear weapons,* long-range missiles that differ less in killing power than one might think from the supposedly smaller TACTICAL NUCLEAR WEAPONS. The amount of fissionable material required to construct a *strategic warhead* is known, naturally, as the *strategic quantity* (for a watered-down version of this, see SIGNIFICANT QUANTITY). On a smaller scale, one of the centerpieces of the war in Vietnam was the Strategic Hamlet Program. (These "hamlets," which bore an uncanny resemblance to refugee camps, were later advertised as "New Life Hamlets.") And for those who want to understand the CIA, it is worth remembering that its bureaucratic predecessor was the Office of Strategic Services.

An especially fine example of a "strategic" whose historical shortcomings have been studiously ignored by most *strategicians* is *strategic bombing.* Before airplanes were invented and *strategic bombing* was possible, attacks on unfortified positions, such as cities, were considered immoral by soldiers of the better sort as well as by civilians on the receiving end. Following the carnage on the battlefields of World War I, however, farsighted military men in Europe and America began looking for ways to shorten the next war. The flyers came up with *strategic bombing,* with Gen. William (Billy) Mitchell and others arguing that no nation would stand up for long against air attacks on its cities ("vital centers," as Mitchell termed them). "A few gas bombs," according to Mitchell, would paralyze a city, and after completely destroying or paralyzing a few cities, the enemy would surrender.

The real meaning of "strategic bombing" was recognized by the public early in World War II, e.g., "Bombing of cities . . . is a true example of strategic bombing" (*Nineteenth Century,* 9/41). And the meaning became even clearer as the war progressed: "Consequently, any plan of strategic bombing to destroy Japan's capacity to make war . . . must include the destruction of these thousands of family factories" (*Reader's Digest,* 5/45). In the end, it is debatable whether *strategic bombing* shortened the war or, by increasing the sense of solidarity among those attacked, lengthened it. Whatever the answer, *strategic bombing* certainly didn't live up to its advance billing by producing a quick, bloodless (for our side) victory.

Nevertheless, all the arguments for *strategic bombing* were trotted out again during the Korean POLICE ACTION and the Vietnam CONFLICT, even though both Korea and Vietnam had rudimentary transportation networks, not susceptible to disruption by bombing, and few other targets worth hitting (see STRUCTURE). Only after a great many tons of bombs were dropped in Vietnam did some of the war's managers begin to realize that the policy wasn't working, e.g.: "It is strategic bombing that seems unproductive and unwise. . . . (The lights have not stayed off in Haiphong, and even if they had, electric lights are in no sense essential to the Communist war effort.) And against this distinctly marginal impact we have to weigh the fact that strategic bombing does tend to divide the U.S. . . . and to accentuate the unease and distemper which surround the war in Vietnam, both at home and abroad" (memo from McGeorge Bundy, special assistant to the president for National Security Affairs, to Lyndon B. Johnson, president, ca. 5/4/67, *The Pentagon Papers*, 1971).

Still, one quails at the thought of *strategic bombing*'s lineal descendent, *strategic nuclear war*, hoping against hope that the words of a former secretary of defense will be remembered: "My personal opinion is . . . we cannot win a nuclear war, a strategic nuclear war, in the normal meaning of the word 'win'" (Robert S. McNamara, as quoted by Arthur M. Schlesinger, Jr., *A Thousand Days*, 1965). Or, in the words of Mr. Galbraith again: "It was the men of relentless strategic mind who guided Lyndon Johnson on Indochina and sent him back to Texas. . . . I would urge [the president] to watch those relentless strategic minds. I, personally, would feel far, far safer with Bert Lance."

For more about the theory and practice of *strategic bombing*, see FLYING FORTRESS and PRECISION BOMBING; for an exception to the rule that "strategic" signifies death and destruction, see the next entry.

strategic movement to the rear. Retreat.

The only kind of "retreat" that proper soldiers recognize is the signal for lowering the flag at sunset. Thus, retreating armies *redeploy* or gracefully RETIRE; they make *changes of base* or engage in *mobile maneuvering*; they conduct RETRO-GRADE MANEUVERS or WITHDRAWALS; they BREAK OFF CONTACT WITH THE ENEMY or make ADJUSTMENTS OF THE FRONT; they may even (as mainly American troops did in 1950 when Chinese VOLUNTEERS entered the Korean POLICE ACTION) resort to "the big bug-out." But they never—well, hardly ever—"retreat."

Since "strategy" comes from *strategos*, the ancient Greek word for "general," it is only natural that "strategic movements" are of some antiquity. Speaking of Antigonus Gonatas, king of Macedonia from 274 to 239 B.C.: "He was also probably the first man to call a retreat a 'strategic movement to the rear'" (A. R. Burn, *A Traveller's History of Greece*, 1965). Gonatas (a nickname, meaning "knee-cap," from the piece of armor that covered it) was a sharp man with words and also deserves to be remembered for his reply to a poet who suggested that he might be divine, i.e.: "The man who carries my chamberpot knows better." See also CHAMBER.

streetwalker. A whore, PROSTITUTE, or, in modern CB lingo, a *pavement princess*. The circumlocutory as well as circumambulatory "streetwalker"—in theory, the phrase could apply to anyone walking the street for any reason whatsoever—has been making her rounds at least since the sixteenth century. For example: "They shold see how these street walkers wil iet in rich garded gowns" (Robert Greene, *A Notable Discovery of Coosnage* or *The Art of Conny Catching*, 1592). And for more about "conny catching," which is not as bad as one might think, see RABBIT.

stress-producing stimulus. An electric shock, as administered by an accredited scientist or doctor. A *stress-producing stimulus* may be used in the course of research in a laboratory on an animal, such as a mouse, or in the course of AVERSION THERAPY in a prison on a person. In either case, the *stress-producing stimulus* may produce, in addition to stress, what is politely, and scientifically, referred to as VOCALIZATION.

striped one. A euphemistic circumlocution for a tiger in lands where tigers run wild and where cautious people do not speak the tiger's true name for fear that one might suddenly appear. "In Sumatra the tiger is mentioned as He With the Striped Coat" (Maria Leach, ed., *Funk & Wagnalls Standard Dictionary of Folklore, Mythology and Legend*, 1972). "When he came to the cave, Fear, the Hairless One, put out his hand and called him 'The Striped One that comes by night,' and the first of the Tigers was afraid of the Hairless One, and ran back to the swamps howling" (Rudyard Kipling, *The Jungle Book*, 1894).

Besides the tiger, many other animals in many lands rate euphemistic names. The lion, for instance, is referred to respectfully by the Algerians as "Mr. John Johnson," while to the Angolans, he is "Sir," and to the South African Botswana, he is "the boy with the beard." In parts of Africa and India, a snake is never called a snake. Instead, on seeing a snake, one might say "There lies a string" (or a "strap" or a "rope"). The hope is that calling it a string will make it lie still like a string; the fear is that labeling it as a snake will make it behave like a snake.

For more about euphemisms for animals and the reasons for them, see GRANDFATHER.

structure. A thatched hut after being blown to smithereens; circa Vietnam ERA. Elevating "huts" into *structures* helped the military rationalize the immense effort that went into destroying so little. By the same token, a dugout canoe was converted into a *vessel*, a sampan into a *waterborne logistic craft*, and a bomb shelter into a *bunker*. Two or more *bunkers*, if connected, became a *network of tunnels*. The heady nomenclature conceals the almost total absence of anything worth blowing up. Even in the more industrial north, the Joint Chiefs of Staff found only eight industrial installations worth listing when first beginning to look for possible targets to bomb—which didn't stop the United States from dropping more bombs on North Vietnam than on Germany in World War II. See also COLLATERAL DAMAGE, FACILITY, and *strategic bombing* in STRATEGIC.

studio. An artistic word for embellishing businesses of various kinds; generally synonymous with PARLOR and SALON. "Studio" is not as popular now as in the 1920s, when the land was littered with *billiard studios*, *candy studios*, and *tonsorial studios* (the barbers then were *tonsorial artists*), as well as—somewhat more legitimately—*movie* and *photography studios*. However, the word still does euphemistic work in real estate ads, where *studio apartments* seldom feature high ceilings and a north light; in the beauty and massage businesses, where Manhattanites (*Yellow Pages*, 1979–80) can choose between David's Haircutting Studio or Ann's Studio (the latter being a licensed, or legitimate, massage parlor); and, finally, in the sex business, where a *rap studio* is the same as a RAP PARLOR and a *co-ed wrestling studio* is an arena where the combatants rarely work up much of a sweat but the spectators do.

submarine. Torture in Uruguay. There are two basic kinds, the "wet" and the "dry":

"When the 'wet submarine' method is used, the prisoner is immersed head down in a tank of putrid water polluted by vomit, excrement and blood. He is suspended until he has almost drowned, a process that is often repeated for hours on end. . . . The 'dry submarine' threatens slow suffocation by tying a plastic bag tightly over the victim's head" (Jari Laber, of Amnesty International, in the *New York Times*, 3/10/76). See also INTERROGATION and WATER CURE.

sudden victory. Sudden death. The upbeat name was suggested over national TV by sportscaster Curt Gowdy for the professional football overtime period in which the first score ends the game. Gowdy has literary company, with Jerzy Kosinski, author of *The Painted Bird* and other works, having devised a rather similar euphemism: Explains Mr. K.: "Deadlines—that is a bad word in English. I am self-employed. I have only myself. I must work on self-lines" (Harper & Row *Bookletter*, 11/22/76). See also INHERITANCE TAX, LIFE INSURANCE, and NO OUTLET.

sugar. A sickly sweet euphemism for "shit"; see also FUDGE and SHUCKS.

summer. In a not-so-subtle reform of the Gregorian calendar, Consolidated Edison Corp. of New York exacts "summer" surcharges from May 15 through October 15, thus squeezing extra money out of its customers by squeezing two extra months into the season. This is the same great "utility" that initially blamed its 1977 blackout on an ACT OF GOD.

sunset years. Old age; the rosy-fingered euphemism has a FOP Index of 2.0. "Hannibal [Missouri] was not a Sturbridge Village, reincarnated from the past, with local citizens dressed up in buckle shoes plying extinct trades. I was grateful for that—I've seen enough blacksmithing and candle dipping to last me well into my sunset years" (William Zinsser, *Smithsonian*, 10/78). The metaphor of the setting sun of life is not new, e.g.: "Old age . . . may be called the sunne set of our dayes" (Thomas Williamson, *Goulart's Wise Veillard or Old Man*, trans. 1621). See also GO WEST and GOLDEN AGE/YEARS.

sunshine. Radiation; a euphemism that failed. "Radiation of any kind was simply not a pleasant thing, and never could be, regardless of one AEC attempt to refer to it as 'sunshine units'" (John G. Fuller, *We Almost Lost Detroit*, 1975). Similarly inspired was "Project Sunshine," the title of the official report on the investigation into the deaths of the Japanese fishermen who were caught in the fallout of an

American H-bomb test in 1956 (from Justus George Lawler, "Politics and the American Language," *College English*, 4/74). For more atomic talk, begin with ABOVE CRITICAL.

superintendent. (1) The person who manages a prison or CORRECTIONAL FACILITY; formerly a warden. (2) A janitor or caretaker; see also CUSTODIAN.

supervisor. A foreman; desexualized newspeak, in which chairman becomes *chair*, draftsman becomes *drafter*, pressman becomes *press operator*, repairman becomes *repairer*, working woman (or girl) becomes *worker*. See also PERSON.

Supreme Being. Another of the many indirect ways of referring to God. Variants include *Supreme Intelligence, Supreme Lord,* and *Supreme One.* "The most tedious of all discourses are on the subject of the Supreme Being" (Ralph Waldo Emerson, *Journals,* 1836). For the general reluctance to speak God's name, see ADONAI

surgical strike. An air raid that theoretically doesn't obliterate anything but the intended, always-strictly-military target; in extended usage, any sharp attack on any opponent, domestic as well as foreign.

The trouble with "surgical strike" in the first sense is that it is rarely, if ever, as clean in practice as in name, a deficiency that has sometimes led planners actually to drop the idea instead of bombs. For example: "The idea of American planes suddenly and swiftly eliminating the missile complex [in Cuba in 1962] with conventional bombs in a matter of minutes—a so-called 'surgical' strike— had appeal to almost everyone first considering the matter, including President Kennedy . . ." (Theodore C. Sorensen, *Kennedy,* 1965). In this case, after realizing that a *surgical strike* was bound to be messier than the name implied, the United States settled on a QUARANTINE. Meanwhile, in the extended sense, a U.S. State Department spokesman said Russia was conducting "a surgical strike against the dissidents," after two were arrested by the Soviet government (*New York Daily News,* 7/9/78). See also PRECISION BOMBING, PREEMPTIVE STRIKE, and SELECTIVE STRIKE.

surplus. To fire. "Executives Who Were 'Surplused'" (*New York Times* headline, 8/14/77). See also the similar EXCESS and REDUNDANCY.

surreptitious entry. A break-in, burglary, or BLACK BAG JOB; frequently abbreviated to the even more opaque "entry."

The usual reasons for a *surreptitious entry* are to search desks, photograph files, or install hidden microphones. The "surreptitious" implies that the "entry" will be accomplished without actually breaking any locks, windows, or whatever, so that the victim of the trespass will not realize an invasion has taken place. In the FBI, which specialized for many years in BLACK BAG JOBS, the newer term is preferred. Thus, at the 1980 trial of two former high-ranking FBI officials for their role in the bureau's break-ins, there occurred this exchange between prosecutor and witness (*New York Times,* 10/6/80):

Q: Did you do a black bag job on Jennifer Dohrn's home?
A: No, I did a surreptitious entry.

And from one of the more chilling documents of our time—Tom Charles Huston's plan for domestic intelligence-gathering (i.e., spying), presented to President Richard M. Nixon in July 1970: "*Surreptitious Entry* . . . Use of this technique is clearly illegal: it amounts to burglary. . . . However, it is also the most fruitful tool and can produce the type of intelligence which cannot be obtained in any other way." Huston's plan was approved by the president. According to a "TOP SECRET" (see TOP SECRET) memorandum of July 15, 1970: "Restraints on the use of surreptitious entry are to be removed." Nixon later said he quickly rescinded his approval, but this was on account of the opposition of FBI Director J. Edgar Hoover, not because of any doubts about his own authority; see ILLEGAL.

surrogate. A substitute; a stand-in. In politics, a *surrogate* usually is a White House aide, cabinet officer, or member of the president's family, who makes a speech in place of the president himself. *Surrogate therapy*, meanwhile, is a form of sex therapy, in which a *surrogate* serves in place of the patient's usual sex partner.

surveillance. Official spying, not necessarily limited to governments, e.g., from a 1976 Gimbels Brothers announcement: "Gimbels security management have evaluated their security procedures used to deter shoplifting and theft and have determined that the surveillance of fitting rooms for apprehension of shoplifters is not necessary." In other words, guards had been secretly watching customers change clothes in dressing and fitting rooms. The reevaluation of policy in the chain's New York division stemmed from the decision of a judge to throw out a case against a woman accused of stealing a scarf on the grounds that the *surveillance* violated "reasonable expectations of privacy" as well as the Fourth Amendment to the United States Constitution, which protects citizens against "unreasonable searches and seizures."

Surveillance comes in two main forms: physical, or eyeball, *surveillance*, and nonphysical, remote *surveillance*, including wiretaps, hidden microphones, and mail watches (see MAIL COVER). Further, both the physical and remote types may be characterized as either *cold surveillance* or *hot surveillance*. In *cold surveillance*, the person being *surveilled* (a new verb, a typical bureaucratic back-formation, thought to have originated in the FBI) isn't supposed to know it. The Gimbels operation would class as physical, *cold surveillance*. In *hot surveillance*, the person, or TARGET, is tailed so obviously, or bugged so crudely, that he or she can't help but know it. The purpose of *hot surveillance* is to harass or intimidate—as in the FBI's famous Counter Intelligence Program (Cointelpro)—for which see TECHNICAL SURVEILLANCE.

swagging. Stealing; a vestige of euphemistic honor among thieves, the term being used among prisoners at New York's Green Haven CORRECTIONAL FACILITY, usually to denote private appropriation of state-owned property (from Susan Sheehan, *The New Yorker*, 10/31/77). See also APPROPRIATE.

swan. Swear; an old and probably obsolete but nevertheless beautiful euphemism for those who wanted to avoid completely even the appearance of swearing. Examples in *A Dictionary of Americanisms* (Mitford M. Mathews, ed., 1951) range in time from 1784 (in which "I swan" is described as an "old saying") to as recently as 1931 (in the *Kansas City Times* of September 11). The basic "I swan" frequently was elaborated into *swan to goodness* and *swan to man*, both of which translate as "swear to God." The expression may derive from "I warrant," which in northern English dialects came out as *I'se warn ye* or *I'se warran*. See also CUSS.

sweet. All-powerful, dreadful. Discussing the shrines along the route of the annual procession conducted in ancient times from Eleusis to Athens: "Next, was the altar of Zeus Melichios, 'Sweet Zeus,' a substitution of a euphemism for a name of dread; for this was Zeus in pre-anthropomorphic, serpent form" (A. R. Burn, *The Lyric Age of Greece*, 1968). See also ADONAI and EUMENIDES.

sweetbread. An interior organ of a calf or other animal when it appears on the menu or dinner plate. The euphemistic value of the phrase can be gauged by trying to imagine how many people would order "pancreas" rather than *stomach sweetbread*. Or think how "thymus gland" would look on the menu of your favorite eatery: The preferred term among gourmets is *neck sweetbread* or, sweeter yet, *throat sweetbread*. It says something about our eating habits that "sweetbread" is a relatively old term, going back at least to the sixteenth century. Even older are the related "chitterlings," for small intestines, first recorded in 1280, according to the *Oxford English Dictionary*, and "tripe," for the stomach of a ruminant, also from pre-1300. (The latter dish, by the way, may have been an Islamic contribution to culinary arts, the Old French *tripe, trippe,* apparently deriving from the Arabic *tharb,* meaning "entrails" or "net.") See also FILET MIGNON, PLUCK, and VARIETY MEATS.

sweetheart. The term of endearment has also been used as a euphemism. From the *Oxford English Dictionary*: "One word alone hath troubled some, because the immodest maid soothing the young man, calls him her Prick. . . . He who cannot away with [i.e., stand for] this, instead of 'my Prick,' let him write 'my Sweetheart'" (H. M., gent., *The Colloquies or Familiar Discourses of D. Erasmus,* trans. 1671). See also PENIS.

swinging. Promiscuity, especially when characterized by one or more of the following: wife-swapping ("mate-swapping," to those who are truly liberated), group sex, and BISEXUAL activity. Frequently, the three factors conjoin:

> VERY INTERESTING MARRIED young cpl in 30s seek attr cpls versatile gals extra select males for discreet friendship and swinging fun. No fatties weirdos. (*Ace,* undated, ca. 1976; see also FUN)

Swinging is a relatively new phenomenon (by this name, that is). Perhaps helped along by Frank Sinatra's 1956 record album, "Songs for Swingin' Lovers," the term became popular during the 1960s. Today, there are *swingers,* some of whom divide their time between partners of different sexes and so are said to *swing both ways.* When three or more *swingers* gather together, the event is known as a *swing party* (i.e., orgy). Plato's Retreat, a *swingers club* in New York City, featured 20 *mini-swing* rooms, each with a carrying capacity of one to three couples. Unmarried, or single *swingers*, are known technically as *swingles*. They are said to make the *swingles scene* at *swingles bars* (which are indistinguishable from "singles bars").

With its meaning having shifted from music to sex, "swing" reverses the transition made earlier by "jazz," which almost certainly was southern black slang for sex long before the turn of this century, when it surfaced as the name of the swinging music that was played in the bawdy houses and honky-tonks in New Orleans and points west. Like "swing," the sexual meaning of "jazz" included practices other than straight COPULATION by straights. Thus, an article on "Homosexual Practices of Institutionalized Females" (Charles A. Ford, *Journal of Abnormal and Social Psychiatry*, 1–3, 1929) quoted a note from one woman prisoner to another, with the following heading:

> You can take my tie
> You can take my coller
> But I'll jazze you
> 'Till you holler.

syndicate. A gang, short for "crime syndicate"; most notably, the Chicago gang of Alfonso Capone (1899–1947). "Syndicate" was popularized by newspapers following Capone's ascension as chief Chicago mobster in 1925. The professional-sounding term received the imprimatur of the BOSS himself, according to an anonymous friend, who reported (*True Detective*, 6/47) that "syndicate" was "picked up by Al from the newspaper stories about him."

tactical nuclear weapon or MINI-NUKE. The "tactical" implies that the bomb (or DEVICE) is small, which is not necessarily the case. "Even the tactical nuclear weapons supposedly designed for 'limited' wars were not an answer. . . . some of these 'small' weapons carried a punch five times more powerful than the bomb that destroyed Hiroshima" (Theodore C. Sorensen, *Kennedy*, 1965). "The main difference between strategic and tactical nuclear weapons is the difference in range. Tactical nuclear weapons have a shorter range but are sometimes more powerful than strategic weapons. . . . The use of 10 percent of the 7,000 U.S. tactical nuclear weapons in Europe would destroy the entire area where such massive nuclear exchanges occurred" (Center for Defense Information, *The Defense Monitor*, 2/75). The strategy for using *tactical nuclear weapons* has been summarized this way: "The NATO doctrine is that we will fight with conventional forces until we are losing, then we fight with tactical nuclear weapons until we are losing, and then we will blow up the world" (Morton Halperin, former deputy assistant secretary of defense, in *The Defense Monitor*, 2/75). See also CLEAN BOMB, EXCHANGE, LIMITED WAR, MEGADEATH, and STRATEGIC.

tail. The ass, usually, but occasionally, and still more euphemistically, the genitals, whether the PENIS (which means "tail" in Latin) or the VAGINA. In the more prevalent sense: "What would become of the fraternity if all of us parked ourselves on our tails?" (Percy Marks, *The Plastic Age*, 1924).

"Tail" can be traced back to the fourteenth century in all senses, making it a leading example of the Rule of the Displaced Referent, whereby euphemisms for unmentionable parts of the body are created by naming mentionable ones in their vicinity. For example, consider the following observation of Geoffrey Chaucer, which is just as true now as it was nearly 600 years ago (ca. 1387–1400), when he wrote the prologue to *The Wife of Bath's Tale*. Herself speaks:

> And after wyn on Venus moste I thynke,
> For al so siker [just as sure] as cold engendreth hayl,
> A likerous [lecherous] mouth moste han a likerous tayl;
> In womman vinolent [being full of wine] is no defence—
> This knowen lechours by experience.

Both the male and female meanings of "tail" were encompassed in "bobtail," as defined by Capt. Francis Grose: "A lewd woman, or one that plays with her tail; also an impotent man, or an eunuch" (*A Classical Dictionary of the Vulgar Tongue*, 1796). And a century later, the anonymous author of *My Secret Life* (ca. 1890) allowed as how "every woman is immodest enough to show her tail, and feel a man's tail at times." Meanwhile, the PROSTITUTE who sold *tail* came to be called "a tail." For instance, the *Lexicon Balatronicum* ("a member of the Whip Club," 1811) illustrated its definition of "cab" in the sense of "brothel" with the following example: "Mother: how many tails have you in your cab? how many girls have you in your bawdy house?"

Finally, in a late, possibly nonce variation, the versatile "tail" was made to stand for yet another piece of nearby anatomy in the film version of *Don't Go Near the Water* (1957) when the newspaperman Gordon Ripwell stormed, "You think you've got me by the tail!"—a peculiar expression for an otherwise ballsy fellow.

See also ARSE, GENITALS, and, for another early "tail" that is not an ass, the "tailis" of the "cattis," of 1401, in CAT HOUSE.

target. A person, especially one whose phone is being tapped, usually illegally (see TECHNICAL SURVEILLANCE), or whose mail is being watched and, probably, opened (see MAIL COVER). People who refer to other people as "targets" tend to have a bombs-away attitude. Consider Tom Charles Huston on the question of "mail coverage": ". . . restrictions on covert coverage should be relaxed on selected targets of priority foreign intelligence and internal security interest" (July 1970 memorandum to President Richard M. Nixon, recommending increased domestic intelligence-gathering, i.e., spying). See also PERSONNEL and SURREPTITIOUS ENTRY.

TB; also **T.B., Tb, Tb., t.b.,** or **tb.** Tuberculosis, or consumption, a killer disease that was euphemized in its time just as cancer is in ours. Attesting to the "tremendous fear [that] surrounded TB," Susan Sontag cited examples from literature and from life: "In Stendhal's *Armance* (1827), the hero's mother refuses to say 'tuberculosis' for fear that pronouncing the words will hasten the course of her son's malady," while Franz Kafka wrote in April 1924 from the SANATORIUM where he was to die two months later: "Verbally I don't learn anything definite, since in discussing tuberculosis . . . everybody drops into a shy, evasive, glassy-eyed manner of speech" (*New York Review of Books*, 1/26/78).

Tuberculosis victims also developed a language of their own. For example, reporting on "'T.B.' Talk" in Arizona: "On reaching the arid southwest the patient finds that he doesn't have consumption, but has t.b. . . . . Often he is referred to as a *lunger*, and sometimes as one who has *the bugs*. The newspapers will refer to him as a *health seeker*, and to enthusiastic, philanthropic ladies he is a *shut-in*. The word 'consumption' is never heard . . ." (Anders H. Anderson, *American Speech*, 2/35). This by no means exhausted the euphemisms of patients. The sanatorium from which so few people returned was known to them as the *san*, and if it featured open-air cabins, it was a *cottage-san* or perhaps a *rest ranch*. To spit (or EXPECTORATE) was to *raise*, and if one was spitting blood, then one was said to *raise color*. A pulmonary hemorrhage was *spilling rubies*. And so it went.

Aside from the many abbreviations, the most popular sobriquet for tuberculosis was *the white plague* (or *the great white plague*), an appellation attributed to Oliver Wendell Holmes, Sr.: "Two diseases especially have attracted attention, above all others, with reference to their causes and prevention; cholera, the 'black death' of the nineteenth century, and consumption, the white plague of the North" (*Medical Essays* [1868], 1883).

For background on the fear of names, see also GRANDFATHER, and for other semantically loaded complaints, continue with LONG ILLNESS and SOCIAL DISEASE.

teacher presence. Attendance. Far be it from teachers to apply to themselves a word that has been contaminated by students; thus, where students "attend" school, teachers reveal their "presence," as in "Teacher presence in Newark schools was normal" (WINS, 5/12/75). *Teacher presence* made news this day because of a threatened SICK OUT.

technical adjustment. A change, usually of stock prices; variants include *technical correction, technical reaction,* and *technical readjustment.* Generally, the different kinds of "technical" serve to conceal the user's ignorance of true causes, as in: "Wall St. labeled the action a technical rally in the absence of any significant news development" (*New York Times,* 12/7/73). This particular "technical rally" just happened to feature the sixth largest daily rise—25.81 points—in the history of the Dow Jones industrial average. See also ADJUSTMENT DOWNWARD.

technical surveillance. Wiretapping and bugging, FBI-ese, as distinguished from simple SURVEILLANCE (spying); also known variously as *electronic surveillance, electronic penetration,* and *trespassory microphone surveillance.* ". . . Cartha D. Deloach, then assistant to Mr. Hoover, set up a special team of agents to conduct 'technical surveillance' (F.B.I. jargon for wiretapping and bugging) and physical surveillance at the convention" (*New York Times,* 1/27/75). The subject, or TARGET, of *technical surveillance* in this particular instance was the Reverend Martin Luther King, Jr., whose activities were MONITORED by at least 16 different wiretaps and eight bugged rooms from 1963 to at least 1965. Technically, the *technical surveillance* of King was part of the FBI's Counterintelligence Program (Cointelpro) for harassing people, parties, and other organizations considered (by the FBI) to be threats to the state (or the FBI). Some people say that Cointelpro activities have been halted; others think they linger on under a new euphemism—*intensive investigation.* See also BLACK BAG JOB and HIGHLY CONFIDENTIAL (or SENSITIVE) SOURCE.

technical trespass. A break-in by an agent of the U.S. government, usually an FBI AGENT. "He acknowledged that the evidence could never be introduced in court because, he said, it was 'tainted,' having been obtained through a 'technical trespass,' without obtaining search warrants or the occupants' consent" (*New York Times,* 10/6/80). This was from the trial testimony of a man who admitted to having participated in 15 to 20 SURREPTITIOUS ENTRIES, but nevertheless insisted they were legal and constitutional. See also BLACK BAG JOB.

technician. An all-purpose label for upgrading job titles. ". . . if you have an oil-tank cleaner, make him a petrochemical technician instead" (Jeremy Rifkin and Randy Barber, *The North Will Rise Again,* 1978). Besides inflating the ego of the worker, "technician" has advantages for the BOSS, since the label replaces traditional craft titles. This fits in with "multi-crafting," which is a new technique for driving unions crazy: Organizers come into a plant looking for plumbers or electricians to unionize and all they can find are *technicians, grade one; technicians, grade two,* etc. Plant efficiency may drop somewhat, since the *technicians, grade one* have been taught only a little bit about plumbing, a little bit about electricity, a little bit about carpentry, with the result that they may not be very proficient at any one of these. But no matter: The union has been beat and that, of course, is the important thing. See also ENGINEER and INDUSTRIAL RELATIONS.

temperance. Literally, "moderation," but a euphemistic stalking-horse in the nineteenth century for voluntary abstention and then involuntary prohibition. Alcohol was not the only enemy: "Tom joined the new order of Cadets of Temperance, being attracted by the showy character of their 'regalia.' He promised to abstain from smoking, chewing, and profanity as long as he remained a member" (Mark Twain, *The Adventures of Tom Sawyer,* 1876).

The first local antialcohol *temperance* societies were founded toward the start of the nineteenth century, and the term still meant moderation, in the sense of voluntary abstention from the stronger spirits, in 1833 when the American Society for the Promotion of Temperance was founded. Just three years later, however, the society changed its pledge to complete abstinence from all liquors, including wine and beer. And a few years after that, as it became clear that moral suasion alone wasn't going to make the nation dry, "temperance" began to mean "prohibition." As early as 1845, New York State enacted a law banning the sale of liquor, a noble experiment that anticipated the national one of 1920–33, but that failed more quickly, New York repealing its law after only two years. A *temperance* drink is, of course, a "soft drink," as in "I'll have an orange temperance, please." See also CLUB, HIGH, and SALOON.

terminate/termination. To end something, as a conversation, a job, or a life; the act of ending something, including any of the above.

In the first, most general sense, "terminate" is a relatively minor offense—typical lawyer talk, e.g., ". . . I terminated the conversation after indicating to him that I would commence work" (*New York Post,* 6/30/73). Next, and more seriously, in the case of jobs, "terminate" becomes a euphemism for "fire." Take the case of a cheerleader for the Chicago Bears football team: "The Honey Bears are still performing for that club, but . . . Jackie Rohrs has been 'terminated' because the team learned that she will appear entirely out of uniform in the December issue of *Playboy*" (*New York Post,* 10/8/78). Finally, when lives are at stake, "terminate" blossoms into a full-fledged euphemism for "kill," as in "Terminate her, immediately" (*Star Wars,* film, 1977). In the last case, art (?) is imitating life, of course. For example: "Other reports said that the Green Berets had been advised by a CIA official in Saigon to 'terminate with extreme prejudice'—an official euphemism for murder—the suspect, and had done so with an injection of morphine, two .22 caliber pistol shots in the head, and the disposal of the weighted corpse in the sea" (*New York Times Encyclopedic Almanac,* 1970). As a clean word for ending a life, "terminate" also pops up frequently in discussions of abortion: ". . . thanks to the development of amniocentesis within the past few years, fetuses with chromosomal defects can be detected early enough in pregnancy to permit the gestation to be terminated" (*Natural History,* 10/78). See also ELIMINATE/ELIMINATION, LET GO, and THERAPEUTIC INTERRUPTION OF PREGNANCY.

terminological inexactitude. A falsehood, a lie; close kin to a CATEGORICAL

testicles

INACCURACY. See also WHITE LIE.

INACCURACY. The young Winston Churchill used the euphemism this way, when sidestepping charges that the British government was condoning slavery of Chinese laborers in South Africa: "It could not, in the opinion of His Majesty's Government, be classified as slavery in the extreme acceptance of the word, without some risk of terminological inexactitude" (speech, House of Commons, 2/22/06). See also WHITE LIE.

testicles. The balls. "Balls" is the word most people use informally, which is most of the time. Thus, even women may be said to be "ballsy" (see LAY for an example). When on their best behavior, however, people tend to turn to the Latinate "testicles," which, like PENIS, has entered the popular vocabulary only within the last generation or so. As recently as the 1930s, the word in newspapers usually was GLANDS. "Testicle" is a relatively old word, however, with the first example in the *Oxford English Dictionary* coming from circa 1425. Even so, the term is not nearly as old in English as the more elemental "balls," with "ballocks" (little balls) traceable to about the year 1000. See THIGH for the curious origin of *testis* (the Latin antecedent of "testicle") as well as, for more on this general subject, the *peloné* in BALONEY, BILATERAL ORCHIDECTOMY, BOLLIXED UP, COJONES, FAMILY JEWELS, FRY, NUTS, PECULIAR MEMBERS, PRAIRIE OYSTERS, ROCKS, and THINGUMBOB(S).

thanatology. The study of death, including its effects on the dying and those around them; from *thanatos*, Greek for "death." There exists a Foundation of Thanatology, and some schools and colleges have begun offering courses in the subject. For example, the American Academy-McAllister Institute of Funeral Service, in New York City, offers an elective in *thanatology* for those who are studying to become undertakers. A duly certified expert in the subject is correctly described as a *thanatologist*. See also FUNERAL DIRECTOR.

that way. Pregnant; the condition is discussed more openly now than once was the case, but euphemisms and circumlocutions still linger on, e. g.: "I saw she was big, but I didn't know she was that way" (resident of Damariscotta, Maine, upon learning that the author's wife was pregnant; summer of 1977). See also EXPECTANT/EXPECTING.

therapeutic accident. The "therapeutic" helps cover up an error by a doctor or other medical person. "In fact the patient leaves 'Admissions' with the feeling that his identification bracelet manacles him to a no-fault system in which a fatal mistake, such as the transfusion of incompatible blood, becomes a 'therapeutic accident'" (Robert Craft, *New York Review of Books*, 9/16/76). See also ACCIDENT and ERRATUM.

therapeutic interruption of pregnancy. An abortion; also called a *pregnancy interruption* or *voluntary interrupted pregnancy* (*VIP*, for short). The induced *therapeutic interruption of pregnancy* contrasts with the spontaneous *interrupted term*, or MISCARRIAGE.

thigh. The balls or testicles, biblical-style. "And the servant put his hand under the thigh of Abraham his master, and sware to him concerning the matter" (Genesis, XXIV, 9, King James Version, 1611).

The ancient custom of holding one's (or as in the case of Abraham's servant, someone else's) balls when making a solemn oath is commemorated in the word "testicle," which comes from the Latin *testis*, meaning "witness." The original idea seems to be that if one swore falsely, one might be rendered impotent. From *testis*-as-witness, we also get such words as "attest," "protest," "protestant," "testament," and the "testimony," which today is offered after swearing on a Bible instead. See also COJONES and TESTICLES.

thing. Verbal shorthand for anything one prefers not to discuss in more vivid detail; an omnibus term, with comparable carrying capacity to IT, PROBLEM, and SITUATION.

The term has been used since medieval times for the sexual parts. Geoffrey Chaucer, in *The Wife of Bath's Prologue* (1387–1400) not only used the word straight out, e.g., ". . . oure bothe thynges smale/Were eek to knowe a femele from a male," but further euphemized it by translating it into French, as in ". . . if I would selle my *bele chose*/I kould walke as fressh as is a rose" (by which the good wife meant she could dress well on her earnings). And in our own time, "thing" has been loaded down with a wide variety of nonanatomical meanings, ranging from the "economic thing," which is a "slump" or RECESSION, to "our thing," which is better known in its Italian original, i.e., Cosa Nostra, to the highly generalized "doing your own thing."

The opaque "thing" also has been made to stand for "tragedy" by those who would rather not acknowledge that one has taken place. Thus, former President Richard M. Nixon referred in a television interview with David Frost to "the Kent State thing" (meaning the killing of four young people and the wounding of nine others when the Ohio National Guard opened fire on university students protesting the Cambodian invasion of 1970). *The White House Transcripts* (1974) are replete with such Nixonian "things" as "the Segretti thing" (3/17/73, meaning dirty tricks); "the executive privilege thing" (3/22/73, meaning the COVER-UP); "the Ellsberg thing, etc.—electronically thing—you know what I mean?" (3/27/73, meaning the work of the PLUMBERS); and "the Mitchell thing" (4/14/73, meaning the effort to get Mitchell to take the rap for everyone else). But the president outdid himself on March 22, 1973, when he allowed as how "we are fighting the situation thing" (meaning, apparently, the Watergate scandal), and then—most ingeniously—improved upon that, on April 16, 1973, saying to John W. Dean III:

> P: It was your job to work for the President, the White House staff and they were not involved in the pre-thing. But then you thought the post-thing. . . .

Dean's reply also is instructive:

> D: I thought we should cut the cancer right off because to keep this whole thing—

thingumbob. A glorified *thing*; an omnibus term for anyone or anything whose name is not known or, if known, not to be mentioned. Thus, recalling life on a

three-letter man

New England farm (ca. 1900), where small heaps of hay were called "tumbles" and larger ones were "cocks": "One proper farmer could never bring himself to use the current name for the larger heaps but always referred to them as thingumbobs" (*American Speech*, 2/53). "Thingumbob" and its many relations (*thingum, thingamajig, thingummy,* and *thingumthangum,* among others) have been with us since at least the seventeenth century, and the euphemistic meaning of "thingumbob" was well established by the mid-eighteenth century, e.g.: "Mr. Thingumbob, a vulgar address or nomination to any person whose name is unknown . . . . Thingumbobs, testicles" (Capt. Francis Grose, *A Classical Dictionary of the Vulgar Tongue,* 1751). "Thingumbobs" also have stood for those UNMENTIONABLE articles, trousers, while "thingummy" has been a euphemism for, in Eric Partridge's discreet definition, "the penis or the pudend" (*A Dictionary of Slang and Unconventional English,* 1970). See also WHAT-YOU-MAY-CALL'EM and, for more about haycocks, ROOSTER.

three-letter man. A homosexual, the three letters in question being "f-a-g." The phrase predates the currently dominant meaning of another three-letter word: GAY. See also the *four-letter man* in FOUR-LETTER WORD.

thrifty. Stingy; the essential meanings of the two words are the same, but "thrifty" has much better vibes (or, as semanticists say, "connotations"). "A game said to have been invented by Bertrand Russell is called 'Conjugating Adjectives.' It is played by mentioning three adjectives having the same denotation but different connotations. Example: I am thrifty; you are tight; he is stingy" (Anatol Rapoport, *Semantics,* 1975). See also ECONOMICAL.

throne. A toilet or, before that, a chamber pot. "The door leading to the toilet room is beautiful, but the comfortable 'throne' inside is even more beautiful" (*The Pop-Up Book of Gnomes,* 1979). See also TOILET.

thunder. Hell; a popular American euphemism that emigrated to England, commonly used in such expressions as *by thunder, go to thunder,* and *what in thunder.* Apparently preceded by "thunderation," which stood for "damnation," the short form became dominant in the hellish sense by the middle of the nineteenth century. For example, after he had captured Savannah at the end of 1864, Maj. Gen. William Tecumseh Sherman quashed the suggestion that he should be promoted to equal or superior rank to Lt. Gen. Ulysses S. Grant, saying: "He stood by me when I was crazy, and I stood by him when he was drunk. And now, by thunder, we stand by each other" (from Richard Wheeler, *Sherman's March,* 1978). And on the other side of the Atlantic: "'How in thunder came you to know anything about it?' he asked" (Conan Doyle, *The Valley of Fear,* 1915). See also BOTHERATION and HECK.

tiger. Nigger—as in the sanitized version of the old counting rhyme:

> Eenie, meenie, minie, mo,
> Catch a tiger by the toe.
> If he hollers, let him go.

During World War II, this rhyme was further amended:

Eenie, meenie, minie, mo,
Catch a Jap [or Hitler] by the toe.
If he hollers, make him say:
"I surrender U.S.A."

Besides "tiger," mothers also encourage their children to use *baby, black cat, feller, rabbit,* and *rooster* in place of the offending term. See also INDIAN and NEGRO.

timberdoodle. The American woodcock, *Philohela minor*—"doodle" being but one of many words beginning with "d" that stands for "penis" or "cock"; see DING-A-LING for a sampling. Somewhat confusingly, two species of woodpecker—the ivory-billed woodpecker and the pileated woodpecker—also used to be known as "woodcocks." See also PECKER and ROOSTER.

tinkle. People as well as pianos go "tinkle, tinkle," and when they do, it is because they are talking potty talk; see WEE WEE.

tittie. The nipple; frequently extended in meaning to include the entire breast. "Tittie" is a diminutive of "tit." Both are regarded by most people today as being on the vulgar side, but not all people have always felt this way. Witness some of America's quainter place names: Wildhorse Tit, Colorado, and Two Tits, California (euphemized on some maps as *Two Teats*). And in the Ozarks, only half a century ago, it was reported that "women of the very best families *give tittie* to their babies in public, even in church, without the slightest embarrassment," but the same women would never say "*breast* in the presence of strange men" (Vance Randolph, "Verbal Modesty in the Ozarks," *Dialect Notes,* vol. VI, Part I, 1928). While the Ozarkians are more sensitive than most people to the nuances of language (see also PETER), they are by no means the only ones to use "tittie" where "breast" would be considered a bit too blunt. There was, for example, the high school girl who, having performed a difficult feat with the bathroom scales, is said to have announced proudly to her boyfriend upon his return home from college, "Look—four ounces of new tittie!" (personal communication, ca. 1954).

"Tit," as a mispronunciation of "teat," may go back to the seventeenth century, and the oldest "titty" in the *Oxford English Dictionary* appears as "tetty" in 1746: "Es wont ha' ma Tetties a grabbled zo" (*An Exmoor Courtship, Gentleman's Magazine,* June). "Tit" also has had a wide variety of other meanings, most of them revolving around the idea of something young, small, or both, as a girl (especially a hussy, a "little tit" being equivalent to a "little chit"); a horse (often a filly); a kitten ("Here tit, tit," was the same as "Here puss, puss"); or a bird (e.g., titlark, titmouse, tomtit). But in the last 100 years, the anatomical sense has become so dominant that hardly anyone ever offers to give "tit for tat" anymore, even though "tit" here actually has nothing to do with "breast," being merely an alliterative conversion of "tip." The original meaning of the expression probably amounted to "blow for blow." For more about breasts, see BOSOM.

tochus. The ass. See TUSHIE.

toilet. A place and a thing that can be discussed only in euphemistic terms for the simple reason that the English language, despite its rich vocabulary, lacks any noneuphemistic words for them.

"Toilet" is a rather recent French import. It comes from *toilette*, dressing room, which is a diminutive of *toile*, cloth. "Toilet" was used in English in various ways before it reached its present state. Thus, from the seventeenth century, the "toilet" was the process of dressing, and in the eighteenth century a "toilet call" was the formal reception of visitors by a lady of fashion while she was in the final stages of making herself fashionable. In the nineteenth century, people began to speak of "toilet articles," "toilet pails" (for slops), "toilet paper" (*Oxford English Dictionary*: "soft paper prepared for shaving, hair-curling, use in lavatories, etc."), and "toilet rooms." The use of "toilet room" in the euphemistic sense of "bathroom" or "lavatory," as contrasted with the original sense of "dressing room," seems to have been an American innovation of the late nineteenth century. Today, the French themselves go to *les toilettes* (or *les cabinets*—*cabinet d'aisances*, in full) when they are not making use of the English WC. French also glories in the explicit *pissoir*, for a public urinal, but this, too, has been euphemized as the VESPASIENNE. The languages of other peoples reveal similar hang-ups. As noted by Mario Pei: "In South Africa they call it 'P.K.,' an abbreviation for the Kaffir *picanin kyah*, 'little house.' Germany has *abort* ('away place'); . . . Spanish and Italian use words which mean 'retreat'; Russian *ubornaya* means 'adornment place' . . ." (*The Story of Language*, 1965). And so it goes. The Dutch call it a *bestekamer* (best room) and the Melanesian islanders even have a Pidgin euphemism: *house-peck-peck*.

In the absence of any precise English word for what we now call a "toilet," euphemisms have flourished, their sheer number indicating the strength of the underlying taboo. For example, out of the pages of history, as well as from our own times, we have such picturesque expressions as:

> *Ajax* (a pun on the older "a jakes," for a chamber pot, popularized by Sir John Harington, Rabelaisian wit and ingenious contriver, who gave his plan for a flush toilet in 1596 in *The Metamorphosis of Ajax*); *altar room, amenity;*
>
> BATHROOM, *bog house* (or *shop*) and *bogs* (from "bog," an old word meaning "To exonerate the bowels," *OED*);
>
> *cabinet; can* (perhaps originally referring to a toilet with a replaceable can beneath the seat);
>
> *Cannes* (a famous watering place); CHAMBER; *chamber of commerce; Chick Sale* (an outhouse of the 1920s, after a comedian who produced a much-admired book on the subject); *cloaca,* CLOAKROOM; *closet* (or *seat*) *of ease* (see EASE); COMFORT STATION; COMMODE; CONVENIENCE; *crap house* (with many variants: *crapper, crappery, crapping castle,* etc.—see CRAP);
>
> *Deauville* (another famous watering place); *dooly; doniker; dunniken* (? "dung" + "ken," i.e., "house");
>
> EARTH CLOSET; *Egypt;*
>
> FACILITY;
>
> *gab room* (for women only); *garderobe* (in medieval castles, and originally a place for keeping clothes, from *garde-r,* keep + *robe*); *growler;*

halfway house; HEAD; *hers/his; holy of holies; honey house* (a septic tank is a *honey bucket*); *house of ease* (or *office*);

IT;

jakes; jane; Joe; JOHN; *Jones' place; jordan* (see LEAK);

LADIES/GENTLEMEN (with many variants: *little girls/boys room, women/men,* etc.); *last resort;* LATRINE; LAVATORY; LOO;

marble palace; member (or *thunder*) *mug* (see MEMBER); MISS WHITE; *Mrs. Jones; municipal relief station* (see RELIEVE);

necessary house (or *place* or *stool:* see NECESSARY); *no-man's-land* (for women only);

old soldiers' home, OUTHOUSE;

peers/peeresses (British); *place; poet's corner; potty* (see WEE WEE); POWDER ROOM; *private office;* PRIVY;

REST ROOM; RETIRING ROOM; *retreat; Ruth;*

sanctuary; sanctum sanctorum; smokehouse; statehouse; STOOL;

temple; THRONE (and *throne room*);

UTENSIL;

WALK; WASHROOM; WASTE-MANAGEMENT COMPARTMENT; WC; WHAT-YOU-MAY-CALL'EM, and *Widow Jones.*

tool. (1) the penis, (2) a weapon, usually (today) a gun. Both usages are old, both were originally Standard English, and both are now considered slang.

As a penis: When a crowd of people get into the palace yard toward the end of William Shakespeare's *Henry VIII* (1613), the porter wonders if "have we some strange Indian with the great tool come to Court, the women so besiege us." Then there are the instructions for a modern Japanese device for increasing a man's sexual prowess: "MORE BIG, OR RUBBER BAND. This may be used by men who have small tools in order to increase sexual pleasure which give unexplainable feeling to women" (from Shirley Green, *The Curious History of Contraception,* 1971).

The "tool" as "weapon" was originally a sword, which is what Chaucer meant in *The Nun's Priest's Tale* (ca. 1387–1400) when cataloging the virtues of a chivalric lover: "We allen desiren, if it myghte be/To han . . . no fool/Ne hym that is agast [afraid] of every tool." More recently, explaining the dramatic reduction in the number of civilians killed by cops in New York City (from 90 in 1971 to 13 in the first half of 1974), the police department's top firearms instructor explained: "We're using weapons less. We're teaching that the gun is designed as a defensive tool" (*New York Times,* 9/23/74). Or, as Agriculture Secretary-designate John R. Block said, when conceding that he had been "a little harsh" in suggesting that food could be used as a "weapon" in United States foreign policy: "Perhaps I should have said a tool for peace, an instrument for peace" ("Good Morning America," WABC-TV, 12/26/80). See also GUN, INSTRUMENT, and PENIS.

top secret. A common governmental COVER-UP for that which is embarrassing or criminal. "Under our system, the American people would not tolerate censorship. Yet, we have high officials who want to protect themselves from embarrassment. So when a document arrives on their desk showing that they have mismanaged their agency, they stamp it TOP SECRET" (Jack Anderson, interview, *Book Review Digest*, 5/79). See also SENSITIVE and, for an example of a "TOP SECRET" plan that included admittedly illegal features, refer to SURREPTITIOUS ENTRY.

touch. To kill. From the diary of Sgt. Alvin York, the World War I hero: "There were thirty of them in continuous action, and all I could do was touch the Germans off as fast as I could. . . . In order to sight me or swing their machine guns on me, the Germans had to show their heads above the trench, and every time I saw a head I just touched it off. . . . Suddenly a German officer and five men jumped out of the trench and charged me with fixed bayonets. I changed to the old automatic and just touched them off, too. I touched off the sixth man first, then the fifth, then the fourth, then the third, and so on. I wanted them to keep coming" (Tom Skeyhill, ed., *Sergeant York, His Own Life Story and War Diary*, 1928).

The very oldest of the many meanings of "touch" involves a hit, stroke, or blow, and this may have been the original sense of the word. Thus, the understated "touch" for "kill" parallels the more common HIT. "Touch" also has acquired other euphemistic meanings. For example, to say that "poor Louise is touched" or "touched in the head" is to say that she is slightly crazy, cracked, insane, or mentally deranged (see MENTAL). The generalized "touch" also has served as a euphemism for close, sexual contact, e.g., ". . . this woman/Most wrongfully accused your substitute,/Who is as free from touch or soil with her/As she from one ungot [i.e., unbegotten]" (William Shakespeare, *Measure for Measure*, ca. 1604).

See also BITE THE DUST.

toupee. A small wig or HAIRPIECE—the French (from *toupet*, a tuft of hair or forelock) helping to hide the baldness. Alexander Pope misguessed when he wrote in *Art of Politicks* (1729):

> Think we that modern words eternal are?
> Toupet, and Tompion, Cosins, and Colmar
> Hereafter will be called by some plain man
> A Wig, a Watch, a Pair of Stays, a Fan.

As for those "stays," their functional equivalent today is the FOUNDATION GARMENT.

tourist. Second class—or worse; a face-saving euphemism for ticket buyers who cannot afford first class but are embarrassed to ask for second or third. "On cruises the QE2 is a one-class ship, but on trans-Atlantic crossings she has two classes—tourist and first" (*New York Times*, 12/4/77). This euphemism is by no means new. From 1895, and the *Oxford English Dictionary*: "The *emigrant sleeping car* is now usually called a *tourist-car*, the latter being preferred by those who patronize them" (John C. Wait, *The Car-Builder's Dictionary*).

With so many carriers offering so many different plans, it is hard to be precise, but where "tourist" equals second class, the euphemism for third class usually is "coach." Another variation is "economy," which stands for "cheap," and may signify either second or third class. Compounding confusion, the euphemism for "second class" becomes FIRST CLASS when "first class" itself is euphemized as DELUXE. If all this sounds like a plot to befuddle the public, that is probably because it is.

traffic expediter. A shipping clerk. Originally a religious term, similar to cleric or clergyman, "clerk" came to signify notarial and secretarial work during the Middle Ages when jobs of this sort were held by religious clerks, who were practically the only people who could read and write. The title was an honorable one then, since "clerk" was considered the equivalent of "scholar," but years of humble work have given the title humble connotations, with the result that modern clerks are as glad to have new handles for themselves, such as *traffic expediter,* as secretaries are to blossom into ADMINISTRATIVE ASSISTANTS.

trail representative. A hired gun in the Old (ca. 1885) West. ". . . a stray calf lost a lot of its appeal when you knew that all the big ranchers moving cattle were paying five or six hired guns, whom they called 'trail representatives' and everybody else called 'enforcers'" (Jane Kramer, *The Last Cowboy,* 1977). See also REPRESENTATIVE.

tramp. A Hollywood euphemism of the 1930s and 1940s, either for a woman of low morals or a man who was a bum. In the first, feminine sense, "tramp" might connote either a cheap whore or a person of higher socioeconomic status who gave out freebies. In the second, masculine sense, "tramp" seems to have been used in order to avoid offending the British, who, when "bum" was mentioned, looked first to their POSTERIORS. It was for this reason that the title of Al Jolson's *Hallelujah I'm a Bum* was changed to *Hallelujah I'm a Tramp* when the picture was shown in England in 1938. (H. L. Mencken, *The American Language, Supplement I,* 1945).

  Although bums spend a lot of time sitting down upon theirs, the vagrant "bum" and the anatomical "bum" do not seem to be connected linguistically. The vagrant "bum" probably is an abbreviation of "bummer," meaning "loafer" or "sponger," which was first recorded in 1855 (Mitford M. Mathews, *A Dictionary of Americanisms,* 1951) and may ultimately come from the German *bummler,* an idler. The anatomical "bum," meanwhile, is a far older word, with the first example in the *Oxford English Dictionary* coming from 1387. Probably not a contraction of BOTTOM, as some have speculated, but of onomatopoetic origin, this "bum" may be related to similar-sounding words with the general meaning of "protuberance" or "swelling," e. g., bumb, an old word for "pimple," and bump. See also ARSE and PROSTITUTE.

transfer of population. Mass eviction and/or deportation. "Millions of peasants are robbed of their farms and sent trudging along roads with no more than they can carry: this is called *transfer of population* or *rectification of frontiers* (George Orwell, "Politics and the English Language," 1946). See also GENERATE/GENERATION.

triage. A soft word for hardhearted neglect. From the French *trier,* to pick or to cull (see CULL), the term began as a method for grading farm products, was later applied to people, and finally to entire nations.

trick

As traditionally practiced, *triage* involves a division into thirds, according to quality. In the eighteenth and nineteenth centuries, for example, coffee beans were separated into three grades, with the lowest, composed of broken beans, being known as "triage coffee." It was during World War I that the French army (which also gave us MATERIEL and PERSONNEL) popularized *triage* as a method for determining which wounded soldiers not to bother treating. As explained by John Keegan in *The Face of Battle* (1976):

> There remained, nevertheless, a brutal selectivity about military surgery which the practitioners did their best to hide from the patients but could not disguise from themselves. It was called "triage" . . . and [it] required surgeons, from the press of casualties flowing in during a battle, to send on those who could stand the journey and to choose, from the group remaining, which men were worth subjecting to serious surgery and which must be left to die; the greater the press of casualties, the larger the latter group.

Finally, in the widest, most modern sense, there is *triage* on the global scale, e.g.: "Triage—a nice clean jargon term for the rather dirty prospect of writing off whole nations who are beyond 'realistic help' and leaving them to suffer while we save the rest of the world from disaster" (John Gribbin, *Future Worlds*, ms, 1978).

See also BENIGN NEGLECT and NO MAYDAY, as well as the basic military CASUALTY.

trick. While the word does have other meanings (e.g., a crime, a jail sentence, a military enlistment), its usual connotations today are sexual. Thus, a *trick* may be a woman (the implication being that she is a PROSTITUTE) or, more commonly, her customer (a JOHN), as from *Bawdyhouse Blues*, a very old jazz song:

> Keep a-knockin' but you can't come in.
> I hear you knockin', but you can't come in.
> I got an all night trick again;
> I'm busy grindin' so you can't come in.
> If you love me, you'll come back again,
> Come back tomorrow at half-past ten.

A customer who engages in unusual or UNNATURAL acts is a *freak trick*. The woman, meanwhile, may also use the word as a verb, e.g., "I tricked with him," or "I just tricked two johns from Nashville." (A companion to *tricking* is *creeping*, which is what the prostitute's girl friend under the bed does in order to steal the wallet of the john, while he is otherwise engaged.) Finally, if the prostitute gets pregnant, the result may be a *trick baby*, formerly known, if male, as a whoreson, or BASTARD.

trouble/troublesome. Disaster/disastrous.

"Trouble" comes in an infinite variety of forms. Some persons have *trouble with the bottle*, in which case they are alcoholics; others *get into trouble*, in which case they have broken a law in some way; and still others *have a trouble* or *get in* (as opposed to *into*) *trouble*, in which case they are female-type PERSONS who have become pregnant without being married. For example, Joan Durbeyfield advised her errant daughter on no account to "say a word of your Bygone Trouble to him. . . . Many a woman—some of the Highest in the Land—have had a Trouble in their time; and why should you Trumpet yours when others don't Trumpet Theirs?" (Thomas Hardy, *Tess of the D'Urbervilles*, 1891).

"Trouble" also makes an excellent blanket for covering things up, e.g.: "A 'troubled child' may be anything from a bed-wetter to a junior grade Jack the Ripper" (Gary Jennings, *Personalities of Language*, 1965). In the plural, the term refers, of course, to Europe's oldest, established, permanent, floating war: the *Troubles* in Northern Ireland. Finally, in the *troublesome*, or disastrous, category, there was the tape recording of the conversation in which President Richard M. Nixon appeared to approve (see EXPLETIVE DELETED) the payment of hush money to E. Howard Hunt, Jr., the Watergate PLUMBER. The president's chief of staff reports: "Then he asked me to listen and take notes on the March 21, 1973, 'troublesome' conference with John Dean—and I ended up with a perjury charge" (H. R. Haldeman, with Joseph DiMona, *The Ends of Power*, 1978). See also PROBLEM.

TS. Tough shit; also euphemized as "tough situation." In the military during World War II, one of the standard retorts to a person whose never-ending complaints had become intolerable was "Fill out a T.S. slip and send it to the chaplain." Some chaplains went so far as to have *TS* slips printed and ready for use. See also BS.

tummy aka **tum** and **tum-tum.** The belly; a nursery-ism, especially beloved by manufacturers of elastic underwear, e.g.: "Hi—I'm Barbara Eden. In the blink of an eye, I made my tummy disappear" (pantyhose ad, WABC-TV, 10/6/79). Which is not to imply that *only* underwear-makers use it: ". . . the hunchback . . . swiftly forced the hand across the panty sheen of her rounded tummy . . ." (Maxwell Kenton, aka Terry Southern, *Candy*, 1965).

The strength of the desire to avoid "belly" is indicated by the euphemism's survival in the face of withering critical fire, e.g.: "*Tummy* is simply disgusting when used by anyone over the age of four" (Bergen Evans and Cornelia Evans, *A Dictionary of Contemporary American Usage*, 1957). Or, as E.B. White advises: "Never call a stomach a tummy without good reason" (William Strunk, Jr., and E. B. White, *The Elements of Style*, 1959). See also ABDOMEN and INTESTINAL FORTITUDE.

turf accountant. A British gentleman's gentlemanly bookie; also called a *commission agent.* Even the basic "bookmaker" has a euphemistic quality to it since, as John Moore points out, "'making a book' seems politer than 'laying the odds'" (*You English Words*, 1961). See also SPECULATE.

turn. To become black; said of neighborhoods. "Although the problems of the city have touched most of the parkway only lightly, there is a distinct fear, especially among those who left racially changing areas in Borough Park and Brownsville, that the neighborhood will 'turn'" (*New York Times*, 1/20/74). Neighborhoods that are kept from *turning* may be described as HARMONIOUS.

tushie, tushy, tush. The ass. ". . . he shakes his tushie with elegant languor" (*New York Post*, 7/23/74).

"Tushie" is a softened version of the Yiddish "tochis," itself spelled variously as *tochos, tochus, tockis, tokas, tokus, tuchis,* and *tuckus.* Whatever the form, the meaning is the same. For example, consider the irate telegram from a writer to a magazine editor who had dropped his column but suggested a face-saving way for the columnist to bow out: "IF YOU WRITE THAT I HAVE GONE ON A SABBATICAL KNOWING THAT IT IS A LIE, I WILL FLOG YOUR TOKAS" (*MORE*, 12/76).

"Tushie/tochos" have been further euphemized in the abbreviations T.O.T. and T.L. The first has been translated variously as *tochis afn tish, tochos oif'n tisch,* and *tookhus auf den tish.* In any case, the meaning is "ass on the table," and the expression is used to describe transactions that are consummated in cash only. Thus, in the furniture business, a couch that is sold T.O.T. must be paid for right away. Or a T.O.T. card game is one in which all losses must be paid immediately, with no credit allowed. T.L., meanwhile, stands for *toches lecker,* a Yiddish phrase delicately translated in *American Speech* (10/47) as "backside kisser."

"T.L." is an example of an abbreviation whose meaning changes considerably depending on the age and ethnic extraction of the user. From one Jewish adult to another, it is, of course, a passably polite way of expressing an impolite thought. However, when one *goy* kid says to another, "I've got a T.L. for you," the initials stand merely for "trade last," by which the speaker means that he or she has a compliment to give (typically, one that originated with a third party), but that the T.L.-user wants to hear something nice about himself or herself before passing it on. Finally, "T.O.T." should not be confused with another Jewish abbreviation, "M.O.T.," which stands for "Member of Our Tribe," as in "He's a M.O.T.," or "That's a M.O.T. fraternity" (*American Speech*, 12/48).

See also ARSE and SHMO.

TV. In personal ads, not "television," but "transvestite" or "transvestism:" "YOUR personal fantasy is MY reality . . . . I specialize in: Bondage, Humiliation, . . . T V." (ad, *Screw*, 8/2/76). See also S/M.

unauthorized use of a motor vehicle. Automobile theft by a white youngster, as distinguished from grand larceny, which is almost always the charge for the same crime when the youngster is black. This distinction was cited as one of a number of "shocking disparities" in the treatment of children of different races and ethnic backgrounds in a 1973 New York Judicial Conference analysis of family court cases. See also APPROPRIATE.

underachiever. A goof-off; educationese.

underarm wetness. Sweat; a Madison Avenue creation and, actually, a double-euphemism, the "underarm" standing for "armpit."

"Zirconium, added to some antiperspirants as an ultimate defense against—pardon the expression—underarm wetness, is suspected of causing serious lung damage" (*New Republic*, 8/29/75). See also ANTIPERSPIRANT and PERSPIRE.

underdeveloped. Poor, backward, primitive; a second-order euphemism (for the sequence, see the third-order DEVELOPING). "It is this concern for sensibilities that gave birth to a euphemism; for it set into motion the search for the softer word, the blunted explanation, the circumlocution aimed at mitigating the harshness of a conclusion, or an evaluation. Thus we . . . speak of . . . 'underdeveloped' when we mean primitive . . . and of 'unaware' when we mean ignorant" (William F. Buckley, Jr., *Up from Liberalism*, 1968).

Underdeveloped lands are usually considered to be foreign lands, making "underdeveloped" more or less an international counterpart to UNDERPRIVILEGED. Occasionally, however, *underdeveloped* parts of the United States are recognized as such, e.g.: "It [the rubber-producing guayule bush] also promises to make federal research dollars flow into underdeveloped areas of the southwestern United States" (*Science*, 10/27/78). See also NATIVE and PRELITERATE.

underprivileged. Poor, usually black or Hispanic. "The university [of Washington] rejected the use of such categories as 'underprivileged' and 'disadvantaged' as being mere euphemisms for the racial classifications they were using openly" (*New York Times*, 4/12/74).

A neologism of the 1930s, when the Great Depression reduced practically everyone to poverty, "underprivileged" originally had a wider, whiter meaning than today. Now it is the domestic equivalent of the international UNDERDEVELOPED (usually applied to nonwhite nations). Which does not mean that "underprivileged" cannot be used in fun, e.g.: "My heart goes out to the underprivileged and that includes people who can't carry a tune and anyone who plays the tuba in public" (Judy Linscott, *Brooklyn* [NY] *Phoenix*, 12/7/78). See also DISADVANTAGED.

understudy. A musician in a feather bed, i.e., one who is hired only to satisfy a requirement that orchestras be of a certain size, regardless of whether all instruments are needed. "Understudy," naturally, is the term the musicians use for themselves; to the people who have to hire them, they are "walkers"—because the hardest part of their job is walking to the theater to get their pay.

undies. Women's underwear; the baby talk changes the frame of reference from adult to prepuberty, thereby desexualizing the subject. (PANTIES work much the same way.)

"Undies" seems to be a British invention of the World War I period, when women's underwear underwent revolutionary changes, as the corset was dropped and the BRASSIERE put on. The oldest example of "undies" in the *Oxford English Dictionary* comes from *Chambers's Journal* (12/1918): "Manufacturing women's under-wear, or 'undies' as they are coyly called, is the greatest commercial industry here." About the best that can be said for "undies" is that it is not quite as gooey as another British term for the same thing, *neathies*—an abbreviation of "neathie-set." Other kinds of babyish clothes, worn by twentieth-century adult women next to their skins, include: *dainties, flimsies, frillies, pullies, pretties, pretty-pretties, scanties, teddies* or *teddy bears* (a one-piece undergarment, combining CHEMISE and drawers, particularly popular in the twenties), *thesies-and-thosies,* and, in wintertime, *fuzzy-wuzzies* and *woollies.* See also LINGERIE and UNMENTIONABLES.

undocumented person (or **worker**). One who has gained unauthorized entry into the United States; a wetback. "Sometimes even euphemisms have euphemisms: *Wetbacks* (a derogation of Mexicans swimming the Rio Grande to slip into the United States) became *illegal aliens,* and are now referred to as *undocumented persons.*" (William Safire, *New York Times Magazine,* 7/23/78). See also DOCUMENT and ILLEGAL.

undoubtedly. Unproved; a signal to the knowing reader to begin doubting. From the *Oxford English Dictionary:* "They affirme undoubtedlie that the deveil plaieth Succubus to the man" (Reginald Scot, *The Discoverie of Witchcraft,* 1584). See also DOUBTLESS.

unfortunate. A Victorian whore; a euphemistic shortening of the apparently older "unfortunate woman," a term that seems to have been devised by "fortunate" women. At least, Capt. Francis Grose defined "unfortunate women" as "Prostitutes; so termed by the compassionate and virtuous of their own sex" (*A Classical Dictionary of the Vulgar Tongue,* 1796). For more about the many words used in place of "whore," see PROSTITUTE.

unfortunate interruption. A war—and an example of the "euphemistic genius" of some of the more rabid anglophiles in Hamburg, Germany, who prefer to gloss over the temporary breach in relations between their country and England caused by World War II (noted by Jane Kramer, *The New Yorker,* 3/20/78). "Unfortunate interruption" has essentially the same appeal to Germans as LATE UNPLEASANTNESS does to American Southerners of the unreconstructed variety.

unit. A bomb—and an uncanny, unofficial parallel to the terminology of official, government bomb-makers in Los Alamos, New Mexico.

Discussing the *modus operandi* of George Metesky, a seemingly gentle resident of Waterbury, Connecticut, who habitually rose early on weekday mornings, put on a business suit, and then, after his two sisters went off to their jobs, hopped into his Daimler and drove it 80-odd feet to the family garage: "Once in the garage workshop he would change to overalls and build what he still calls his 'units.' He assembled their charges with gun powder taken from rifle bullets" (*New York Times*, 12/13/73). Metesky built an unknown number of *units* during the 1940s and 1950s, taking them by Daimler to New York City, then transferring to subway to spot them around town. Thirty-seven of his *units* went off, wounding a few people seriously but killing no one. He always gave advance warning and even halted operations during World War II out of "patriotism." Finally caught in 1957, he spent the next 17 years in a STATE HOSPITAL. Mr. Metesky is best remembered by New Yorkers by his sobriquet, "The Mad Bomber."

For the terminology of the sane citizens of Los Alamos, see DEVICE.

Universal Time. Greenwich Mean Time. *Universal Time* is reckoned from the same meridian as Greenwich Mean Time—so-called because the meridian runs through the London borough in which the Royal Observatory is located. The cosmic name is preferred by those who wish to demonstrate that their mental horizons are no longer bound by those of planet Earth, but it does seem a mite pretentious. One can't help wondering how often *UT* is used for synchronizing watches by the BEM (Bug-Eyed Monsters) that are said to inhabit other worlds. It seems possible, too, that the BEM have a different idea of what constitutes MU (Miss Universe). See also PERPETUAL CARE and WORLD SERIES.

university. College. That the proliferation of *universities* on the American landscape diluted the term somewhat is revealed, albeit unintentionally, by the boast of a patriot of the 1870s: "There are two universities in England, four in France, ten in Prussia, and thirty-seven in Ohio" (from Arthur M. Schlesinger and Dixon Ryan Fox, eds., *A History of American Life*, 1927). The distinction between "college" and "university" began to be drawn more carefully after the founding of Johns Hopkins University in 1876. Still, some 60 years later, H. L. Mencken could note: "Euphemisms for things are almost as common in the United States as euphemisms for avocations. Dozens of forlorn little fresh-water colleges are called *universities* . . ." (*The American Language*, 1936). See also CITY.

unmentionables. The ultimate euphemism, not merely softening the offending word but blotting it out altogether. Apparently a product of the early nineteenth century, "unmentionables" originally stood for breeches and trousers, e.g., "A blue coat . . . with a pair of blue 'unmentionables,' white fleecy stockings, and short black gaiters . . ." (William Glascock, *Sailors and Saints; or Matrimonial Manoeuvres*, 1829). In our own century, now that it is permissible to refer publicly to men's outerwear, "unmentionables" has taken on new life as a euphemism for the underwear of children and women (a common coupling; see PANTIES and UNDIES). Because women wear so many different kinds of underclothes, it is sometimes necessary to be more precise, referring to their *lower unmentionables* and their *upper unmentionables* (see BRASSIERE). In speaking of children, the single word will do, e.g., "His little man-o'-war top and unmentionables were full of sand . . ." (James Joyce, *Ulysses*, 1922).

"Unmentionables" is one of a long series of similar euphemisms for trousers and associated garments—not the oldest (that honor seems to go to

unnatural

INEXPRESSIBLES, ca. 1790), but the one that is showing the most staying power. Herewith, a list of "unmentionable's" mentionable synonyms: *indescribables, indispensables, ineffables, in-* (and *un-)explicables, inexpressibles, innominables, unhintables, unspeakables, untalkaboutables, unutterables,* and *unwhisperables.* It would be too much to hope that this listing is complete. In addition, there are the allied *don't-mention'ems* and *mustn't-mention'ems* (both women's underwear); *conveniences, etherials, nether garments, netherlings* (all trousers); the marginally more specific *sit-in'ems, sit-down-upons,* and *sit-upons* (more trousers); *small clothes* (breeches); and *subtrousers* (underdrawers). Though some of these terms may have been introduced in fun, the original impulse and its many permutations are a tribute to the strength of the taboo against "leg," which is so strong that people don't even want to talk about the clothing that comes in contact with the lower EXTREMITY. See also LIMB and SIT-ME-DOWN-(UPON).

unnatural. Homosexual—and a loaded word if there ever was one, the meaning depending entirely upon the proclivities of the user. For example, consider the parade of subjective terms in the following definition of "unnatural carnal copulation," offered in 1967 by the Louisiana Supreme Court. Opined the court: ". . . this phrase simply means 'any and all carnal copulation or sexual joining and coition that is devious and abnormal because it is contrary to the natural traits and/or instincts intended by nature, and therefore does not conform to the order ordained by nature'" (from Jonathan Katz, *Gay American History,* 1976). Of course, it is impossible to tell from the court's definition just what all the shooting was about—a common symptom of euphemistic talk. In this case, the *unnatural* crime was "oral copulation" between two women (i.e., CUNNILINGUS). The women had been sentenced to 30 months in jail for what they did, and the state supreme court affirmed their convictions.

"Unnatural" has been used in this same, formless sense for many years. For example, from Katz's work one also learns that in 1636, the Reverend John Cotton (grandfather of Cotton Mather) wanted "unnatural filthiness" to be punishable by death in the Massachusetts Bay Colony. To a later generation, the fighting phrase was "unnatural familiarity." Here is how a committee of the Unitarian Church of Brewster, Massachusetts, reported in 1866 on the actions of a man who was soon to win fame for his books about boys:

> That Horatio Alger, Jr., who has officiated as our Minister for about 15 months has recently been charged with gross immorality and a most heinous crime, a crime of no less magnitude than the abominable and revolting crime of unnatural familiarity with *boys.* . . . the committee sent for Alger and to him specified the charges and evidence of his guilt which he neither denied or attempted to extenuate but received it with apparent calmness of an old offender—and hastily left town on the very next train for parts unknown. (From Katz, *op. cit.*)

Of course, society's rather fuzzy definitions of what is "natural" and what isn't go back to the Bible, e.g., ". . . even their women did change the natural use into that which is against nature: And likewise also the men, leaving the natural use of the woman, burned in their lust one toward another . . ." (Epistle of Paul, the Apostle, to the Romans, I, 26–27, King James Version, 1611). Society's heavy penalties for *unnatural* acts also are sanctioned by the Bible· 'If a man also lie with mankind, as he lieth with a woman, both of them have committed an abomination: they shall surely be put to death; their blood *shall be* upon them" (Leviticus, XX, 13, King James Version). See also GAY and LIE/LIE WITH.

unthinkable. Unspeakable, usually with the implication that the *unthinkable* thought is unspeakable because it is immoral. Since anything the mind conceives is "thinkable," the grotesque "unthinkable" actually is an interior contradiction. If the term has any meaning at all, it is as a shorthand description of thoughts of things that are so numerous or so nebulous that the mind is unable to fully grasp them. The word is an old one, dating to at least the fifteenth century, but its present popularity is due to the *unthinkable* thoughts (*On Thermonuclear War*, 1959, and *Thinking About the Unthinkable*, 1962) of Herman Kahn, the 350-pound guru of Hudson Institute (an *unthinkable* tank?). After thinking about it in excruciating detail, Kahn decided that thermonuclear war was tolerable ("people can and do rise to the occasion"), a judgment that most lesser minds felt was immoral as well as wrongheaded. For some of those who thought differently about this *unthinkable*, see the opinions of John F. Kennedy in EXCHANGE, Robert S. McNamara in STRATEGIC, and Morton Halperin in TACTICAL NUCLEAR WEAPON.

upchuck. To puke or vomit. Back in the Roaring Twenties and Depressing Thirties, when college students swallowed quantities of alcohol as well as goldfish, "puke" and "vomit" were considered to be coarse words, while "upchuck" was smart. See also MOTION DISCOMFORT and STOMACHACHE.

urinate/urination. Medical Latin for "piss." "Urination is easy to avoid as a word, if not as a process; the commonly used term, verb or noun, process or object, is *piss*" (Edward Sagarin, *The Anatomy of Dirty Words*, 1962). Compared to DEFECATE/DEFECATION, whose present meanings go back only to the nineteenth century, "urinate" and "urination" are relatively antique, having been employed in their modern senses at least since the sixteenth century, while doctors have been asking their patients to piss into glass vials called "urinals" since the thirteenth. Those who enjoy the sport of skindiving may be interested to know that they were once known as "urinators," e.g.: "It is observed, that a barrell or cap . . . will not serve a Urinator or Diver for respiration" (Bishop John Wilkins, *Mathematicall Magick; or, The Wonders That May Be Performed by Mechanicall Geometry*, 1648). See also PEE.

utensil. A chamber pot, i.e., in full, "a chamber utensil." Thus, from Jonathan Swift's "Strephon and Chloe" (1731):

> The nymph . . .
> Steals out her hand, by nature led,
> And brings a vessel into bed;
> Fair utensil, as smooth and white
> As Chloe's skin, almost as bright.

See also CHAMBER and TOILET.

V 🐦

Vagina. The most common Latin substitute for one of the most tabooed of the
FOUR-LETTER WORDS, "cunt." "Vagina" means "sheath" in Latin (to the Romans,
the PENIS was a *gladius*, or sword), and it has been in the English language for only
three centuries or so. The oldest example of "vagina" in the *Oxford English
Dictionary* comes from 1682 (predating the first "penis" by two years). "Cunt," by
contrast, is a legitimate (nonslang) language word of the very oldest stock. It has
cognates in the Romance languages (the French *con* and the Latin *cunnus*) as well
as Old Norse (*kunta*), Old Frisian (*kunte*), and even, from a language that may
stem from Europe's Stone Age, cave-dwelling inhabitants, the Basque (*kuna*). It
also has suspicious resemblances to, among other words, "cunabula," a cradle or
place where anything is nurtured at its beginning (and hence, also, to
"incunabula"); to "cunicle," an obsolete word for an underground passage; to
"coney," an old word for RABBIT, a critter that lives in "cunicular" passages or
burrows; and to QUEEN. Meanwhile, the Latin *cunnus* also has given us *cunnilingus*.

The Romans extended the meaning of *cunnus* to include "whore," in much
the same way that English-speakers have used "cunt" as a pejorative term for
"woman" as well as for the anatomical part. As long ago as the first century B.C.
Cicero held that *cunnus* should be avoided as obscene, but English-speakers have
not always been so fastidious. The City of London once (ca. 1230) boasted a
Gropecuntelane and Geoffrey Chaucer used the word unblushingly in his
Canterbury Tales (ca. 1387–1400), though with a different spelling. As the lusty,
much-married Wife of Bath put it in the Prologue to her tale:

> What eyleth yow to grucche thus and grone?
> Is it for ye wolde have my queynte allone?

As times became more refined, however, people began to shy away from the old
word. Thus, William Shakespeare titillated his audience by spelling out what was
fast becoming unpronounceable (in public, at least) even among otherwise frank-
speaking Elizabethans. In *Twelfth Night* (1600–01), the steward, Malvolio, upon
picking up a letter, deciphers the handwriting (mistakenly, as it happens, the
letter being forged) this way:

> By my life, this is my lady's hand.
> These be her very C's, her U's, and ['n]
> her T's; and thus makes she her great P's.

This indirect mention (and a visual pun, too, since "cut" meant the same
thing in Elizabethan slang) was practically the last appearance of the term in
aboveground literature for the next 300 years. Dirty-minded boys might scrawl it
on walls (see MONOSYLLABLE) and bawdy poets might dare it occasionally, as in
The Royal Angler or *Windsor*, a ditty on the subject of Charles II's Nell Gwyn,
commonly though perhaps mistakenly attributed to John Wilmost, second earl of
Rochester (1647–1680).

> However weak and slender be the string
> Bait it with Cunt, and it will hold a king.

Not long after this (ca. 1700), society closed ranks even more, and use of the word, previously regarded as vulgar, was deemed to be obscene in a legal, prosecutable sense. Even Capt. Francis Grose, though his subject was slang, dared not print the word in full, resorting to asterisks when defining such terms as "biter," i.e., "A wench whose **** is ready to bite her a-se; a lascivious, rampant wench" (*A Classical Dictionary of the Vulgar Tongue*, 1796). A similar f⸱ befell Robert Burns: When his *Merrie Muses of Caledonia* (ca. 1800) finally was pu lished (1911), his language was toned down for public consumption thusly:

> For ilka hair upon her c——t,
> Was worth a royal ransom.

And Eric Partridge, the great modern authority on slang, still was requireu ⸲ use dashes when annotating Grose in 193⸳, e.g.: "Among the soldiers in 1914–1918 the word was perhaps heard most often in some such phrase as 'you silly *or* great c——,' though its literal application was frequent."

The euphemistic dashes might have been eliminated sooner if Sir James Murray, editor of the *Oxford English Dictionary*, had not had a failure of nerve when the C's went to press in 1888–93, "cunt" being one of the two (the other is "fuck") most conspicuous omissions from the monumental, standard-setting *Oxford English Dictionary* (to which, curiously, other "vulgarisms," such as "cock," "prick," and "twat" were admitted). As it was, the beginning of the word's return to public printability, if not respectability, can be dated to James Joyce's *Ulysses* (published in 1922 but banned from the United States until 1931), in which Leopold Bloom ruminates on, among other things, the geography of the Holy Land and the Dead Sea, or, as he thought of it, "the grey sunken cunt of the world." Of course, the taboo did not collapse because of this single breach. Even after the Second World War, which, like the First, helped loosen the restrictions on language, "cunt" (along with "prick") was excised from the manuscript of James Jones's *From Here to Eternity* (1951), though many a "fuck" and "shit" was allowed to stand (Edward Sagarin, *The Anatomy of Dirty Words*, 1962). Not until D. H. Lawrence's *Lady Chatterley's Lover* (1928) was finally cleared legally for publication in the United States (1959) and in the United Kingdom (1960) did it become entirely safe to print all the words that schoolchildren know—and which the Wife of Bath used unblushingly nearly 600 years ago.

As a result of the long-standing ban on "cunt," a host of euphemisms and circumlocutions have been created to fill the linguistic vacuum. Their number reflects the strength of the underlying taboo and also, apparently, the amount of gossiping that men do about sex, it being mainly the words of men that are preserved in literature.

Some 650 synonyms for the dread word (about double the number for "prick") are included in the great *Slang and Its Analogues* (J. S. Farmer and W. E. Henley, 1890–94) and it seems unlikely that twentieth-century man, even with his febrile imagination, has been able to add many terms to this remarkable list. Herewith, a lightly annotated sampling of synonyms, grouped in three categories: the general, the physical, and the poetical:

vagina

1. General, more-or-less opaque references, some of which served for the PENIS, too: *article,* BUSINESS; *commodity* ("the private parts of a modest woman, and the public parts of a prostitute" Grose, *op. cit.*); GENITALS (from the Latin for "to beget"); IT (an omnibus term of many misuses); MONOSYLLABLE (the chief euphemism for most of the eighteenth and nineteenth centuries); *natural* (another omnibus term); *novelty, piece,* PUDENDUM (literally "that of which one ought to be ashamed"); *quim* (seventeenth to twentieth centuries, perhaps from the Spanish *quemar,* to burn); THING (yet another omnibus term, whose sexual possibilities were fully realized by Geoffrey Chaucer), *thingummy* (see THINGUMBOB); *toy, twat* (of obscure origin and sufficiently obscure meaning that Robert Browning, searching for words to lend an archaic mood to *Pippa Passes,* 1841, latched on to this one by mistake, thinking that it meant an article of clothing worn by, of all people, nuns: "The owls and bats, Cowls and twats, Monks and nuns, in a cloister's moods"); *what-do-you-call-it* (see WHAT-YOU-MAY-CALL'EM), and YOU-KNOW-WHAT.

2. Physical references, often generalized to the extent of including the adjacent pubic region: *aperture, basket* (also slang for the scrotum); *box* or *hot-box* (from Pandora's box?); *bun* (see RABBIT), *bushes, can; case, cauliflower* (Grose, *op. cit.,* explained the origin of the term this way: "A woman, who was giving evidence in a case wherein it was necessary to express those [private] parts, made use of the term cauliflower; for which the judge on the bench, a peevish old fellow, reproved her, saying she might as well call it an artichoke. Not so, my Lord, replied she; for an artichoke has a bottom, but a **** and a cauliflower have none"); *circle, cleft; crack* (also a "whore"); *crinkum-crankum* (a variant of "crinkle-crankle," meaning "a winding way"); FANNY (an anatomical displacement); *fig* (an old metaphor, dating perhaps to Roman times, with "giving the fig"—or sometimes "the fig of Spain"—being the Mediterranean equivalent of our own well-known hand gesture with middle finger upraised); *fish pond,* KEISTER (a container, also the anus); *motte* (a popular Victorian term, from the French word for "mound"); *muff* (from at least the seventeenth century, when the toast, "To the well wearing of your muff, mort," translated as "To the happy consummation of your marriage," a "mort" being any woman but also a PROSTITUTE); *nick; nock* (see KNOCK UP); *nooky* (also meaning COITION, from "nook"?); *notch; O; orifice,* PRIVATE PARTS, PUSSY, *slit, slot, sluice, snatch* (perhaps from "snatch" in the sense of "snare" or "trap," but more likely from the "snatch" that is a quick grab or other act, as in, from Robert Burton's *The Anatomy of Melancholy,* of 1621: "They had rather go to the stewes, or haue now and then a snatch . . . then haue wiues of their owne"); TAIL (an extremely versatile term, used also for the PENIS and the ass, or ARSE, since the fourteenth century).

3. More-or-less poetical or picturesque references: *aphrodisiacal tennis court, bower of bliss; carnal trap, Carvel's ring* (from a possibly apocryphal story, as related by Grose, *op. cit.,* of "Hans Carvel, a jealous old

doctor, being in bed with his wife, dreamed that the Devil gave him a ring, which, so long as he had it on his finger, would prevent his being made a cuckold: waking, he had got his finger the Lord knows where"); *centrique part, coffee house* ("To make a coffee-house of a woman's ****; to go in and out and spend nothing" Grose, *op. cit.*); *Cupid's alley* (less delicately, *cock alley* or *cock lane*); *delicate glutton, Eve's Custom House* ("where Adam made his first entry" Grose, *op. cit.*); *eye that weeps, furnace mouth; garden* (from Garden of Eden?); *green grocery* (probably from GREENS); *hat* ("because frequently felt," Grose, *op. cit.*); *honeypot; Lapland; living fountain; love's lane; love's paradise; most when most pleased; Mother of all Masons* (or *Saints* or *St. Patrick* or *Souls*); *poontang* (originally reserved for blacks or mulattoes, perhaps from *putain*, whore, by way of French-speaking New Orleans, and also used for INTERCOURSE generally, as in "It's good for the constitution to have a little poontang regularly"); *postern gate to the Elysian field; seminary; sensible part; temple of Venus; Venus's mark;* and, finally, *yum-yum.*

Which may seem like a lot but which is, really, only a sampling.

variety meats. Organs or the parts of organs; the euphemistic generalization covers up such all-too-vivid particulars as the kidneys and tongue. See also FILET MIGNON and SWEETBREAD.

venison. Deer meat; from the French (*venaison* is the modern form), and ultimately from the Latin *venari*, to hunt. *Venison* tastes much better than "deer," just as veal (from *veau*) is more palatable than the more-recognizable "calf," and the term has been used in English at least since the thirteenth century. In keeping with the Latin root, it was originally applied to the flesh of any animal killed in the chase—boar, hare, rabbit, as well as to deer. For more about Frenchifying the names of the animals we eat, see FILET MIGNON.

Venusian. Venereal. Reporting the results of Russian and American probes of Venus, even the best science writers produced such sentences as "An unexpectedly large amount of argon was discovered in the Venusian atmosphere," although the proper adjective for "Venus" is "Venereal." (Acceptable alternates include Venerean, Venerial, Venerian, and Venerien.) However, "Venereal" is so infected with sex that it seems certain "Venusian" will survive. See also SOCIAL DISEASE.

verbalize. Talk, with a FOP Index of 2.75. The word originally meant "to talk verbosely," and its meaning has been changed by those who do.

Vertical Transportation Corps. At Hahnemann Hospital in Philadelphia, Pennsylvania, the insignia of the elevator operators proclaim their membership in the "Vertical Transportation Corps." This contribution to the cause of occupational upgrading received an honorable mention when the Committee on Public Doublespeak of the National Council of Teachers of English handed out its Doublespeak Awards for 1977. See also AIR SUPPORT, EGRESS, and ENGINEER.

vespasienne. A *pissoir*, or public urinal, in France. The euphemism honors the Roman emperor, Vespasian (A.D. 9–79), who not only taxed people to build public urinals but raised more money by selling the contents to launderers, who used urine for bleaching clothes. See also TOILET.

vichyssoise. The French has a certain *je ne sais quoi* that is lacking from "cold potato soup," but during World War II the "vichy" left a bad taste in patriotic mouths. As the 1941 edition of *The Escoffier Cook Book* explains: "Vichyssoise, now called Crème Gauloise, is made by adding cream and chilling." By the way: The final "s" of "vichyssoise" should be pronounced (as in "swäz"), which is only fitting for a dish of domestic origin: It was devised by Louis Diat, chef at the old Ritz Carlton Hotel in New York City. See also LIBERTY CABBAGE.

Victory girl or **V-girl.** A woman with a fatal fondess for military uniforms, circa World War II; an amateur PROSTITUTE, aka *patriotute*. At the outset of the war, a "Victory girl" was a woman factory worker, but this meaning was dropped like a hot potato as the other caught on—another demonstration of the application of Gresham's Law to language. See also B-GIRL.

vocalization. A scream, squeak, squeal, or some combination thereof. "Electric shocks were applied to the tails of mice, and if 'vocalization' did not occur after 5 minutes the animals were considered insensitive" (Louis Goldman, *When Doctors Disagree*, ms, 1976). Technically, the shock that causes *vocalization* is known as a STRESS-PRODUCING STIMULUS.

voluntary. Forced, required, involuntary; pure, unadulterated doubletalk.
President Jimmy Carter established *voluntary* pay-price guidelines in 1978, following in the footsteps of President Richard M. Nixon, who imposed *voluntary* wage and price controls in 1971. In both instances, employees who failed to get the salary increases they expected found the *voluntary* aspect hard to appreciate. Employers, too, while perfectly willing to limit pay raises, were something less than free agents. Speaking of the 1971 controls, for example: "Voluntary compliance for the great bulk of business was the rule to be followed, with the threat of heavy fines for violations" (*The 1972 World Book*).
Though Carter and Nixon apparently had forgotten it, the true meaning of "voluntary" in their sense was explained a long time ago by another American president, Theodore Roosevelt, in a speech attacking yet a fourth president, Woodrow Wilson. This speech, made in 1916, is a landmark in the history of doubletalk, for in it Roosevelt popularized the phrase "weasel words" to describe ambiguous talk, usually by politicians. In TR's words: "You can have universal training, or you can have voluntary training, but when you use the word *voluntary* to qualify the word *universal*, you are using a weasel word; it has sucked all the meaning out of *universal*. The two words flatly contradict each other" (*Brewer's Dictionary of Phrase and Fable*, rev. by Ivor H. Evans, 1970). "Voluntary," to refer to yet another contribution of TR to the language, could be described as a lot of MUCK.

volunteer. In civilian life, "volunteer" is a relatively innocuous euphemism for "unpaid," as in "Matilda is doing volunteer work for the Red Cross," but in the military, sergeants "humorously" reverse the basic meaning of the word, declaring, as they pick out men for various dirty details, "I want three volunteers for KP—you, you, and you." On a larger scale, but in much the same manner, the Chinese sent an army of *volunteers* into Korea in 1950, e.g.: "Under the blue and white banner of the United Nations, the United States and, to a lesser extent, 15 other nations battled the North Koreans and later a force of 700,000 'volunteer' Chinese Communists for three years" (David Eggenberger, *A Dictionary of Battles*, 1967). See also POLICE ACTION.

W

walk. A nineteenth-century public toilet or rest room. ". . . 'Ladies' Walk, 'Gentlemen's Walk,' i.e., a privy. This absurd piece of squeamishness is common at hotels and at railroad-stations" (John Russell Bartlett, *Dictionary of Americanisms,* 1877). See also TOILET.

walking/walk out. To court, as in "Let's go walking," or "Let's walk out"; relics of the pre-Automobile Age, before teen-agers learned to *park,* NECK, or PET.

wanna go out? A WORKING GIRL's way of asking a passerby if he wants to have some FUN (personal communication, frequently, New York City, 1970–80). In the nineteenth century, before inflation had reduced the value of a penny to almost nothing, the standard question of flower girls and news girls who were more interested in selling themselves than their wares was "Give me a penny, mister?" See also PROSTITUTE.

War Between the States, the. The Civil War, aka the LATE UNPLEASANTNESS. Southerners prefer "War Between the States" because it legitimizes the great cause of States' Rights even in defeat. When a national politician adopts this terminology, it is a sure sign that he is courting the white, southern vote. The phrase may also be used out of force of habit, long after the national politician has removed himself from the possibility of ever running again for office, e.g.: "Well, what I, at root I had in mind I think was perhaps much better stated by Lincoln during the War Between the States" (Richard M. Nixon, interview with David Frost, 5/18/77).

warrantless investigation. Illegal investigation; FBI-ese. In the words of the former head of the bureau's New York City office: "Mr. [J. Wallace] LaPrade's assertion about what he described as 'warrantless investigations'—or cases in which the F.B.I. allegedly broke into homes without search warrants and placed electronic eavesdropping devices without court approval—were made at a hastily called news conference . . ." (*New York Times,* 4/14/78). See also BLACK BAG JOB and SURREPTIT'OUS ENTRY.

washlady/washerlady. Pre-Bendix niceties for "washwoman" and "washerwoman," e.g., "'Blanchisseuses,' what some folks here call 'washladies'" (*Brooklyn Standard Union,* 5/29/04) See also LADY.

washroom. An Americanism for "toilet," dating to the nineteenth century; the functional and euphemistic equivalent of BATHROOM and LAVATORY. The oldest "washroom" in *A Dictionary of Americanisms* (Mitford M. Mathews, ed., 1951) comes from 1853: "Tabby came from the wash-room just then." Naturally, if anyone were to ask, Tabby would have said that she had been "washing her hands" in the *washroom.* Or, as Miss Cartwright told Julian English, after having had a couple of drinks: ". . . I'd feel a thousand percent better if you'd let me wash my hands. . . . my back teeth are floating" (John O'Hara, *Appointment in Samarra*, 1945). See also TOILET and POWDER MY NOSE.

waste. A euphemism, whether as a noun, in the form of bodily "waste," or as a verb, in the form of "to waste" a person—a true parallel in both senses to ELIMINATE/ELIMINATION. For example: "Dog waste is a blight" (*Park Slope* [Brooklyn, NY] *Civic News*, 6/78). New York City, as it happens, has some 700,000 dogs, who among them produce perhaps 350,000 pounds of *waste* per day, a "blight" that has been only slightly alleviated by enactment of canine *waste* law. See also DOG DIRT/LITTER/WASTE. The other, more-obnoxious kind of "waste" seems to be a product of the Vietnam ERA. As a byword for "kill," it began to penetrate the public consciousness about the time of the trial in 1971 of Lt. William L. Calley for his part in the murder three years before of some 300 to 500 civilian residents of the South Vietnamese village of My Lai, e.g.: "Of course, the ultimate low in word—and soul—pollution was William Calley's account of 'wasting' (killing) civilians. It makes murder seem painless, like wasting unwanted food" (Grace Hechinger, *Wall Street Journal*, 10/27/71).

"Waste" had other meanings before it obtained its lethal one, and the later meaning seems to be a compound of the earlier senses. For example, the only definition for the verb in Eugene Landy's *The Underground Dictionary* (1971) is "hit very hard and hurt (someone)." (See HIT in this regard.) Meanwhile, as an adjective "wasted" was popular among drug users, meaning so loaded, wiped out, or zonked on a drug as to be nonfunctioning (i.e., "dead" to all appearances). The development of "waste" to mean "kill" may have been reinforced by the particular nature of the Vietnam War, in which all deaths were a *waste*, more so than in any other war that comes quickly to mind. This is "waste" in its conventional, primary meaning of "To use or expend thoughtlessly, uselessly, or without return . . ." (*Funk & Wagnalls Standard College Dictionary*, 1973). In this respect, the modern military "waste" and "wasted" were clearly foreshadowed by "used up" in the eighteenth century. As Capt. Francis Grose defined it in *A Classical Dictionary of the Vulgar Tongue* (1796):

USED UP. Killed: a military saying, originating from a message sent by the late General Guise, on the expedition at Carthagena, where he desired the commander in chief to order him some more grenadiers for those he had were all used up.

See also CASUALTY and EXPENDABLE.

waste-management compartment. A toilet in orbit. "[Capt. Alan L.] Bean glided into [*Skylab's*] bathroom . . . The bathroom—or waste-management compartment as NASA called it—was a small room about the size of a similar compartment on an airplane . . ." (Henry S. F. Cooper, Jr., *A House in Space*, 1976). See also TOILET.

water cure. Water torture. "At the beginning of the new century, the systematic infliction of torture upon war prisoners, in what was politely termed the 'water cure,' by the American Army in the Philippines [helped] set the stage for the epoch we now confront, with its steadily augmenting horrors, from Buchenwald to Vietnam" (Lewis Mumford, *My Works and Days*, 1979).

watering hole

There are several different kinds of water torture: The victim's head may be immersed in water, as in the wet SUBMARINE; or water may be poured into a gauze bag in the throat, gradually forcing the gauze into the victim's stomach; or—much more sophisticated—water may be poured, ever so slowly, drop by drop by drop, on a particular spot on the victim's body. Still different was the *water cure,* as used by Americans to interrogate Filipino nationalists (1899–1902). According to an account in the *New York Evening Post* (4/8/02), the victim was pinned to the ground, while up to five gallons of water were poured down his throat, making the body an "object frightful to contemplate." Since the prisoner, even if willing, couldn't talk in this condition, the next step was to get the water out. This might be done by squeezing the victim or sometimes, as one young soldier told the *Post,* "we jump on them to get it out quick." After one or two doses of the *water cure,* the prisoner was either talking freely or dead. For more about this war, see CONCENTRATION CAMP.

watering hole or **place.** A jocularity for a bar or SALOON, i.e., an establishment whose stock consists principally of firewater. See also HIGH.

water landing. Airline-ese for ditching, as in "Please use the exit over the wing in the event of a water landing." Meanwhile, back at the airport, passengers waiting for the plane in the water will be told that their departure has been delayed "due to late arrival of equipment." See also CUSHION FOR FLOTATION, EQUIPMENT, MOTION DISCOMFORT, and SEAT BELT.

water sports or **golden showers.** Playing with urine; specifically, voiding it upon another person, who thereby obtains sexual gratification. For example:

> TRUCKDRIVER TRAVELS ALL 48 states. Would like to meet fem any age or race. Enjoy fr gr and all water sports. (*Ace,* ca. 1976)

See also MICTURATE/MICTURITION and PEE.

WC. An English water closet or TOILET. Although "water closets," as such, date to the mid-eighteenth century, it was several generations before they became common. A seminal work appears to have been John Phair's, of 1814: *Observations on the Principles and Construction of Water Closets, Chimneys and Bell Hanging*—a combination that is not as odd as it seems, since bellhangers ran their wires along the perpendicular paths of *water closet* pipes. Still, nearly 40 years later, the mere presence of a *water closet* could be cause for favorable comment. Thus, the anonymous author of *My Secret Life* (ca. 1890) had this to say of the appointments of a seaside lodging house which, interior evidence of his autobiography suggests, must have been built shortly before 1851: ". . . the bedroom . . . was entered from the staircase-landing, as was the lodgers' water-closet, a convenience which few such houses had then." This location—off the landing, halfway up the stairs from the first to the second story—was frequently picked when householders made the great decision to install indoor plumbing, and this led to a second-order euphemism for the *WC,* i.e, *halfway house.* See also EARTH CLOSET.

Wealthy One, the. Just as people have always been circumspect about speaking the names of their gods (see ADONAI), their devils (see DEVIL, THE), and other dread beings, real as well as supernatural (see GRANDFATHER and GOOD PEOPLE), so they have been hesitant when referring to Death, or to the Angel of Death. In all instances, the underlying fear is that to speak the name will cause the being to appear. Thus, the ancient Greeks usually referred to Hades, lord of the underworld, as Pluto, "the Wealthy One" (hence also "plutocracy"). The euphemism alluded to the agricultural wealth that came from Hades's domain. Of course, the god of the underworld also was wealthy in souls, as suggested by another of his euphemistic names, Polydectes, "gatherer of many." Other aliases of Death include *The Arch Foe; The Destroying Angel; that fell sergeant* and *that grim ferryman* (both Shakespeare); *The Grim Reaper; The Pale Horseman* (or more poetically, *pale horse, pale rider); The Spoiler;* and *The Twin Brother of Sleep.*

weapon. In the battle between the sexes, the *weapon* is the PENIS. ". . . and now, disengag'd from the shirt, I saw, with wonder and surprise, what? not the plaything of a boy, not the weapon of a man, but a maypole of so enormous a standard, that had proportions been observ'd, it must have belong'd to a young giant" (John Cleland, *Memoirs of a Woman of Pleasure,* 1749). The *Woman* of the title is, of course, the famous Ms. Fanny Hill, who also observes that "generally speaking, it is in love as it is in war where the longest weapon carries it."

The *weapon* analogy is very old, dating to before the year 1000, and it is a key element in the complex of associations between sex, violence, and death. (See ACTION, DIE, and GUN.) Cleland's work, meanwhile, is of additional interest for being not only the most famous of all dirty (aka ADULT) novels but also perhaps the most discreetly written. Not once does Ms. Hill sully her ruby lips—or the reader's eyes—with a FOUR-LETTER WORD. For example, the *penis,* when not a "weapon" (or a "maypole"), parades under a host of other names. It may be an AFFAIR, an *engine,* an INSTRUMENT, a MEMBER, a *machine,* an ORGAN, a stake, a truncheon, or even, most poetically, *love's true arrow,* but it is never, never, never an ANGLO-SAXON WORD. See also PENIS.

wee wee. Potty talk for urine, synonymous with PEE, and also, in the case of males, a euphemism for the responsible anatomical part. "Specimen of wee-wee . . . taking it to the hospital for a urinalysis" (Carson McCullers, *Reflections in a Golden Eye,* 1941).

Potty talk is the regressive language adopted by grown-ups who do not wish to use ADULT words for vital functions and organs. ("Potty" itself is something of a euphemism, being the "cute" diminutive of the "pot" in "chamber pot"; see CHAMBER.) When lapsing into potty talk, otherwise adult people announce that they are going to the LITTLE BOYS' ROOM or LITTLE GIRLS' ROOM. When reaching their destination, they will do NUMBER ONE AND/OR TWO, or perhaps one or the other of the following. BM, *boom boom, caca* (from the Latin *cacare,* to defecate); *cis cis* (or *sis sis); doo doo,* PEE, PIDDLE; *poo poo* (see DIDDLY-POO); *poop* (whence comes POOPER-SCOOPER); or TINKLE.

welfare. Relief, alms; the fare is not as good as it sounds. In general, "on welfare" equals "poor," a correspondence that received official recognition in 1969 when the U.S. Labor Department listed the criteria that had to be satisfied in order for a person to qualify as DISADVANTAGED, i.e., "A person is deemed poor if he is a member of a family that receives cash welfare payments . . ." (*The Official Associated Press Almanac*, 1973).

"Welfare," as we now know it, seems to have been invented around 1904 in Dayton, Ohio—about the same time that two citizens of that city, Wilbur and Orville Wright, were getting their act together. *Welfare* programs naturally led to *welfare* centers, child *welfare*, *welfare* administrators, and so forth. Today, however, the term seems to be on the way out, its "poor" connotations having caught up with it. Thus, New York City's Welfare Department is now known as the Department of Social Services (it operates a string of *income maintenance* centers). By the same token, the city's old Bureau of Child Welfare is now the *Office of Direct Child Care Special Services* and Blackwell's Island, where the city prison used to be, was converted into *Welfare Island* and then *Roosevelt Island*. All this is just part of a national trend. Thus, everything is up to date in Cleveland, Tennessee, where, Calvin Trillin reports (*The New Yorker*, 1/10/77), the old Welfare agency is now called *Human Services*—a new handle that would do credit to euphemists of the Big Apple. See also CLIENT, CORRECTIONAL FACILITY, and LOW-INCOME.

welfare meeting. A non-Muslim religious service in Saudi Arabia, where such meetings are officially banned. Thus, as Joseph Kraft reported in *The New Yorker* (10/20/75), an announcement at the American embassy of a forthcoming *welfare meeting* means that a religious service will be held. The person who conducts a *welfare meeting* of this sort is referred to as the *lecturer*. The faithful understand that when the *lecturer* is said to be available for *private interviews*, they will be able to make their confessions. For another discreet evasion of Muslim law, see COMMISSION.

Welsh rarebit. Affected menu-ese for "Welsh rabbit," itself a euphemistic joke for a strictly meatless concoction of melted cheese on toast or crackers.

Lacking sufficient meat for their tables, the Welsh managed to develop a taste for cheese, as noted in the eighteenth century by Capt. Francis Grose, in his definition of "Welch [*sic*] rabbit," i.e.: "The Welch are said to be so remarkably fond of cheese, that in cases of difficulty their midwives apply a piece of toasted cheese to the *janua vitae*, to attract and entice the young Taffy, who on smelling it makes most vigorous efforts to come forth" (*A Classical Dictionary of the Vulgar Tongue*, 1796). "Taffy," by the way, is a corruption of "David," patron saint of Wales. See also CAPE COD TURKEY.

wet affair or **wet stuff.** A Russian intelligence operation in which blood is shed; especially, a political murder (*mokrye dela*, as the Ruskies say). Thus, on the subject of the Komitet Gosurdarstvennoi Bezopasnosti (Committee for State Security): "Western analysts believe the K.G.B. has abandoned its practice of 'wet affairs'—the Soviet euphemism for covert actions like assassinations" (*New York Times*, 6/2/75). For the American side of the coin, alas, see ASSASSINATION in general and EXECUTIVE ACTION in particular.

what-you-may-call'em. An omnibus term for anyone or anything a person forgets or, as a euphemism, prefers not to name; a modern (nineteenth–twentieth century) British equivalent of the American *whatchamacallit* and of the older *what-d'ye-call'em* (or *call him, her, it,* or *um*). "'He has discovered gold under the sitting room hearth, a body under the what-you-may-call'em in the downstairs bathroom, and two wells'" (Josephine Tey, *The Singing Sands*, 1953). See also ARSE, THINGUMBOB(S), and YOU-KNOW-WHAT.

white dielectric material. Pigeon shit—to a scientist who had to get rid of it in order to confirm one of the most remarkable astronomical discoveries of the modern era.

The *white dielectric material* became an issue in 1964 after two radio astronomers, Arnold A. Penzias and Robert W. Wilson, detected surprisingly strong radiation at the 7.35 centimeter wavelength. The radiation seemed to be of cosmic origin, but they had to check out their antenna at the Bell Telephone Laboratories site in Holmdel, New Jersey, just to be sure the noise was not coming from the apparatus itself. Unfortunately, a pair of pigeons had been living within the 20-foot, horn-shaped antenna, and "in the course of their tenancy, the pigeons had coated the antenna throat with what Penzias delicately calls 'a white dielectric material,' and this material might at room temperature be a source of electrical noise" (Steven Weinberg, *The First Three Minutes*, 1977). Early in 1965, the antenna was cleaned out, but without substantially reducing the level of microwave radiation, which was soon identified as the background remnant of the primeval fireball ("The Big Bang") in which our universe apparently was created. In 1978, as deferred compensation for their struggles with the *white dielectric material*, Penzias and Wilson received Nobel Prizes.

See also DEFECATE/DEFECATION.

white lie. A lie; the addition of the extenuating "white" produces a FOP Index of 3.3. The distinction between regular lies and the supposedly small, harmless, perhaps even well-intentioned *white lies* reflects the ancient distinction between black (bad) magic and white (good) magic. People have been telling *white lies* for the past couple of centuries at the very least, with the first example of "white lie" in the *Oxford English Dictionary* coming from 1741. The essential nature of *white lies* also has long been recognized, e.g.: "White lies always introduce others of a darker complexion" (William Paley, *The Principles of Moral and Political Philosophy*, 1785).

Naturally, people with forked tongues have found many ways not to use the words "lie" and "lying." See also CATEGORICAL INACCURACY, EMBROIDER THE TRUTH, ERRONEOUS REPORT, FABRICATION, FIB, HEAVENLY DECEPTION, INOPERATIVE, MISSPEAK, NO RECALL OF, PREVARICATE, STORY, and TERMINOLOGICAL INEXACTITUDE.

white meat. In England, a euphemism for a meatless dairy product, such as milk and cheese, and in the United States, a euphemism for the unspeakable "breast" (or BOSOM) of a fowl. As a nineteenth-century Englishman noted of American table manners: "And some of them would scarcely hesitate to ask for the breast of a chicken, though almost all call it 'white meat,' in contradistinction to the 'dark meat,' as all ladies and gentlemen designate the legs of poultry" (Thomas C. Grattan, *Civilized America*, 1859). See also DRUMSTICK, LIMB, and PENGUIN.

wild oats. An old metaphor for the indiscretions of youthful males, up to and including the sowing of the seeds that grow into bastards. "That wilfull and vnruly age, which lacketh rypeness and discretion, and (as wee saye) hath not sowed all theyr wyeld Oates" (Thomas Newton, *Lemnie's Touchstone of Complexions,* trans. 1565).

The *wild oat* is a tall grass with a long twisted awn. Probably similar to the wild ancestor of the cultivated oat, it frequently appears as a weed in cornfields. The metaphor alludes to the folly of sowing wild oats rather than good grain. See also LOVE CHILD.

with child. Pregnant—and an example of how great a difference a single letter can make, with the phrase, "a woman with child," conjuring up an entirely different image than "a woman with a child." A now-obsolete variant, for someone newly pregnant, was *young with child.* See also FAMILY WAY, IN A.

withdrawal. Retreat; sometimes further disguised as *phased withdrawal* or *strategic withdrawal.* The euphemistic difference between an official "withdrawal" and an unofficial "retreat" is evident from the following denouement to the INCURSION of 1971: "It was not until some of the [South Vietnamese] commanders on the ground threatened to take the troops out and the retreat had already begun that the order for withdrawal was formally given" (Frances FitzGerald, *Fire in the Lake,* 1972). See also STRATEGIC MOVEMENT TO THE REAR.

woman. A common circumlocution for "girl," whose pejorative connotations have been so greatly magnified by advocates of Women's Liberation that it has become very risky to utter the word at all. (It is virtually impossible to conceive of the Gibson Girl being reincarnated today or—another measure of how quickly the language has changed—anyone now daring to release a movie called *Les Girls,* a delightfully innocent film of 1957.) A good example of the lengths to which careful speakers will go to avoid saying "g-i-r-l" was provided on the TV show "Straight Talk" (WOR, NYC, 12/7/76), when a discussion of prostitution was carefully couched in terms of *working women, working people,* and *professional women,* as opposed to WORKING GIRLS or *professional girls*—the terms used by the "girls" themselves. The objections to "girl" are various, revolving around its secondary, formerly euphemistic meanings (servant, mistress, whore), but in general are much the same as those of liberated men (and women) to the contemptuous, demeaning, also-formerly euphemistic BOY.

"Woman" itself has a curious history, which may be of some consolation to female readers, since it shows that they are not, linguistically at least, mere derivatives of the other sex. "Woman," superficial appearance to the contrary, does not come from "man," but from the Old English "wif-mann," where "wif" meant "female" and "mann" meant a human being of either sex. As late as 1752, the philosopher David Hume could use "man" in the original sense, when contending that ". . . there is in all men, both male and female, a desire and power of generation more active than is ever universally exerted." What happened as the language evolved, of course, was that males gradually arrogated the generic "mann" to themselves, while the old word for female, "wif," was diminished into "wife," i.e., man's appendage, aka *the little woman, the old woman,* and *my woman.* Today, some men still insist that when they use "man" in such constructions as "The proper study of Mankind is Man," or "Man is a tool-making animal," they do not intend to imply that their sex is the superior, but they are fighting the tide of our time.

The word "woman" *has* had its share of ups and downs. In the first part of the nineteenth century, it was considered entirely too common for polite conversation; the preferred euphemisms then were FEMALE and LADY, e.g.: "A female negro is called 'a wench,' or a 'woman'; and it is this, perhaps, which makes the term 'woman' so offensive to American ears, when applied to white females, who must all be called 'ladies'" (James A. Buckingham, *The Slave States of America*, 1842). Aside from slaves and SERVANTS, "women" of this era were mostly likely encountered in the form of FALLEN WOMEN or as the lower-class people served by such institutions as Philadelphia's Lying-In Charity for Attending Indigent Women in Their Homes. "Female" gradually began to acquire some of the unsavory connotations of "woman," however, while "lady," which always seemed a bit British to Americans, also demonstrated a lack of staying power. As early as 1838, James Fenimore Cooper plumped firmly for "woman" instead of "lady" in *The American Democrat* (see SABBATH for details), and in 1845, that freethinking person, Margaret Fuller, published *Woman in the Nineteenth Century*, without being ostracized for her choice of words. Other radicals also favored "woman," e.g., the crusaders who founded the National Woman's Suffrage Association and the American Woman's Suffrage Association in 1869, followed by the Woman's Christian Temperance Union in 1874. As their causes gained respectability, so did their choice of words. By the start of the next century, the *Times* of London could report (10/18/08): "The writer is a 'newspaper woman'—which is, she tells us, 'the preferred American substitute for the more polite English term "lady journalist."'"

In our own time, "woman" is still preferred to "female" on grounds that it refers specifically to adult, nonmale persons, while the latter applies to a sexual distinction common to almost all creatures, great and small. Even so, "woman's" place in the language is being threatened as modern liberationists advance from the joys of recognizing sexual differences to the apparently more sublime delights of blotting them out. Thus, feminists of a generation ago were pleased to accept the title "chairwoman," but their daughters today are not, with unfortunate linguistic consequences in some organizations, where the opposite number of a committee "chairman" is not a "chairwoman" but a "chairperson."

The men have only themselves to thank for all this. Just as "girl" was tarred by its secondary meanings, so the desire to avoid "woman" will be increased each time the word is used insultingly—as in the invective-filled trial of the Chicago Eight in 1969, when Black Panther leader Bobby G. Seale topped off his taunts of Judge Julius J. Hoffman, with the shout: "You're just a woman!" Mr. Seale had also addressed the judge as a "racist," a "fascist," and a "pig," but observers believed "woman" to be the word that cut most deeply, leading to the edifying spectacle of a black man, gagged and in chains, in an American courtroom. One hardly dares imagine the judge's response if Mr. Seale had gone so far as to call him a "girl."

See also PERSON.

wonderful personality. "Brunnhilde has a wonderful personality" is a conventional way of saying "Brunnhilde is not good looking," i.e., she is, at best, homely.

wood colt (or **woods colt**). A bastard, the comparison being to a horse of unknown paternity. "He raved, swore, called the boy a wood's colt and his instrument a thump keg" (*Saturday Evening Post*, 6/16/49). Similar rural round-abouts for illegitimacy include *catch colt, old field colt,* and *wild colt.* See also LOVE CHILD.

wood up. To consume alcohol; a euphemism of the steamboat age, when stops for taking on firewood became occasions for stretching the legs and partaking REFRESHMENT. "[He] made a straight bend for Sander's 'Grocery,' and began to 'wood up'" (Jonathan F. Kelly, *The Humors of Falconbridge,* ca. 1856). See also HAPPY HOUR and HIGH.

word from our sponsor, and now a. A standard lead-in to what inevitably proves to be more than a single word, i.e., an advertisement or MESSAGE.

working girl. A whore, especially a STREETWALKER, as distinguished from a higher-class CALL GIRL or COURTESAN. "They call themselves 'working girls.' . . . Their work is a 'business,' or even . . . a 'social service.' . . . By the prostitute's code, prostitution is moral . . . 'what's immoral is giving it away free, sleeping around with anyone'" (*New York Times,* 8/9/71). See also, in the order just mentioned, BUSINESS, SERVICE, IT, and SLEEP WITH.

working to rule. A slowdown on the job; a British JOB ACTION. "'Working to rule' is what air-controllers do when they are said in the press to be 'on strike'" (*New York Review of Books,* 2/22/79). Production drops whenever employees begin *working to rule* because the rules that have been agreed upon by union and management negotiators rarely reflect the realities of the workplace. *Working to rule* is but one aspect of a general rebellion by bored and discontented employees against the nature of much of modern work. Other aspects have been labeled "voluntary inefficiency," "efficiency resistance," and "sabotage."

World Series. Since 1903, the pennant winners in the American and National leagues have been meeting in a World Series to determine the "World" championship of baseball. For most of this time, "World" translated as "United States," but in 1969, the Montreal Expos took the field, and the meaning of "World" was enlarged to "United States and Canada." Obviously out-of-this-world, since his team was never eligible for the *World Series* was Sadaharu Oh, first baseman of the Yomiuri Giants, who surpassed Hank Aaron's lifetime home-run record when he belted number 756 on September 3, 1977, at Korakuen Stadium, Tokyo, Japan. It would be fitting if the moment for starting the *World Series* each year were figured in UNIVERSAL TIME. See also FREE WORLD.

XYZ

X. The symbol for a kiss, as on the flap of an envelope, "X," or sometimes, "XXXXXXXX," to demonstrate especial ardor.

Yah! Yah! Kill! Kill! To the members of the silent generation of the 1950s, who couldn't imagine feeling strongly enough about anything to actually fight for it, one of the more grotesque bits of basic training in the army came during bayonet instruction class when they were required to yell, just as loudly as they could, "Kill! Kill!" with each mock thrust of their weapons. Someone's mother must have complained to her congressperson because the official yell was changed during the Vietnam ERA to "Yah! Yah!" Unofficial report even has it that the army wanted to dispense with bayonets altogether back when the M14 NATO-round rifle was being designed. It was the marines who insisted that bayonets be kept, and they were. The newer M16 takes them, too. *Yah! Yah!*
    See also HIT.

yard. The penis—and not necessarily just a case of wishful thinking, since "yard" meant "stick," "staff," or "rod," before the equivalency with "three feet" or "thirty-six inches" was established. The use of "yard" for "penis" began at least as early as the fourteenth century and persisted into the nineteenth. William Shakespeare, in about the middle of this period, knew the euphemism and punned upon it in *Love's Labor's Lost* (1593):

> PRINCESS OF FRANCE: Speak, brave Hector. We are much delighted.
> DON ADRIANO DE ARMADO: I do adore the sweet Grace's slipper.
> BOYET [*Aside to Dumain*]: Loves her by the foot.
> DUMAIN [*Aside to Boyet*]: He may not by the yard.

    See also PENIS.

you know. A meaningless expression, traditionally associated with drug addicts, teen-agers, and other vacant-minded types, e.g., "I was going down the street, you know, when I saw these two girls, you know." Unfortunately, the disease is contagious. Even usually precise speakers have been known to suffer from it. Critiquing his performance in an interview with Walter Cronkite, one of the more effective public speakers of our time explained the cause of the disease and the means of curing it:

> *"Too many 'you knows.'"* These came from starting to answer before I had thought out what I was going to say. "You knows" are sound fillers. Don't answer a question until you know the answer you're prepared to give. (John Dean III, *Blind Ambition*, 1976)

    See also AT THIS POINT IN TIME.

you-know-what. Euphemisms are so DOGGONE easy to slip into that almost everyone uses them from time to time, even the greatest of semanticists. Thus, during the course of a United States Senate committee hearing on June 14, 1978, on the subject of teen-age pregnancy, the distinguished author of *Language in Thought and Action* and other works, Sen. S. I. Hayakawa (R., California), spoke with unaccustomed imprecision when he observed (more than once—he apparently liked the phrase) that "flirtation leads to you-know-what." As a euphemistic catchall, "you-know-what" compares favorably with the British WHAT-YOU-MAY-CALL'EM.

young. Middle-aged, a journalistic euphemism for *young* people in the public eye. ". . . anybody on the White House staff who would not be embarrassed to take an intelligence test is commonly described as 'brilliant.' Anyone under the age of 49 is 'young'" (Russell Baker, *New York Times*, 1/16/72). See also LATENCY PERIOD and MATURE.

yours truly. I—with a fine FOP Index of 13.0. "Yours truly, sir, has an eye for a fine woman and a fine horse" (Wilkie Collins, *Armadale*, 1866). Americans of the tonier sort also use the expression: "'Wish he'd stuck to [Skull and] Bones,' said Schley. 'Yours truly would feel more hopeful'" (Owen Johnson, *Stover at Yale*, 1931).

youth-oriented merchandise. Drug-taking paraphernalia, e.g., coke spoons and hash pipes, as in "Some publications specialize in ads for youth-oriented merchandise."

Zionist. An anti-Semite's euphemism for a Jew. "The Soviet Union . . . never attacks Jews, just Zionists. But, Jews over the millennia have come to know the anti-Semite without regard to the euphemisms he employs" (letter to the *New York Times*, from Rep. [and future New York City Mayor] Edward I. Koch, 1/14/74). See also HEBREW.

zounds. The euphemistic abbreviation of "by God's wounds," circa sixteenth–nineteenth centuries. (See ODDS BODKINS for a similarly constructed phrase.) "Zounds" provides a heartfelt ending to this book, thanks to William Shakespeare's *The Life and Death of King John* (1590–91?):

Zounds! I was never so bethumped with words